Katie Stewart's

— COOKBOOK —

Katie Stewart's
COOKBOOK

with best wishes

Katie Stewart

1986.

LONDON
VICTOR GOLLANCZ LTD
1983

British Library Cataloguing in Publication Data
Stewart, Katie
    Katie Stewart's cookbook.
    1. Cookery
    I. Title
    641.5   TX717

ISBN 0-575-03278-2

Phototypeset in Great Britain by
Rowland Phototypesetting, Bury St Edmunds and London

Printed in Italy by New Interlitho SpA, Milan

Contents

Illustrations

Photographer: Bryce Attwell
Stylist: Roisin Nield

Introduction

Who would have thought that cooking would become so fashionable and food such a topic of discussion? For my part I have always concentrated on recipes that are unashamedly straightforward but, I hope, none the less special for that. I believe in good food simply prepared, in exploiting seasonal ingredients to the full and presenting dishes attractively, not with fussy ideas, but by cooking food thoughtfully and serving it looking fresh and inviting. Here you will find a personal approach that reflects a style of cooking that has evolved from my years of working with food.

This is the book I have always wanted to write. I have collected my best recipes as well as useful cookery hints and tips that I have discovered during the course of my work. Cooking can be exasperating but it is also very rewarding and there is always something new to learn. I love to indulge in discussions about food – the recipes, the exchange of ideas that make cooking more enjoyable and easier, techniques and even the aspects of food which take away some of the mystery of why ingredients react the way they do – this has fascinated me right from the beginning. I have listed my hints and tips with care because I know they will help you follow the recipes in this book with confidence.

I am indebted to my housekeeper Mamie Eeckhout whose continental influence in our household made me completely rethink my own very traditional approach to food; many of the best soup, vegetable and fruit recipes were inspired by her. In putting together this book, I had invaluable assistance from my secretary, Cheryl McCarthy, and from Sarah Jane Haws who spent many hours typing the manuscript, and to Nancy Anthony, who edited the manuscript with the utmost care and sympathy for my ideas, I am very grateful indeed.

MEASUREMENTS

Both imperial and metric measurements are given in the recipes. As their equivalents are not exact, the metric measurements have been rounded out. Tin, packet and carton sizes are given according to the manufacturers' labels. Use either imperial or metric measures, but don't switch from one to the other.

1

First Courses

A good first course will whet the appetite for the meal ahead. Go for simple combinations of ingredients that will tempt the palate and have eye-catching appeal.

First Courses

Dips

Dips are delicious mixtures with tangy flavours. I like to make them with soft cream cheese which has a naturally bland taste and takes added flavours very well. Mix dips in advance and leave to stand so flavours develop. Then serve surrounded with salty biscuits, potato crisps or raw vegetables (crudités) for dipping. Recipes that follow serve 12 guests.

Quick dip: Take any flavoured cream cheese and blend it with soured cream to a soft dipping consistency. Try cream cheese flavoured with garlic and herbs or liptauer cheese. Use approximately 8 oz (225g) flavoured cream cheese blended with ¼ pint (150ml) soured cream.

Avocado dip: Halve 2 ripe avocados and remove the stones. Scoop the flesh into a mixing bowl and mash with a fork. Add 8 oz (225g) fresh cream cheese, juice of ½ lemon, 1 teaspoon onion juice (twist an onion half on a lemon squeezer), ½ level teaspoon salt, dash of Worcestershire sauce and 2 tablespoons single cream. Beat until smooth and soft. Or purée ingredients in a blender or food processor. Spoon into a serving bowl and cover with cling film placed close to the surface to retain the colour until ready to serve.

Horseradish dip: Put 8 oz (225g) fresh cream cheese into a mixing bowl. Add 2–3 tablespoons single cream, 3 tablespoons prepared horseradish relish (not sauce). Mix until smooth and soft, then add a dash of Worcestershire sauce and a seasoning of salt to taste. Spoon into a serving bowl.

Party dip has a pretty pink colour. Put 2 tablespoons oil and vinegar dressing and 8 oz (225g) fresh cream cheese into a mixing bowl and mix until smooth and soft. Then beat in 2 tablespoons tomato ketchup, 2 teaspoons finely chopped onion and 1 teaspoon anchovy essence. Spoon into a serving bowl.

Ideas for party snacks

● Cut firm cheese into small cubes and spike them on cocktail sticks along with tinned mandarin orange segments, seeded black grapes or maraschino cherries. The contrast of colours looks pretty on a tray.

● Hand round plates of thinly sliced salami or garlic sausage. Both are spicy and pleasant to eat.

● Spread mini melba toasts with smoked cod's roe that has been blended with lemon juice and freshly milled pepper to taste. Sprinkle a little finely chopped onion on top.

● Wrap melon balls in wafer thin pieces of Parma ham and spike on to cocktail sticks.

● Offer peeled quail eggs arranged on a bed of lettuce and spiked with a cocktail stick. On the same plate have a dish of sea salt or flavoured salt for dipping the eggs.

● Prunes or fresh dates with cream cheese make a wonderful cocktail snippet. (Immerse tenderized prunes in boiling water for 2 minutes only, then drain and cool.) Split the prunes or dates and remove stones, then fill with slightly salted cream cheese. The quickest and nicest way to do this is to pipe the cheese using a star nozzle. Decorate with a pinch of chopped parsley or paprika.

● Celery stalks are tasty piped with smoked cod's roe pâté or smoked mackerel pâté and cut in bite-sized pieces.

● For hot bacon savouries wrap pineapple cubes in pieces of trimmed streaky bacon. Stretch the rashers with a knife to make them thin and cut in half across. Thread wrapped pineapple on kebab skewers. Grill until bacon is cooked, turning once or twice, then spike individual savouries with a cocktail stick.

● Smoked salmon pinwheel sandwiches (page 290) look tempting arranged decoratively on a plate with a garnish of lemon wedges.

Canapé suggestions

Use bite-sized squares of mini melba toast, small cocktail pumpernickel and rye bread or rounds cut from a French loaf. All will stand up to a variety of toppings without becoming soggy. Prepare ahead, cover with cling film and leave in a cool place until ready to serve.

● Soften 8 oz (225g) fresh cream cheese to a spreading consistency with 2 tablespoons lemon juice. Then fork in contents of a 3½ oz (100g) jar lumpfish caviar. Drop generous teaspoonfuls on mini melba toasts.

● Generously spread your own kipper pâté (page 17) or taramasalata (page 17) on buttered rounds of French bread. Spicy liptauer cheese and teewurst, a German spreading sausage, are also good. Garnish some with a sprinkling of chopped parsley and the others with paprika.

● Trim slices of smoked salmon to fit thin slices of pumpernickel spread with unsalted butter, then cut in bite-sized pieces. Or place wafer thin slices of Westphalian or Parma ham on rye bread.

● Soften 8 oz (225g) fresh cream cheese to a spreading consistency with single cream and season with salt and freshly milled pepper. Drop generous spoonfuls on pumpernickel and top with chopped smoked salmon, black lumpfish caviar and chopped chives. Arrange on a serving plate in alternating colours of pink, black and green.

● Squeeze the contents of a chub pack of smoked buckling pâté or smooth liver pâté into a large piping bag fitted with a star nozzle. Pipe on to lightly buttered rounds of pumpernickel – the flavour combination is delicious. Top some with sieved hard-boiled egg yolk and the others with chopped egg white.

● Spread mini melba toasts lightly with butter, then top with pieces of marinated kipper (page 68) and a slice of pickled onion.

Cocktail pizzas

Sift the flour, baking powder and salt into a mixing bowl. Add the fat in pieces and rub in with the fingertips. Stir in the grated cheese. Add the milk and sufficient water to mix to a soft but not sticky dough. Turn on to a floured work surface and knead just long enough to remove the cracks. Cover with upturned mixing bowl and allow to rest for 10 minutes.

Heat the oven to 425°F (220°C) or Gas no. 7. Peel and finely chop the onions for the topping. Heat the oil in a saucepan over low heat, add the onions and fry gently for 5 minutes to soften but not brown. Draw off the heat and stir in the tomato purée.

Roll out rested dough on a floured work surface to a rectangle about ¼ inch (5mm) thick, trim the edges and slide on to a greased baking sheet. Alternatively, press dough over the base of a 9 × 13 inch (22.5 × 34.5cm) baking tin. Prick the surface with a fork.

Spread the onion and tomato mixture on top, then sprinkle over the cheese and herbs. Season with salt and pepper and garnish with the anchovy fillets. Bake above centre in preheated oven for 20–25 minutes. Slice the pizza 5 times lengthways and 5 times crossways to make 36 pieces. You can bake this in advance and reheat wrapped in kitchen foil (to keep mixture soft) in an oven heated to 350°F (180°C) or Gas no. 4 for 10 minutes.

Makes 36

12 oz (350g) self-raising flour
3 level teaspoons baking powder
1 level teaspoon salt
3 oz (75g) white cooking fat
2 oz (50g) grated hard cheese
¼ pint (150ml) milk
4 tablespoons water

Topping
3 medium-sized onions
3 tablespoons oil
3 tablespoons concentrated tomato
    purée
2 oz (50g) grated hard cheese
2 teaspoons dried mixed herbs
salt and freshly milled pepper
2 × 1¾ oz (50g) tins anchovy fillets

Cheese sablées

Sift the flour into a mixing bowl. Add the cayenne and a seasoning of salt and pepper. Add the butter in pieces and rub in with the fingertips. Stir in the grated cheese. Lightly mix together the egg yolk and water, add to the flour mixture and mix to a rough dough with a fork. Turn on to a floured work surface and knead just long enough to remove the cracks. Shape into a long roll about 1 inch (2.5cm) in diameter. Wrap in cling film and chill the dough until firm.

Heat the oven to 375°F (190°C) or Gas no. 5. Grease three baking sheets. With a sharp knife, slice dough about ¼ inch (5mm) thick and place 12 rounds on each prepared sheet. Lightly beat the egg white and use to brush each round, then sprinkle with poppy seeds, caraway seeds, almonds or walnuts. Or use a combination of toppings for variety. Place in preheated oven and bake for 10–12 minutes until golden. Allow to cool for 1 minute, then transfer the cheese sablées to a wire rack and leave them until completely cool.

Makes 36

6 oz (175g) plain flour
pinch of cayenne pepper
salt and freshly milled pepper
4 oz (100g) butter
3 oz (75g) grated hard cheese
1 egg yolk
1 tablespoon cold water

Topping
1 egg white
poppy seeds, caraway seeds, finely
    chopped almonds or walnuts, for
    sprinkling

Mussels with garlic butter

Serves 4

3 lb (1.4kg) fresh mussels

Garlic butter
6 oz (175g) butter
2 cloves garlic
3 tablespoons finely chopped parsley
salt and freshly milled pepper

Thoroughly clean the mussels by shaking them in several changes of cold water until the water remains clean and free of grit. Discard any open ones. Scrape shells clean and pull off the 'beards'. Put mussels into a large saucepan, cover with a lid and steam over moderate heat for 2–3 minutes until shells open. Shake the pan occasionally so those on top work downwards. Allow mussels to cool in the pan (so they stay moist), then tip them into a colander and discard any that have remained closed. Detach the top shells, leaving the mussels in their half-shells.

Cream the butter until soft. Peel and mash garlic cloves to a purée with salt. Mix into the butter along with the chopped parsley and a seasoning of salt and pepper. Fill each mussel with the soft garlic butter and spread level.

Divide filled mussels between four individual ovenproof serving dishes. Place in an oven heated to 425°F (220°C) or Gas no. 7 for 10–12 minutes, or until butter is bubbling hot. Serve with plenty of warmed French bread to mop up the delicious butter.

Moules à la marinière

Serves 4

3 lb (1.4kg) fresh mussels
1 small onion
4 tablespoons dry white wine
1½ oz (40g) butter
1 level tablespoon plain flour
freshly milled pepper
chopped parsley, for sprinkling

illustrated facing page 17

Thoroughly clean the mussels by shaking them in several changes of cold water until the water remains clean and free of grit. Discard any open ones. Scrape shells clean and pull off the 'beards'. Peel and finely chop the onion.

Using a buttered paper, thoroughly butter the inside of a large saucepan. Sprinkle the onion in the pan and add the wine. Simmer for 1–2 minutes to soften the onion. Then transfer mussels straight from the washing water to the saucepan. Cover with a lid and steam over high heat for 2–3 minutes, until mussels have opened. Shake pan from time to time and those on top will work their way down to the bottom. Draw off the heat. Discard any mussels that remain closed and arrange in hot soup plates or deep bowls. Reserve the cooking liquid.

Cream the butter and flour together on a plate to make a beurre manié. Add to the hot cooking liquid in small pieces. Stir until butter has melted and blended, then return pan to the heat and bring to the boil, stirring all the time. Check seasoning – there's no need to add salt as mussels release a lot of salty water but a little pepper may be required. Pour the thin sauce over the mussels and sprinkle with chopped parsley. Use whole mussel shells as pinchers for picking up mussels and provide a spoon for the sauce. Pass hot crusty bread for mopping up the delicious sauce.

Scallops with mushrooms

Scrub six of the deep scallop shells, rub with oil and set aside. Otherwise grease six pretty white china scallop dishes or ramekins. Cut the scallops in thick slices, leaving the coral whole, and put into a saucepan. Slice the mushrooms and add to the pan along with the wine, water and parsley. Simmer for 5 minutes. Strain ½ pint (300ml) cooking liquid into a measuring jug and reserve for making the sauce. Keep the scallops and mushrooms hot and discard the parsley.

Melt 1½ oz (40g) of the butter in a saucepan over low heat. Stir in the flour and cook for 1 minute. Gradually stir in the hot cooking liquid. Bring to the boil, stirring all the time to make a smooth sauce. Simmer for 2–3 minutes and draw off the heat. Blend the egg yolk with the cream and stir into the sauce. Add a squeeze of lemon juice and half the grated cheese and season with salt and pepper. Pour about two-thirds of the sauce into the scallops and mushrooms and mix together. Spoon into the prepared serving dishes. Top each dish with the remaining sauce, sprinkle with remaining cheese and dot with remaining butter. Bake in an oven heated to 375°F (190°C) or Gas no. 5 for 20 minutes, until sauce is hot and bubbling.

Variation **Scallops in a cream sauce:** For a simple yet extravagant first course, gently fry the scallops in 2 oz (50g) butter for 5 minutes. Season with salt and pepper and stir in ¼ pint (150ml) double cream. Bring just to the simmering point and draw off the heat. Spoon into the prepared dishes and serve with crusty bread to mop up the tasty sauce.

Serves 6

6–8 fresh scallops
4 oz (100g) button mushrooms
¼ pint (150ml) dry white wine
¼ pint (150ml) water
few sprigs parsley
2 oz (50g) butter
1 oz (25g) plain flour
1 egg yolk
3 tablespoons single cream
squeeze of lemon juice
2 oz (50g) grated Gruyère cheese
salt and freshly milled pepper

Devilled soft roes

Separate the herring roes, rinse and carefully pull away the thread. Take care when handling not to break the very thin membrane surrounding them or they will lose their shape. Mix together the flour and curry powder and season with salt and pepper, then evenly coat the roes in the seasoned flour.

Melt the butter in a frying pan over moderate heat, add the roes and fry gently for 3–4 minutes, turning once. The roes should be firm but not crisp. Add a dash of Worcestershire sauce and vinegar. Serve on hot buttered toast.

Variation: Herring roes are also very good simply fried in butter, and seasoned with salt and pepper. Add a squeeze of lemon juice just before serving.

Serves 4

¾–1 lb (350–450g) soft herring
   roes
1 tablespoon plain flour
1 level teaspoon curry powder
salt and freshly milled pepper
2 oz (50g) butter
dash of Worcestershire sauce
dash of vinegar
4 slices hot buttered toast

Aubergine caviar

Serves 4–6

3 large aubergines
1 medium-sized onion
3 tablespoons oil
1 clove garlic
3 tablespoons concentrated tomato
    purée
juice of ½ lemon
½ level teaspoon sugar
salt and freshly milled pepper
chopped parsley, to garnish

Prick the skins of the aubergines with a fork. Place in a baking tin and cook in an oven heated to 375°F (190°C) or Gas no. 5 for 40–45 minutes, until aubergines feel quite soft. Allow to cool, then cut in half lengthways and scoop out the soft flesh with a spoon. Discard the skins. Coarsely chop the flesh and set aside.

Peel and finely chop the onion. Heat the oil in a frying pan over low heat, add the onion and fry gently for 5 minutes to soften but not brown. Peel and crush the garlic with salt and add to the pan along with the chopped aubergine, tomato purée, lemon juice and sugar. Season with salt and pepper. Simmer gently, uncovered, until the mixture is quite thick and most of the juices have evaporated. Stir occasionally to prevent mixture from sticking to the pan. Check seasoning and allow to cool completely. Sprinkle with chopped parsley. Serve with hot crusty French bread or toast in the same way as for a pâté or spread.

Potted salmon

Serves 4

8 oz (225g) cooked salmon
3 anchovy fillets
5 oz (125g) unsalted butter
pinch of ground mace
salt and freshly milled pepper
4 lemon slices

This is a useful way to use up any leftover salmon from a whole fish. Flake the salmon flesh and discard any skin and bone. Pound the anchovies in a mixing bowl with the back of a wooden spoon, then add the salmon and mix together well. Add 4 oz (100g) of the butter and beat until creamy. Add the mace and season with salt and pepper. Spoon into a small serving pot or four ramekin dishes and spread level. Melt the remaining butter in a saucepan and pour it over the top. Garnish with lemon slices. Chill for at least 3 hours. The butter will form a crust and keep the salmon moist and fresh. Serve with hot toast.

Eggs mayonnaise

Serves 6

6 eggs
4 crisp lettuce leaves
4 rounded tablespoons mayonnaise
2 tablespoons single cream
chopped chives or lumpfish caviar,
    to garnish

illustrated facing page 33

Boil the eggs for 6 minutes from cold. (The eggs will be set but still slightly soft in the centre.) Drain and plunge into cold water to arrest cooking. Shell the eggs and submerge them in a bowl of water until cold.

Using a wetted knife, cut eggs in half lengthways. Place crisp lettuce on four individual serving plates and arrange the eggs in pairs on top, cut side up. Blend the cream with the mayonnaise to soften the consistency and spoon it on to the centre of each egg half. Garnish with chopped chives or lumpfish caviar. Serve with thinly sliced brown bread and butter.

Variations: Omit the mayonnaise and cream and coat the eggs with a seafood mayonnaise (page 121) or curry mayonnaise (page 121). Garnish the eggs with curls of anchovy fillets or sprinkle them with paprika.

Illustrated: Selection of cocktail snacks – melon with Parma ham, smoked salmon pinwheels, seasoned cream cheese on pumpernickel, all page 12

Kipper pâté

Put the kipper fillets in a jug, pour over boiling water to cover and leave for 2–3 minutes, then drain. When cool enough to handle, remove the skin and flake the kipper flesh. Melt the butter in a saucepan over low heat.

Place kipper flesh in a blender or food processor, add the melted butter, reserving a little, and blend to a purée. Transfer ingredients to a mixing bowl and stir in the double cream and lemon juice and season with pepper. Spoon into a serving dish and spread level. Spoon over the reserved melted butter and spread evenly. Garnish with lemon slices. Chill for at least 3 hours.

This makes a good first course with hot toast. Use as a stuffing for hard-boiled eggs, as a topping for canapés or a tasty sandwich filling with lettuce.

Serves 6

1 lb (450g) boned kipper fillets
7 oz (200g) butter
¼ pint (150ml) double cream
juice of 1 lemon
freshly milled pepper
2 lemon slices

Smoked mackerel pâté

Remove the skin from the smoked mackerel and flake the flesh on to a plate. Cream 2 oz (50g) of the butter in a mixing bowl until soft, then beat in the cream cheese. Add the flaked fish, lemon juice, tomato purée and a good seasoning of salt and pepper and beat until smooth. Alternatively, blend ingredients in a blender or food processor. Spoon the mixture into a serving dish and spread level. Melt the remaining butter in a saucepan and pour it over the top. Decorate with a bay leaf. Chill for at least 3 hours.

This pâté is lovely with wholemeal toast, French bread or spooned on to tiny biscuits or rounds of pumpernickel. Use this tasty pâté to stuff stalks of celery and serve with drinks.

Serves 4

2 medium-sized smoked mackerel
**   fillets**
3 oz (75g) butter
4 oz (100g) cream cheese
juice of ½ lemon
1 teaspoon concentrated tomato
**   purée**
salt and freshly milled pepper
1 bay leaf

Taramasalata

Put the smoked cod's roe into a mixing bowl, pour over boiling water to cover and leave to soak for 2–3 minutes to loosen the skin. Drain, then peel the skin. Coarsely chop the roe and return to the bowl. Add 2 tablespoons of the oil and mix together. Allow to stand for 15 minutes to soften, then press through a sieve into a mixing bowl to make a smooth mixture.

Beat in 1 tablespoon of the lemon juice. Gradually beat in the oil, 1 tablespoon at a time, beating in the remaining lemon juice half-way through adding the oil. Stir in the chopped parsley and onion and season with pepper. Spoon into a serving dish, cover with cling film, and chill. Wrap tightly, otherwise other foods will take up the strong flavour. The flavour will improve if the taramasalata is made 1–2 days before serving and it will keep for a week. Spread on hot pitta bread or unbuttered toast.

Serves 6

8 oz (225g) smoked cod's roe
¼ pint (150ml) oil
2 tablespoons lemon juice
2 tablespoons finely chopped
**   parsley**
1 tablespoon finely chopped onion
freshly milled pepper

Illustrated: Moules à la marinière, page 14

Smooth liver pâté

Serves 6

1 lb (450g) chicken livers
1 onion
1 clove garlic (optional)
3 oz (75g) butter
4 tablespoons chicken stock
salt and freshly milled pepper
¼ pint (150ml) double cream
2 eggs
1 level tablespoon cornflour
4 tablespoons dry sherry

Trim the chicken livers. Peel and finely chop the onion and garlic, if using it. Melt 2 oz (50g) of the butter in a saucepan over low heat, add the onion and fry gently for 5 minutes to soften but not brown. Add the garlic, chicken livers and stock and season with salt and pepper. Cook gently, covered with a pan lid, for 10–15 minutes, until livers are lightly cooked.

Spoon the mixture with juices into the goblet of a blender or food processor and blend to a smooth purée. Pour into a mixing bowl and stir in the cream and eggs. Blend the cornflour with the sherry, add to the bowl and mix together well.

Pour the very soft mixture into a 2 pint (1.1 litre) greased baking dish and cover with a lid or kitchen foil. Place in a roasting tin and fill the tin to a depth of 1 inch (2.5cm) with water. Cook in an oven heated to 325°F (160°C) or Gas no. 3 for 1–1½ hours until firm when pressed in the centre. Allow to cool. Melt the remaining butter in a saucepan and pour it over the surface to cover. Chill overnight. This smooth-textured pâté will keep for up to 3 days. Serve with hot toast and butter.

Choosing a mould

Use a simple ring mould, a fluted savarin mould or a plain sided charlotte russe tin for moulding savoury recipes and keep the very decorative mould with intricate designs for lending interest to dessert recipes. Don't be tempted to use one of those Victorian china moulds because unmoulding gelatine mixture from these needs patience and can be unreliable – remember thin metal makes unmoulding easier. Rinse your mould with cold water before pouring in the mousse mixture and this will help it to slip out more easily afterwards. If you need more details turn to page 207.

Cucumber mousse

Serves 6

1 cucumber
2 tablespoons coarse salt
¼ pint (150ml) chicken stock
½ oz (15g) powdered gelatine
1 lb (450g) cream cheese or
    2 × 8 oz (227g) cartons cottage
    cheese
1 tablespoon chopped chives
salt and freshly milled pepper
¼ pint (150ml) double cream
squeeze of lemon juice or dash of
    wine vinegar

Peel the cucumber, cut in half lengthways and scoop out the seeds with a teaspoon. Dice the cucumber, place in a colander and sprinkle with coarse salt. Leave to stand for 30 minutes to draw some of the juices. Thoroughly rinse cucumber and press dry in absorbent paper.

Put 4 tablespoons of the stock into a saucepan, sprinkle in the gelatine and leave to soak for 5 minutes. Meanwhile, put the cream cheese into a mixing bowl and beat until soft. Or press cottage cheese through a sieve into a mixing bowl. Stir the stock and gelatine over low heat (do not boil) until the gelatine has dissolved. Draw off the heat and add the remaining stock.

Slowly stir the stock into the cheese and blend. Add the cucumber, chives and a good seasoning of salt and pepper. Whip the cream until soft peaks form and fold into the mixture. Add a squeeze of lemon juice or a dash of wine vinegar to sharpen the flavour. Pour into a 1½ pint (900ml) wetted ring mould and chill for at least 3 hours or overnight. Unmould on to a serving plate. Serve with thinly sliced brown bread and butter.

Avocado mousse with prawns

Pour the cold water into a small saucepan, sprinkle in the gelatine and leave to soak for 5 minutes, then stir over low heat until the gelatine has dissolved (do not boil). Draw off the heat and add the stock. Set aside to cool.

Halve the avocados and remove the stones, then scoop out the flesh with a spoon. In a mixing bowl, mash the avocado flesh with a fork. Add onion juice (twist an onion half on a lemon squeezer), Worcestershire sauce and season with salt and pepper. Slowly stir in the cooled gelatine and mix together well. When mixture begins to thicken and shows signs of setting, whip the cream until soft peaks form and fold into the mixture along with the mayonnaise.

Pour into a wetted 1½ pint (900ml) ring mould and chill for at least 3 hours. Unmould mousse on to a serving plate. Combine prawns with oil and vinegar dressing and spoon into the centre. Serve with thinly sliced brown bread and butter.

Serves 6

¼ pint (150ml) cold water
½ oz (15g) powdered gelatine
¼ pint (150ml) chicken stock
3 avocados
1 teaspoon onion juice
2 teaspoons Worcestershire sauce
salt and freshly milled pepper
¼ pint (150ml) double cream
¼ pint (150ml) mayonnaise
1 × 8 oz (225g) packet frozen peeled prawns, thawed
3–4 tablespoons oil and vinegar dressing

Smoked cod's roe mousse

Put the smoked cod's roe into a mixing bowl, pour over boiling water to cover and leave to soak for 2–3 minutes to loosen the skin. Drain, then peel the skin. Coarsely chop the roe and return to the bowl. Add the oil and mix together. Leave to stand for 15 minutes to soften, then press through a sieve into a mixing bowl. Add the lemon juice and season with pepper. Mix together until well blended.

Put 4 tablespoons of the cold water into a saucepan, sprinkle in the gelatine and leave to soak for 5 minutes, then stir over low heat until the gelatine has dissolved (do not boil). Draw off the heat and stir in remaining water. Slowly add to the cod's roe, stirring all the time. When mixture begins to thicken and shows signs of setting, whip the cream until soft peaks form and whisk the egg whites until stiff peaks form, then fold first the cream, then the egg whites into the mixture. Spoon into a serving dish and spread level. Chill for at least 3 hours. Sprinkle with the chopped chives or parsley. Serve the mousse with thinly sliced brown bread and butter.

Serves 6

8 oz (225g) smoked cod's roe
3 tablespoons oil
juice of 1 lemon
freshly milled pepper
6 tablespoons cold water
½ oz (15g) powdered gelatine
½ pint (300ml) double cream
2 egg whites
1 tablespoon chopped chives or parsley

Curried egg mousse

Serves 6

6 eggs
½ cucumber
1 tablespoon coarse salt
¼ pint (150ml) chicken stock
½ oz (15g) powdered gelatine
½ pint (300ml) mayonnaise
2 level teaspoons curry powder
juice of ½ lemon
salt and freshly milled pepper
¼ pint (150ml) double cream

Boil the eggs for 8 minutes from cold. Drain and plunge into cold water to arrest cooking. Shell and submerge eggs in a bowl of water until cold. Peel the cucumber, cut in half lengthways and scoop out the seeds with a teaspoon. Dice the cucumber, place in a colander and sprinkle with the coarse salt. Leave to stand for 30 minutes to draw some of the juices. Thoroughly rinse and press dry in absorbent paper to remove excess moisture.

Pour the chicken stock into a saucepan, sprinkle in the gelatine and leave to soak for 5 minutes. Meanwhile, combine mayonnaise, curry powder and lemon juice in a mixing bowl. Coarsely chop the eggs and stir into the mayonnaise mixture. Add the diced cucumber. Stir the stock and gelatine over low heat until the gelatine has dissolved (do not boil), then slowly stir into the egg mixture and blend well. Season with salt and pepper. When mixture begins to thicken and shows signs of setting, whip the cream until soft peaks form and fold into the mixture. Pour into a wetted 1½ pint (900ml) ring mould and spread level. Chill for at least 3 hours. Unmould on to a serving plate. Serve with thinly sliced brown bread and butter.

Smoked haddock mousse

Serves 6

1 lb (450g) smoked haddock fillet
slice of onion
few parsley stalks
1 bay leaf
1 pint (600ml) water
½ oz (15g) powdered gelatine
juice of ½ lemon
freshly milled pepper
½ pint (300ml) double cream
2 hard-boiled eggs
lemon aspic jelly (page 119)

Cut the smoked haddock into pieces and put into a saucepan along with the onion, parsley stalks, bay leaf and water. Bring to the boil, cover with a lid and cook gently for 10 minutes, or until haddock is tender. Transfer fish to a plate and when cool enough to handle, flake the flesh discarding skin and bones. Strain ½ pint (300ml) cooking liquid into a measuring jug and pour into the rinsed pan. Sprinkle in the gelatine and leave to soak for 5 minutes.

Replace pan over low heat and stir until the gelatine has dissolved. Do not allow to boil. Pour the fish liquid into a medium-sized bowl and allow to cool. When mixture begins to thicken and shows signs of setting, stir in the flaked haddock, lemon juice and a seasoning of freshly milled pepper. Add salt only if necessary.

Whip the cream until soft peaks form and fold into the mixture. Spoon into a serving dish and spread level. Decorate the top with slices of hard-boiled egg and spoon over sufficient lemon aspic jelly to make a thin covering. Chill for 2–3 hours or overnight. Remove smoked haddock mousse from refrigerator at least 30 minutes before serving. Serve with thinly sliced brown bread and butter.

Melon with ginger sugar

Cut the melon lengthways and scoop out the seeds, then slice each half in 2 or 3 wedges. Using a sharp knife, cut between the juicy melon flesh and rind but leave in place, then cut the flesh crossways in slices.

Combine the sugar and ginger in a serving bowl or, better still, put sugar and ginger into a sugar sifter. Ginger sugar is a good idea – it makes the ginger less potent and you can afford to be more generous with it. Pass the ginger sugar and lemon wedges separately for sprinkling on the melon and eat the melon with a fruit knife and fork.

Serves 4–6

1 ripe honeydew melon
lemon wedges, for serving

Ginger sugar
3 oz (75g) castor sugar
1 level teaspoon ground ginger

Avocado and mozzarella salad

Scald the tomatoes and peel away the skins. Slice tomatoes and arrange a few slices on each of six serving plates. Slice the mozzarella cheese thinly and arrange on each of the plates alongside the tomatoes.

Halve and stone the avocados. Place each half, cut side down, on a work surface and run a knife point along the centre back, cutting the skin only. Peel back sections of skin and remove to reveal the green flesh, then cut crossways in slices. Arrange avocado slices alongside cheese and immediately spoon over the dressing. Sprinkle with oregano and grate over a little pepper.

This salad, with its neat rows of contrasting colours, also looks lovely arranged on a single large plate for a buffet. Mozzarella is a bland cheese and one of the few cheeses that goes well with an oil and vinegar dressing.

Serves 6

4 ripe tomatoes
6 oz (175g) mozzarella cheese
2 ripe avocados
¼ pint (150ml) oil and vinegar dressing
pinch of dried oregano
freshly milled pepper

Avocado and apple salad

Halve and stone the avocados. Place each half, cut side down, on a work surface and run a knife point along the centre back, cutting the skin only. Peel back sections of skin and remove to reveal the green flesh, then cut crossways in ¼ inch (5mm) thick slices. Put the slices into a mixing bowl and immediately spoon over the oil and vinegar dressing.

Peel, quarter and core the apples. Cut the apples crossways in ¼ inch (5mm) thick slices. Add the apple slices and chopped walnuts to the bowl and toss to coat in the dressing. Spoon on to six serving plates and serve.

Variation: Scoop avocado flesh from each shell. Chop flesh and mix with salad ingredients. Spoon salad into the avocado shells and serve.

Serves 6

3 ripe avocados
¼ pint (150ml) oil and vinegar dressing
2 dessert apples
3 tablespoons chopped walnuts

Avocado with orange

Serves 6

**3 oranges
3 ripe avocados
freshly milled pepper**

Dressing
**dash of French mustard
2 tablespoons lemon juice
salt and freshly milled pepper
6 tablespoons oil**

illustrated facing page 48

Combine the mustard, lemon juice and a seasoning of salt and pepper in a mixing bowl. Beat in the oil and blend well.

Slice the top and bottom off each orange. Using a sharp knife, cut downwards and around the sides to remove the peel and white pith. Hold prepared fruits over the mixing bowl to catch juices, cut into segments and turn them into the dressing.

Halve and stone the avocados. Place each half, cut side down, on a work surface and run a knife point along the centre back cutting the skin only. Peel back sections of skin and remove to reveal the green flesh, then cut crossways in slices. Arrange a fan of avocado slices on six individual serving plates. Spoon over dressing and arrange orange segments in a fan shape alongside the avocados – this looks very pretty. Grate over a little pepper.

Variation: Halve and stone the avocados. Pile orange segments into the hollow of each one and spoon over dressing. Add a grating of freshly milled pepper.

Grapefruit as a first course

Never underestimate how refreshing and appetizing grapefruit can be. These recipes serve 6.

Grilled grapefruit: Cut a sliver off the top and bottom of 3 grapefruits so they stand upright. Then cut in half crossways. Using a grapefruit knife, cut around the segments in each half to loosen. Melt 1 oz (25g) butter and using a pastry brush, dab melted butter over the surface of each grapefruit half, then sprinkle generously with demerara sugar. Set grapefruit halves under a hot grill about 2 inches (5cm) from the heat. Grill for about 5 minutes until sugar has melted and is bubbling. Set in individual serving glasses.

Baked grapefruit: Prepare 3 grapefruits as directed above. Then arrange grapefruit halves in a baking tin. Spoon 1 teaspoon sherry on to each grapefruit half, sprinkle with demerara sugar then dot the surfaces with 1 oz (25g) butter cut in flakes. Bake in an oven heated to 400°F (200°C) or Gas no. 6 for 15 minutes. Set in individual serving glasses and spoon over juices from the tin.

Florida cocktail: Cut a slice off the top and bottom through to the flesh of 3 grapefruits. For best colour contrast include 1 pink grapefruit, if possible. Stand each grapefruit upright and using a sharp knife, cut downwards and around to remove white pith and peel. Then hold prepared fruits over a mixing bowl to catch juices, cut in between each segment to loosen and turn them into the bowl. Discard pips. Prepare 2 oranges the same way. Add 2 oz (50g) castor sugar. Stir fruits and refrigerate for at least 1 hour so sugar and juices form a syrup. This mixture looks best in a clear glass bowl or spoon it into individual serving glasses with sugared rims.

Grapefruit with crème de menthe: Prepare 4 grapefruits as above, turning segments into a bowl. Add 2 oz (50g) castor sugar and chill for several hours. Then stir in 2 tablespoons crème de menthe and grapefruit will take the pretty green colour. Chilling the grapefruit emphasizes the cool taste of the liqueur. Serve in individual serving glasses, with sugared rims.

Pears with Roquefort cream

In a mixing bowl, mash the Roquefort and cream cheese together with a fork. Beat in the single cream to make a smooth mixture and season with freshly milled pepper. Chill until required.

Peel the pears and place in a bowl of cold water with lemon juice added to retain the colour. Combine all the ingredients for the dressing except chopped parsley. Halve the pears and scoop out the core with a teaspoon to make a hollow for the cheese mixture. Turn the pears in the prepared dressing and arrange them cut side up on crisp lettuce – allow two pear halves per person on individual plates. Spoon the Roquefort cream into the cavity of each pear half. Add chopped parsley to the dressing and spoon dressing over the filled pears. The pears for this recipe must be fully ripe – juicy Comice or Williams pears are the best. The flavour of fresh pear and sharp Roquefort cream is delicious.

Serves 6

3 oz (75g) Roquefort cheese
4 oz (100g) fresh cream cheese
2–3 tablespoons single cream
freshly milled pepper
6 ripe dessert pears
crisp lettuce, for serving

Dressing
salt and freshly milled pepper
pinch of sugar
juice of 1 lemon
3–4 tablespoons oil
1 tablespoon chopped parsley

Eggs baked in the oven

The traditional cocotte dishes for this recipe are small and hold 1 egg perfectly. Generously grease four cocotte dishes or individual ramekin dishes with butter. Warm the dishes in the oven, then carefully break 1 egg into each dish and season with salt and pepper. Place the dishes in a roasting tin and pour boiling water into the tin to come half-way up the sides of the dishes.

Bake in an oven heated to 350°F (180°C) or Gas no. 4 for about 6 minutes, until the whites are just set. Remove from the oven and spoon a little cream over each egg, then bake for a further 2 minutes. The egg whites should be set but the yolks still runny. Remember that the eggs will continue to cook in the hot dishes after they have been removed from the oven.

Variations: A spoonful of lightly cooked mushrooms, chopped fried bacon, chopped red and green pepper softened in butter, or fresh tomatoes (peeled, seeded and coarsely chopped) can be added to each dish before cracking in the egg. Or, sprinkle the tops with chopped fresh parsley, chives or tarragon after adding the cream; a little grated cheese or lumpfish caviar is also nice.

Crack 2 eggs into each ramekin dish if you wish to serve this as a light lunch or supper dish.

Serves 4

4 eggs
butter, for greasing
salt and freshly milled pepper
¼ pint (150ml) double cream

Smoked fish

A first course of smoked fish is the answer for a busy hostess. Take your pick from the suggestions below. All are good served on individual plates, accompanied by lemon wedges, a plate of thinly sliced brown bread and butter and a pepper mill of black peppercorns.

Smoked salmon is always served cut in very thin slices. It can be bought as a whole side, a pre-sliced side, in packs of slices, or it can be sliced to order. Allow 2 oz (50g) per serving and arrange slices spread out on the plate. If slicing a whole side, use a sharp knife, and cut at a slant, starting about 3 inches (7.5cm) from the tail. Keep surface of uncut smoked salmon lightly oiled so it does not dry out.

Smoked trout is a whole smoked fish. Cut off head and tail, lift away the skin and serve smoked trout on the bone. It's particularly nice served with soured cream horseradish sauce (page 122).

Smoked cod's roe is delicious just as it is. Simply cut the smoked roe in slices about ¼ inch (5mm) thick. Arrange 2–3 slices per person on lettuce leaves and sprinkle with a very little finely chopped onion.

Smoked buckling is a type of smoked herring, gutted but not opened out. It has already been cooked when smoked so only needs the skin removed and flesh lifted off the bones before serving. Smoked buckling is large so one should be enough to serve 4.

Smoked eel is rich and satisfying. Lift away skin and cut smoked eel in 3–4 inch (7.5–10cm) lengths, then lift the flesh off the bone and arrange on crisp lettuce.

Smoked mackerel are sold whole or in fillets. Excellent vacuum-packed ones come from Cornwall; these can be plain or coated with black peppercorns – the latter are my favourite. Smoked mackerel are large so half a fish is adequate for one serving. Plain smoked mackerel are very good served with soured cream horseradish sauce (page 122).

2

Soups

It's hard to go wrong with soups. Not only are
they easy to make, but with good ingredients and
a little imagination you will be constantly
surprised and delighted at the many varieties of
soups you can make.

Soups

How to make better soups

● Flavour is always better if you stir-fry soup vegetables in butter before adding the stock.

● Thicken green soups such as lettuce, leek, spinach or watercress by adding a diced potato to the pan. Use a floury maincrop variety.

● Cut vegetables small so they cook more quickly and simmer the soup gently to slowly release the flavour. Soups should never be boiled fast or they will just evaporate and reduce.

● A meat bone or chicken carcass boiled up to make a simple stock will improve the flavour of any soup, but the lack of one should not deter you. Vegetable soups can be made with water; you can also use vegetable cooking water or a chicken stock cube with water.

● Add milk to soups after the soup is puréed and before reheating to avoid the risk of milk separation, especially if vegetables are acid, such as tomato and watercress. Soups with milk added will easily boil over, so watch the pot.

● Soups passed through a food mill or sieve have more character, but use the blender when you want them very smooth and creamy.

● Season soups carefully and recheck seasoning before serving. Soups served cold will need more seasoning than those served hot.

● When making puréed soups to serve chilled, keep butter to a minimum and make sure you skim off every particle of fat before refrigerating. Or avoid butter altogether by using oil.

● A tablespoon of cream added to any soup will make it richer, and a liaison of egg yolk and cream makes it satiny smooth. A blend of 1 egg yolk with 2–3 tablespoons cream to 2 pints (1.1 litres) soup is the usual proportion. Add cream or a liaison at the very end after the pan has been drawn off the heat.

● Soups thicken as they cool, especially pulse soups. When reheating do not add extra liquid because the soup will thin again with heating. For serving soups chilled, however, add extra cream, stock or milk to make a thin consistency.

● Some soups taste better the day after making, particularly vegetable soups. Allow soup to cool to room temperature, then chill. Reheat just before serving and check seasoning.

Soup garnishes

● Chopped parsley makes an attractive garnish for any soup and it blends with most flavours.

● Freeze chopped parsley in ice cubes made with a little water or stock. A parsley cube can then be dropped into the hot soup at the last moment when the ice will dissolve to release the fresh parsley. Do the same with fresh chives.

● A lump of plain butter or parsley butter (page 117) stirred into a vegetable soup at the last moment will enrich the flavour.

● A spoonful of double cream swirled over the top of a deep-coloured soup will make it look very appetizing.

● Just a pinch of paprika is pretty sprinkled over a pale-coloured soup.

● Hot garlic or herb bread (page 286) is delicious served with chilled soups.

● Sprinkle grated hard cheese on vegetable soups when serving, or pass a bowl round separately.

All-purpose stock

Makes 2 pints (1.1 litres)

2 carrots
1 onion
1 leek (optional)
1 stalk celery (optional)
1 chicken carcass or raw meat bone
4 pints (2.4 litres) cold water
2 level teaspoons salt
4–6 black peppercorns
1 bay leaf

Peel and chop the carrots and onion. Trim and chop the leek and celery, if using them. Put the carcass in large pieces or the raw meat bone into a large saucepan. Add the water, salt and peppercorns. Slowly bring to the boil, removing scum when it rises to the surface. Add the bay leaf and vegetables, and simmer gently, uncovered, for 2 hours. A gentle simmer prevents the stock from turning cloudy.

Strain through a fine sieve and check seasoning. Allow to cool, then chill. Skim the fat from the surface of the chilled stock. Use within 3 days of making.

Variations: Other suitable flavourings for stocks are bacon trimmings or mushroom trimmings. You can also make stock with a turkey carcass or a cooked meat or ham bone.

Chilled avocado soup

Serves 6

2 ripe avocados
1½ pints (900ml) chicken stock
¼ pint (150ml) single cream
juice of 1 lemon
salt and freshly milled pepper
2 tablespoons chopped chives

Halve the avocados lengthways and remove the stones. Scoop out avocado flesh with a tablespoon and put into the goblet of an electric blender or food processor. Immediately add 1 pint (600ml) of the cold chicken stock. Cover and blend to a purée – the soup should be pale green and beautifully smooth.

Pour soup into a mixing bowl and stir in remaining stock, the cream, lemon juice and season with salt and pepper. Cover bowl with cling film and chill for several hours. Stir in freshly chopped chives about 10 minutes before serving. Serve in chilled soup bowls. Avocado soup looks cool and inviting with a few ice cubes floating in it.

Cucumber and yoghurt soup

Chop the unpeeled cucumber and place in a mixing bowl. Peel and finely chop the garlic and add to the bowl along with the salt, yoghurt, chopped walnuts and oil.

Ladle half the ingredients into the goblet of an electric blender or food processor. Cover and blend to a purée then pour into a second mixing bowl. Repeat with remaining ingredients. Stir in the cream and lemon juice and season with pepper. Taste and add more salt and pepper if necessary. This soup is a delicate pale green flecked with dark pieces of cucumber peel. A few drops of green food colouring can be added at this stage, if a darker shade is liked.

Cover bowl with cling film and chill for several hours. Serve in chilled soup bowls. Sprinkle with chopped chives or mint. This is wonderfully refreshing on a hot summer day.

Serves 6

1 large cucumber
1 clove garlic
½ level teaspoon salt
1 pint (600ml) natural yoghurt
1 oz (25g) chopped walnuts
1 tablespoon oil
½ pint (300ml) single cream
juice of ½ lemon
freshly milled pepper
few drops of green food colouring (optional)
1 tablespoon chopped chives or mint

Lettuce soup

Peel and finely chop the onion. Melt the butter in a large saucepan over low heat, add the onion and fry gently for 5 minutes to soften but not brown. Meanwhile, peel and cut the potato in even-sized chunks. Add the stock to the onions; season with salt and pepper and bring to the boil. Add the potato, lower the heat and simmer gently, covered, for 15 minutes until potato is tender.

Coarsely shred the lettuce leaves. (The lettuce may consist of outer leaves from two or more heads reserving the hearts for salad.) Add to the pan and bring to the boil, then draw off the heat. Pass soup mixture through a food mill, or purée in an electric blender or food processor. Return the soup to the rinsed pan. Reheat and check seasoning. Stir in the cream and serve.

Variations: For **chilled lettuce soup,** allow the puréed soup to cool, then chill. Stir in ¼ pint (150ml) single cream. Ladle the soup into chilled soup bowls and sprinkle with chopped chives.

Sorrel soup: Use a mixture of fresh sorrel leaves and lettuce in about equal quantities, though proportions may vary according to the flavour you like. Sorrel looks like spinach and has an astringent flavour. It is not readily available in shops but can be easily grown.

Spinach soup: Use 8 oz (225g) young spinach leaves, well washed with ribs removed, in place of lettuce. Simmer gently for 5 minutes after bringing to the boil. Then finish in the same way.

Serves 6

1 medium-sized onion
1 oz (25g) butter
1 large potato
1½ pints (900ml) chicken stock
salt and freshly milled pepper
1 medium-sized lettuce
2–3 tablespoons single cream

Watercress soup

Serves 6

2 bunches watercress
1 medium-sized onion
1 oz (25g) butter
1 lb (450g) potatoes
1½ pints (900ml) chicken stock
1 bay leaf
salt and freshly milled pepper
½ pint (300ml) milk
2–3 tablespoons single cream

illustrated facing page 32

Pick off the leafy tops from the watercress and set aside a small handful for the garnish. Peel and finely chop the onion. Melt the butter in a large saucepan over low heat, add the onion and fry gently for 5 minutes to soften but not brown. Meanwhile, peel and cut the potatoes in even-sized chunks. Pour the stock into the pan, add the bay leaf and season with salt and pepper. Bring to the boil, add the potatoes, then lower the heat and simmer gently, covered, for 15 minutes, until potatoes are tender. Add the watercress and bring back to the boil. Draw off the heat, discard bay leaf and stir in the milk. Pass soup mixture through a food mill, or purée in an electric blender or food processor.

Return the soup to the rinsed pan. Reheat and check seasoning. Draw off the heat, stir in the cream, and garnish with chopped watercress. Ladle the soup into warmed soup bowls and serve.

Variations: For **chilled watercress soup**, allow the puréed soup to cool, then chill. Stir in ¼ pint (150ml) single cream.

Parsley soup: Use 2 oz (50g) fresh parsley in place of the watercress. Omit the bay leaf.

Cream of cucumber soup

Serves 6

2 large cucumbers
2½ oz (65g) butter
½ level teaspoon sugar
salt and freshly milled pepper
½ pint (300ml) milk
½ onion
1 bay leaf
1 oz (25g) flour
¾ pint (400ml) chicken stock
2–3 tablespoons single cream

Peel the cucumbers, cut in half lengthways, scoop out the seeds with a teaspoon and chop the flesh. Blanch in boiling water for 2 minutes to preserve the nice green colour, then drain. Dice a little cucumber and reserve for garnish. Melt 1 oz (25g) of the butter in a medium-sized saucepan and add the cucumber, sugar and a seasoning of salt and pepper. Cover with a pan lid and cook gently for 15 minutes, or until soft.

Meanwhile, heat the milk with the onion and bay leaf in a separate saucepan. Draw off the heat and allow flavours to infuse for 10 minutes. Melt the remaining butter in a saucepan over low heat. Stir in the flour and cook gently for 1 minute. Gradually pour in the milk (discard onion and bay leaf), stirring all the time, and bring to the boil. Cook gently for 2–3 minutes, stirring, to make a thick smooth sauce. Add the chicken stock and white sauce to the cucumbers. Cook gently, covered, for 15 minutes. Pass soup mixture through a food mill, or purée in an electric blender or food processor. Return the soup to the rinsed pan. Reheat and check seasoning. Stir in the cream and serve garnished with diced cucumber.

Variation: For **chilled cucumber soup**, allow the puréed soup to cool. Stir in ¼ pint (150ml) extra chicken stock or ¼ pint (150ml) single cream and chill.

Cream of spinach soup

Tear away coarse midribs of the spinach and wash spinach in several changes of cold water. Peel and finely chop the onion and garlic. Melt 1 oz (25g) of the butter in a large saucepan over low heat, add the onion and garlic and fry gently for 5 minutes to soften the onion but not brown. Add the wet spinach leaves, cover with a pan lid, and cook gently for 10 minutes until tender.

Meanwhile, heat the milk with the bay leaf in a separate saucepan. Draw off the heat and allow flavours to infuse for 10 minutes. Melt the remaining butter in a saucepan over low heat. Stir in the flour and cook gently for 1 minute. Gradually pour in the milk (discard bay leaf), stirring all the time, and bring to the boil. Cook gently for 2–3 minutes, stirring, to make a thick smooth sauce. Add the chicken stock and sauce to the spinach and season with salt and pepper. Cook gently, covered, for 10 minutes. Pass soup mixture through a food mill, or purée in an electric blender or food processor.

Return the soup to the rinsed pan and add a little grated nutmeg. Reheat and check seasoning. Stir in the cream and serve at once. Or ladle the hot soup into six warmed soup bowls and swirl the cream on top.

Serves 6

1 lb (450g) fresh spinach
1 medium-sized onion
1 clove garlic
2½ oz (65g) butter
½ pint (300ml) milk
1 bay leaf
1 oz (25g) flour
1 pint (600ml) chicken stock
salt and freshly milled pepper
grated nutmeg
4 tablespoons single cream

Celery soup with cheese

Separate the celery stalks, scrub well and then shred the stalks and finely chop the leaves. Peel and dice the potatoes. Peel and finely chop the onion.

Melt the butter in a large saucepan over low heat. Add the onion and fry gently for 5 minutes to soften but not brown. Add the celery and potato and cook gently for a further 5 minutes without allowing them to take colour. Add the stock and season with salt and pepper. Bring to the boil, then lower the heat and simmer, covered, for 30–40 minutes, or until the vegetables are quite tender. Pass soup mixture through a food mill or purée in an electric blender or food processor.

Return the soup to the rinsed pan. Reheat and check seasoning. Stir in the cream off the heat. Ladle into warmed soup bowls and serve with grated cheese sprinkled over the top.

Serves 6

1 head of celery with leaves
1 lb (450g) potatoes
1 medium-sized onion
2 oz (50g) butter
1½ pints (900ml) chicken stock
salt and freshly milled pepper
¼ pint (150ml) single cream
2–3 oz (50–75g) grated hard
  cheese

Chestnut soup

Serves 6

1 lb (450g) chestnuts
1 medium-sized onion
2–3 stalks celery
1 oz (25g) butter
2 pints (1.1 litres) chicken stock
salt and freshly milled pepper
¼ pint (150ml) single cream
1–2 tablespoons medium sherry
chopped parsley, to garnish

Use fresh chestnuts and buy the best – the larger ones are easier to peel. Cut a slit on the flat side of each chestnut. Immerse in boiling water for about 2 minutes and both inner skins and outer shell should peel off easily, but only boil about one-third at a time or chestnuts will cool before they can all be peeled.

Peel and finely chop the onion and chop the celery. Melt the butter in a large saucepan over low heat. Add the onion and celery and fry gently for 5 minutes to soften but not brown. Add the chestnuts and toss them in the hot butter, then pour in the stock and season with salt and pepper. Bring to the boil, then lower the heat and simmer gently, covered, for 35–40 minutes, or until chestnuts are tender. Reserve a few broken pieces of chestnut for garnish and pass soup through a food mill, or purée in an electric blender or food processor.

Return the soup to the rinsed pan. Reheat and check seasoning. Draw off the heat and stir in the cream and sherry. Add reserved pieces of chestnut and a sprinkling of chopped parsley. Ladle into warmed soup bowls and serve. This soup is rich and luxurious and would make a good first course for a special occasion.

Jerusalem artichoke soup

Serves 6

2 lb (900g) Jerusalem artichokes
1 medium-sized onion
1 oz (25g) butter
1 pint (600ml) chicken stock
salt and freshly milled pepper
½ pint (300ml) milk
1 egg yolk
3 tablespoons single cream
1 tablespoon chopped parsley

Peel the artichokes, placing each one when peeled in cold water with a little vinegar or lemon juice to prevent discoloration, then cut them up. Peel and finely chop the onion.

Melt the butter in a large saucepan over low heat. Add the onion and fry gently for 5 minutes to soften but not brown. Add the artichokes and toss them in the hot butter. Stir in the stock and season with salt and pepper. Bring to the boil, then lower the heat and simmer gently, covered, for 30 minutes, or until the vegetables are quite soft. Draw off the heat and add the milk. Pass soup mixture through a food mill, or purée in an electric blender or food processor.

Return the soup to the rinsed pan. Reheat and check seasoning. Blend egg yolk with cream in a small bowl and stir into the soup off the heat. Sprinkle with chopped parsley. Ladle into warmed soup bowls and serve.

Illustrated: Cold soups – watercress, carrot and orange, and vichyssoise, pages 30 and 34

Carrot and parsley soup

Peel and slice the carrots. Peel and finely chop the onion. Peel and dice the potato. Melt the butter in a large saucepan over low heat. Add the onion and fry gently for about 5 minutes until soft and lightly browned. Stir in the stock and bring to the boil.

Add the carrot and potato, the sprig of thyme, and a seasoning of salt and pepper. Lower the heat and simmer gently, covered, for about 40 minutes until carrots are tender. Add the sprigs of parsley and cook for a further 1 minute, then draw off the heat. Discard the thyme.

Pass soup mixture through a food mill, or purée in an electric blender or food processor. Return the soup to the rinsed pan. Reheat and check seasoning. Ladle into warmed soup bowls and serve. Carrot and parsley soup is very filling and makes a good snack or light lunch.

Serves 6

1 lb (450g) carrots
1 medium-sized onion
1 large potato
2 pints (1.1 litres) chicken stock
salt and freshly milled pepper
1 sprig thyme
6–8 parsley sprigs

Marrow soup with melon balls

Peel the marrow and cut in half lengthways. Scoop out the seeds and cut marrow flesh in chunks. Blanch in boiling water for 2 minutes, then drain. Melt 1 oz (25g) of the butter in a large saucepan over low heat. Add the marrow, sugar, parsley and a seasoning of salt and pepper. Cover with a pan lid and cook gently for 15 minutes until soft.

Meanwhile, heat the milk with the onion and bay leaf in a separate saucepan. Draw off the heat and allow flavours to infuse for 10 minutes. Melt remaining butter in a saucepan over low heat. Stir in the flour and cook gently for 1 minute. Gradually pour in the milk (discard onion and bay leaf), stirring all the time, and bring to the boil. Cook gently for 2–3 minutes, stirring, to make a smooth thick sauce. Add the chicken stock and white sauce to the marrow. Cook gently, covered, for a further 15 minutes. Discard parsley and pass soup mixture through a food mill, or purée in an electric blender or food processor. Allow to cool, then chill.

Scoop out the melon flesh with a melon baller. Divide between six chilled soup bowls. Ladle the soup into the bowls and sprinkle with paprika.

Variation: For **hot marrow soup**, do not allow soup to cool, but return to the rinsed pan, reheat and check seasoning. Omit the honeydew melon.

Serves 6

1 small tender marrow
2½ oz (65g) butter
pinch of sugar
bouquet of parsley sprigs
salt and freshly milled pepper
½ pint (300ml) milk
½ onion
1 bay leaf
1 oz (25g) plain flour
1 pint (600ml) chicken stock

Garnish
½ honeydew melon
paprika

Illustrated: Eggs mayonnaise, page 16

Chilled courgette soup

Serves 6

1 large onion
2 tablespoons oil
1 lb (450g) courgettes
1½ pints (900ml) chicken stock
salt and freshly milled pepper
¼ pint (150ml) natural yoghurt
1 tablespoon finely chopped chives

Peel and finely chop the onion. Heat the oil in a large saucepan over low heat, add the onion and fry gently for 5 minutes to soften but not brown.

Trim and slice the courgettes and add to the saucepan. Stir in the stock and bring to the boil, then lower the heat and simmer gently, covered, for about 30 minutes, until courgettes are soft. Draw off the heat and season with salt and pepper. Pass soup mixture through a food mill, or purée in an electric blender or food processor. Allow to cool, then stir in the yoghurt and chill. About 10 minutes before serving, stir in the chopped chives and check seasoning. Serve in chilled soup bowls.

Variation: For **hot courgette soup**, omit yoghurt, do not allow soup to cool but return to the rinsed pan, reheat and check seasoning. Stir in 1 tablespoon chopped parsley and serve.

Chilled carrot and orange soup

Serves 6

1 lb (450g) new carrots
1 onion
1 oz (25g) butter
1½ pints (900ml) chicken stock
1 level teaspoon castor sugar
salt and freshly milled pepper
juice of 4 oranges
¼ pint (150ml) single cream
2 tablespoons chopped chives

illustrated facing page 32

Scrape and thinly slice the carrots. Peel and finely chop the onion. Melt the butter in a large saucepan over low heat, add the carrots and onion, cover with a pan lid, and cook gently for 5 minutes to soften the onion but not brown.

Pour the stock into the pan, add the sugar and season with salt and pepper. Bring to the boil, then lower the heat and cook gently, covered, for 40 minutes until carrots are soft. Pass soup mixture through a food mill, or purée in an electric blender or food processor. Stir in the orange juice. Allow to cool, then chill. Stir in the cream and finely chopped chives. Serve in chilled soup bowls.

Vichyssoise

Serves 6

2 lb (900g) leeks
1 medium-sized onion
1 oz (25g) butter
1 lb (450g) potatoes
1½ pints (900ml) chicken stock
salt and freshly milled pepper
½ pint (300ml) milk
¼ pint (150ml) single cream
2 tablespoons chopped chives

illustrated facing page 32

Trim the tops and roots from the leeks, leaving only the white part. Cut in half lengthways and wash well, then finely chop the leeks. Peel and finely chop the onion. Melt the butter in a large saucepan over low heat, add the leeks and onion, cover with a pan lid, and cook gently for 5 minutes until softened and translucent. Meanwhile, peel and cut the potatoes in even-sized chunks.

Stir in the stock and season with salt and pepper. Bring to the boil, add the potatoes, then lower the heat and simmer gently, covered, for 30 minutes until potatoes are tender. Draw off the heat and add the milk. Pass soup mixture through a food mill, or purée in an electric blender or food processor. Pour into a bowl and allow to cool. Stir in the cream and chill. About 10 minutes before serving stir in the chopped chives.

Gazpacho

Trim the crust from the bread and soak the bread in a little cold water for a few minutes. Scald the fresh tomatoes, if using them, and peel away the skins, then halve and deseed them. Trim and chop the spring onions. Peel and chop the cucumber. Halve, deseed and chop the green peppers. Peel the clove of garlic and crush to a purée with salt.

Place all the vegetables (including garlic) in a mixing bowl along with the oil. If canned tomatoes are being used, add them at this stage with their juices. Squeeze the excess liquid from the bread and add to the bowl. Mix ingredients together. Ladle mixture into the goblet of an electric blender or food processor and blend to a coarse purée. Pour into a bowl and stir in the cold stock, sugar and vinegar and season with salt and pepper. Chill for several hours. Stir in chopped parsley and ladle soup into chilled soup bowls.

Serves 6

1 thick slice white bread
2 lb (900g) ripe tomatoes or 2 ×
   14 oz (396g) tins peeled tomatoes
6–8 spring onions
½ cucumber
2 green peppers
1 small clove garlic
4 tablespoons olive oil
1½ pints (900ml) chicken stock
1 teaspoon castor sugar
3 tablespoons wine vinegar
salt and freshly milled pepper
1 tablespoon chopped parsley

Hot beetroot soup

Peel the skins from the beetroot and potato, then cut them in even-sized chunks. Peel and finely chop the onion. Melt the butter in a large saucepan over low heat, add the onion and fry gently for 5 minutes to soften but not brown. Stir in the stock, season with salt and pepper and bring to the boil. Add the beetroot and potato, lower the heat, and cook gently, covered, for 40 minutes until vegetables are very soft. Pass soup mixture through a food mill, or purée in an electric blender or food processor.

Return the soup to the rinsed pan. Reheat and check seasoning. Ladle the soup into six warmed soup bowls and add a dash of Worcestershire sauce to each bowl. If you like, swirl cream over the top of each serving.

Serves 6

1 lb (450g) fresh beetroots
1 large potato
1 medium-sized onion
1 oz (25g) butter
2 pints (1.1 litres) chicken stock
salt and freshly milled pepper
Worcestershire sauce, for serving
2–3 tablespoons single cream
   (optional)

Parsnip soup

Peel and cut the parsnips and potato in even-sized chunks. Peel and finely chop the onion. Melt the butter in a large saucepan over low heat. Add the onion and fry gently for 5 minutes to soften but not brown. Stir in the curry powder and cook gently for a further 1 minute to draw out the flavour. Stir in the stock and season with salt and pepper.

Add the parsnips and potatoes and bring to the boil, then lower the heat and simmer gently, covered, for 40 minutes until parsnips are tender. (Test by squashing one with the back of a wooden spoon.) Pass soup mixture through a food mill, or purée in an electric blender or food processor. Return the soup to the rinsed pan. Reheat and check seasoning.

Serves 6

1 lb (450g) parsnips
1 large potato
1 large onion
1 oz (25g) butter
1 level teaspoon curry powder
2 pints (1.1 litres) chicken stock
salt and freshly milled black pepper

Pheasant soup

Serves 6

3–4 rashers streaky bacon
4 oz (100g) lamb liver
1 medium-sized onion
2 oz (50g) butter
2 roast pheasant carcasses
4 pints (2.4 litres) water
pinch of ground mace
bouquet garni of thyme, parsley
   and bay leaf
salt and freshly milled pepper
beurre manié (page 117)
2 tablespoons medium sherry

Trim and dice the bacon. Cut the lamb liver in bite-sized pieces. Peel and finely chop the onion. Melt the butter in a large saucepan over low heat, add the bacon and onion and fry gently for 5 minutes to soften the onion but not brown. Add the liver and toss with the butter and onions. Add the pheasant carcasses, water, mace and bouquet garni and season with salt and pepper. Bring to the boil and skim the surface, then lower the heat and simmer gently, covered, for 2 hours – the slower the cooking the better the soup will taste.

Strain the soup and return the stock to the rinsed pan. Lift any bits of pheasant meat from the carcasses. Pass pheasant meat, bacon, liver and a little of the stock through a food mill, or purée in an electric blender or food processor, then add to the pan. Add the beurre manié in small pieces to the soup and stir to blend. Return to the heat and bring to the boil, stirring all the time, so soup thickens evenly. Stir in the sherry and check seasoning.

Seafood chowder

Serves 4–6

1 lb (450g) smoked haddock fillet
1 pint (600ml) milk
1 bay leaf
few sprigs parsley
1 large onion
1 lb (450g) potatoes
1 oz (25g) butter
1 pint (600ml) water
1 × 8 oz (225g) packet frozen
   prawns, thawed
1 oz (25g) cornflour
freshly milled pepper
dash of tomato ketchup
squeeze of lemon juice
chopped parsley, to garnish

Rinse the fish and cut in 4 pieces. Put into a large saucepan along with the milk, bay leaf and parsley. Simmer gently (do not boil or milk may separate), covered, until fish is tender. Strain cooking liquid into a jug. When cool enough to handle, flake the fish discarding skin and bones.

Peel and finely chop the onion and peel and dice the potatoes. Melt the butter in the rinsed and dried saucepan over low heat. Add the onion and fry gently for about 5 minutes to soften but not brown. Then add the potatoes and ¾ pint (400ml) of the water. Bring to the boil, then lower the heat and simmer gently, covered, for 10 minutes. Add the reserved cooking liquid and peeled prawns. Blend the cornflour with the rest of the cold water and stir into the soup. Bring just to the boiling point and draw off the heat. Season with freshly milled pepper, add the flaked fish, a dash of tomato ketchup and a squeeze of lemon juice. Ladle into warmed soup bowls and sprinkle with chopped parsley. Chowder is filling enough to make a good lunch or supper dish. Serve with crusty bread or rolls and butter.

Freezing soups

● The best soups to freeze are vegetable or pulse soups. If cream or a liaison of cream and egg is to be added, do this after the soup is thawed and reheated for serving.

● Pour cold soup into cartons leaving ½ inch (1cm) head space to allow for expansion; freeze in amounts you are likely to use at one time.

● Partially thaw frozen soup in the refrigerator. Or stand carton of frozen soup in cold water to loosen, then transfer contents to a saucepan. Bring frozen soup for serving hot just to the boiling point.

● Thawed soup will blend perfectly as it is stirred and brought to the boil. For serving soup cold, thaw in refrigerator and if necessary, purée in the blender to achieve original smooth consistency.

Sweetcorn and prawn soup

Drain the sweetcorn and put into a large saucepan along with the stock. Cook gently, covered, for 10 minutes, until sweetcorn is quite soft. Pass mixture through a food mill, or purée in an electric blender or food processor. Reserve for adding to the soup.

Peel and finely chop the onion. Melt the butter in the rinsed and dried saucepan over low heat, add the onion and fry gently for 5 minutes to soften but not brown. Stir in the flour and cook gently for 1 minute. Gradually add the milk, stirring all the time, and bring to the boil. Simmer for 2–3 minutes, stirring, to make a smooth sauce. Stir in the reserved corn purée, season with salt and pepper and reheat to simmering. Stir in the cheese, prawns and cream. Ladle the soup into warmed soup bowls and sprinkle with chopped parsley.

Serves 6

2 × 11 oz (326g) tins sweetcorn
¾ pint (400ml) chicken stock
1 small onion
1½ oz (40g) butter
1 level tablespoon flour
1 pint (600ml) milk
salt and freshly milled pepper
4 oz (100g) grated hard cheese
1 × 8 oz (225g) packet frozen
   peeled prawns, thawed
2–3 tablespoons single cream
chopped parsley, to garnish

Butter bean soup

Soak the butter beans overnight and drain. Peel and chop the carrots. Peel and cut the potatoes in even-sized chunks. Trim and coarsely chop the celery. Peel and finely chop the onion. Melt the butter in a large saucepan over low heat, add the onion and fry gently for 5 minutes to soften but not brown. Add the prepared vegetables to the pan and toss them in the hot butter and onions.

Add the butter beans and pour in the water. Crumble the stock cube into the pan, add the bay leaf and tomato purée and season with salt and pepper. Bring to the boil, then lower the heat and simmer gently, covered, for 1 hour, until beans are tender. (Test by biting a bean – they can have a hard centre even when they feel soft on the outside.) Discard the bay leaf and pass soup mixture through a food mill, or purée in an electric blender or food processor. Return the soup to the rinsed pan. Reheat and check seasoning. Serve with fried croûtons sprinkled on top.

Serves 6

6 oz (175g) dried butter beans
2 carrots
2 medium-sized potatoes
2 stalks celery
1 large onion
2 oz (50g) butter
2½ pints (1.5 litres) water
1 chicken stock cube
1 bay leaf
1 tablespoon concentrated tomato
   purée
salt and freshly milled pepper

Lentil soup

Peel and finely chop the onion. Melt the butter in a large saucepan over low heat, add the onion and fry gently for 5 minutes to soften but not brown. Meanwhile, peel and cut the carrots and potatoes in even-sized chunks. Add to the pan and toss the vegetables in the hot butter.

Add the lentils to the pan along with the stock and bay leaf and season with salt and pepper. Bring to the boil, then lower the heat and simmer gently, covered, for 45 minutes until lentils are tender. (Test by squeezing a lentil between the fingers.) Discard bay leaf and pass soup mixture through a food mill, or purée in an electric blender or food processor. Return the soup to the rinsed pan. Reheat and check seasoning.

Serves 6

1 medium-sized onion
1 oz (25g) butter
2–3 carrots
2 medium-sized potatoes
6 oz (175g) split red lentils
2½ pints (1.5 litres) chicken stock
1 bay leaf
salt and freshly milled pepper

Green pea and leek soup

Serves 6

6 oz (175g) green split peas
2 large leeks
1 medium-sized onion
2 oz (50g) butter
2 medium-sized potatoes
2 pints (1.1 litres) water
1 chicken stock cube
salt and freshly milled pepper
nut of butter

Soak the split peas overnight and drain. Trim the leeks, cut in half lengthways and wash well, then shred finely, reserving a little of the white part for garnish. Peel and finely chop the onion. Melt the butter in a large saucepan over low heat, add the onion and leeks and fry gently for 5 minutes to soften but not brown. Meanwhile, peel and cut the potatoes in even-sized chunks. Add to the pan and toss them with the onion and leeks.

Add the split peas and pour in the water. Crumble the stock cube into the pan and season with salt and pepper. Bring to the boil, then lower the heat and simmer gently, covered, for 45 minutes until peas are tender. (Test by squeezing a split pea between the fingers.) Pass soup mixture through a food mill, or purée in an electric blender or food processor.

Return the soup to the rinsed pan. Reheat and check seasoning. Gently fry the reserved leek in a nut of butter to soften. Ladle the soup into warmed soup bowls and garnish with the leek.

French onion soup

Serves 4

1 lb (450g) onions
1 oz (25g) butter
2 pints (1.1 litres) chicken stock
salt and freshly milled pepper
1 oz (25g) cornflour
4 tablespoons cold water

Garnish
4 slices day-old French bread
butter, for spreading
2 oz (50g) grated hard cheese

Peel and finely slice the onions. Melt the butter in a large saucepan over low heat, add the onions and toss them in the butter. Cover with a pan lid and cook gently for about 30–40 minutes so that the onions stew in their own juices and are soft and translucent. Remove the pan lid and cook the onions briskly, stirring occasionally, until lightly browned.

Add the stock and season with salt and plenty of pepper. Simmer gently, uncovered, for 20–30 minutes. Blend the cornflour with the cold water and stir into the soup, then bring to the boil stirring all the time, until soup thickens. Simmer gently for 2–3 minutes, stirring, and check seasoning.

Toast the bread on one side under a hot grill. Remove from the grill and spread each slice with a little butter and sprinkle over a little grated cheese, then grill until bread is crisp and cheese is melted. Put 1 teaspoon grated cheese into four warmed soup bowls. Ladle in the hot soup and float the cheese bread on top. This soup is filling enough to serve as a lunch or supper dish. Or serve as a first course for 6, in which case use 6 slices of bread.

Croûtons and Melba Toast

● *Croûtons* are made with white bread cut in medium-sized dice and fried in hot butter until crisp and golden. They are delicious sprinkled over vegetable or pulse soups. Fry croûtons and serve straight away so they are crunchy and warm. Toasted bread cubes are nice but not so crisp.

● Use day-old bread slices from a sliced loaf to make *melba toast*. Start by toasting bread slices on both sides. While hot, trim away the crusts, then slice the toast in half horizontally. Cut each half diagonally into a triangle and toast the untoasted sides. The melba toast will curl up and become crisp. Allow to cool and serve at once or store in an airtight tin.

3

Light Meals

Eggs, cheese and pasta are the basis of some of the most satisfying lunch and supper dishes. From a simple omelette to an elegant cheese soufflé or a filling quiche, you will find they are quick to make and always sure to please.

Light Meals

Eggs

Eggs are marvellous for quick meals and are convenient because they always seem to be on hand. Keep them cool – the lowest section of the refrigerator is the best place in most kitchens, but let eggs come to room temperature before you cook them.

Boiled eggs: Soft-boiled eggs are nice with hot asparagus and hard-boiled eggs can be stuffed with sardines or smoked cod's roe.

● Eggs should not be cooked at a full rolling boil. Place them in cold water to cover and bring just to the boiling point, then lower the heat and simmer – 4 minutes for soft-boiled eggs and 8 minutes for hard-boiled eggs.

● When serving eggs cold, such as in salads, the eggs are more digestible if the yolk is set but still moist – 6 minutes is the time I use.

● Before cooking, prick a small hole in the shell at the rounded end with an egg pricker or needle to prevent shells cracking.

● Stir eggs gently as they come to the boil to get yolks that set in the centre of the egg.

● Drain eggs as soon as they are cooked and plunge into a bowl of cold water for a moment to arrest cooking.

● Roll eggs between the palms of the hand or on work surface to crack the shells all over and they will be easier to peel. New-laid eggs are always obstinate; eggs that are 4-5 days old will peel best.

● For salad, peeled eggs can be kept in a bowl of cold water to cover for up to 24 hours to keep the whites moist.

Poached eggs: Serve these on Welsh rarebit to make buck rarebit, on a spinach purée with cheese sauce topping or try them on poached smoked haddock cutlets.

● Use the freshest eggs possible – the white is tighter and doesn't spread so much.

● Use a shallow pan; a frying pan is best as it's more roomy. There's no need to add salt or vinegar to the water.

● Crack the egg into a teacup, and holding the cup close to the water surface, tip the egg into simmering water. Cook until egg white is set, basting with the simmering water.

● Lift poached eggs from the pan with a perforated spoon to drain off the water.

● Eggs can be poached in advance: leave cooked

eggs covered with cold water. To reheat, immerse them in simmering water for 30 seconds.

Scrambled eggs: Serve on toast or buttered biscottes and top with grated cheese or a little lumpfish caviar.

● Mix eggs lightly with a fork to blend yolks and whites; season with salt and pepper.

● Add 1 tablespoon milk per egg to enrich the mixture; use single cream for a special occasion.

● Cook gently over direct heat; let the butter melt in the pan first, then add the eggs. A silicone-lined pan makes washing up afterwards easier.

● Don't stir scrambled eggs. Instead, draw mixture up with a spoon in creamy folds as eggs begin to set.

● Draw pan off the heat when mixture is set but still moist – the heat of the pan will continue to cook it.

● A nut of butter added at the end of cooking helps keep scrambled eggs moist and soft.

Omelettes: Fill omelettes with mushrooms, prawns, cooked mussels tossed in hot butter or hot ratatouille.

● Mix eggs lightly with a fork to blend yolks and whites. Add salt and pepper and 1 teaspoon water per egg to lighten the mixture.

● Use the right pan – an omelette pan which is about 6–8 inches (15–20cm) in diameter is ideal. Otherwise use a small frying pan so the mixture does not spread too thin.

● Add unsalted or clarified butter to the hot pan and tilt pan to grease evenly. Then add egg mixture and cook quickly.

● Use a fork to stir, then draw edges of mixture to centre so uncooked egg on top flows on to hot pan surface.

● When set but still moist, loosen edges and slide omelette to edge of pan away from the handle. Add hot filling at this stage and turn sides of omelette to centre. Hold pan edge close to serving dish and tip out quickly so omelette turns over on to plate.

Curried supper eggs

Serves 4

6 eggs
8 oz (225g) long-grain rice
½ oz (15g) butter

Sauce
1 medium-sized onion
1 oz (25g) butter
½ cooking apple
2 level tablespoons curry powder
1 level tablespoon plain flour
¾ pint (400ml) hot chicken stock
2 teaspoons mango chutney
1 tablespoon soft light brown sugar
juice of ½ lemon
1 oz (25g) sultanas

Boil the eggs for 8 minutes from cold. Drain and plunge into cold water. Shell and submerge eggs in a bowl of water until cold. Sprinkle the rice into a pan of boiling salted water and cook for 8–10 minutes, then drain. Turn into a greased ovenproof dish, add a few flakes of butter and cover with kitchen foil. Place in an oven heated to 325°F (160°C) or Gas no. 3 for 30 minutes to dry.

Peel and finely chop the onion. Melt the butter in a saucepan over low heat. Add the onion and fry gently for 5 minutes to soften but not brown. Peel, core and dice the apple. Add to the pan along with the curry powder. Cook gently for 1 minute to draw out the flavour of the curry powder. Stir in the flour and gradually add the hot stock. Bring to the boil, stirring all the time to make a smooth sauce. Lower the heat and add the chutney (chop up any large pieces), sugar, lemon juice and sultanas. Cover with a pan lid and simmer gently for 30 minutes, stirring occasionally.

Cut the eggs in quarters and add to the sauce. Fluff the rice with a fork and transfer to a warmed serving dish. Spoon the curried eggs on top and serve.

Pizza omelette

Make the topping: peel and finely chop the onion. Melt the butter in a saucepan over low heat, add the onion and fry gently for 5 minutes to soften but not brown. Meanwhile, trim and chop the bacon rashers and fry gently in a dry pan until the fat runs and bacon is crisp. Add the tomato purée and herbs to the onion and cook for a further 1 minute, then draw off the heat.

Thoroughly heat an omelette pan or small heavy-based frying pan over low heat. Crack the eggs into a mixing bowl. Add the water and season with salt and pepper. Beat with a fork until eggs are runny – do not aerate. Add the butter to the heated pan and tilt pan to grease it. Pour the egg mixture into the hot pan. Cook gently, drawing the edge of the omelette to the centre with a fork so pools of liquid egg run on to the pan. When underside is brown and the mixture is set but still moist, draw off the heat. Spread the tomato and onion mixture on top and sprinkle with the bacon and cheese. Place the omelette under a hot grill to melt the cheese and brown the top. Slide omelette on to a hot plate. Serve with hot herb bread and a green salad.

Serves 2

4 eggs
1 tablespoon cold water
salt and freshly milled pepper
1 oz (25g) butter

Topping
1 medium-sized onion
1 oz (25g) butter
3–4 rashers lean bacon
1 tablespoon concentrated tomato
    purée
pinch of dried mixed herbs
2 oz (50g) grated hard cheese

Eggs Nova Scotia

Crack the eggs into a mixing bowl, add the cream and season with salt and pepper. Beat with a fork until eggs are runny.

Arrange smoked salmon slices on the slices of buttered toast. Melt the butter in a frying pan over low heat. Pour the egg mixture into the hot butter. Cook gently, drawing the egg mixture into soft folds with a spoon as it begins to set (do not stir). The eggs should have a creamy soft consistency. Immediately spoon on to salmon toast. Sprinkle with cayenne pepper and garnish with lumpfish caviar. This makes a grand breakfast or brunch dish or a delicious lunch.

Serves 4

8 eggs
¼ pint (150ml) single cream
salt and freshly milled pepper
4 oz (100g) smoked salmon
4 slices of buttered toast
2 oz (50g) butter
cayenne pepper, for sprinkling
black lumpfish caviar, to garnish

Chicken livers in a mustard and cream sauce

Trim the chicken livers. Melt the butter in a frying pan over low heat, add the chicken livers and cook for 5–6 minutes, turning the livers fairly frequently. Combine mustard and cream in a small bowl and set aside.

Add a seasoning of salt and pepper to the pan, then sprinkle over the flour and turn the livers so the flour absorbs the hot butter. Add the mustard and cream and slowly bring just to the boiling point, stirring all the time as sauce thickens. Draw the pan off the heat and sprinkle with chopped parsley. Serve the livers and sauce with plain boiled rice.

Serves 4

1 lb (450g) chicken livers
2 oz (50g) butter
2 teaspoons made English mustard
¼ pint (150ml) double cream
salt and freshly milled pepper
1 rounded teaspoon plain flour
chopped parsley, to garnish

Pissaladière

Serves 4

shortcrust pastry, made using 4 oz
(100g) self-raising flour (page
167)

Filling
1 lb (450g) ripe tomatoes
1 medium-sized onion
1 clove garlic
1 oz (25g) butter
bouquet of parsley stalks and thyme
2 tablespoons concentrated tomato
purée
2 eggs
4 oz (100g) grated hard cheese
freshly milled pepper
1 × 1¾ oz (50g) tin anchovy fillets
6 black olives or sweet pickled
prunes (page 306)

Roll out prepared pastry to a circle on a lightly floured work surface and use to line an 8 inch (20cm) round quiche tin or flan ring set on a baking tray. Chill the pastry while preparing the filling.

Scald the tomatoes in boiling water and peel away the skins. Peel and finely chop the onion. Peel the garlic and crush to a purée with a little salt. Melt the butter in a saucepan over low heat. Add the onion and fry gently for 5 minutes to soften but not brown. Add the garlic, chopped tomatoes, herbs and tomato purée. Cover with the pan lid and simmer for 30 minutes, stirring occasionally, to make a thick purée. Draw off the heat and allow to cool until the hand can be comfortably held against the side of the pan.

Heat the oven to 375°F (190°C) or Gas no. 5. Stir the eggs, grated cheese and a seasoning of pepper into the tomato mixture. Pour mixture into the pastry case. Arrange a lattice of anchovy fillets on top and decorate with black olives or pickled prunes. Place in preheated oven and bake for 40 minutes. Serve as newly cooked or bake ahead and reheat for 10 minutes in an oven heated to 350°F (180°C), or Gas no. 4.

To serve pissaladière at a summer party or barbecue place it in a large attractive earthenware or porcelain dish and cut it in thin slices. Served this way, pissaladière makes a tasty appetizer.

Ratatouille flan

Serves 4

shortcrust pastry, made using 4 oz
(100g) self-raising flour (page
167)
2 oz (50g) grated hard cheese

Filling
1 medium-sized onion
1 green pepper
2 tablespoons oil
1 lb (450g) courgettes
4 tomatoes
1 level teaspoon castor sugar
salt and freshly milled pepper
3 eggs

Roll out prepared pastry to a circle on a lightly floured work surface and use to line an 8 inch (20cm) quiche tin or flan ring set on a baking tray. Chill while preparing the filling.

Peel and slice the onion. Halve, deseed and finely chop the green pepper. Heat the oil in a medium-sized saucepan over low heat. Add onion and pepper to the pan, cover with a pan lid, and cook gently for 10 minutes until softened. Meanwhile, slice the courgettes. Scald the tomatoes, peel away the skins and scoop out seeds. Chop tomato flesh. Add courgettes, tomatoes and sugar to the pan and season with plenty of salt and pepper. Cover with a pan lid and cook gently for about 30 minutes, or until vegetables are soft. Draw off the heat and allow to cool.

Heat the oven to 375°F (190°C) or Gas no. 5. Break up the eggs with a fork and stir into the vegetable mixture. Pour mixture into pastry case and sprinkle with the grated cheese. Place in the centre of preheated oven and bake for 40 minutes. Serve warm or cold.

Asparagus quiche

Roll out prepared pastry to a circle on a lightly floured work surface and use to line an 8 inch (20cm) quiche tin or flan ring set on a baking tray. Chill while preparing the filling.

Scrape and trim the asparagus. Place them lying flat in a pan of boiling salted water and cook for 15 minutes, or until tender. Drain well and trim the tender green tops.

Heat the oven to 375°F (190°C) or Gas no. 5. Peel and finely chop the onion. Melt the butter in a frying pan over low heat, add the onion and fry gently for 5 minutes to soften but not brown. Toss the asparagus tips in the hot onion and butter. Spoon mixture over base of pastry case and sprinkle with the grated cheese.

Lightly mix together the eggs and cream and season with salt and pepper. Strain into a jug and pour the mixture over asparagus. Place in centre of preheated oven and bake for 40 minutes until set. Serve warm.

Serves 4

shortcrust pastry, made using 4 oz (100g) self-raising flour (page 167)

Filling
1 lb (450g) fresh asparagus
1 small onion
½ oz (15g) butter
1 tablespoon grated Parmesan cheese
3 eggs or 2 whole eggs and 1 egg yolk
½ pint (300ml) single cream
salt and freshly milled pepper

Smoked salmon quiche

Heat the oven to 375°F (190°C) or Gas no. 5. Roll out the prepared pastry to a circle on a lightly floured work surface and use to line a 10 inch (25cm) quiche tin (with removable base) or flan ring set on a baking tray. Chill while preparing the filling.

Lightly mix together the eggs, single cream and soured cream and season with salt and pepper. Strain into a jug. Trim and cut the smoked salmon in bite-sized pieces and arrange evenly over the base of the pastry case. Pour in the cream mixture and dot the surface with flakes of butter. Place in the centre of preheated oven and bake for 40 minutes until set. Serve warm.

Variation: Instead of the salmon use 8 oz (225g) peeled prawns, thawed and thoroughly drained if frozen.

Serves 6

shortcrust pastry, made using 6 oz (175g) self-raising flour (page 167)

Filling
4 eggs or 3 whole eggs and 1 egg yolk
½ pint (300ml) single cream
¼ pint (150ml) soured cream
salt and freshly milled pepper
6 oz (175g) smoked salmon
1 oz (25g) butter

Crab and Cheddar cheese quiche

Heat the oven to 375°F (190°C) or Gas no 5. Roll out the prepared pastry to a circle on a lightly floured work surface and use to line a 10 inch (25cm) quiche tin (with removable base) or flan ring set on a baking tray. Chill while preparing the filling.

Lightly mix together the eggs and cream and season with salt and pepper. Strain into a jug and add the sherry. Flake the crabmeat (remove any sinews or bone) over the base of the pastry case and sprinkle evenly with the grated cheese. Pour in the cream and egg mixture. Place in the centre of preheated oven and bake for 40 minutes until set. Serve warm.

Serves 6

shortcrust pastry, made using 6 oz (175g) self-raising flour (page 167)

Filling
4 eggs
¾ pint (400ml) single cream
salt and freshly milled pepper
1 tablespoon sherry
8 oz (225g) crabmeat
2 oz (50g) grated Cheddar cheese

Chilled prawn curry

Serves 6

1 × 12 oz (350g) packet frozen
    peeled prawns, thawed
1 small onion
1 tablespoon oil
1 level tablespoon curry powder
4 tablespoons chicken stock or water
1 rounded teaspoon concentrated
    tomato purée
juice of ½ lemon
2 rounded tablespoons sweet chutney
½ pint (300ml) mayonnaise
3 tablespoons single cream
salt and freshly milled pepper
8 oz (225g) long-grain rice
3–4 tablespoons oil and vinegar
    dressing
2 hard-boiled eggs, to garnish

Drain the prawns thoroughly, otherwise the juices will dilute the dressing. Peel and finely chop the onion. Heat the oil in a saucepan over low heat, add the onion and fry gently for 5 minutes to soften but not brown, then stir in the curry powder and cook for a further 1 minute to draw out the flavour. Stir in the stock or water, tomato purée, lemon juice and chutney. Bring to the boil, stirring all the time, then lower the heat and simmer for 5 minutes. Strain into a mixing bowl and set aside until completely cool.

Stir the mayonnaise and cream into the cooled curry sauce and season with salt and pepper. Add the prawns and chill. Sprinkle the rice into a pan of boiling salted water and cook for 8–10 minutes, or until just tender. Drain and while hot, toss with oil and vinegar dressing. Leave until completely cool, then chill. Spoon rice salad on to one-half of six individual serving plates or china scallop shells and spoon prawns in curry sauce alongside. Cut the eggs in quarters and use to garnish the dishes.

How to cook perfect pasta

● Use a large pan with plenty of boiling salted water so pasta has room to move around.

● Stir pasta for a moment once it's in the water to prevent it sticking together, and cook fast with the pan uncovered.

● Test by lifting out a strand and biting into it – it should be tender but still firm. Follow packet directions for cooking time; fresh pasta will cook in only 2–3 minutes. When cooked pasta will rise to the surface.

● Drain pasta in a colander as soon as it is cooked. If allowed to stand in the cooking water it will soften.

● Turn cooked pasta immediately into a hot serving bowl and toss with a knob of butter. If you let pasta stand without a coating it will stick together.

● Try cooking a mixture of plain noodles and green, or spinach, noodles together – they look very pretty for serving.

● Fresh tagliatelle cooked and tossed in butter are a good accompaniment to dishes having a rich sauce or gravy. Season with freshly milled pepper.

● Parmesan cheese is best if you grate it yourself, or use hard, dry pieces of Cheddar cheese that will grate easily.

Tagliatelle with ham and mushrooms

Serves 4

1 medium-sized onion
4 oz (100g) button mushrooms
4 oz (100g) sliced cooked ham
2 oz (50g) butter
freshly milled pepper
2 egg yolks
¼ pint (150ml) double cream
8 oz (225g) fresh green tagliatelle
grated Parmesan cheese, to serve

Peel and chop the onion. Wipe and thinly slice the mushrooms and cut the ham in thin strips. Melt 1½ oz (40g) of the butter in a frying pan over low heat, add the onion and cook gently for 10 minutes until tender and beginning to brown. Add the sliced mushrooms and ham and season with pepper. Cook gently for a further 2–3 minutes. Combine egg yolks and cream in a small bowl and set aside.

Add the tagliatelle to a saucepan of boiling salted water, bring back to the boil and cook noodles for 2–3 minutes, or until tender. Drain in a colander. Turn cooked noodles into a warmed deep serving bowl, add the remaining butter and toss to coat. Add the egg and cream mixture and toss the noodles again. Then add the mixture of onion, mushrooms and ham and toss again. Serve with grated Parmesan cheese for sprinkling over the top.

Spaghetti with bacon and cream

Serves 4

8 oz (225g) spaghetti
1 tablespoon oil
6 rashers lean bacon
1 oz (25g) butter
4 tablespoons dry white wine
3 egg yolks
¼ pint (150ml) double cream
2 oz (50g) grated Parmesan cheese
freshly milled pepper

Add spaghetti to a saucepan of boiling salted water, bring back to the boil and cook for 8–10 minutes, or until spaghetti is tender. Drain in a colander. Add the oil and toss to coat the spaghetti to prevent sticking.

Trim and chop the bacon rashers. Return rinsed saucepan to the heat. Add the butter and bacon and fry over moderate heat until the fat runs and bacon begins to brown. Add the wine, bring to the boil and boil for 1 minute. Return the cooked spaghetti to the pan, lower the heat and let the spaghetti heat through when it will absorb the wine.

In a mixing bowl, combine the egg yolks, cream, grated Parmesan cheese and a seasoning of freshly milled pepper. Draw the saucepan of spaghetti off the heat and add the egg and cream mixture. Toss ingredients together. The heat of the pan will be sufficient to thicken the sauce. Turn into a hot dish and serve.

Mushroom and cheese risotto

Serves 4

4 lean bacon rashers
1 medium-sized onion
2 oz (50g) butter
8 oz (225g) long-grain rice
1 pint (600ml) hot chicken stock
8 oz (225g) button mushrooms
4 oz (100g) Cheddar cheese

Trim away rinds and chop bacon rashers. Peel and finely chop the onion. Melt half the butter in a saucepan over low heat, add the bacon and onion and fry for about 5 minutes until onion is soft but not brown. Stir in the rice and mix well. Add the hot stock and bring to the boil, stirring all the time. Lower the heat, cover with the pan lid and simmer gently for 20 minutes. As the rice cooks it will absorb the stock. No seasoning will be needed unless stock is very lightly flavoured.

Trim and slice the mushrooms. Melt the remaining butter in a frying pan over low heat. Add the mushrooms and turn them in the butter for a few minutes only so they are glazed and softened but not overcooked. Using a fork, fold the mushrooms into the cooked rice along with half the grated cheese. Turn the mixture into a hot serving dish and sprinkle remaining cheese on top. Serve with a crisp green salad.

Tips on using cheese

● If a hard cheese such as Cheddar dries out, grate it and store in a screw-topped jar in the refrigerator where it will keep for weeks. It comes in handy for flavouring savoury dishes.

● Cheddar or other hard cheeses freeze very well when grated. Store in polythene and use straight from the freezer as there is no need to thaw the cheese; frozen grated cheese stays free flowing.

● Go easy on the salt in a recipe that has cheese as an ingredient. Salt is added to cheese to preserve it and improve the flavour.

● All cheese should be cooked gently and for a short time. Too much heat and the protein in cheese tightens and squeezes out natural oils causing cheese to separate. When adding cheese to sauces, draw the pan off the heat, then add the cheese and stir until melted. The heat of the pan will be sufficient to do this.

● For a crunchy topping combine dry white breadcrumbs and grated cheese in equal parts, then sprinkle mixture over the dish and place under the grill. The cheese melts and the breadcrumbs absorb the oil of the cheese, making a crunchy brown topping.

● To make the best *toasted cheese*, toast bread slices on one side, lay cheese slices on untoasted side and grill to a golden, bubbling brown. I like to sprinkle a little paprika on the cheese before grilling – it gives the cheese a lovely brown colour.

Cheese soufflé

Serves 6

2 oz (50g) butter
1½ oz (40g) plain flour
½ pint (300ml) milk
4 egg yolks
salt and freshly milled pepper
½ level teaspoon made English
   mustard
4 oz (100g) grated Gruyère or
   mature Cheddar cheese
5 egg whites

Melt the butter in a large saucepan over low heat. Stir in the flour and cook gently for 1 minute. Gradually pour in the milk, stirring all the time, and bring to the boil. Simmer gently for 2–3 minutes, stirring, to make a thick sauce and draw off the heat.

Lightly break up the egg yolks with a fork and gradually add to the sauce, beating well all the time. Season with salt and pepper, add the mustard and stir in the grated cheese. Whisk the egg whites until stiff peaks form and gently fold into the mixture with a metal spoon. Turn into a greased 8 inch (20cm) soufflé dish and bake in the centre of an oven heated to 350°F (180°C) or Gas no. 4 for 35–40 minutes until well risen and brown.

Macaroni cheese

Serves 4

4 oz (100g) macaroni
1 tablespoon soft white
   breadcrumbs
½ oz (15g) butter

Sauce
2 oz (50g) butter
2 oz (50g) plain flour
1 pint (600ml) milk
salt and freshly milled pepper
4–6 oz (100–175g) grated Cheddar
   cheese
½ level teaspoon made English
   mustard
dash of Worcestershire sauce

Cook the macaroni in a large pan of boiling salted water until tender. Meanwhile, melt the butter for the sauce in a saucepan over low heat. Stir in the flour and cook gently for 1 minute. Gradually pour in the milk, stirring all the time, and bring to the boil. Simmer gently, stirring, for 2–3 minutes to make a smooth sauce. Draw off the heat and season with salt and pepper. Stir in two-thirds of the cheese, the mustard and a dash of Worcestershire sauce.

Thoroughly drain the macaroni and add to the cheese sauce. Pour the mixture into a greased ovenproof dish. Sprinkle the remaining cheese on top along with the breadcrumbs (essential for a golden crisp crust as the crumbs absorb the oil that comes from the cooked cheese). Dot with flakes of butter. Bake above centre in an oven heated to 375°F (190°C) or Gas no. 5 for 15–20 minutes, until bubbling. Place under a hot grill to brown the top.

Illustrated: Avocado with orange, page 22

Soufflé rarebit

Serves 4

Melt the butter in a saucepan over low heat. Add the grated cheese, milk or whisky, mustard and a seasoning of salt and pepper. Stir until the cheese has melted and the mixture is smooth. Do not overcook at this stage or cheese will become oily. Draw off the heat and allow to cool slightly. Meanwhile, separate the egg and whisk the egg white until stiff peaks form. Stir the egg yolk into the cheese mixture, then fold in the egg white.

Have the hot toast slices ready and place on a grill-pan rack. Spoon the rarebit mixture on to each slice and spread evenly. Place under a hot grill and the rarebit mixture will puff up and brown beautifully.

½ oz (15g) butter
6 oz (175g) grated Cheddar cheese
1 tablespoon milk or whisky
dash of made English mustard
salt and freshly milled pepper
1 egg
4 slices hot buttered toast

Swiss cheese tart

Serves 4

Roll out prepared pastry to a circle and use to line an 8 inch (20cm) quiche tin or flan ring set on a baking tray. Chill while preparing the filling.

Heat the oven to 375°F (190°C) or Gas no. 5. Peel and finely chop the onion. Melt the butter in a saucepan over low heat. Add the onion and fry gently for 5 minutes to soften but not brown. Mix the grated cheese and flour together and sprinkle this over the pastry case. Add the softened onions. Lightly beat the eggs, cream, a seasoning of salt and pepper and a little grated nutmeg in a mixing bowl. Strain into a jug, then pour over the cheese and onion mixture to fill the pastry case.

Place in the centre of preheated oven and bake for 40 minutes until the filling turns a beautiful brown. Serve warm or cold. This tart is lovely served with tomato and spring onion salad (page 153).

shortcrust pastry, made using 4 oz (100g) self-raising flour (page 167)

Filling
1 medium-sized onion
1 oz (25g) butter
4 oz (100g) grated Gruyère cheese
1 level teaspoon plain flour
3 eggs or 2 whole eggs and 1 egg yolk
½ pint (300ml) single cream
salt and freshly milled pepper
grated nutmeg

Gouda cheese fondue

Serves 4

Rub the inside of a medium-sized saucepan with a crushed clove of garlic. Discard the garlic. Add the wine and lemon juice and bring to just below the boiling point, then add the grated cheese, stirring all the time until melted. Blend the cornflour with the gin, add to the pan and stir until fondue thickens and comes just to the boil, then draw off the heat. Add the nutmeg and season with freshly milled pepper.

Have the French bread cut in cubes. Pour fondue into an earthenware fondue dish and set over a spirit heater to keep it hot. Stir the fondue to prevent the cheese from sticking to the dish. Arm guests with fondue forks for dipping the bread into the fondue.

Variation: Serve with boiled new potatoes for dipping into the fondue, if liked. Any leftover fondue can be spread on toast and grilled to make toasted cheese.

1 clove garlic
¼ pint (150ml) dry white wine
1 teaspoon lemon juice
14 oz (400g) grated Gouda cheese
1 tablespoon cornflour
1½ tablespoons gin
pinch of grated nutmeg
freshly milled black pepper
1–2 loaves of French bread

Illustrated: Home-made curd cheese with oatcakes, pages 53 and 260

Smoked haddock pancakes

Serves 4–6

12 pancakes (page 268)
1½ oz (40g) butter
1 oz (25g) grated hard cheese

Filling
1 lb (450g) smoked haddock fillet
½ pint (300ml) milk
few sprigs parsley
1 bay leaf
2 hard-boiled eggs
1½ oz (40g) butter
1 oz (25g) plain flour
freshly milled pepper
squeeze of lemon juice
1 egg yolk
3 tablespoons double cream

Cut the smoked haddock in pieces and put into a saucepan along with the milk and sufficient water to cover. Add the parsley and bay leaf, cover, and poach for 10 minutes. Transfer the fish to a plate and when cool enough to handle, flake the fish, discarding skin and bones. Strain ½ pint (300ml) of the cooking liquid into a measuring jug. Chop the hard-boiled eggs.

Melt the butter for the filling in a saucepan over low heat. Stir in the flour and cook gently for 1 minute. Gradually stir in the reserved cooking liquid. Bring to the boil, stirring well all the time to make a smooth sauce. Simmer for 2–3 minutes, add a squeeze of lemon juice and season with pepper. Add salt, only if necessary. Draw off the heat. Blend the egg yolk with the cream and stir into the sauce. Stir in the flaked fish and chopped egg and allow mixture to cool.

Spoon a little of the filling down the centre of each pancake and roll up carefully. Arrange pancakes in a greased ovenproof serving dish. Melt the butter in a saucepan over low heat, pour it over the pancakes and sprinkle with the grated cheese. Cover with kitchen foil and heat through in an oven heated to 375°F (190°C) or Gas no. 5 for 20–30 minutes until bubbling hot.

Pancakes with spinach and cheese

Serves 4–6

12 pancakes (page 268)

Filling
1 lb (450g) fresh spinach
1½ oz (40g) butter
1½ oz (40g) plain flour
¾ pint (400ml) milk
4 oz (100g) grated Gruyère cheese
salt and freshly milled pepper

Tear away coarse midribs and thoroughly wash spinach in cold water. Pack wet spinach into a saucepan, cover with a pan lid and cook over moderate heat for 10 minutes until spinach is tender. (The water clinging to the leaves will provide sufficient cooking liquid.) Drain well by pressing the spinach in a colander, then finely chop or pass through a food mill.

Melt the butter in a saucepan over low heat. Stir in the flour and cook gently for 1 minute. Gradually stir in ½ pint (300ml) of the milk. Bring to the boil, stirring well all the time to make a smooth sauce. Simmer for 2–3 minutes to thicken. Draw off the heat. Stir in 3 oz (75g) grated cheese and season with salt and pepper. Stir half the sauce into the spinach purée. Spoon a little spinach filling down the centre of each prepared pancake and roll up carefully. Arrange pancakes in a greased ovenproof dish.

Add the remaining milk to the rest of the sauce and bring to the boil. Check seasoning and pour the sauce over the spinach pancakes. Sprinkle with the remaining grated cheese and heat through in an oven heated to 375°F (190°C) or Gas no. 5 for 20–30 minutes until bubbling hot and brown.

Chicken liver stuffed pancakes

Trim the chicken livers. Melt 1 oz (25g) of the butter in a saucepan over low heat, add the chicken livers, stock or red wine and herbs. Cover with a pan lid and simmer for 10 minutes to cook the livers. Draw off the heat and pass mixture through a food mill into a mixing bowl or purée mixture in a blender or food processor.

Peel and finely chop the onion. Put into a saucepan and pour over cold water to cover. Bring to the boil, then lower the heat and simmer, covered, for 10 minutes to soften the onion. Drain, reserving onion and ¼ pint (150ml) onion stock for the sauce.

Melt the remaining butter in a saucepan over low heat. Stir in the flour and cook gently for 1 minute. Gradually stir in the reserved hot onion stock, then stir in the cold milk. Bring to the boil, stirring well all the time to make a smooth sauce. Simmer gently for 2–3 minutes and season with salt and pepper. The sauce will have a mild onion flavour. Add half the sauce and the reserved onion to the chicken liver purée and mix together well.

Spoon a little filling down the centre of each prepared pancake and roll up carefully. Arrange pancakes in a greased ovenproof dish. Thin remaining sauce with the milk. Check seasoning and pour the sauce over the pancakes. Heat through in an oven heated to 375°F (190°C) or Gas no. 5 for 20–30 minutes until the sauce is bubbling hot.

Serves 4–6

12 pancakes (page 268)

Filling
1 lb (450g) chicken livers
2½ oz (65g) butter
4 tablespoons chicken stock or red wine
pinch of dried mixed herbs
1 medium-sized onion
1½ oz (40g) plain flour
½ pint (300ml) milk
salt and freshly milled pepper
3 tablespoons milk

Luncheon liver pâté

Trim the liver and pork or bacon and cut in pieces. Pass the cut pieces and anchovy fillets through a mincer into a mixing bowl. Or chop the ingredients in a food processor. Peel and mash the garlic to a purée with salt, if using it. Add to the minced ingredients and season with salt and pepper. Set aside.

Peel the onion and put into a saucepan along with the milk and bay leaf. Heat the milk and allow flavours to infuse off the heat for 10 minutes. Melt half the butter in a saucepan over low heat. Stir in the flour and cook gently for 1 minute. Gradually stir in the milk (discard onion and bay leaf). Bring to the boil, stirring well all the time to make a smooth sauce. Simmer for 2–3 minutes to thicken. Add the sauce to the minced ingredients. Lightly break up the eggs with a fork, add to the bowl and mix together well.

Pour mixture into a greased 2 pint (1.1 litre) terrine. Cover with a lid or buttered kitchen foil and set in a roasting tin. Fill the tin to a depth of 1 inch (2.5cm) with water. Cook in an oven heated to 325°F (160°C) or Gas no. 3 for 1½–2 hours. Allow to cool overnight. Melt the remaining butter in a saucepan and pour it over the surface, then chill. Serve with crispbread or toast.

Serves 6–8

1 lb (450g) lamb liver or chicken livers
8 oz (225g) belly of pork or streaky bacon
3–4 anchovy fillets
1 clove garlic (optional)
salt and freshly milled pepper
½ onion
½ pint (300ml) milk
1 bay leaf
2 oz (50g) butter
1 oz (25g) plain flour
2 eggs

Home-made yoghurt

Makes 2 pints (1.1 litres)

¼ pint (150ml) natural yoghurt
2 pints (1.1 litres) UHT milk

Home-made yoghurt has the most delicious fresh taste – especially if you transfer it to the refrigerator as soon as it has set. The flavour stays sweet, without becoming too sharp and acid. You can make your own yoghurt without any special equipment though a thermometer will ensure the temperature is right.

The yoghurt must be at room temperature so that it does not alter the temperature of the milk. Pour the milk into a saucepan and heat to slightly hotter than lukewarm (a drop on the wrist should feel hot but not burning) or 110°F (43°C) and draw off the heat.

Whisk the yoghurt into the milk and pour the contents of the pan into a warmed serving bowl. Cover with a warmed plate and insulate the bowl with towels placed under, around and over the top. Leave undisturbed in a warm place for 6–8 hours. As soon as the yoghurt has set, transfer the bowl to the refrigerator for at least 12 hours until thick and firm.

Once yoghurt is stirred it takes on a creamy consistency. Stir in any fruit purée such as strawberry sauce (page 227), blackcurrant sauce (page 228) or your own prepared apricot or banana purée to make flavoured yoghurt.

If the yoghurt separates into curds (because the milk was too hot or the yoghurt was left too long) just drain the curds as for yoghurt curd cheese to make a simple cheese.

Serving yoghurt

● I like yoghurt best when spooned straight from the dish, sprinkled with sugar and served with summer fruit compote (page 193).

● Spoon yoghurt into a bowl of muesli with added chopped apple, banana or stewed damsons and serve for breakfast.

● Mix with grapefruit segments and brown sugar. Or add snipped dried apricots and brown sugar and leave to stand for several hours so apricots soften.

● Lighten mayonnaise for dressing by mixing half and half with yoghurt.

● Use half yoghurt and half lightly whipped double cream to make a delicious topping for strawberries or trifle.

● Sweeten with sugar and stir to a creamy consistency, then spoon the yoghurt over baked apples or fruit pie.

● Stir into chilled soups or swirl over the top of chilled soups as you would cream.

● Add a spoonful to the milk used for mixing scones to give them a light texture.

● Dilute with milk to a pouring consistency for milk shakes.

● Yoghurt dressings are refreshing and especially good with spicy barbecue foods. Combine ¼ pint (150ml) natural yoghurt with a squeeze of lemon juice, pinch of sugar, seasoning of salt and freshly milled pepper and 1 tablespoon chopped chives.

Yoghurt curd cheese

Home-made soft curd cheese has a wholesome taste and can be used to make delicious toppings and spreads. Fresh farm milk sours naturally, but pasteurized milk does not sour because the milk has been heat treated which destroys the natural souring bacteria. You can sour pasteurized milk the old-fashioned way if you add a starter such as yoghurt.

Put the milk and skimmed milk powder, which increases the quantity of curds, in a saucepan and set over low heat. Warm the milk, stirring to dissolve milk powder, to 110°F (43°C), or when a drop on the wrist feels hot but not burning, and draw off the heat. Stir in the yoghurt and blend well. Pour into a warmed bowl of about 3 pint (1.7 litres) capacity and leave in a warm place covered with a cloth for 24 hours. When ready the milk will have set into solid curds.

Cut through the curds with a knife to separate the whey from the curds. Line a colander set over a dish with a square of scalded muslin and tip the curds into the colander. Knot the four corners of the muslin and hang the curds to drain for about 24 hours. Refrigerate and use within 3 days.

Makes 8 oz (225g) soft curd cheese

2 pints (1.1 litres) milk
2 oz (50g) skimmed milk powder
¼ pint (150ml) natural yoghurt

illustrated facing page 49

Using yoghurt curd cheese

Use yoghurt curd cheese to make savoury spreads and toppings such as the following which can also be made with store-bought curd cheese or soft cream cheese.

Herb cheese: Turn 8 oz (225g) yoghurt curd cheese into a mixing bowl. Add a seasoning of salt and freshly milled pepper and stir with a fork. Stir in 1 tablespoon chopped spring onion and 1 teaspoon chopped chives or parsley. Serve on hot toast or as a topping for baked jacket potatoes.

Caviar cheese: Turn 8 oz (225g) yoghurt curd cheese into a mixing bowl. Add a seasoning of salt and freshly milled pepper and stir with a fork. Stir in a little onion juice (twist an onion half on a lemon squeezer) to flavour. Add 1–2 tablespoons lumpfish caviar and a squeeze of lemon juice. Stir gently to mix and check seasoning: add extra pepper if necessary, but remember lumpfish caviar is salty. This makes a good dinner party first course when served on hot toast.

Garlic and herb cheese: Turn 8 oz (225g) yoghurt curd cheese into a mixing bowl and stir with a fork. Crush 1 clove garlic to a purée with a little

salt and add to the cheese along with a seasoning of freshly milled pepper – no extra salt is necessary. Add 1–2 teaspoons chopped chives or parsley and mix through. Cover with cling film and chill for 1–2 hours to allow flavours to develop.

Smoked salmon cheese: Mince or finely chop 6 oz (175g) smoked salmon and put into a mixing bowl along with 8 oz (225g) yoghurt curd cheese, 2–3 tablespoons double cream and a seasoning of freshly milled pepper. Mix together well. Pile into a dish and garnish with chopped parsley. Serve with granary bread and lemon wedges for squeezing over. This makes a good first course.

Liptauer cheese: In a mixing bowl, cream 2 oz (50g) butter until soft. Add 8 oz (225g) yoghurt curd cheese and mix together. Add 1 teaspoon anchovy paste, 1 teaspoon made English mustard, 2 teaspoons chopped capers, 2 teaspoons chopped chives and a seasoning of freshly milled pepper. Mix well – the cheese will be a pretty salmon pink colour. Spoon into a serving dish and sprinkle with chopped parsley. Serve with hot toast or French bread.

Ham croquettes

Serves 4

8–10 oz (225–255g) cold cooked
    ham or gammon
1 small onion
1½ oz (40g) butter
1 oz (25g) plain flour
¼ pint (150ml) milk
dash of made English mustard
2 oz (50g) grated Cheddar cheese
salt and freshly milled pepper
1 egg
toasted breadcrumbs, for coating
butter, for frying

Trim and mince the cold ham or gammon. Peel and finely chop the onion. Melt the butter in a saucepan over low heat, add the onion and fry gently for 5 minutes to soften but not brown. Stir in the flour and cook for 1 minute. Gradually stir in the milk. Bring to the boil, stirring well all the time to make a smooth sauce. Simmer for 2–3 minutes to thicken and draw off the heat.

Stir the minced ham, mustard and grated cheese into the sauce and season with salt and pepper. Separate the egg and stir the egg yolk into the mixture. Set mixture aside until completely cool.

Using a fork, lightly break up the egg white in a soup plate. Divide the mixture into 8 portions and with wetted fingers, roll each one to a ball and flatten slightly. Coat each one in the egg white, then coat in the toasted breadcrumbs. Chill for at least 1 hour to firm the coating.

Melt the butter for frying in a frying pan over moderate heat. Fry the croquettes in batches for 6 minutes, turning once, until heated through and brown all over. Serve on slices of hot buttered toast or with a crisp green salad.

Variation: Use a bacon knuckle in place of the ham: soak the knuckle overnight, then drain. Place the knuckle in a large saucepan and pour over cold water to cover. Do not salt. Bring to the boil, then lower the heat and simmer for 30 minutes. Allow to cool and remove meat from the bone then mince the meat.

Cheese croquettes with lemon

Serves 6

2 oz (50g) butter
2 oz (50g) plain flour
½ pint (300ml) milk
salt and freshly milled pepper
8 oz (225g) grated Cheddar cheese
1 egg
toasted breadcrumbs, for coating
butter, for frying
lemon wedges, to serve

Melt the butter in a saucepan over low heat. Stir in the flour and cook gently for 1 minute. Gradually stir in the milk. Bring to the boil, stirring well all the time to make a smooth sauce. Simmer for 3–5 minutes to thicken. Draw off the heat, season with salt and pepper and stir in the cheese. Separate the egg, set aside the white and beat the yolk into the cheese mixture. Allow mixture to become completely cold.

Using a fork, lightly break up the egg white in a soup plate. Spoon out tablespoonsful of the cheese mixture and with wetted fingers shape in small croquettes – you should get about 12. Coat each one in the egg white, then coat in the toasted breadcrumbs. Chill for at least 1 hour to firm the coating.

Melt butter for frying in a frying pan over moderate heat. Fry the croquettes in batches for 6 minutes, turning once, until heated through and brown all over. Serve with lemon wedges – the lemon juice counteracts the richness of the cheese and sharpens the flavour. Serve on slices of hot toast if liked.

4

Fish

Freshness is all important as is the right method of cooking to bring out the fine flavour of fish. Its marvellous flavour also comes through to advantage in cold dishes, making fish an excellent choice for buffets and summertime menus.

Fish

Popular fish

Cod is a firm white-fleshed fish which is very popular because of its mild flavour. Cod is sold as fillets, cutlets or steaks and sometimes small whole cod is available. Poach or bake fillets and serve with a sauce. Snip the bone out of cod steaks with scissors, then press a stuffing in the spaces and bake. Flaked cooked cod is excellent for fish casseroles and fish cakes. *Smoked cod fillet* can be used along with fresh cod to add extra flavour to fish pie or fish cakes.

Coley is also known as saithe. The greyish-pink flesh turns white on cooking, expecially if you first rub it with lemon juice. Use coley as an economical substitute for cod.

Haddock: Though more expensive than cod, haddock is worth the price for its fine flavour. Large haddock are cut in fillets and can be cooked, then flaked and used to make a number of fish dishes or it can be topped with a sauce. In Scotland, small fresh haddock are sold boned and opened out and are very tasty when crumbed and fried or baked. *Smoked haddock* is best bought on the bone because it will have more flavour — it's worth the extra effort to remove the bones. *Arbroath smokies* and *Finnan haddock* are two of the finest smoked haddocks you can buy.

Halibut: This large member of the flat fish family has firm white flesh and a wonderful flavour. It is expensive but filling so portions can be small. Halibut steaks on the bone are delicious when simply grilled and served with lemon. Cold flaked halibut is especially nice in fish dishes made with mayonnaise.

Herrings are pretty silvery grey fish with oily flesh. They are sold whole or as boned fillets. When grilling whole herrings, slash the sides of the fish right through to the flesh so the fish cooks more quickly; serve with mustard butter (page 117). Boned herring fillets are good dipped in oatmeal and fried with bacon. *Kippers* are smoked gutted herrings. Cook them the fisherman's way: place kippers in a deep dish or jug. Pour over boiling water to cover and leave for 10 minutes. Drain and serve with a large lump of butter on top — they will be beautifully tender and juicy.

Huss used to be called rock salmon but the Trades Description Act changed all that, probably because the fish bears no resemblance in taste or appearance to salmon. Huss is sold in long skinned fillets and is a firm meaty fish, making it good to use in soups or stews because it doesn't disintegrate during cooking.

Mackerel has an òily flesh and flavour that goes well with sharp sauces like gooseberry or horseradish. Mackerel must be very fresh to be appreciated. Whole fish are good grilled. Alternatively, have the fish filleted, season with salt and pepper and fry in butter and serve with a good squeeze of lemon juice.

Monkfish is a firm fleshed fish that is usually sold without its head as it's very ugly. The flesh flakes into chunky pieces and has a flavour similar to lobster. Soak chunks of fish in oil and vinegar dressing and grill them on kebab skewers. Or egg and crumb them, then fry until golden.

Plaice is easily recognized by its orange-spotted skin. A member of the flat fish family, plaice is usually sold in fillets. Take the time to remove the skin from plaice fillets — they will be much nicer to eat. The fish has a mild flavour so squeeze plenty of lemon juice over fried fillets.

Salmon: A luxurious fish with a pretty pink flesh, salmon is prized for its fine flavour. Salmon is seasonal but farm reared fish are available all year round. Cook salmon whole or in large pieces of at least 1½–2 lbs (700–900g). Serve hot or cold with hollandaise (page 118) or mayonnaise. Salmon steaks are good when simply grilled and served with lemon. Flaked cooked salmon can be used to turn traditional fish dishes into marvellous party food — try salmon kedgeree or salmon fish cakes.

Salmon trout: No relation to salmon, but this fish has a similar pink-coloured flesh and fine flavour. Smaller salmon trout are good grilled. Slash sides of the fish with a sharp knife and cut the flesh so fish cooks more quickly. Whole salmon trout can be wrapped in kitchen foil and baked in the oven. Serve it hot, or cold with a tarragon mayonnaise.

Sea bass: This fish has a white flesh that is delicately flavoured and tastes very good served cold with a herb mayonnaise (page 121). A whole sea bass makes an impressive part of a cold-table or buffet. Cook as for fresh salmon.

Skate: The large fins, called wings, are the edible meat of this unusual looking fish. Poach the wings in water with vinegar or lemon juice added to help tenderize them; they are most easily skinned after they are cooked. Serve skate the classic way with black butter (page 60); it is also very good served cold in salads.

Sole: The firm, plump fillets of sole are good wrapped round stuffing, then poached and served in delicious sauces. Whole fish can be grilled. Ask the fishmonger to remove the skin for you. *Lemon sole* has a yellow-brown skin and is a little smaller than the famous *Dover sole*, which has grey-brown skin and the most exquisite flavour.

Trout: Best known is the *rainbow trout* which is farm-reared on an extensive scale. The common river, or *brown trout* is a game fish and only available in season and locally — well worth looking for. Trout are best cooked whole — first gut the trout, then either grill or fry in butter.

Turbot: This very expensive flat fish has a delicious creamy white flesh. Turbot is usually available in summer which makes it popular for serving cold with light sauces. Turbot steaks can be poached and served with hollandaise (page 118) or flaked and used in salads.

Whitebait: The small silvery fry of the herring family, whitebait are so tiny you eat the whole fish. They are most popular when deep fried and served with lemon and thinly sliced brown bread and butter. Make sure whitebait are patted dry, then roll about a quarter of the fish at a time in seasoned flour. Deep fry in small batches for 2–3 minutes, then reheat the fat and add all the fried whitebait for one quick fry to crisp them up.

Popular shellfish

Crab is often sold ready-cooked but live crabs are also available. Both the white flesh found in the legs and claws and the brown meat from the body are delicious. A little goes a long way to add a special succulence and flavour to seafood salads. Crabmeat can be used to flavour sauces and stuffings for fish. Dressed crab is also sold — the fishmonger will have removed the crabmeat and replaced it attractively in the shell.

Crawfish: Similar in appearance to lobster, crawfish are easily distinguished because they have no claws. The flesh has a good flavour, some say better than lobster, and there's more of it. It should be prepared and served in the same way as lobster.

Lobster: Renowned for its rich juicy meat, lobster is a real luxury. Because it is not fished in great numbers it remains a very expensive shellfish. Choose a lobster that feels heavy for its size — the tail should be resilient and spring back when straightened and released. Lobsters are usually sold cooked and can be cut in half lengthways (follow the natural line down head and centre back). Serve cold with home-made mayonnaise (page 120). Live lobsters are best when simply boiled in salted water — allow about 15 minutes per 1lb (450g). Serve hot with melted butter and lemon wedges to squeeze over the meat.

Mussels: Buy mussels that are tightly closed, wet and fresh looking. Nowadays mussels that are sold are mostly farmed but you should still wash them in several changes of cold water to remove any grit, otherwise they will be very unpleasant to eat. The simplest way to cook mussels is to pop them all in a saucepan, cover with a lid, and set over moderate heat to steam them open. You can eat them just as they are with lemon and brown bread and butter. Discard any that have remained closed. Mussels cooked this way are wonderful added to omelettes or tossed in a mayonnaise dressing and served with brown bread and butter.

Oysters: Their exquisite taste of the sea is what makes oysters so special. Oysters gathered from our own waters are only available during the colder months of the year—those months having the letter 'R' in them. Keep unopened oysters with the deep shell downwards so the oyster remains moist in its natural juice. Served in the half shell on a bed of crushed ice with plenty of lemon, they make a wonderful first course.

Prawns: The best prawns come from the cold waters of the North Sea. I find frozen North Atlantic prawns are very tasty and delicious in salads, but thaw them completely and discard the juice or it will dilute delicate dressings.

Scallops: Fresh scallops are sold sitting in their pretty shells. Frozen scallops are sold without their shells. The delicately flavoured white flesh can be thickly sliced, but take care to leave the coral whole or it will break up when cooked. Scallops respond best to simple treatment and need only a few minutes cooking time.

Scampi: Once caught near Dublin, scampi are also known as Dublin Bay prawns, as well as by their French name, *langoustines*. The plump tails hold the fleshy edible part. Scampi are sold both raw and cooked and are best when served cold with a mayonnaise dressing. Most frozen scampi are already breadcrumbed, which rather limits the way you can cook and serve them.

How to cook better fish

● Fish cooks as quickly as tender cuts of meat and will spoil if the temperature is too fierce or the cooking time too long.

● Like meat, fish is best cooked on the bone, which makes grilled fish steaks or baked whole fish a real treat.

● Haddock, cod and plaice fillets will all taste better if their skins are first removed. Place fillets on a work surface skin side down. Dip your fingers in salt and grip the tail end. Using a sharp knife, slice under the flesh as close as possible to the skin. Hold tail of fish firmly, and with knife blade held horizontal, cut along the skin so the flesh comes away as cleanly as possible.

● Add 1 tablespoon of oil to the beaten egg for coating fish fillets to make the egg go further.

● Make your own toasted breadcrumbs for coating by placing biscottes or melba toast in a polythene bag and crushing finely with a rolling pin. These are a more attractive colour than the ones you buy.

● Use dry cider, which is as nice as white wine, for baking fish in the oven. Or try vermouth which has a delicious flavour. Dilute vermouth with an equal quantity of water and use some of the liquid to make the sauce.

● Very salty water is best for poaching whole fish – sea water is good too. Add 1 teaspoon salt to every 1 pint (600ml) water and use for cooking fresh salmon.

● White fish is ready when flesh loses that translucent look and becomes white or creamy.

● You can also tell it's cooked when the flesh flakes, or falls easily into natural divisions, when pressed gently. Test near the bone for fish steaks.

● A squeeze of lemon juice over fried or grilled fish fillets or steaks brings out the flavour.

● For toppings or borders over and around cooked fish dishes, beat an egg yolk into mashed potato and you will find it browns beautifully under the grill.

Grilled salmon steaks

Serves 4

4 salmon steaks, each about 1 inch
    (2.5cm) thick
2 oz (50g) butter
seasoned flour, for dusting
parsley butter (page 117)

illustrated facing page 64

Heat the grill to moderate. Melt the butter under the grill in a flameproof dish or the grill pan (remove rack). When hot and foaming but not brown, place the salmon steaks in the dish or pan and immediately turn them over so that both sides are coated in butter. Grill on one side for about 3 minutes.

Turn salmon steaks, dust with seasoned flour and grill for a further 6 minutes, basting well 2 or 3 times with the buttery pan juices, until the fish flakes when pressed near the bone. Top each steak with a slice of parsley butter and serve.

Variation **Grilled halibut steaks:** Use 4 halibut steaks, each weighing about 4–6 oz (100–175g), and cook in the same way. Omit the parsley butter and melt 1 oz (25g) butter in a saucepan, add a squeeze of lemon juice and pour the butter over the steaks.

Skate with black butter

Serves 4

1½–2 lb (700–900g) skate wings
1 small onion
1 bay leaf
salt
3 tablespoons wine vinegar
3 oz (75g) butter
2 teaspoons capers
1 teaspoon chopped parsley

Skate is a fish best skinned after cooking. Cut skate wings in 4 portions. Place in a pan large enough for the skate to lie in one layer. Peel and thinly slice the onion. Add to the pan along with the bay leaf. Pour over boiling water (from the kettle) to cover. Add salt and 1 tablespoon of the vinegar. Bring to a simmer, cover with a pan lid, and cook gently for 15–20 minutes. Using a perforated spoon, transfer the skate to a work surface. Remove the skin from both sides. Place skate on a warmed serving platter and keep hot.

Cook the butter in a saucepan over moderate heat until golden and pour it over the skate. Add the remaining vinegar to the pan. Bring just to a simmer, add the capers and chopped parsley. Pour this over the skate and serve.

Herrings in oatmeal

Serves 4

4 herrings
medium oatmeal, for coating
salt and freshly milled pepper
8 rashers streaky bacon
1 tablespoon oil

illustrated facing page 65

Clean the herrings and cut off the heads. Place on a work surface and spread out flat, skin side up. Press along the back to loosen the bone, then turn each herring over and gently pull away the bone. Put the oatmeal on to a plate and season with salt and pepper. Coat the herrings by firmly pressing each side in the oatmeal. Shake away loose oatmeal.

Trim the bacon. Heat the oil in a large frying pan over moderate heat, add the bacon and fry until crisp. Push the bacon over to one side of the pan. Fry the herrings in the hot bacon fat for 5–6 minutes, turning once. Serve with the fried bacon rashers.

Baked salmon trout

Baking a whole fish in foil helps prevent overcooking: the fish remains moist and all the juices are preserved. Clean the fish leaving on the head. Rub with oil and season with salt and pepper. Place fish in the centre of a large square of kitchen foil. Arrange a few thin slices of lemon on top of the fish. Seal the foil over the top and turn up ends to completely enclose the fish in a baggy parcel. Place on a baking tray and cook in an oven heated to 350°F (180°C) or Gas no. 4, allowing 20 minutes per 1 lb (450g). Unwrap the salmon trout and remove the skin. Separate the flesh from the centre bone and lift the flesh away in neat serving portions. Serve with melted butter or hollandaise (page 118).

Variation: To serve cold, leave the wrapped fish until completely cool, then chill overnight. Unwrap and serve with green mayonnaise (page 120).

Serves 6

2½–3 lb (1.2–1.4kg) fresh whole
    salmon trout
oil
salt and freshly milled pepper
few lemon slices

Oven-fried fish

Melt the butter in a saucepan over low heat and allow to cool until warm to the touch. Meanwhile, remove the skin from the plaice fillets. Beat the egg with the warm butter and salt and pour into a soup plate. Dip each fillet in the mixture, then turn each fillet in the breadcrumbs, pressing the crumbs in firmly to coat all over.

Arrange the coated fish on an ungreased baking sheet. Cook in an oven heated to 400°F (200°C) or Gas no. 6 for 20 minutes. (Do not turn the fillets over.) Serve hot with lemon wedges.

Serves 4

2 oz (50g) butter
8 plaice fillets
1 egg
pinch of salt
toasted breadcrumbs, for coating
lemon wedges, for serving

Scallops in curry sauce

Cut the scallops in thick slices, leaving the coral whole, and set aside. Peel and finely chop the onion. Heat the oil in a saucepan over low heat. Add the onion and fry gently for 5 minutes to soften but not brown. Add the curry powder and cook for 1 minute, stirring occasionally, to draw out the flavour, then stir in the flour. Add the tomato purée and water. Bring to the boil and add the chutney (chop any large pieces of fruit) and lemon juice, then simmer for 5 minutes. Strain the curry sauce and reserve.

Melt the butter in a frying pan over moderate heat. When hot and foaming, add the scallops (and coral) and fry for 2–3 minutes. Stir in the curry sauce and bring to the boil. Draw off the heat and stir in the cream. Serve with hot buttered rice.

Variation **Prawns in curry sauce:** Use 12 oz (350g) peeled prawns in place of the scallops.

Serves 4

6 fresh scallops
2 oz (50g) butter

Curry sauce
1 small onion
1 tablespoon oil
1 level tablespoon curry powder
1 level tablespoon plain flour
1 teaspoon concentrated tomato
    purée
¼ pint (150ml) water
1 tablespoon sweet chutney
juice of ½ lemon
4 tablespoons double cream

Baked fish Provençal

Serves 4

1–1½ lb (450–700g) cod or
  haddock fillet
1 medium-sized onion
1 clove garlic
1 small green pepper
1 oz (25g) butter
1 × 14 oz (396g) tin peeled
  tomatoes
1 level teaspoon castor sugar
pinch of dried mixed herbs
salt and freshly milled pepper

Topping
1 oz (25g) butter
2 tablespoons soft white
  breadcrumbs
2 tablespoons grated hard cheese

Skin and cut the fish in 4 equal pieces. Place in a greased ovenproof dish. Peel and finely chop the onion and peel and crush the garlic to a purée with salt. Halve, deseed and finely chop the green pepper.

Melt the butter in a saucepan over low heat. Add the onion and garlic, cover with a pan lid, and cook for 5 minutes until the onion is soft and translucent. Add the tomatoes with juice, green pepper, sugar and herbs and season with salt and pepper. Bring to the boil, then lower the heat and simmer gently, covered, for 15 minutes. Pour the vegetable mixture over the fish.

Melt the butter for the topping in a saucepan over low heat and draw off the heat. Add the breadcrumbs and using a fork, toss to coat the crumbs, then stir in the grated cheese. Sprinkle the mixture over the fish. Cook in an oven heated to 400°F (200°C) or Gas no. 6 for 30 minutes, until the fish is tender and the topping is crisp and brown. Serve from the dish.

Old-fashioned fish pie

Serves 4–6

1½ lb (700g) cod fillet
½ pint (300ml) milk
¼ pint (150ml) water
1 bay leaf
1 oz (25g) butter
1 oz (25g) plain flour
1 heaped tablespoon chopped
  parsley
squeeze of lemon juice
salt and freshly milled pepper

Topping
1½ lb (700g) potatoes
1–2 tablespoons milk
1 oz (50g) butter
salt and freshly milled pepper

Skin and cut the fish in pieces. Put the fish into a saucepan along with the milk, water and bay leaf. Bring to the boil, then lower the heat and simmer, covered, for 15 minutes. Meanwhile, cut the potatoes for the topping in even-sized chunks. Add to a pan of boiling salted water and cook until tender, then drain. Return to the hot saucepan and shake over the heat until dry, then mash and beat in the milk and half the butter. Season with salt and pepper and set aside.

Lift out the cooked fish and place on a work surface. When cool enough to handle, flake the fish, discarding the skin and bones. Strain ½ pint (300ml) cooking liquid into a measuring jug.

Melt the butter in a saucepan over low heat. Stir in the flour and cook gently for 1 minute. Gradually stir in the reserved fish liquid. Bring to the boil, stirring well all the time to make a smooth sauce. Simmer for 2–3 minutes and draw off the heat. Fold in the fish and parsley. Add the lemon juice and a seasoning of salt and pepper.

Turn the mixture into a greased 1½ pint (900ml) ovenproof dish. Cover with the mashed potato, mark the surface with a fork and dot with the remaining butter in flakes. Cook in an oven heated to 375°F (190°C) or Gas no. 5 for 20 minutes until heated through, then put under a hot grill to brown and crisp the top.

Variations: Add 1 chopped hard-boiled egg or 2 oz (50g) grated hard cheese or 1 teaspoon anchovy essence when adding the flaked fish to the sauce. Sprinkle the top with grated hard cheese, if liked, before grilling.

Haddock with lemon sauce

Skin and cut the haddock fillet in 4 pieces. Peel and finely chop the onion. Grease a baking dish and sprinkle with the onion. Arrange haddock pieces in the dish, season with salt and pepper and pour over the wine. Cover with a buttered paper and cook in an oven heated to 350°F (180°C) or Gas no. 4 for 30 minutes. Transfer the fish to a warmed flameproof serving dish and keep hot. Strain the cooking liquid into a measuring jug and make up to ½ pint (300ml) with milk. Reserve for the sauce.

Melt the butter in a saucepan over low heat. Stir in the flour and cook for 1 minute. Gradually stir in the reserved liquid. Bring to the boil, stirring well all the time to make a smooth sauce. Simmer for 2–3 minutes and draw off the heat. Blend the egg yolk with the cream and stir into the sauce, then add the lemon juice and season with pepper. Pour the lemon sauce over the haddock. Place the dish under a hot grill for 3 minutes until the sauce is bubbling hot and brown.

Variation: Use water and vermouth in equal parts in place of the white wine for cooking the fish.

Serves 4

1½ lb (700g) fresh haddock fillets
½ small onion
salt and freshly milled pepper
¼ pint (150ml) dry white wine

Lemon sauce
1½ oz (40g) butter
1 oz (25g) plain flour
milk (see recipe)
1 egg yolk
3 tablespoons single cream
juice of ½ lemon
freshly milled pepper

Party kedgeree

Cut each haddock in 4 pieces and put into a saucepan along with the water, bay leaf, parsley and lemon. Simmer for about 10 minutes. Lift out the cooked fish and keep warm. Strain exactly 2 pints (1.1 litres) of the cooking liquid into a measuring jug then pour into the rinsed pan and set aside.

Peel and finely chop the onion. Melt half the butter in a separate saucepan over low heat. Add the onion and fry gently for 5 minutes to soften but not brown. Add the curry powder and cook for 1 minute, stirring occasionally, to draw out the flavour. Bring the reserved fish liquid to the boil. Add the rice to the onion and toss together, then pour in the boiling fish liquid. Bring to the boil, stirring all the time, then lower the heat, cover with a pan lid, and cook gently for 20–30 minutes, until rice is tender and liquid has been absorbed.

Meanwhile, flake the fish, removing skin and bones, and chop the hard-boiled eggs. Draw the pan of rice off the heat, add the remaining butter in pieces, the flaked fish and lemon juice. Season with pepper and gently mix together with a fork. Turn into a warmed serving dish. Sprinkle with the chopped eggs and parsley and serve. If you wish, you can press the hard-boiled egg yolks through a sieve instead of chopping them. This makes a finer texture and looks pretty sprinkled over the rice mixture.

Serves 8

2 smoked haddock on the bone,
   each weighing about 1½ lb
   (700g)
2 pints (1.1 litres) water
1 bay leaf
few sprigs parsley
1 slice lemon
1 medium-sized onion
4 oz (100g) butter
pinch of curry powder
1 lb (450g) long-grain rice
4 hard-boiled eggs
juice of ½ lemon
freshly milled pepper
chopped parsley, to garnish

Smoked haddock in puff pastry

Serves 4–6

puff pastry, made using 8 oz (225g)
   strong white flour (page 171)
beaten egg, for glazing

Filling
12 oz (350g) smoked haddock
   fillet
milk (see recipe)
2 oz (50g) long-grain rice
1 medium-sized onion
4 oz (100g) button mushrooms
2 hard-boiled eggs
2 oz (50g) butter
1 tablespoon chopped parsley
freshly milled pepper

Cut the haddock in large pieces and poach in milk to cover for about 10 minutes. Sprinkle the rice into a saucepan of boiling salted water and simmer for 8–10 minutes until tender. Meanwhile, peel and finely chop the onion. Trim and coarsely chop the mushrooms and chop the hard-boiled eggs. Drain the rice and put into a mixing bowl. Drain the fish and when cool enough to handle, flake the fish, discarding the skin and bones.

Melt 1 oz (25g) of the butter in a saucepan over low heat. Add the onion and fry gently for 5 minutes to soften but not brown. Draw off the heat, add the remaining butter and when melted, add to the rice along with the haddock, mushrooms, parsley and a seasoning of pepper. Gently fold the hard-boiled eggs into the mixture. Leave mixture until it becomes cool.

Roll out the prepared pastry on a lightly floured work surface to a 12 × 14 inch (30 × 35.5cm) rectangle. Trim the edges straight and slide pastry on to a baking sheet. Spoon filling down the centre of the pastry and pat into a neat shape with the fingertips. Using a floured sharp knife, cut the pastry diagonally on both sides of the filling at 1 inch (2.5cm) intervals to make strips, then criss-cross the strips over the filling and fold in the ends of the pastry. Chill for at least 30 minutes.

About 15 minutes before baking, heat the oven to 425°F (220°C) or Gas no. 7. Brush pastry with beaten egg. Place in the centre of preheated oven and bake for 30 minutes. Serve hot or cold.

Trout meunière

Serves 4

4 rainbow trout
seasoned flour
4 oz (100g) butter
1 tablespoon oil
juice of ½ lemon
1 teaspoon chopped parsley

This is one of the most straightforward methods of cooking fish and one best used for small delicately flavoured fish like trout. The secret is the extra butter and lemon juice added to the pan after cooking the fish. Clean the trout leaving on the heads. Holding each one by the tail, roll in seasoned flour to coat all over.

Heat half the butter and the oil in a large frying pan over moderate heat and when hot and foaming, add the fish one at a time. Fry for about 6–8 minutes until browned, turning once. Transfer to a hot serving platter and keep hot.

Pour away the hot butter and quickly wipe out the frying pan with absorbent paper. Melt the remaining butter in the hot pan, add the lemon juice and chopped parsley. When hot and foaming, pour the butter over the fish and serve.

Variation **Trout with almonds:** Fry 1–2 oz (25–50g) flaked almonds in the remaining 2 oz (50g) butter until golden, then add the lemon juice. Omit the parsley.

Illustrated: Grilled salmon steaks with parsley butter, pages 60 and 117

Cold salmon mayonnaise

Determine the amount of water required for cooking the fish by placing the fish in a large pan and pouring over cold water to completely cover, then remove the fish. Salt the water and add the vinegar. Bring to the boil, then carefully lower in the salmon and return to a full rolling boil and boil for exactly 2 minutes.

Draw off the heat and cover with a tight-fitting lid. Set in a cool place and leave undisturbed until cold – about 12 hours. The fish will continue to cook in the liquid. (This method works for any size – even whole – salmon.)

Transfer the cold salmon to a work surface and remove the skin – the flesh will be moist and beautifully pink. Place the salmon on a serving platter and surround the fish with crisp lettuce. Cut the eggs in half and top with spoonfuls of mayonnaise and a little lumpfish caviar, if liked. Arrange eggs on the lettuce. Serve with extra mayonnaise or green mayonnaise (page 120) passed separately.

Any leftover salmon is delicious in salads. Try using it in Niçoise salad (page 154) in place of tuna fish. Or use salmon to make potted salmon (page 16) for a summer picnic.

3 lb (1.4kg) middle cut of salmon
salt
1 tablespoon vinegar

Garnish
crisp lettuce leaves
3 hard-boiled eggs
mayonnaise
lumpfish caviar (optional)

Seafood mayonnaise with tomato aspic

Drain the prawns thoroughly, otherwise the juices will dilute the dressing. Combine the mayonnaise, tomato ketchup, cream and Worcestershire sauce in a mixing bowl and add a squeeze of lemon juice to sharpen the flavour. Chill for at least 1 hour so flavours combine.

Put the lemon juice and water for the tomato aspic into a teacup, sprinkle in the gelatine and leave to soak for 5 minutes. Bring the tomato juice to the boil in a saucepan and draw off the heat. Add the soaked gelatine to the hot tomato juice and stir until dissolved. The heat of the pan will be sufficient. Add the sugar and season with salt and pepper. Pour into a wetted 1½ pint (900ml) ring mould and chill until set firm.

Unmould tomato aspic on to a serving plate or into a serving bowl (contains the shape best). Fill the centre with the prawn mixture and sprinkle with chopped parsley. Serve with hot herb bread.

Variation: Instead of prawns, quartered hard-boiled eggs are nice in the dressing.

Serves 6

1 × 1 lb (454g) packet frozen
  peeled prawns, thawed
4 rounded tablespoons mayonnaise
4 tablespoons tomato ketchup
4 tablespoons double cream
1 teaspoon Worcestershire sauce
squeeze of lemon juice
chopped parsley, to garnish

Tomato aspic
juice of ½ lemon
1 tablespoon water
2 level tablespoons powdered
  gelatine
2 × 14 fl oz (415ml) tins tomato
  juice
1 level teaspoon castor sugar
salt and freshly milled pepper

Illustrated: Herrings in oatmeal, page 60

Smoked salmon mousse

Serves 6–8

1 lb (450g) smoked salmon or
    smoked salmon trimmings
1½ oz (40g) butter
1½ oz (40g) plain flour
½ pint (300ml) milk
4 oz (100g) unsalted butter
juice of 1 lemon
salt and freshly milled pepper
¼ pint (150ml) double cream
lemon aspic jelly (page 119)

Trim the smoked salmon and discard any tiny pieces of skin and bone. Reserve 1 or 2 nice pieces for garnish and finely chop or mince the remainder.

Melt the 1½ oz (40g) butter in a saucepan over low heat. Stir in the flour and cook gently for 1 minute. Gradually stir in the milk. Bring to the boil, stirring well all the time to make a smooth sauce. Simmer for 2–3 minutes to thicken and turn on to a plate. Cover with a circle of wetted greaseproof paper and leave until completely cool.

Cream the unsalted butter in a medium-sized mixing bowl until soft. Beat in the smoked salmon, then beat in the white sauce and the lemon juice. Season with plenty of pepper and add salt only if necessary. Whip the cream until soft peaks form and fold into the mixture. Spoon into a serving dish and spread level. Decorate with the reserved smoked salmon slices and spoon over sufficient liquid lemon aspic jelly to make a thin covering. Chill for several hours or overnight. Serve as a first course with hot toast or as a main dish with a green salad. The smoked salmon mousse is rich so portions should be small.

Variations **Fresh salmon mousse:** Use 1 lb (450g) fresh salmon that has been cooked and cooled (page 65). Flake the flesh, discarding the skin and bones. Decorate this delicious mousse with sliced lemon.

Kipper mousse: Separate 1 lb (450g) kipper fillets and pull away the silvery skin. Place in a shallow dish, pour over the juice of 2 lemons and marinate for 1 hour. Flake the flesh, discarding the bones, and add to the unsalted butter along with a little of the marinade in place of the juice of 1 lemon. For best results purée this mixture in a blender or food processor. Decorate the mousse with sliced lemon.

Prawns in mayonnaise

Serves 6

1 × 1 lb (454g) packet frozen
    peeled prawns, thawed
2 tablespoons mayonnaise
1 tablespoon chopped parsley
squeeze of lemon juice
1 firm lettuce heart
2 hard-boiled eggs

Drain the prawns thoroughly, otherwise the juices will dilute the dressing. Combine the prawns, mayonnaise and parsley in a mixing bowl and add a squeeze of lemon juice to sharpen the flavour. Chill for at least 1 hour so flavours blend.

Place crisp lettuce leaves in a shallow serving dish and spoon the prawn mixture on top. Cut the eggs in quarters and arrange them around the prawn mixture. Serve with a tossed green salad and plenty of wholemeal bread and butter.

Variation **Crabmeat in mayonnaise:** For a luxurious cold-table dish, use 1 lb (450g) crabmeat in place of the prawns.

Soused mackerel with mustard dressing

Clean the mackerel and remove the heads. Place in an ovenproof dish. Cut the tail fins off, if necessary, so the fish fit into the dish. Peel and thinly slice the onion. Arrange on top of the fish along with the lemon slices, peppercorns and bay leaves. Mix together the vinegar and water and pour it over the fish to cover. Add more vinegar and water in equal parts to cover the fish, if necessary. Cover the dish with kitchen foil and cook in an oven heated to 350°F (180°C) or Gas no. 4 for 45 minutes. Allow mackerel to cool in the liquid, preferably overnight.

Combine the mustard, vinegar, sugar, if using it, water and a seasoning of salt and pepper in a bowl. Beat in the oil until the dressing is well blended.

Transfer the fish to a work surface and carefully remove the skin, then lift the fish from the bones. Arrange the crisp lettuce on a serving plate and place the fish on top. Hand the dressing separately. Serve with thinly sliced brown bread and butter.

Serves 4

2 medium-sized mackerel
1 medium-sized onion
2–3 thin lemon slices
few black peppercorns
2 bay leaves
about ¼ pint (150ml) wine vinegar
about ¼ pint (150ml) water
crisp lettuce, for serving

Mustard dressing
1 teaspoon French mustard
1 tablespoon wine vinegar
pinch of sugar (optional)
3 tablespoons water
salt and freshly milled black pepper
4 tablespoons oil

Pickled herrings

Clean the herrings and remove the heads and tails. Place on a work surface and spread them out flat, skin side up. Press along the back to loosen the bone, then turn each herring over and gently pull away the bone. Cut each fish in half down the centre to make 2 fillets. In an earthenware or china dish, arrange fillets in layers, sprinkling each layer with salt to cover and finishing with a sprinkling of salt. Cover and leave herrings in a cool place for at least 24 hours.

Remove herring fillets from the salt and carefully peel away the silvery skins. Soak in cold water for 1 hour, changing the water once or twice, then drain. Meanwhile, peel and finely chop the onion and put into a saucepan along with the vinegar, water, sugar and spices. Bring to the boil and draw off the heat. Leave until completely cool.

Thoroughly drain the soaked herring fillets and place in an earthenware or china dish. Pour over the pickling liquid, cover and leave for at least 48 hours in a cool place. The herrings will keep in the refrigerator for several weeks.

Lift out the number of fillets required for serving and cut in thin strips. Arrange in a serving dish and spoon over a little of the pickling liquid. Garnish with chopped raw onion and quartered hard-boiled eggs. Serve with rye bread and butter.

6–8 fresh herrings
coarse salt
1 medium-sized onion
½ pint (300ml) wine vinegar
¼ pint (150ml) water
6 oz (175g) granulated sugar
4 black peppercorns
1 teaspoon mixed pickling spice

Garnish
chopped raw onion
hard-boiled eggs

Herring rollmops

Clean the herrings and remove the heads and tails. Place on a work surface and spread them out flat, skin side up. Press along the back to loosen the bone, then turn each herring over and gently pull away the bone.

Season the flesh side with salt and pepper. Roll up the herrings skin side out and pack tightly in a baking dish so herrings remain closed. Put the vinegar, water, bay leaf, peppercorns and sugar in a saucepan and bring to the boil. Pour the liquid over the herrings. Cover with a lid or foil and cook in an oven heated to 350°F (180°C) or Gas no. 4 for 40 minutes. Leave herrings to cool overnight in the cooking liquid to absorb flavour. Lift from the liquid for serving – the herrings will be firm and easy to handle.

Serves 6

6 fresh herrings
salt and freshly milled pepper
¼ pint (150ml) white wine vinegar
¼ pint (150ml) water
1 bay leaf
few black peppercorns
1 teaspoon soft light brown sugar

Swedish herring salad

Cut herrings in bite-sized pieces and place in a mixing bowl. Peel and finely chop the onion. Dice the beetroot and potato. Add the vegetables to the bowl along with the gherkin. Quarter, core and dice the apples and add to the bowl.

Blend the soured cream with the mayonnaise and fold into the salad. Toss together – the salad will take on a pink colour from the beetroot – and season with salt and pepper. Chill until ready to serve. Cut the eggs in quarters and use to garnish the salad. Serve with rye bread and butter.

Variation: Pickled herrings are sold in jars. They come ready-cut in pieces. Drain them from the liquid and use instead of your home-made ones.

Serves 4

4 pickled herring fillets
   (page 67)
1 medium-sized onion
4 oz (100g) cooked beetroot
8 oz (225g) cooked potato
1 tablespoon chopped gherkin
2 dessert apples
¼ pint (150ml) soured cream
2 tablespoons mayonnaise
salt and freshly milled pepper
2 hard-boiled eggs, to garnish

Marinated kipper fillets

Allow frozen kipper fillets to thaw until they can be separated. Pull away the silvery skin from the back of each kipper fillet and arrange the fillets in a shallow serving dish. Peel and slice the onion into rings and arrange on top. Add the bay leaves.

Put the sugar, vinegar and a seasoning of salt and pepper into a mixing bowl. Stir to dissolve the seasonings and then beat in the oil. Pour the marinade over the kipper fillets. Leave kippers to marinate for 6–8 hours or overnight in a cool place. Serve with thinly sliced brown bread and butter. Any leftovers make excellent brown bread sandwiches with lettuce.

Serves 4

1 packet (6–8) boned kipper fillets
1 small onion
2 bay leaves
1 level teaspoon castor sugar
3 tablespoons wine vinegar
salt and freshly milled pepper
4 tablespoons oil

5

Poultry and Meat

Plain cooked poultry and meat will always be
favourites, and cooking them with spicy,
well-flavoured sauces or seasonings is what
makes them so versatile and delicious.

/

Poultry and Meat

How to cook better poultry

● Chickens sold today are young and tender. A supple breastbone is always a good guide that the chicken will be tender when cooked.

● Make certain frozen poultry is completely thawed, so cooking times are accurate. Remember chicken and turkey must be well cooked through.

● Cut up a whole bird for chicken portions – you'll find pieces are neater (there's less bone), you can crowd more in a pan for cooking and you will have the bonus of a carcass for stock.

● Leave skin on chicken portions unless you are coating them with egg and breadcrumbs.

● Always truss a whole chicken for cooking. Legs will not dry out so much if they are tied close to the body.

● For best flavour, use butter for frying chicken and add a little oil to prevent butter from over-browning at high temperatures.

● Chicken and turkey are bland meats so are always best teamed with other flavours such as lemon, herbs, spicy tomato mixtures or curry. They are also good served with pickled fruits and preserves.

● A squeeze of lemon juice perks up grilled or fried chicken; the breast meat will be whiter if rubbed with lemon before poaching.

● Test poultry by pushing a skewer or fork deep into the thigh (or the thickest part). If juices run clear – no tinges of pink – then poultry is cooked.

Roast chicken

A whole chicken is good value for money. I always buy a bird large enough to provide leftover meat for serving cold.

● Fresh chilled and frozen chickens are available all year round. Allow 8–12 oz (225–350g) oven-ready weight per person; a 4 lb (1.8kg) oven-ready bird will serve 4 people with some left over.

● A frozen chicken must thaw completely before cooking and remember to remove the neck, giblets and any loose fat from the body cavity (page 75).

● A lemon and parsley stuffing is especially nice with chicken. Or put a lump of butter inside the cavity to keep the flesh moist and add some chopped herbs – tarragon is wonderful. Truss chicken with string (see below) to keep a good compact shape.

● Spread the breast with soft butter and cover the chicken with buttered paper. Roast in an oven heated to 375°F (190°C) or Gas no. 5, allowing 20 minutes per 1 lb (450g).

● Leave a hot roast chicken to stand for 5–10 minutes before carving so juices settle. Serve chicken with pan gravy and cranberry sauce or corn fritters (page 141).

● If you plan to serve cold roast chicken, leave bird to cool at room temperature and meat will slice best. A cold roast chicken is very good with green beans in an oil and vinegar dressing, sweet pickled peaches (page 157) or a delicious curry mayonnaise (page 121).

● To roast chicken portions, trim the pieces and place skin side up in a buttered roasting tin. Brush with melted butter and season with salt and pepper. Roast, uncovered, in an oven heated to 400°F (200°C) or Gas no. 6 for 45–50 minutes. Baste occasionally but do not turn pieces over.

Roast turkey

Roast turkey is very economical when you are serving a lot of people especially for parties and buffets.

● When choosing a fresh bird look for a breast that is broad in proportion to its length; this

Trussing a chicken or turkey

Trussing a chicken or turkey will give it a neat, compact shape which helps the bird roast evenly. Doing it yourself makes a neater job and takes only a moment if you use a trussing needle and a good length of fine string. A trussing needle is sturdy, about 10 inches (25cm) long and has a large eye. The pointed end of the needle is flattened, rather like a knife tip, so that it penetrates the flesh easily. You cannot substitute anything else because a trussing needle has to be long enough to go into the chicken or turkey and out on the opposite side in one go. You can buy a trussing needle at most good kitchen equipment shops. I've had mine for years and wouldn't be without it.

● Thread a trussing needle with an 18 inch (45cm) length of fine string. Set chicken or turkey on work surface with neck end facing you.

● Pull the front flap of skin over the neck cavity and under the bird. Then twist wings back and under so tips lie neatly underneath. Push the needle into the wing on one side, catch the neck underneath using an in-and-out stitch, and bring the trussing needle out through the wing on the opposite side.

● Draw the needle through, but leave a length of string where you started. Pass the needle back through the thickest part of the thigh joint (on the same side) and draw it out through the thigh on the opposite side, so that you finish back where you started.

● Remove the needle and tie the two ends of string in a tight bow knot to hold the wings and legs close to the body of the bird.

● With a second piece of string neatly tie ends of the legs close to the tail, or parson's nose. Don't forget to remove the string before carving. You can draw the whole length from the main body of the bird in one pull.

means there will be plenty of tender white meat. A flare of white up either side of the breast indicates a thin layer of fat under the skin which will baste the flesh and keep it moist when roasting.

● Remember one-third of the weight will be lost when a fresh bird is drawn so allow for this when you estimate size. Frozen birds are sold oven-ready. Allow 12 oz (350g) oven-ready weight per person. From a 5 lb (2.3kg) turkey you get 5 portions; from an 8 lb (3.7kg) turkey, 9–10 portions; from a 12 lb (5.5kg) turkey, 16 portions.

● Let frozen turkey thaw completely (page 75). Remove the neck, giblets and loose fat from the body cavity.

● Turkey usually has two stuffings: one in the neck and a second in the body cavity. The neck stuffing is most important because it gives the roast bird a good shape. A chestnut stuffing is always popular. When the breast is carved you should take a slice of the stuffing with it. A lump of butter and a few blanched onions can go in the body cavity. Truss turkey with string to make a compact shape.

● For a traditional roast, spread turkey with soft butter, cover with bacon rashers and buttered paper or with a square of double-thickness butter muslin – you can baste right through the muslin. Roast in an oven heated to 425°F (220°C) or Gas no. 7 for the first 30 minutes, then lower oven temperature to 350°F (180°C) or Gas no. 4 for a turkey up to 12 lb (5.5kg); or 325°F (160°C) or Gas no. 3 for a turkey over 12 lb (5.5kg) for the rest of the roasting time.
Cooking times are: 8–10 lb (3.6–4.5kg), 3–3½ hours; 10–14 lb (4.5–6.4kg), 3½–4 hours; 14–18 lb (6.4–8.2kg), 4–4½ hours and 18–20 lb (8.2–9.1kg), 4½–5 hours.

● For a slow roast set the bird in an oven heated to 325°F (160°C) or Gas no. 3. Calculate 25 minutes per 1 lb (450g) for a turkey up to 12 lb (5.5kg) and 20 minutes per 1 lb (450g) for a turkey over 12 lb (5.5kg). Large turkeys are excellent cooked this way. On a roasting thermometer a temperature of 190°F (90°C) will indicate that the turkey is cooked.

● Put 1 tablespoon of flour in a roasting tin and place turkey on top; during roasting flour absorbs drippings and takes colour. The flour contributes to making a rich gravy (page 89).

● Allow roast turkey to stand for at least 15 minutes before carving. If skin is not cut or pierced it will hold in the heat. Juices get a chance to settle and the meat slices better.

● Hot roast turkey is great with cranberry preserve or relish and gravy. Cold sliced turkey can be served with sweet pickled fruits and is very good with Cumberland sauce.

Roast duckling

Roast duckling is very succulent and roasts beautifully since it bastes itself. Cold roast duckling is especially nice.

● Ducklings are available year round, fresh or frozen. As a guide a 5 lb (2.3kg) oven-ready duckling will serve 4 people and two 4 lb (1.8kg) oven-ready birds will serve 6 people.

● Spoon stuffing of your choice into body cavity – sage and onion is the most popular. Or put a cut up orange, apple or onion into the cavity to enhance the flavour and discard before serving. Truss or skewer closed.

● Duckling is very fatty. Prick the skin all over with a fork so fat drains off during roasting and rub the skin with salt. Place duckling on a trivet in a roasting tin with just 2–3 tablespoons cold water in the tin.

● Roast, uncovered, in an oven heated to 350°F (180°C) or Gas no. 4, allowing 30 minutes per 1 lb (450g). Do not baste, but pour or ladle off fat as it accumulates. For a crisp skin, increase oven temperature to 425°F (220°C) or Gas no. 7 for the last 15 minutes roasting time.

● Hot roast duckling is good served with apple sauce, red cabbage and apple, glazed onions and cranberry or orange sauce.

● For cold duckling, strip meat from the carcass and cut in bite-sized pieces. If you take off the skin and place it under a hot grill until really crisp, it can be cut in strips or crumbled and used as a garnish along with crunchy salad vegetables and fruits tossed in an oil and vinegar dressing.

● To roast duckling portions, prick skin all over and rub with salt. Set, skin side up, on a trivet in a roasting tin. Roast, uncovered, in an oven heated to 400°F (200°C) or Gas no. 6 for 1 hour. Rub the skin with grated orange rind and squeeze over the orange juice before cooking the duckling, if liked.

Roast goose

Roast goose is a luxury. It's very fatty, which makes it succulent and tender, especially when served cold, but there is a considerable weight loss when goose is cooked – an uncooked bird looks very deceiving.

● Goose is seasonal from September to January and if you want a fresh bird you will need to order one. Allow just over 1 lb (450g) oven-ready weight per person. An average 10 lb (4.5kg) goose will serve 8 people.

● Spoon stuffing of your choice into body cavity. Mixtures with fruit flavours like apple or prune are popular, or use sage and onion. Then truss or skewer closed.

● Prick skin all over with a fork so fat drains off during roasting and rub the skin with salt. Place on a trivet in a roasting tin with just 3–4 tablespoons cold water in the tin.

● Roast the goose in an oven heated to 425°F (220°C) or Gas no. 7 for 20 minutes. Then lower oven temperature to 350°F (180°C) or Gas no. 4 and roast, allowing 15 minutes per 1 lb (450g). Have the goose covered with a buttered paper during the first 40 minutes roasting time. Do not baste but pour or ladle off the fat as it accumulates in the tin.

● Increase the oven temperature for the last 15 minutes roasting time to get a crisp, golden skin.

● Roast goose goes well with red cabbage and apple, fried apple rings or apple sauce. Serve cold roast goose with Cumberland sauce or a salad including fruit such as oranges or apples and something crunchy like chicory or celery.

Roast pheasant

Pheasant tastes like tough old chicken if it's not well hung. In muggy weather 4–5 days is enough, but when it's crisp and cold pheasant can hang for up to 2 weeks. Birds are ready when a tail feather is easy to pull out.

● If your pheasant comes oven-ready from the supermarket, you will have to take a chance on its age. With a freshly shot bird in your hand you will get some indication if you look at its feet: they should be soft and supple; long spurs on the back of the legs in a cock pheasant indicate an older one. It's harder to tell with a hen pheasant but since she's juicier and more tender anyhow it doesn't really matter. One pheasant is enough to serve 2 persons.

● Truss a pheasant in the same way as chicken (page 72). If the bird is bought from a poulterer, it will have a slice of larding fat tied over the breast. Otherwise, you will have to use streaky bacon rashers because pheasant meat is very lean and needs added fat.

● Put a piece of butter the size of a walnut inside the body cavity to keep it moist; you can push in some herbs such as thyme or marjoram, too. A bed of roasting vegetables – thick slices of carrot, onion and celery – under the bird adds flavour both to the bird and the gravy.

● I like to roast pheasant upside down for most of the cooking time and then turn it right way up towards the end. This helps to keep the breast moist. A traditional method is to cover each pheasant with a square of double-thickness butter muslin soaked in melted butter instead of using the bacon rashers and basting through the muslin with hot butter from the tin.

● For a crisp skin, remove bacon rashers or other coverings towards the end of the cooking time and baste the bird, then dredge lightly with flour, called frothing. Baste again and return to the oven for the remainder of the time with the heat turned up a little. Roast pheasant in an oven heated to 400°F (200°C) or Gas no. 6 for 50–60 minutes.

● Cold roast pheasant is lovely for a buffet supper. Cut off legs first, then thinly slice the breast. It is delicious with shredded red cabbage salad or cold chestnut purée.

To thaw frozen poultry

● All frozen poultry must be completely thawed – as slowly as possible – before cooking.

● Leave the frozen bird in its plastic wrapper slit open and set in a cool place on an upturned plate, so that the bird doesn't sit in a pool of liquid as it thaws.

● Make sure you allow plenty of time by starting the thawing well in advance. The size of the bird will make a difference to the time needed:

Bird and oven-ready weight	Time
chicken or duck up to 5 lb (2.3kg)	24 hours
turkey or goose up to 8 lb (3.6kg)	36 hours
turkey 9–12 lb (4.1–5.4kg)	48 hours
turkey 13–20 lb (5.9–9.1kg)	2–3 days

● If you're in a rush and faced with a bird that is still frozen, don't dunk it in hot water; instead submerge the bird in cold water for a while.

● As soon as the bird is pliable, remove giblets from the body cavity to speed up thawing.

● It is essential that the interior is defrosted if you are going to stuff the bird. Frozen poultry is properly thawed when there are no ice crystals in the body cavity and the legs are flexible. Once poultry is thawed it is very perishable and should be cooked as soon as possible.

Jointing a chicken

For servings of four to six, you'll find it more satisfactory to buy a whole bird and joint it yourself, then you have the carcass to boil up for stock. There is another advantage: chicken joints cut from a whole bird are neater and there is less bone, which makes it easier to fit them in one pan – something you will appreciate when you're cooking for a party.

● From a 4 lb (1.8kg) oven-ready chicken, you will be able to cut 8 pieces. Using a sharp knife, cut the legs from each side of the bird, then cut through each leg at the joint to make 4 pieces.

● Turn chicken so neck-end is nearest you and carefully cut along one side of the breastbone. Lift the chicken flesh away from carcass and then cut through the wing joint to detach from the carcass. Trim off wing pinions (the meatless wing tips) and set aside for stock.

● Lay the breast portion flat on the work surface and cut neatly in half – at a slant like French bread – to get 2 even-sized portions.

● Repeat the procedure with the breast portion on the second side and you will finish up with 8 chicken portions and a carcass and two wing tips for the stock pot.

Roast chicken with herbs

Wipe chicken and remove giblets. Cream 2 oz (50g) of the butter with the herbs and a little grated lemon rind and season with salt and pepper. Spoon the butter into the body cavity.

Place the chicken resting on one breast in a buttered roasting tin and spread exposed surface with the remaining butter. Roast in an oven heated to 400°F (200°C) or Gas no. 6. After 20 minutes roasting time, turn the bird on its other side and baste. After a further 20 minutes, turn the chicken upright and baste again. Roast for a final 20 minutes – a total of 1 hour cooking time. This method of roasting will keep the chicken succulent and juicy. Allow chicken to cool for 10 minutes, then carve. Spoon over the melted butter and herbs from the body cavity and serve at once.

Serves 4

3 lb (1.4kg) oven-ready chicken
3 oz (75g) butter
1 tablespoon finely chopped parsley
1 tablespoon finely chopped chives
finely grated lemon rind, to taste
salt and freshly milled pepper

Honey roast duck

Serves 4

4 lb (1.8kg) oven-ready duckling
salt
2 tablespoons water
2 tablespoons clear honey
1 tablespoon boiling water
2–3 oranges, to garnish
1 bunch watercress, to garnish
3–4 tablespoons oil and vinegar
    dressing

Wipe duck and remove giblets. Prick the skin all over with a fork and rub well with salt which will make the skin crisp when cooked. Place in a roasting tin and add the water. Roast in an oven heated to 350°F (180°C) or Gas no. 4, allowing 30 minutes per 1 lb (450g).

After 1 hour of roasting time, pour the duck fat from the roasting tin. Blend the honey with the boiling water and generously brush a little over the skin of the duck. Return to the oven and complete the roasting time, basting two or three times with the honey mixture (not with drippings in the pan or glaze will lose its lustre). Leave duckling until completely cool.

Cut the duck in serving portions and arrange on a serving platter. Peel and cut the oranges in segments and arrange around the meat along with the watercress. Sprinkle the oil and vinegar dressing over the oranges and watercress and serve.

Chicken in a basket

Serves 6

12 chicken drumsticks
1 egg
1 tablespoon oil
seasoned flour
soft white breadcrumbs, for coating
oil, for deep frying

Remove the skin from the chicken drumsticks. Lightly beat together the egg and oil in a soup plate. Coat the chicken pieces in seasoned flour and dip each piece in the egg and drain slightly, then roll in the breadcrumbs to coat evenly. Chill for at least 1 hour to firm the coating.

Deep-fry 4 drumsticks at a time for 8–10 minutes until crisp and golden brown. Drain on absorbent paper and keep warm while frying the remaining chicken. Wrap a little kitchen foil around the bone end of chicken drumsticks so they can be picked up and eaten with the fingers. Arrange chicken in a basket lined with a pretty napkin and serve.

Provençal chicken

Serves 6

4 lb (1.8kg) oven-ready chicken,
    jointed
3 tablespoons oil
1½ lb (700g) ripe tomatoes
1–2 cloves garlic
6 anchovy fillets
¼ pint (150ml) dry white wine
1 teaspoon concentrated tomato purée
1 level teaspoon castor sugar
freshly milled pepper
12 stoned black olives
chopped fresh basil, to garnish
illustrated facing page 80

Trim the chicken pieces. Heat the oil in a large frying pan. Add chicken pieces and fry over moderate heat for 10 minutes to brown on both sides. Scald the tomatoes and peel away the skins. Remove seeds and chop tomato flesh coarsely. Peel the garlic (flavour is milder if you leave it whole) and chop the anchovies.

Add the wine and tomato purée to the frying pan and bring to the boil. Then add the tomatoes, garlic, castor sugar and a seasoning of freshly milled pepper. Cover with a pan lid and cook gently for a further 30 minutes. Add the anchovies and olives and heat through. Serve chicken with sauce from the pan and sprinkle with chopped basil. This is a summer recipe – when basil is out of season use chopped parsley for colour or omit altogether.

Stuffings for poultry

● A good stuffing makes all the difference to a roast bird. Team fruit mixtures with richer duck and goose. Tasty herb or oatmeal mixtures are good with turkey or chicken.

● Assemble stuffing ingredients beforehand. Then lightly mix ingredients together and stuff a bird just before roasting – do not pack stuffing too tightly into the cavity.

● Remember to remove stuffing after the first hot serving and store separately in the refrigerator. Stuffing is perishable and should be used up quickly.

● You can cook a stuffing separately, except those with oatmeal, by wrapping the mixture in buttered foil and cooking in an oven heated to 350°F (180°C) or Gas no. 4 for 1 hour. Or place stuffing alongside bird for the last hour of the cooking time. For serving cold, let stuffing cool in the wrapping; serve it sliced with cold roast chicken or turkey.

● Allow 4 oz (100g) breadcrumbs for every 5 lb (2.3kg) oven-ready weight of poultry to calculate the amount required. Above 15 lb (6.8kg) oven-ready weight for turkey there is no need to increase the amounts, since body cavity remains the same size and the extra weight is from the meat of the bird.

Lemon and parsley: Combine 4 oz (100g) fresh white breadcrumbs, finely grated rind of 1 lemon and 4 tablespoons chopped parsley. Season with salt and freshly milled pepper. Using a fork, stir 2 oz (50g) melted butter and 1 lightly beaten egg into ingredients. Use for roast chicken and turkey.

Spiced apple: Peel, core and dice 2 medium-sized cooking apples and add to 4 oz (100g) fresh white breadcrumbs along with a seasoning of salt and freshly milled pepper, 1 level tablespoon castor sugar and a pinch of ground cinnamon. Using a fork, stir 3 oz (75g) melted butter into ingredients. Use for roast duck or goose.

Oatmeal and onion: Peel and finely chop 1 medium-sized onion and place in a mixing bowl along with 4 oz (100g) medium oatmeal, 2 oz (50g) shredded beef suet and a good seasoning of salt and freshly milled pepper. Mix together to make a loose stuffing which you spoon into the body cavity. During cooking oatmeal will swell and absorb poultry juices and cook to a delicious nutty flavour. Use for any roast poultry.

Orange and walnut: Combine 4 oz (100g) fresh white breadcrumbs with 1 tablespoon chopped parsley, grated rind of 2 oranges, 1 oz (25g) chopped walnuts and a seasoning of salt and freshly milled pepper. Peel and finely chop 1 medium-sized onion. Melt 2 oz (50g) butter over low heat. Add the onion and fry gently for 5 minutes to soften but not brown. Using a fork stir butter and softened onion and the juice of 1 orange into ingredients. This makes a delicious stuffing for roast turkey, chicken or goose.

Fried turkey escalopes

Trim the turkey escalopes. Lightly beat the egg in a soup plate and season with salt and pepper. Dip each escalope in the egg and drain slightly, then coat them in the breadcrumbs, pressing the coating on firmly. Chill for at least 30 minutes to firm the coating.

Heat the butter and oil in a large frying pan over moderate heat. When hot and foaming, add the turkey escalopes and fry on both sides to seal, then lower the heat and fry gently for about 15–20 minutes until tender and golden.

Using a fish slice, transfer escalopes to a hot serving dish. Add the lemon juice to the hot butter and oil in the pan and stir and scrape to pick up coagulated pan juices. Pour the pan juices over the escalopes and serve.

Serves 4

4 turkey escalopes
1 egg
salt and freshly milled pepper
toasted breadcrumbs, for coating
2 oz (50g) butter
1 tablespoon oil
juice of ½ lemon

Grilled chicken with bacon

Serves 4

4 chicken portions
2 oz (50g) butter
salt and freshly milled pepper
4 lean bacon rashers
juice of ½ lemon

Trim the chicken portions. Heat the grill to moderate and lightly grease the grill-pan rack. Melt the butter in a saucepan over low heat. Place the chicken on the grill-pan rack, skin side down (bone towards the grill conducts heat more quickly), brush with melted butter and season with salt and pepper.

Place the grill pan at least 3 inches (7.5cm) below the heat and grill the chicken portions for 10 minutes, then turn the chicken, baste with butter, and grill for a further 10–15 minutes. Trim the bacon rashers and grill alongside chicken for the last 3–5 minutes cooking time. Increase the heat towards the end of cooking time if you like a crisp chicken skin and crisp bacon. The chicken is cooked if the juices run clear when the meat is pierced in the thickest part with the tip of a knife. Squeeze lemon juice over chicken portions and serve with grilled bacon rashers.

Duck with orange

Serves 6

2 × 4 lb (1.8kg) oven-ready
   ducklings
salt
2 oranges
2 tablespoons water

Orange sauce
4 tablespoons granulated sugar
2 tablespoons water
2 tablespoons wine vinegar
3 oranges
1 rounded tablespoon orange
   marmalade
½ pint (300ml) stock, made using
   the giblets
4 level teaspoons cornflour
2 tablespoons water

Wipe duck and remove giblets. Prick the skins all over with a fork and rub well with salt. Cut the 2 oranges in chunks and push half inside each body cavity, then skewer the cavities closed. Place in a roasting tin and add the water. Roast in an oven heated to 350°F (180°C) or Gas no. 4, allowing 30 minutes per 1 lb (450g).

Put the granulated sugar for the sauce into a dry saucepan and stir over moderate heat until the sugar melts and turns a golden brown. Draw off the heat and stir in the water to make a caramel syrup. (Take care as the mixture bubbles up when water is added.) Add the wine vinegar, juice of 1 of the oranges, orange marmalade and stock. Bring to the boil, then lower the heat and simmer covered, for 30 minutes. Strain the sauce and return it to the rinsed pan. Set aside.

Thinly pare the rind from the remaining 2 oranges using a vegetable peeler. Cut in the narrowest possible julienne strips. Put into a saucepan, pour over cold water to cover and simmer for 15 minutes until tender. Remove the white pith from the oranges and cut them in segments. Drain the orange strips and reserve. Blend the cornflour with the water and stir into the strained orange sauce. Bring to the boil, stirring all the time as sauce thickens and clears, then add the orange strips and reserved orange segments. Draw off the heat and keep hot.

Cut the duck in serving portions and arrange on a warmed serving platter. Spoon over the sauce and serve.

Chicken Maryland

Trim the chicken pieces. Lightly beat together the egg and oil in a soup plate. Coat the chicken pieces in seasoned flour and dip each piece in the egg mixture and drain slightly, then coat all over in the breadcrumbs. Chill for at least 1 hour to firm the coating. Trim bacon rashers, cut in half crossways and roll up, then thread them on skewers.

Heat the oven to 400°F (200°C) or Gas no. 6. Melt 2 oz (50g) of the butter in a roasting tin placed in the heating oven. Remove from the oven, add the chicken pieces and baste. Cook chicken for 45 minutes, basting and turning occasionally. About 15 minutes before the end of cooking time, add the skewers of bacon rashers to the tin.

Peel the bananas, cut in half lengthways and roll each half in a little flour. Gently fry in the remaining butter for 2–3 minutes until lightly browned.

Transfer the chicken to a warmed serving platter. Surround the meat with the bacon rolls (removed from the skewers) and bananas. Serve with corn fritters (page 141).

Serves 6

4 lb (1.8kg) oven-ready chicken, jointed
1 egg
1 tablespoon oil
seasoned flour
soft white breadcrumbs, for coating
6–8 streaky bacon rashers
3 oz (75g) unsalted butter
3 bananas
plain flour, for coating

Chicken with tarragon butter sauce

Trim chicken portions neatly and season them with salt and pepper. If using fresh tarragon strip the leaves from the stems and chop finely to make about 1 tablespoon chopped tarragon. Using a knife blade, mash the butter and tarragon together on a plate to make a tarragon-flavoured butter.

Place chicken pieces in a roasting tin with skin side upwards. Spread the tarragon butter over each one. Place in an oven heated to 350°F (180°C) or Gas no. 4 and cook for 1 hour. Baste chicken portions occasionally with the butter as it melts in the roasting tin. About 10 minutes before the end of the cooking time, pour the cream over the chicken and complete cooking time.

Transfer chicken portions to a warmed serving platter. Stir up the cream and tarragon butter in the tin to a sauce consistency, spoon over the chicken and serve.

Variations: This recipe can be made using other herb-flavoured butters such as parsley (page 117). Or try making it with mustard-flavoured butter (page 117).

Serves 4

4 chicken breast portions
salt and freshly milled pepper
4–6 sprigs fresh tarragon or 2 tablespoons dried tarragon
2 oz (50g) butter
¼ pint (150ml) double cream

Italian-style chicken

Serves 6

4 lb (1.8kg) oven-ready chicken,
  jointed
seasoned flour
2 oz (50g) butter
1 tablespoon oil
2 small onions
1–2 cloves garlic
8 oz (225g) button mushrooms
1 lb (450g) ripe tomatoes
4 fl oz (125ml) dry white wine
½ pint (300ml) chicken stock
1 tablespoon concentrated tomato
  purée
bouquet garni
salt and freshly milled pepper
chopped parsley, to garnish

Trim the chicken pieces and roll in seasoned flour. Heat the butter and oil in a frying pan (with lid) over moderate heat. When hot and foaming, add the chicken pieces and fry for 10 minutes, turning occasionally, until brown all over. Meanwhile, peel and thinly slice the onions and peel and crush the garlic with salt. Trim the mushrooms. Scald the tomatoes and peel away the skins then chop them. Remove the chicken from the pan and keep warm until required.

Add the onions to the hot fat remaining in the pan and fry gently for 10 minutes until golden, then add the garlic and mushrooms. Return the chicken to the pan, add the chopped tomatoes, wine, stock, tomato purée and bouquet garni. Season with salt and pepper. Bring to the boil, then lower the heat and simmer, covered, for 30 minutes, until tender. Discard bouquet garni.

Transfer the chicken and mushrooms to a warmed serving platter and keep hot. Press the sauce through a sieve and return to the rinsed pan. Boil rapidly for 4–5 minutes, stirring occasionally, to reduce the sauce and concentrate the flavours. Spoon the sauce over the chicken and sprinkle with chopped parsley. Serve with saffron rice (page 150).

Barbecued chicken casserole

Serves 6

4 lb (1.8kg) oven-ready chicken,
  jointed
2 oz (50g) butter
1 small orange

Barbecue sauce
1 medium-sized onion
1 tablespoon oil
2 oz (50g) soft light brown sugar
1 level tablespoon cornflour
2 teaspoons made English mustard
1 teaspoon Worcestershire sauce
juice of ½ lemon
1 × 2¼ oz (64g) tin concentrated
  tomato purée
½ pint (300ml) water
salt and freshly milled pepper

Trim the chicken pieces. Melt the butter in a frying pan over low heat. When hot and foaming, add the chicken pieces and fry for 10 minutes, turning occasionally, until brown all over. Meanwhile, peel and slice the orange. Peel and finely chop the onion for the sauce. Heat the oil in a saucepan over low heat, add the onion and fry gently for 5 minutes to soften but not brown. Transfer the chicken to a casserole, add the orange slices and keep hot.

Combine the brown sugar, cornflour, mustard, Worcestershire sauce, lemon juice, tomato purée and water in a mixing bowl and season with salt and pepper. Add to the onion and bring to the boil, stirring all the time, then lower the heat and simmer for 5 minutes, stirring occasionally.

Pour the sauce over the chicken, cover casserole with a lid and cook in an oven heated to 350°F (180°C) or Gas no. 4 for 1 hour. Serve straight from the casserole or spoon chicken and sauce on to a warmed serving platter. Serve with buttered rice and a crisp green salad.

Illustrated: Provençal chicken, page 76

Chicken paprika

Peel and thinly slice the onion and peel and finely chop the garlic. Halve, deseed and finely chop the pepper. Trim the chicken pieces and season with salt and pepper. Melt the butter in a frying pan over low heat. When hot and foaming, add the chicken and fry gently, turning occasionally, until brown all over. Transfer chicken to an ovenproof casserole and keep hot.

Add the onion to the hot butter in the frying pan and cook gently for 10 minutes until golden. Add the garlic and sprinkle in the paprika. Stir in the hot stock and tomato purée and bring to the boil. Pour the contents of the pan over the chicken and add the green pepper. Cover casserole with a lid and cook in an oven heated to 350°F (180°C) or Gas no. 4 for 1 hour. Transfer chicken pieces to a warmed serving platter and keep hot.

Put the soured cream into a mixing bowl, sift over the flour and beat until blended and smooth. Add a little of the casserole juices, mix together well and turn soured cream mixture into the casserole. Bring sauce to the boil, stirring all the time, then simmer until thickened. Check seasoning and spoon the sauce over the chicken.

Serves 6

1 medium-sized onion
1 clove garlic
1 medium-sized green pepper
4 lb (1.8kg) oven-ready chicken, jointed
salt and freshly milled pepper
1 oz (25g) butter
1 level tablespoon paprika
¾ pint (400ml) hot chicken stock
1 tablespoon concentrated tomato purée
¼ pint (150ml) soured cream
1 level tablespoon plain flour

Chicken liver pilaff

Trim and chop the bacon and peel and finely chop the onions. Melt half the butter in a heavy-based saucepan or flameproof casserole over low heat, add the bacon and onion and fry gently for 5 minutes to soften the onion but not brown. Bring the stock to the boil. Stir the rice into the pan of onions and bacon and pour in the boiling stock. Season with salt and pepper. Bring to the boil, then lower the heat and simmer, covered, for about 20–30 minutes, until rice is tender and liquid has been absorbed. Alternatively, transfer casserole to an oven heated to 350°F (180°C) or Gas no. 4 and cook for 45 minutes–1 hour.

Meanwhile, trim the mushrooms and chicken livers. Melt 2 oz (50g) of remaining butter in a frying pan over low heat, add the mushrooms and cook for 5 minutes, then transfer them to a warmed plate and keep hot. Add chicken livers to the pan and toss them in the butter for 1–2 minutes (just to set but not cook through) and then lift them out and place on a work surface. Cut livers in slices and return to the pan. Fry over moderate heat for about 2 minutes.

Add the mushrooms and chicken livers to the rice, mixing them in carefully with a fork so as not to crush the rice grains. Check seasoning and turn pilaff on to a warmed serving platter. Dot with remaining butter in flakes and sprinkle with grated cheese. Serve with hot garlic bread and a crisp salad.

Serves 8

8 oz (225g) rashers streaky bacon
2 medium-sized onions
6 oz (175g) butter
1 lb (450g) long-grain rice
2 pints (1.1 litres) chicken stock
salt and freshly milled pepper
8 oz (225g) button mushrooms
8 oz (225g) chicken livers
2–3 oz (50–75g) grated hard cheese

Illustrated: Cold chicken with lemon sauce, page 83

Chicken chasseur

Serves 6

**4 lb (1.8kg) oven-ready chicken,
   jointed**
salt and freshly milled pepper
2 oz (50g) butter
6 oz (175g) button mushrooms
1 tablespoon brandy
**1 tablespoon concentrated tomato
   purée**
4 fl oz (125ml) dry white wine
brown sauce (page 113)
chopped parsley, to garnish

Trim the chicken pieces and season with salt and pepper. Melt the butter in a frying pan over moderate heat. When hot and foaming, add the chicken pieces and fry for 10 minutes, turning occasionally, until brown all over. Lower the heat, cover with a pan lid, and cook gently for 30 minutes until tender. Trim and slice the mushrooms.

Add the brandy to the frying pan and set alight – shake pan gently so flames spread over the contents of the pan. Flaming burns off excess fat and greatly adds to the flavour of the dish. When flames go out, add the mushrooms, tomato purée and white wine. Boil the sauce, stirring occasionally, for at least 5 minutes to reduce and concentrate the flavour. Add the prepared brown sauce and heat through. Check seasoning and spoon chicken pieces and sauce on to a hot serving platter. Sprinkle with chopped parsley and serve.

Chicken Waldorf

Serves 6

1 lb (450g) cold cooked chicken
1 tablespoon finely chopped onion
2 stalks celery
3 dessert apples
¼ pint (150ml) natural yoghurt
¼ pint (150ml) mayonnaise
salt and freshly milled pepper
1 oz (25g) chopped walnuts
crisp lettuce leaves, for serving

Trim and dice the chicken and put into a mixing bowl. Add the finely chopped onion. Trim and finely chop the celery stalks. Quarter, core and dice the apples (but do not peel). Add celery and apples to mixing bowl.

Combine yoghurt and mayonnaise in a mixing bowl and season with salt and pepper. Add to the chicken mixture and toss together. Fold in the chopped walnuts. Spoon on to crisp lettuce leaves arranged on a serving platter. Serve with thinly sliced brown bread and butter.

Chicken fricassee

Serves 6

4 lb (1.8kg) oven-ready chicken
1 medium-sized onion
few black peppercorns
2–3 stalks celery
1 bay leaf
3 oz (75g) butter
2 oz (50g) plain flour
¼ pint (150ml) double cream
1 egg yolk
squeeze of lemon juice
salt and freshly milled pepper

Wipe the chicken and remove giblets. Place in a deep pan with salted cold water to cover. Peel the onion and add to the pan along with the peppercorns, celery and bay leaf. Bring to the boil, then lower the heat and cook gently, covered, for 40 minutes until tender. Allow to cool in the liquid for several hours or overnight. Strain 1 pint (600ml) of the chicken stock into a measuring jug and reserve for making the sauce.

Melt 2½ oz (65g) of the butter in a saucepan over low heat. Stir in the flour and cook gently for 1 minute. Gradually stir in the hot chicken stock. Bring to the boil, stirring well all the time to make a smooth sauce. Simmer for 2–3 minutes and draw off the heat. Combine cream and egg yolk in a small bowl. Add a little of the hot sauce, blend together and add to the sauce. Add a squeeze of lemon juice and remaining butter and season with salt and pepper.

Joint the chicken, remove skin and lift chicken meat from the bones. Cut in bite-sized pieces and add to the sauce. Heat through for serving. This makes an excellent filling for pancakes or vol-au-vents or serve with saffron rice (page 150).

Cold curried chicken with melon

Wipe the chickens, remove the giblets and place a little of the butter inside body cavities. Rub the skins of the birds with remaining butter, place in a roasting tin and cover with kitchen foil. Roast in an oven heated to 400°F (200°C) or Gas no. 6 for 1 hour. Allow the chickens to cool.

Joint birds, remove skin and lift chicken meat from the bones. Cut in bite-sized pieces and put into a mixing bowl. Trim and finely chop the celery stalks. Halve the melon, scoop out the seeds, remove the rind and dice the flesh, then add to the chicken. Cover and chill. Combine mayonnaise, lemon juice, curry powder and cream in a mixing bowl. Cover and chill for at least 2 hours for flavours to blend. Combine mayonnaise dressing with chicken mixture and turn on to a serving plate lined with crisp lettuce.

Serves 12

2 × 3 lb (1.4kg) oven-ready
   chickens
3 oz (75g) butter
1 head celery
1 medium-sized melon
crisp lettuce leaves, for serving

Dressing
½ pint (300ml) mayonnaise
juice of ½ lemon
1 level teaspoon curry powder
2–3 tablespoons single cream

Cold chicken with lemon sauce

Wipe the chicken and remove the giblets. Place in a deep pan with salted cold water to cover. Peel the onion and add to the pan along with the peppercorns and bay leaf. Cover with a pan lid and cook gently for 40 minutes until tender. Allow to cool in the liquid for several hours or overnight so chicken flesh remains moist.

Skim fat from chicken stock and measure ½ pint (300ml) stock for the sauce. Joint the bird, remove skin and lift chicken meat from the bones. Melt the butter in a saucepan over low heat. Stir in the flour and cook gently for 1 minute. Gradually stir in the chicken stock. Bring to the boil, stirring all the time to make a smooth sauce. Simmer gently for 3–4 minutes. Season with salt and pepper and draw off the heat. Stir in grated lemon rind and lemon juice. Blend the egg yolks with the cream and stir into the sauce. Check seasoning. Allow the sauce to cool, stirring occasionally to prevent a skin forming.

Cut chicken in bite-sized pieces and arrange on a serving plate, then spoon the lemon sauce over the chicken. Garnish with cooked cold asparagus tips or green grapes – any green vegetable or fruit is pretty with this dish. Serve with rice salad (page 157). This is a good dish to make the day before serving.

Serves 6

4 lb (1.8kg) oven-ready chicken
1 medium-sized onion
3 black peppercorns
1 bay leaf
asparagus tips or green grapes, to
   garnish

Lemon sauce
1 oz (25g) butter
1 oz (25g) plain flour
salt and freshly milled pepper
grated rind and juice of 1 lemon
2 egg yolks
½ pint (300ml) single cream

illustrated facing page 81

Turkey tetrazzini

Serves 4–6

¾–1 lb (350–450g) cold roast
   turkey
8 oz (225g) dried tagliatelle
8 oz (225g) button mushrooms
2 oz (50g) butter
squeeze of lemon juice
1 oz (25g) plain flour
1 pint (600ml) hot turkey or
   chicken stock
salt and freshly milled pepper
¼ pint (150ml) double cream
2 tablespoons dry sherry
1 oz (25g) soft white breadcrumbs
1 oz (25g) grated Parmesan cheese

Cut the turkey in bite-sized pieces and set aside. Cook the noodles in boiling salted water for 8 minutes, or until just tender. Meanwhile, slice and lightly fry the mushrooms in half the butter, add a squeeze of lemon juice and draw off the heat. Melt the remaining butter in a saucepan over low heat. Stir in the flour and cook gently for 1 minute. Gradually stir in the hot stock. Bring to the boil, stirring well all the time to make a smooth sauce. Simmer for 2–3 minutes, then season with salt and pepper and draw off the heat. Stir in the cream and sherry.

Thoroughly drain the noodles and put them into a greased ovenproof dish. Add a little of the hot sauce and the fried mushrooms and toss together well. Add the turkey pieces to the sauce and spoon the mixture over the noodles. Mix together the breadcrumbs and grated cheese and sprinkle the mixture over the casserole. Heat through in an oven heated to 375°F (190°C) or Gas no. 5 for about 20 minutes until the top is crisp and brown.

Casserole of pheasant with chestnuts

Serves 6

1 brace oven-ready pheasant
8 oz (225g) chestnuts
8 oz (225g) small onions
1 oz (25g) butter
1 level tablespoon plain flour
1 pint (600ml) hot chicken stock
1 tablespoon redcurrant jelly
2–3 large pieces thinly pared orange
   rind
juice of 1 orange
1 teaspoon wine vinegar
1 bay leaf
salt and freshly milled pepper
chopped parsley, to garnish

Cut each pheasant into 4 pieces with game shears. Slit the flat sides of the chestnuts, add to a pan of boiling water and boil for 2 minutes. Drain and peel away the outer shells and inner skins. Peel the onions. Melt the butter in a frying pan over low heat. When hot and foaming, add the pheasant and fry gently, turning, until brown all over. Transfer the pheasant to a casserole. Toss the onions and chestnuts in the hot butter until the onions are lightly browned. Using a perforated spoon, transfer onions and chestnuts to the casserole.

Add the flour to the butter remaining in the pan. Cook gently, stirring all the time, for 5 minutes until brown, then add the hot stock and bring to the boil. Add the redcurrant jelly, pared orange rind, orange juice and wine vinegar. Whisk to break up the redcurrant jelly, then pour the contents of the pan over the pheasant and add the bay leaf. Cover the casserole with a lid and cook in an oven heated to 350°F (180°C) or Gas no. 4 for 1 hour until the pheasant is cooked through.

Transfer pheasant pieces, onions and chestnuts to a warmed serving platter and keep hot. Strain the cooking liquid into a saucepan and boil for 5 minutes to reduce the liquid and concentrate the flavours. Season with salt and pepper and pour the sauce over the pheasant. Sprinkle with chopped parsley and serve.

Duck terrine

Wipe duckling and remove the giblets, reserving the liver. Place duckling in a roasting tin, add the water and roast in an oven heated to 425°F (220°C) or Gas no. 7 for 30 minutes. When cool enough to handle, remove the meat from the bones, discarding the skin. (The flesh will still be quite pink.) Dice the breast pieces and put into a shallow bowl along with the orange-flavoured liqueur or brandy and set aside to marinate.

Trim the pork fillet and belly of pork and cut in pieces. Pass the remaining duck flesh, duck liver, pork fillet and belly of pork through a mincer into a mixing bowl. Or chop ingredients in a food processor. Add the eggs, salt and a good seasoning of pepper. If pistachio nuts are used (colour is pretty) blanch in boiling water for 1 minute, then rub off skins in a clean cloth. Add the nuts and the reserved diced duck breast along with liqueur or brandy. Mix together well.

Press the mixture into a greased 2 pint (1.1 litre) terrine. Top with the bay leaves. Cover with a lid or buttered kitchen foil and place in a roasting tin. Fill roasting tin to a depth of 1 inch (2.5cm) with water. Cook in an oven heated to 325°F (160°C) or Gas no. 3 for 2 hours. Leave to cool overnight pressed under a weight. Melt the butter in a saucepan and pour it over the surface, then chill. Serve in slices with salad.

Serves 8

4 lb (1.8kg) oven-ready duckling
2 tablespoons water
2 tablespoons orange-flavoured liqueur or brandy
1 lb (450g) pork fillet
8 oz (225g) belly of pork
2 eggs
2 level teaspoons salt
freshly milled pepper
2 tablespoons shelled pistachio nuts (optional)
1–2 bay leaves
1 oz (25g) butter

Pheasant terrine

Rub the pheasant with a little butter and place in a roasting tin. Roast in an oven heated to 400°F (200°C) or Gas no. 6 for 20 minutes until partially cooked. When cool enough to handle, remove the pheasant meat from the bones, discarding the skin. Trim and cut the belly of pork in pieces. Trim the chicken livers.

Pass the pheasant flesh, belly of pork and chicken livers through a mincer into a mixing bowl. Or chop ingredients in a food processor. Crush the juniper berries and add to the bowl along with the wine, brandy, egg, salt and a good seasoning of pepper. Mix together well with a wooden spoon and leave to stand for about 1 hour in a cool place.

Trim the bacon rashers. Press the mixture into a greased 2 pint (1.1 litre) terrine and top with the bacon. Cover with a lid or buttered kitchen foil and place terrine in a large roasting tin. Fill tin to a depth of 1 inch (2.5cm) with water. Cook in an oven heated to 325°F (160°C) or Gas no. 3 for 2 hours. Allow to cool overnight pressed with a heavy weight. Then, discard bacon rashers and chill for at least 12 hours. Serve with hot toast or crusty bread and butter.

Serves 8

1 oven-ready pheasant
butter (see recipe)
1½ lb (700g) belly of pork
4 oz (100g) chicken livers
4 juniper berries
4 fl oz (125ml) red or white wine
2 tablespoons brandy
1 egg
2 level teaspoons salt
freshly milled pepper
4 rashers streaky bacon

How to cook better meat

● For best results, meat should be at room temperature before cooking.

● Use wetted hands, not floured, for rolling meat balls and shaping meat loaf – flour gets sticky.

● Season meat with salt and pepper just before cooking. The exception is steak – salt makes it stick to the pan. Salt rubbed into the fat on roast beef will make it crisp.

● Wet meat won't brown. Thawed cuts of meat, particularly escalopes and chops, should be patted dry in absorbent paper before frying, and if meat is marinated make sure you pat it dry, too.

● Rare roast meat is more tender, especially for serving cold. Lamb is very good when still pink, but pork must be well cooked.

● Serve leftover roast meat hot by simmering the gravy, then add meat slices and bring back to a simmer. The flavour is better than when meat is heated in gravy from the start.

● Some casseroles taste better when reheated, especially spicy dishes. Be sure to heat casseroles until bubbling hot. This will take about 30–40 minutes in an oven heated to 350°F (180°C) or Gas no. 4.

● Fruit flavours go well with meat dishes. Try adding soaked prunes to beef stew; serve apricot halves filled with mint jelly with roast lamb and peach halves filled with horseradish sauce with beef. Cold meats are extra good served with sweet pickled fruits.

Roast beef

● Beef should be well hung to improve the flavour and make the meat more tender. There is no way to recognize this in raw meat – find a good butcher and rely on him.

● Colour is not important, beef just tends to darken when cut. Look for marbling – the tiny rivulets of fat open up the meat and baste it while cooking. Scotch beef has very good marbling.

● Cuts from the forequarter of the animal are cheaper and need longer, slower cooking than those from the rear quarters, which include the best grilling and roasting cuts.

● The best cuts for roasting are sirloin, ribs and topside in that order. Look for a layer of fat on a joint for roasting, then beef will baste naturally. A joint weighing over 3 lb (1.4kg) will roast better.

● Let a chilled joint stand at room temperature for 1–2 hours before cooking. Prick the fat all over with a fork and rub in salt for a crisp brown crust. Set the joint in the roasting tin, fat side up, and put a spoonful of flour on the tin directly under the roast and you'll find it absorbs fat and sediments during roasting to provide a delicious thickener for gravy afterwards.

● Start beef in an oven heated to 425°F (220°C) or Gas no. 7 for 15 minutes, then lower the heat to 375°F (190°C) or Gas no. 5 for the rest of the cooking time. Allow 15 minutes per 1 lb (450g) for rare or 20 minutes per 1 lb (450g) for medium. For a boned and rolled joint, allow 25 minutes per 1 lb (450g).

● For complete accuracy use a meat thermometer to test the internal temperature. Push thermometer into a lean part and not touching any bone. When thermometer reading shows 150°F (65°C) meat is rare and at 160°F (70°C) it is medium.

● Let roast joint stand at room temperature for 15 minutes before carving so juices settle and meat carves better. If joint is for serving cold leave meat to cool at room temperature.

● Roast beef is best with gravy, Yorkshire pudding and horseradish sauce. Cold roast beef is delicious with soured cream horseradish sauce (page 122).

Roast lamb

● Lamb is available year round with the meat coming in from one source or another. Our own Scotch lamb is a good buy in autumn.

● Because the animal is young you'll find lamb is a very tender meat and all cuts, apart from the scrag end neck and shank, are suitable for roasting. It's a small animal so you'll find you can easily recognize the cuts.

● Remember lamb goes well with fruit flavours, especially in stuffings and sauces.

● Popular roasting joints are shoulder, which can be boned and rolled, and leg, either whole or cut into the shank end and fillet end. Rack of lamb from the best-end is usually sold as cutlets, but if you ask the butcher he will cut it in one piece. This is the cut to use for a lamb guard of honour or crown roast and it's also good for serving as a small mid-week roast.

● Let chilled meat come to room temperature. Then stand lamb on a bed of vegetables such as a carrot and onion cut in thick slices. During roasting the vegetables caramelize at the edges and give flavour and colour to the gravy.

● Roast lamb slowly. Set in a roasting tin and place a knob of dripping on top. Roast in an oven heated to 350°F (180°C) or Gas no. 4, allowing 20 minutes per 1 lb (450g) plus 20 minutes. For a boned and rolled joint, allow 25 minutes per 1 lb (450g) plus 25 minutes.

● For added flavour make small slits and insert slivers of garlic. Best of all, about 20 minutes before the end of the roasting time spread the fat with about 1 tablespoon redcurrant jelly, mint jelly or rowan jelly. The jelly caramelizes and looks and tastes delicious.

● Try your roast lamb medium rare for a change. On a meat thermometer the temperature reading should show 180°F (80°C) for well cooked or 160°F (70°C) for medium rare.

● Good accompaniments for roast lamb include redcurrant jelly, rowan jelly or mint sauce.

● Leftover cold roast lamb can be chopped and used to make shepherd's pie (page 99).

Roast venison

● A roast cut of venison makes a lovely party dish and there's no mystery about the cooking – just treat venison like beef.

● Venison is dark with a close grain and has no natural covering of fat. To help overcome the dryness, first season the meat with salt and pepper, then rub the surface with 1–2 tablespoons oil, working the oil into the meat very thoroughly with your fingertips. Leave the meat to soak for several hours.

● Alternatively, season meat with salt and pepper and wrap it in streaky bacon rashers. Or, spread some lard over the surface of the meat, being more generous than you would be with a cut of beef.

● Marinate venison (page 106) for several hours or overnight. Then pat dry and rub the surface with oil or wrap in bacon.

● The natural covering of fat in other joints bastes the joint and as it cooks keeps the meat succulent. You can roast venison in an open tin with a tent of foil over the top, or use a covered roasting tin. Towards the end of the cooking time open the foil or remove lid and dust the joint with flour, then baste with the juices.

● For cooking time, roast in an oven heated to 400°F (200°C) or Gas no. 6 allowing 20 minutes per 1 lb (450g) plus 20 minutes extra.

● Venison drippings make a lovely gravy with a good gamey flavour. Try putting a tablespoon of flour in the roasting tin underneath the joint right at the start. During roasting it will absorb pan drippings and can then be used as a delicious thickener for the gravy.

● Unlike other meats, venison should not be left to stand before serving, but should be carved in very thin slices immediately it is cooked. Serve on very hot plates. This way venison stays moist and juicy.

● Redcurrant jelly or rowan jelly are the usual accompaniments for venison, but try Cumberland or cranberry sauce. A purée of chestnuts also goes very well with it.

Roast pork

● With modern refrigeration pork is no longer seasonal, these days it is available year round.

● If your pork is frozen it's very important to thaw it correctly to ensure proper cooking. Thaw in the refrigerator, allowing 12 hours for chops and small joints. For joints over 3 lb (1.4kg) allow 24 hours in a cool place. Remember it's easier to score the rind of pork while it's still frozen.

● Pork is a rich meat which needs a minimum of additional flavours, but lends itself perfectly to a variety of accompaniments, particularly those with fruit or a sweet sharp flavour.

● All cuts of pork are tender and suitable for roasting; best cuts are ones with a good area of rind for crackling, such as cuts from the leg or loin. Pork has a good covering of fat, so joint bastes naturally and there are usually tasty drippings for making gravy.

● Make sure the rind is well scored by the butcher and rub in salt for a crisp finish. Put a spoonful of flour directly under the joint and it will absorb fat and sediments during cooking to provide a delicious gravy thickener.

● Since it is important to cook pork thoroughly I recommend a meat thermometer. Push thermometer into a lean part and not touching the bone. When pork is cooked the temperature will read 190°F (90°C).

● Set pork joint rind side up in a roasting tin and roast in an oven heated to 425°F (220°C) or Gas no. 7, allowing 25 minutes per 1 lb (450g) plus 25 minutes. For a boned and rolled joint, roast at 375°F (190°C) or Gas no. 5, allowing 35 minutes per 1 lb (450g) plus 35 minutes.

● Increase oven heat for last 10 minutes of cooking time to crisp the crackling. Or you can lift off the rind with a knife, crisp it under a hot grill and serve separately.

● Let roast stand at room temperature for 15 minutes before carving and meat will be juicier. You'll find pork goes well with accompaniments like baked apples, apple sauce, red cabbage with apple or pickled peaches.

Bacon and gammon

● Bacon and gammon joints can be boiled or roasted and are excellent served cold when they slice beautifully.

● Gammon is the hind leg of a bacon pig. It is sold whole – good for a party – or in smaller joints such as middle gammon, gammon corner, slipper or hock. Always check the weight of your joint.

● Bacon comes from the fore, or shoulder, cuts of a bacon pig and is less expensive. The middle cut provides bacon rashers.

● These cuts have been salt cured so it's best to soak them overnight in cold water. Or put the joint straight into a pan of cold water and bring to the boil. Then drain and cover bacon or gammon with fresh cold water.

● Add a peeled onion, bay leaf or sprig of rosemary to the water for boiling bacon or gammon. Simmer gently, covered, skin side down. Allow 30 minutes per 1 lb (450g) and top up the pan with extra boiling water to keep the joint covered. The liquid makes a good stock for lentil soup.

● For roasting in the oven, wrap the joint in foil with a bay leaf or sprig of rosemary added and place in a roasting tin with a little water in the tin. Bake in an oven heated to 375°F (190°C) or Gas no. 5, allowing 30 minutes per 1 lb (450g). On a roasting thermometer the internal temperature will read 180°F (80°C) when meat is cooked.

● Strip off the rind with a knife while the joint is hot; press on toasted breadcrumbs when the fat is hot – they stick better. Or you can score the fat in a criss-cross pattern and glaze.

● Glaze by spreading the fat with French mustard and press on demerara sugar. Or spread with orange marmalade or redcurrant jelly. Place joint in a roasting tin, uncovered, and set in the oven with temperature increased to 400°F (200°C) or Gas no. 6 for about 15 minutes and the glaze will caramelize.

● For serving cold, allow joint to cool for 24 hours, then slice thinly. Serve with sweet pickled fruits, especially peaches (page 157) or garnish with sugared grapes.

How to make perfect gravy

● A well flavoured stock is important; make it using the giblets from poultry or game, or use vegetable cooking water along with a stock cube.

● Put a sliced onion or carrot under the roast – the natural sugars caramelize in the roasting tin and add to the colour. An old-fashioned trick is to put a teaspoon of sugar in the corner of the tin – this caramelizes during cooking and adds colour to the gravy.

● Try putting 1 tablespoon flour directly under the roast before cooking. During roasting it absorbs drippings and browns. When it's time to make the gravy and the fat is poured off, you have a thickener already there.

● For steaks, chicken joints, hamburgers or most pan-fried foods make a thin gravy for serving by deglazing the pan with stock, wine or water. Use butter for initial frying and when meat is removed from the pan, add a few tablespoons liquid to the hot pan. Using the back of a fork or a whisk stir or whisk over high heat to pick up coagulated pan juices. Boil liquid to a syrupy consistency and pour the liquid over the meat.

To make a thin gravy: Strain off all the fat from the roasting tin leaving behind the dark drippings and coagulated pan juices. Add ½–¾ pint (300–400ml) hot stock and bring to the boil, stirring and scraping to pick up all the dark flavouring bits. Simmer to reduce and concentrate the gravy. Strain into a hot gravy boat.

To make a thick gravy: Strain off all but 1 tablespoon of the fat and leave behind all the dark drippings and coagulated pan juices. Sprinkle 1 tablespoon flour into the tin and cook over the heat for a few moments to brown the mixture. Stir in ½–¾ pint (300–400ml) hot stock and bring to the boil, whisking all the time. Simmer for 2–3 minutes then strain into a hot gravy boat. If you've added 1 tablespoon flour to the tin before roasting the joint, it won't be necessary to add any extra flour to the pan.

Cold roast beef fillet

Trim the fillet and neatly tie with string (butcher will do this). Season with freshly milled pepper, then rub the oil all over the fillet with your fingers. Leave to stand for 3–4 hours at room temperature.

Calculate the cooking time at 12 minutes per 1 lb (450g). Place fillet in a roasting tin and flash roast in an oven heated to 450°F (230°C) or Gas no. 8 for calculated cooking time, or until the meat has a nice brown crust and is pink and juicy inside. Leave until completely cool, preferably overnight. Remove string, carve in thick slices and arrange on a serving platter.

Variations **Beef niçoise:** Arrange the meat slices on a serving platter and surround the meat with cold French beans in oil and vinegar dressing, quartered hard-boiled eggs and sliced tomatoes.

For a stunning party dish, glaze the beef slices by thinly brushing them with chilled consommé. Or surround the meat with assorted sweet pickles.

Serves 8–12

2–3 lb (.9–1.4kg) beef fillet
freshly milled pepper
3 tablespoons oil

illustrated facing page 96

Beef in pastry

Serves 8

2 lb (900g) beef fillet
2 oz (50g) butter
salt and freshly milled pepper
puff pastry, made using 8 oz (225g)
 strong white flour (page 171)
beaten egg, for glazing

Ask the butcher to cut the meat from the thick end of the fillet and trim and tie it for you. Melt the butter in a roasting tin over low heat. Brown the beef fillet all over in the butter and season with salt and pepper. Then transfer the tin to the centre of an oven heated to 425°F (220°C) or Gas no. 7 and roast for 15–20 minutes. Remove the meat from the pan and leave until completely cool, then remove string.

Roll out the pastry on a lightly floured work surface to a rectangle about three times wider than the beef fillet and about 4 inches (10cm) longer. Trim the edges straight and reserve the trimmings. Place the beef fillet on the pastry at one long edge and roll it up in the pastry – it should fit almost exactly. Any extending pastry should be trimmed away and reserved for decoration. Fold up ends, brushing pastry with a little egg, and seal the joins. Place the meat and pastry seam side down on a wetted baking tray and brush the pastry all over with beaten egg. Use the pastry trimmings to make leaves to decorate or strips to criss-cross over the top. Brush pastry decorations with beaten egg. Chill pastry for at least 30 minutes.

Bake in an oven heated to 425°F (220°C) or Gas no. 7 for 30 minutes, until pastry is golden brown. Serve cut in thick slices.

Whole baked gammon

Serves 30

1 whole gammon, smoked or
 unsmoked, on the bone, weighing
 about 16 lb (7.2kg)
1 tablespoon French mustard
2 tablespoons dark bitter
 marmalade or redcurrant jelly
24 cloves
sugared grapes (page 321) or pickled
 peaches (page 157), to garnish

Soak the gammon for 2 days in cold water, changing the water each day. Check the weight of the gammon to calculate the cooking time and allow 15 minutes per 1 lb (450g) plus an extra 15 minutes. Wrap the gammon in a sheet of kitchen foil and place in a large roasting tin.

Cook in an oven heated to 350°F (180°C) or Gas no. 4 for calculated cooking time. If you have an oven roasting thermometer push it into the centre of the meat avoiding any bone. A thermometer reading is reassuring with a really big piece of meat. When the temperature reaches 180°F (80°C) the gammon will be cooked to perfection. About 15–20 minutes before the end of the cooking time, remove the gammon from the oven and open up the foil. Increase the oven temperature to 425°F (220°C) or Gas no. 7.

Using a sharp knife, carefully strip the rind from the gammon. Then score the fat in an attractive criss-cross pattern. Smear the fat with the French mustard and then with marmalade (remove any chunky pieces of peel) or redcurrant jelly. Push the cloves into the fat, distributing them evenly. Return the uncovered joint to the oven to complete cooking time. The gammon will be beautifully glazed and golden brown. Leave until completely cool – at least 12 hours. Transfer to a large serving platter and garnish with sugared grapes or pickled peaches. Carve in thin slices.

Hot gammon with cider and apples

Soak the gammon overnight in cold water. Peel, quarter and core the apples and put into a large pan. Peel the onion. Push the cloves into the onion and add to the pan along with the bay leaf. Place the soaked gammon rind side up on top of the apples and add the cider to completely cover the apples. Bring to the boil, then lower the heat and simmer, covered, for 1½–2 hours.

Lift out gammon and place on a work surface. Using a sharp knife, strip away the the rind and score the fat in a criss-cross pattern. Spread with French mustard and sprinkle over the demerara sugar. Set in a roasting tin and cook in an oven heated to 400°F (200°C) or Gas no. 6 for 15 minutes until glazed.

Meanwhile, strain off the cooking liquid into a separate saucepan. Discard onion and bay leaf and return the apples to the heat. Simmer, stirring occasionally, to thicken. Press apple mixture through a nylon sieve to make a purée and stir in the sugar and butter. Keep warm in a serving bowl.

Boil the reserved cooking liquid until reduced and concentrated in flavour. Blend the cornflour with the water and stir into the liquid. Bring to the boil, stirring all the time, to make a thick gravy. Check seasoning and pour into a warmed sauceboat. Slice the hot gammon and serve with the apple sauce and gravy.

Serves 8

3 lb (1.4kg) corner gammon
2 lb (900g) cooking apples
1 medium-sized onion
2 cloves
1 bay leaf
about 1 pint (600ml) dry cider
1 tablespoon sugar
½ oz (15g) butter
1 level tablespoon cornflour
2 tablespoons water

Glaze
1 teaspoon French mustard
2–3 tablespoons demerara sugar

Honey glazed rack of lamb

Each piece of best-end will have 6–7 cutlets and for rack of lamb you should trim back the fat to reveal the cutlet bones. Cut away a 2 inch (5cm) strip of fat from the bone tips. Then with a small sharp knife, cut and scrape around each cutlet bone to clean it. Wrap bone tips in kitchen foil to prevent them from scorching during roasting.

Place trimmed racks in a roasting tin so they lie flat with fat side up to baste the meat. Place in an oven heated to 350°F (180°C) or Gas no. 4, and roast for 1 hour if you prefer your lamb pink. Allow an extra 15 minutes if you prefer lamb well done. Combine honey and boiling water to make a glaze. About half-way through the cooking time, remove lamb from the oven. Score the fat in a criss-cross pattern with a sharp knife and brush with some honey glaze. Return lamb to the oven to complete roasting time. Brush with more glaze once or twice as the fat begins to turn an attractive golden brown.

Remove foil from cutlet tips and transfer racks of lamb to a serving platter. Carve by cutting in between the bones and allow 2 cutlets per person. This is wonderful with summer vegetables, especially buttered new potatoes and green beans or mange-tout.

Serves 6

2 joints best-end of lamb
2 tablespoons clear honey
1 tablespoon boiling water

Lamb guard of honour with apricots

Serves 6

**2 joints best-end of lamb, each
 having 6–7 cutlets, chined
1 × 1 lb 3 oz (539g) tin apricot
 halves
mint jelly, to garnish**

Cut away a 2 inch (5cm) strip of fat from the bone tips of the lamb and scrape bones clean. Wrap the bone tips with kitchen foil to prevent them from scorching during roasting. Drain the apricots and reserve the juice. Place the 2 joints of lamb in a roasting tin, fat side up, so that they lie flat and pour over the apricot juice. Roast in an oven heated to 350°F (180°C) or Gas no. 4 for 1¼ hours, basting occasionally with the fruit juices in the tin. About 10 minutes before the end of the cooking time, spoon the apricot halves around the meat to heat through.

Stand the 2 joints, fat side out, on a warmed serving platter and criss-cross the rib bones like the swords in a military row. Remove the foil from the bone tips and slip on cutlet frills, if liked. Surround the meat with the apricot halves and garnish each one with a little mint jelly. Carve by cutting in between the bones and allow 2 cutlets per person. Serve with a little of the hot fruit juice from the roasting tin.

How to cook better steaks

● Steaks come in various sizes, shapes and degrees of tenderness. Fillet steak is known for its tenderness; sirloin steak, also called entrecôte steak, is regarded for its fine flavour and rump steak for its good value and flavour if well hung.

● Thicker cuts are better for grilling as it's difficult to judge the degree of doneness when meat is very thin – it cooks so quickly. Steaks should be at room temperature before cooking.

● Use freshly milled pepper to season steaks on both sides, but do not add salt until after cooking. For a subtle flavour, rub a crushed clove of garlic over raw steak. Brush steaks with melted butter or oil and use it for basting during grilling.

● When frying steaks it's vital to heat the pan really well before you start cooking. Add butter to the hot pan and when hot and foaming add the steaks one at a time so fat retains the heat and meat seals quickly. Lower heat to moderate for cooking and leave steaks undisturbed for half the cooking time (Don't lift or peek). Turn just once.

● For grilling, heat the grill to high for at least 5 minutes and adjust level of grill pan. Thin minute steaks should be placed close to the source of heat and thicker steaks should be at least 3 inches (7.5cm) away. Keep grill heat high; the control of cooking is obtained by the distance of the meat from the heat.

● The thickness of a steak determines the cooking time, not its size or weight. Steaks about 1 inch (2.5cm) thick need about 5 minutes to be rare or 6–8 minutes to be medium. The best method to check if steak is cooked to your liking is to test by the feel of the meat. Press down gently on centre of steak with your finger or the back of a spoon. If the meat gives easily, then steak is rare; if flesh resists but is still soft, it's medium done, and if flesh feels firm then steak is cooked right through, or well done.

● The advantage of frying steaks is that you can use the drippings to make a delicious gravy. The best gravy is made by deglazing the pan with water, stock or wine. Add a few tablespoons of liquid to the pan and stir over the heat to pick up coagulated pan juices, at the same time rapidly boiling to make a syrupy consistency. For a variation, add sherry, vermouth or brandy to the hot drippings and reduce by half, then stir in double cream and bring to just below boiling point to make a deliciously flavoured sauce.

● Grilled steaks are best with a squeeze of lemon. Or top them with flavoured butters or a little melted butter with chopped spring onion added.

Pork escalopes with orange and ginger

Trim the fat and sinew from the pork fillets. Cut each fillet crossways in 1½ inch (4cm) thick slices to make 12 slices. Using a rolling pin, pound each slice between two squares of wetted greaseproof paper to flatten.

Thinly pare the rind from 1 orange using a vegetable peeler, then cut rind in narrow julienne strips. Cook in boiling water for 15 minutes, then drain and set aside. Squeeze the juice from both oranges and make up to ½ pint (300ml) with cold water. Put the brown sugar, wine vinegar, ground ginger and cornflour into a mixing bowl and season with salt and pepper. Add the orange juice, stir to blend and set aside.

Melt the butter in a large frying pan over low heat, add the pork escalopes, a few at a time, and fry for about 5 minutes, turning once. Transfer to a warmed serving platter and keep hot while frying the remaining escalopes. Stir the sauce ingredients again, pour into the pan and stir until boiling and thickened. Check seasoning and add the orange strips. Pour the sauce over the pork escalopes and serve.

Serves 6

2 × 1½ lb (700g) pork fillets
2 oranges
4 oz (100g) soft light brown sugar
4 tablespoons wine vinegar
½ level teaspoon ground ginger
1 level tablespoon cornflour
salt and freshly milled pepper
2 oz (50g) butter

Pork escalopes in a mushroom and cream sauce

Trim the fat and sinew from the pork fillets. Cut the meat crossways in 1½ inch (4cm) thick slices to make 12 slices. Using a rolling pin, pound each slice between two squares of wetted greaseproof paper to flatten. Place escalopes in a shallow dish. Mix the ingredients for the marinade together and pour it over the pork. Marinate for about 30 minutes.

Peel and finely chop the onion and trim and slice the mushrooms. Melt the butter in a large frying pan over low heat, add the onion and mushrooms and fry gently for 5 minutes until onion is soft but not brown. Using a perforated spoon, transfer the onion and mushrooms to a bowl and keep hot.

Lift a few pork escalopes from the marinade and drain slightly. Add to the hot butter in the pan and fry escalopes for 5 minutes, turning once. Transfer to a warmed serving platter and keep hot while frying the remaining escalopes.

Add the sherry to the hot pan and boil briskly, stirring to pick up bits in the pan, until sherry is reduced and concentrated in flavour. Return cooked onion and mushrooms to the pan, season with salt and pepper and add the cream. Bring just to the boiling point, stirring all the time. Pour the cream sauce over the pork escalopes and serve.

Serves 6

2 × 1½ lb (700g) pork fillets

Marinade
3 tablespoons oil
1 tablespoon lemon juice
1 small clove garlic
freshly milled pepper
few sprigs parsley

Sauce
1 medium-sized onion
6 oz (175g) button mushrooms
2 oz (50g) butter
3 tablespoons dry sherry
salt and freshly milled black pepper
½ pint (300ml) double cream

Oriental beef and pineapple

Serves 6

2 lb (900g) lean braising steak
1 oz (25g) butter
2–3 stalks celery
1 × 8 oz (227g) tin pineapple pieces
1 medium-sized onion
2 level tablespoons cornflour
1 oz (25g) soft light brown sugar
2 tablespoons wine vinegar
1 tablespoon soy sauce
¾ pint (400ml) beef stock
freshly milled pepper

Trim the meat and cut into strips. Melt the butter in a frying pan over moderate heat. Add the meat and fry to seal the pieces all over. Transfer to a casserole. Shred the celery. Strain the pineapple pieces and reserve the juice. Add the pineapple pieces and celery to the beef in the casserole.

Peel and chop the onion and add to the butter remaining in the frying pan. Cook over low heat for 5 minutes until onion is soft and beginning to brown. Meanwhile, blend the cornflour, brown sugar, wine vinegar and soy sauce together in a mixing bowl. Stir in the pineapple juice and stock and pour into the browned onion in the pan. Bring to the boil, stirring all the time; then add to the meat and pineapple in the casserole along with a seasoning of pepper. Cover with casserole lid and cook in an oven heated to 325°F (160°C) or Gas no. 3 for 2 hours. Serve the beef with plain boiled rice.

Venison pot roast

Serves 6

2 lb (900g) haunch of venison
1 onion
2 carrots
2 stalks celery
1 oz (25g) white cooking fat
thinly pared rind and juice of 1
  orange
½ pint (300ml) chicken stock
1 tablespoon redcurrant jelly
salt and freshly milled pepper
beurre manié (page 117)

Marinade
1 onion
6 juniper berries
1 bay leaf
4 black peppercorns
½ pint (300ml) red wine
1 tablespoon oil

Place the venison in a deep dish. Peel and slice the onion for the marinade and arrange over the meat. Crush the juniper berries and add to the meat along with the bay leaf and peppercorns. Pour over the red wine and oil and marinate overnight.

Peel and thickly slice the onion and carrots. Trim and coarsely chop the celery. Drain the meat, reserving the marinade, and pat dry. Melt the cooking fat in a flameproof casserole over low heat and brown the venison all over. Lift from the pan and keep hot.

Add the onion, carrots and celery to the hot fat and fry gently for 4–5 minutes until lightly browned. These form a bed of braising vegetables. Place the venison on top. Pour in the reserved marinade and add the pared orange rind. Add sufficient stock to cover the vegetables and bring to the boil. Cover with a lid and transfer to an oven heated to 325°F (160°C) or Gas no. 3, and cook, allowing 30 minutes per 1 lb (450g) plus 30 minutes extra – about 1½ hours.

Transfer the meat to a warmed serving platter and keep hot. Strain the cooking liquid into a saucepan, add the orange juice and redcurrant jelly and season with salt and pepper. Add the beurre manié in small pieces to the liquid and stir until melted and blended. Bring to the boil, stirring all the time until gravy has thickened. Check seasoning. Slice the venison and pour over a little of the gravy. Pass the remaining gravy separately in a warmed sauceboat.

Barbecued pork ribs

Place the ribs in a single layer in a roasting tin. Sprinkle with salt and cook in an oven heated to 400°F (200°C) or Gas no. 6 for about 30 minutes.

Meanwhile, prepare the barbecue sauce. Peel and finely chop the onion. Heat the oil in a saucepan over low heat, add the onion and fry gently for about 5 minutes to soften but not brown. Combine the tomato ketchup, vinegar, brown sugar, mustard and Worcestershire sauce in a mixing bowl and add to the onion in the saucepan. Bring to the boil and draw off the heat.

Lower the oven temperature to 350°F (180°C) or Gas no. 4. Pour off the fat from the roasting tin, then pour the barbecue sauce over the pork ribs. Return to the oven and cook for a further 30 minutes, until meat is crispy at the edges. Transfer the pork ribs to a serving platter and spoon over the sauce. Provide finger bowls and plenty of napkins as the meat is best eaten with your fingers. Serve with a green salad and hot bread.

Serves 3–4

2–3 lb (0.9–1.4kg) pork ribs
salt

Barbecue sauce
1 medium-sized onion
1 tablespoon oil
4 tablespoons tomato ketchup
2 tablespoons wine vinegar
1 tablespoon soft light brown sugar
1 tablespoon made English mustard
1 tablespoon Worcestershire sauce

Pork chops in sweet and sour sauce

Trim the pork chops and place in a roasting tin. Dot the fat on the chops. Cook above centre in an oven heated to 400°F (200°C) or Gas no. 6 for about 15 minutes, turning the chops once, to brown on both sides.

Meanwhile, prepare the sauce. Drain the pineapple and make up the syrup to ½ pint (300ml) with water. Combine the syrup with the vinegar, brown sugar, soy sauce and salt. Put the cornflour into a saucepan and moisten with a little of the liquid to make a smooth paste. Stir in the remaining liquid and cook over moderate heat until boiling and thickened. Add the pineapple cubes and draw off the heat.

Lower the oven temperature to 350°F (180°C) or Gas no. 4. Pour off the fat in the roasting tin, then pour the sauce over the chops, coating each one thoroughly. Cover with a square of kitchen foil, return to the oven and cook for a further 45–50 minutes, basting once or twice. Using a fish slice, transfer the pork chops to a warmed serving platter and spoon over the sauce from the roasting tin. Serve with croquette potatoes (page 147) or plain boiled rice.

Serves 4

4 pork chops
1 oz (25g) white cooking fat

Sauce
1 × 12 oz (340g) tin pineapple
  cubes
4 tablespoons wine vinegar
3 oz (75g) soft light brown sugar
1 tablespoon soy sauce
¼ level teaspoon salt
2 level tablespoons cornflour

Ragout of kidneys in red wine

Serves 6

6–8 lamb kidneys
8 oz (225g) 'mini' chipolata
   sausages
2 medium-sized onions
2½ oz (65g) butter
1 level tablespoon plain flour
1 × 2¼ oz (64g) tin concentrated
   tomato purée
¾ pint (400ml) chicken stock
¼ pint (150ml) red wine
salt and freshly milled pepper
8 oz (225g) button mushrooms
1 × 8 oz (225g) packet frozen petits
   pois
chopped parsley, to garnish

Remove the suet from around fresh kidneys and using a pair of scissors, snip deep into each one and cut out the core. Remove the thin membrane and slice the kidneys in half lengthways. Separate the sausages. Peel and thinly slice the onions. Melt 2 oz (50g) of the butter in a large frying pan over low heat, add the onions and fry gently for 5 minutes to soften but not brown. Increase the heat to moderate, add the kidneys and sausages and fry for about 3 minutes to brown all over. Using a perforated spoon, transfer the onion, kidneys and sausages to a casserole dish.

Melt the remaining butter in the hot frying pan over low heat. Stir in the flour and cook gently for 5 minutes until browned. Stir in the tomato purée, stock and red wine and season with salt and pepper. Bring to the boil, stirring all the time. Strain the sauce into the casserole. Cover with a lid and cook in an oven heated to 350°F (180°C) or Gas no. 4 for 1½ hours. About 20 minutes before the end of the cooking time, trim and slice the mushrooms and add to the casserole along with the frozen peas. Sprinkle with chopped parsley and serve.

Beef stew with mustard dumplings

Serves 4

1½ lb (700g) lean braising steak
seasoned flour
2 medium-sized onions
1 lb (450g) carrots
1 oz (25g) white cooking fat
1 bay leaf
1 pint (600ml) beef stock
salt and freshly milled pepper
1 teaspoon wine vinegar

Dumplings
2 oz (50g) self-raising flour
½ level teaspoon mustard powder
¼ level teaspoon dried mixed herbs
1 oz (25g) shredded beef suet
2–3 tablespoons cold water

Trim the fat from meat and cut meat in bite-sized pieces, then coat in seasoned flour. Peel and thinly slice the onions. Peel and dice the carrots. Melt the fat in a frying pan over moderate heat. Add the meat and fry to brown all over. Transfer to a casserole and add the onions, carrots and bay leaf.

Add 1 level tablespoon seasoned flour to the hot fat remaining in the frying pan. (If necessary, add extra fat to the pan.) Stir over low heat for 5 minutes until the flour begins to brown. Gradually stir in the hot stock and bring to the boil, stirring all the time. Check seasoning with salt and pepper and strain the liquid over the meat and vegetables. Cover with casserole lid and cook in an oven heated to 325°F (160°C) or Gas no. 2 for 2 hours.

About 30 minutes before end of cooking time, prepare the dumplings. Sift the flour and mustard powder into a mixing bowl. Add the herbs and suet, and season with salt and pepper. Sprinkle in sufficient water to mix to a soft scone-like dough. With floured hands, divide dough in 4 portions and roll each one into a ball. Place dumplings on top of meat and vegetables (do not submerge), cover the casserole and return to oven for the last 20 minutes cooking time. Beef stew with mustard dumplings makes a complete meal. All that is needed is a crisp green salad.

Illustrated: Cold roast beef fillet with sweet pickles, pages 89, 306, 307 and 308

Pork with apples

Trim the pork chops of excess fat. Melt half the butter in a frying pan, add the pork chops and fry for 5–6 minutes, turning once, to brown both sides. Remove chops from the pan. Deglaze the hot pan with the water, stirring and scraping to pick up coagulated pan juices, and reserve.

Peel and slice the onions. Peel, core and slice the apples. Arrange in the base of a greased ovenproof dish. Sprinkle with the sugar and sage. Place pork chops on top and season with salt and pepper. Pour in the pan juices and cider. Combine breadcrumbs and grated cheese and sprinkle mixture over the chops. Dot with flakes of the remaining butter. Cook, uncovered, in an oven heated to 375°F (190°C) or Gas no. 5 for 1 hour. Serve from the dish with baked jacket potatoes.

Serves 4

4 boneless pork loin chops
1 oz (25g) butter
3–4 tablespoons water
2 medium-sized onions
2 medium-sized cooking apples
1 level tablespoon castor sugar
½ level teaspoon powdered sage
salt and freshly milled pepper
¼ pint (150ml) dry cider
4 heaped tablespoons soft white
   breadcrumbs
4 tablespoons grated hard cheese

Kebabs of lamb

Cut lamb into bite-sized pieces and place them in a shallow bowl. Combine the oil, lemon rind, lemon juice, brown sugar, ground ginger and a seasoning of pepper for the marinade and pour this over the lamb. Leave lamb to marinate for at least 1 hour, turning meat occasionally.

Peel and quarter the onions and separate the layers. Thread lamb on to 6 skewers alternating the pieces with the onions. Grill under a moderate grill about 3 inches (7.5cm) from the heat for 15–20 minutes, turning to cook lamb evenly and basting with the marinade. Serve with wedges of lemon to squeeze over. A Greek summer salad (page 156) with its crunchy texture makes a suitable accompaniment.

Serves 6

2 lb (900g) boned leg of lamb
4 medium-sized onions
lemon wedges, for serving

Marinade
4 tablespoons oil
finely grated rind of ½ lemon
2 tablespoons lemon juice
1 tablespoon soft light brown sugar
½ level teaspoon ground ginger
freshly milled pepper

Fried liver and bacon

Trim and cut the liver in very thin slices. Soak in milk for about 1 hour, then drain and pat dry. Dip both sides of each slice in seasoned flour. Trim the bacon rashers and grill until crisp.

Meanwhile, melt the butter in a frying pan over moderate heat. When butter is hot and foaming, add the liver and fry briskly for 4 minutes, turning once, until the liver is browned and still pink in the centre. Squeeze over the lemon juice. Transfer liver to a warmed serving platter and pour over the butter and juices. Serve with the grilled bacon.

Serves 4

1 lb (450g) lamb liver
milk, for soaking
seasoned flour
8 streaky bacon rashers
2 oz (50g) butter
squeeze of lemon juice

Illustrated: Kebabs of lamb with Greek summer salad, see above and page 156

Oxtail casserole

Serves 4

2–3 lb (0.9–1.4kg) oxtail pieces
bouquet garni or bay leaf
2 large onions
2 carrots
1 oz (25g) white cooking fat
1 rounded tablespoon plain flour
1 level teaspoon curry powder
1 tablespoon concentrated tomato
   purée
salt and freshly milled pepper
chopped parsley, to garnish

Put the oxtail pieces into a pan and pour over cold water to cover. Add the bouquet garni or bay leaf and bring to the boil, then lower the heat and simmer, covered, for about 2 hours. Strain the liquid and leave to cool. Carefully skim off the fat. Pour the liquid into a measuring jug and make up to 1 pint (600ml) with water, if necessary. Set aside.

Peel and slice the onions and carrots. Place the vegetables in a casserole dish and arrange the oxtail pieces on top. Melt the fat in a frying pan, stir in the flour and cook gently for 5 minutes, stirring occasionally, until a golden brown colour. Stir in the curry powder and tomato purée, then add the reserved cooking liquid and bring to the boil, stirring all the time, and season with salt and pepper. Pour the liquid into the casserole dish. Cover with a lid and cook in an oven heated to 325°F (160°C) or Gas no. 3 for about 2 hours, or until the meat falls away from the bone when pierced with a knife. Sprinkle with chopped parsley. Serve with mashed potatoes.

Beef in beer

Serves 4

1½ lb (700g) lean braising steak
seasoned flour
1 oz (25g) butter
¼ pint (150ml) water
1 medium-sized onion
1 slice day-old white bread
1 teaspoon made English mustard
1 tablespoon soft light brown sugar
½ pint (300ml) lager
salt and freshly milled pepper
6–8 soaked prunes
1 level tablespoon plain flour
1 tablespoon wine vinegar

Trim the meat and cut in bite-sized pieces. Roll the meat in seasoned flour. Melt the butter in a frying pan, add the meat and fry gently to brown all over. Transfer meat to a flameproof casserole. Add the water to the frying pan, stir and scrape to pick up coagulated pan juices and bring to the boil. Pour the liquid over the beef.

Peel and finely chop the onion and add to the casserole. Trim the bread crust and spread the bread with the mustard. Add to the casserole along with the sugar and lager, which should be enough to cover the meat. Season with salt and pepper. Cover the casserole and cook in an oven heated to 325°F (160°C) or Gas no. 3 for about 2 hours. About 20 minutes before the end of cooking time, add the soaked prunes.

Blend the flour with the wine vinegar and stir into the casserole. Cook the casserole over direct low heat, stirring all the time, until the sauce has thickened. Check seasoning and serve.

Variation **Rabbit in beer:** Use 2 lb (900g) jointed rabbit in place of the beef.

Beef goulash

Trim the beef and cut in bite-sized pieces. Peel and thinly slice the onions. Heat the oil in a flameproof casserole over moderate heat, add the meat and fry to brown all over. Add the sliced onions. Peel the garlic and mash together with the caraway seeds. Add to the pan along with the paprika and season with salt and pepper. Stir well, cover with a lid, lower the heat and cook gently for 1 hour, stirring occasionally. Do not add any water – sufficient juices come from the onions, which make the flavour very good.

Sprinkle in the flour and stir to blend. Add the tomato purée and stock and bring to the boil. Transfer to an oven heated to 350°F (180°C) or Gas no. 4 and cook for a further 1 hour, or until the meat is tender.

Stir in the soured cream or yoghurt and sprinkle with chopped parsley. Check seasoning. Serve with buttered noodles.

Serves 4

1½ lb (700g) lean braising steak
1 lb (450g) onions
2 tablespoons oil
1 clove garlic
1 level teaspoon caraway seeds
1 rounded tablespoon paprika
salt and freshly milled pepper
1 level tablespoon plain flour
1 tablespoon concentrated tomato
  purée
¾ pint (400ml) beef stock
2–3 tablespoons soured cream or
  yoghurt
chopped parsley, to garnish

Beef curry casserole

Trim the meat, cut in bite-sized pieces and place in an ovenproof casserole. Peel and finely slice the onions. Melt the butter in a saucepan over low heat, add the onions and fry gently for 5 minutes to soften but not brown. Add the curry powder according to taste and cook gently for a further 1–2 minutes, stirring all the time, to draw out the flavour. Stir in the flour and cook for 1 minute. Gradually pour in the stock and bring to the boil, stirring all the time. Add the chutney or apricot jam, brown sugar and lemon juice and season with salt and pepper. Simmer the sauce for 2–3 minutes, stirring occasionally.

Pour the curry sauce over the meat. Cover with a lid and cook in an oven heated to 325°F (160°C) or Gas no. 3 for 2 hours, or until the meat is tender. Serve with plain boiled rice. The beef has a very good flavour because it's cooked in the curry sauce.

Serves 4

2 lb (900g) lean braising steak
2 medium-sized onions
1 oz (25g) butter
3–4 level tablespoons curry powder
1 level tablespoon plain flour
¾ pint (400ml) beef stock
1 rounded tablespoon mango
  chutney or apricot jam
1 rounded tablespoon soft light
  brown sugar
juice of ½ lemon
salt and freshly milled pepper

Shepherd's pie

This recipe makes a tasty dish using leftovers from a Sunday joint. Trim the fat from the meat and pass the meat through a mincer. Peel and finely chop the onion. Melt 1 oz (25g) of the butter in a saucepan over low heat, add the onion and fry gently for 5 minutes to soften but not brown. Add the minced meat, curry powder, mixed herbs and gravy and season with salt and pepper. Mix together well.

Spoon into a greased pie dish, cover with mashed potato and dot with the remaining butter. Heat through in an oven heated to 350°F (180°C) or Gas no. 4 for 30 minutes.

Serves 4

10–12 oz (275–350g) cold roast
  beef or roast lamb
1 onion
1½ oz (40g) butter
¼ level teaspoon curry powder
¼ level teaspoon dried mixed herbs
¼ pint (150ml) thickened gravy
salt and freshly milled pepper
1–1½ lb (450–700g) mashed
  potato

Steak and kidney pie

Serves 4–6

1 onion
1½ lb (700g) lean braising steak
8 oz (225g) ox kidney
seasoned flour
pinch of dried mixed herbs
salt and freshly milled pepper
¼ pint (150ml) beef stock or red
   wine
puff pastry, made using 8 oz (225g)
   strong white flour (page 171) or
   1 × 13 oz (370g) packet frozen
   puff pastry, thawed
beaten egg, for glazing

Peel and finely chop the onion. Trim and cut the steak in bite-sized pieces. Snip out the core, remove the thin membrane and cut kidney in bite-sized pieces. Roll steak and kidney in seasoned flour. In a 1½ pint (900ml) pie dish, arrange the steak with kidney in layers sprinkled with the onion, herbs and seasoning. Mound meat in the centre and add the stock or red wine.

On a floured work surface, roll out pastry at least 1 inch (2.5cm) larger than the rim of the pie dish, and cut out the pie lid. Grease pie dish rim and place pastry trimmings on the dish. Cut a small cross in the centre of the pastry lid and turn pastry under to make a hole. Brush pastry rim with water and cover the pie with the lid. Trim the edges, knock up and flute. Cut pastry leaves from trimmings to decorate. Glaze the pie with beaten egg, place on decorations and glaze the decorations.

Cook above centre in an oven heated to 425°F (220°C) or Gas no. 7 for 30 minutes. Then lower oven temperature to 350°F (180°C) or Gas no. 4 and cook for a further 1½ hours. When pastry is a deep golden colour, wrap pie crust with a double thickness of wetted greaseproof paper, wet side out, to prevent over-browning.

Lasagne verdi

Serves 6

8 oz (225g) green lasagne
1 oz (25g) grated Parmesan cheese

Meat sauce
1 medium-sized onion
1 clove garlic
2 tablespoons oil
1 lb (450g) lean minced beef
1 × 14 oz (400g) tin chopped tomatoes
2 tablespoons concentrated tomato
   purée
¼ pint (150ml) chicken stock
1 level teaspoon salt
freshly milled pepper

Cheese sauce
2 oz (50g) butter
2 oz (50g) flour
1 pint (600ml) milk
salt and freshly milled pepper
6 oz (175g) grated hard cheese
½ teaspoon made English mustard

Cook the lasagne in boiling water for about 10 minutes, or until just tender. Drain well and spread out on a clean cloth. Peel and finely chop the onion and garlic. Heat the oil in a large saucepan, add the onion and fry gently for 5 minutes to soften but not brown. Add the garlic and minced beef and stir until beef loses its red colour. Add the tomatoes with juices, tomato purée, stock and salt and season with pepper. Cover with a pan lid and cook gently for 1 hour. Check seasoning.

Melt the butter for the sauce in a saucepan over low heat. Stir in the flour and cook gently for 1 minute. Gradually stir in the milk. Bring to the boil, stirring well all the time to make a smooth sauce. Simmer for 2–3 minutes to thicken and season with salt and pepper. Draw off the heat and stir in the cheese and mustard.

To assemble lasagne, spread a little meat sauce over the base of a greased 3 pint (1.7 litre) oblong ovenproof dish, then cover with a layer of lasagne and spoon over half the remaining meat sauce. Cover with lasagne and spread with half the cheese sauce, then top with another layer of lasagne. Spoon over the remaining meat sauce, cover with lasagne and finish with a layer of cheese sauce. Sprinkle with the Parmesan cheese.

Heat through in an oven heated to 350°F (180°C) or Gas no. 4 for 30–40 minutes. Leave to stand for 5 minutes so layers settle, then cut in six portions with a knife and lift out with a fish slice.

Meat loaf

Peel and finely chop the onion and put into a mixing bowl, add the minced beef and mix together with a fork. Set aside to allow the flavours to combine. Trim the bread crust. Crumble the bread into a small mixing bowl and add the milk. Leave to soak for a few minutes until the bread has absorbed the milk, then mash with a fork. Add the bread, egg, salt and nutmeg, if using it, to the minced beef and onion and season with pepper.

Thoroughly mix together the ingredients with a fork. Texture at this stage is important: if the meat loaf is going to be juicy and succulent the mixture must be moist, but not soft or difficult to handle. Using wetted fingers, shape the meat mixture into a fat oval, patting the mixture to make a compact, smooth shape.

Melt the butter in a large frying pan over low heat. When hot and foaming, add the meat loaf and fry gently to brown. Give the pan an occasional shake so that the loaf rolls over to brown all over. Carefully transfer the meat loaf to a roasting tin. Add the water to the hot fat in the frying pan and stir and swirl the mixture over the heat to pick up the coagulated pan juices. Pour the liquid over the meat loaf and cover with a roasting tin lid or kitchen foil. Cook in an oven heated to 350°F (180°C) or Gas no. 4 for 45 minutes – the meat loaf should be pink in the middle and keep its shape.

Serve cut in slices with gravy made from the pan juices (page 89). To serve cold, leave several hours or overnight and serve with hot new potatoes or sweet pickled fruit.

Serves 4

1 small onion
1 lb (450g) lean minced beef
1 slice white bread
2 tablespoons milk
1 egg
1 level teaspoon salt
grated nutmeg (optional)
freshly milled pepper
1–2 oz (25–50g) butter
3 tablespoons hot water

Moussaka

Leave aubergines unpeeled and slice them thinly, then dust with seasoned flour. Heat 3–4 tablespoons oil in a frying pan, add a few aubergines and fry for 2–3 minutes. Drain aubergine slices on absorbent kitchen paper. Add more oil to the pan as necessary to fry all the aubergines. Peel and slice the onions. Heat 2 tablespoons oil in a saucepan, add the onions and fry gently for 5 minutes to soften but not brown. Add the minced meat and cook gently, stirring, until meat loses its red colour. Season with salt and pepper and stir in the chopped parsley, tomato purée and red wine or stock. Cook gently for 20 minutes to make a thick sauce.

Arrange layers of aubergine and meat mixture in a shallow ovenproof dish, starting and finishing with layers of aubergine. In a mixing bowl, blend the eggs, flour and yoghurt for the topping. Pour the topping over the aubergines. Place in the centre of an oven heated to 375°F (190°C) or Gas no. 5 and cook for 45 minutes until top is golden brown and set. Serve hot with a crisp green salad.

Serves 6

2 lb (900g) aubergines
seasoned flour
8–10 tablespoons oil
2 medium-sized onions
2 lb (900g) lean minced lamb or
  beef
salt and freshly milled pepper
2 tablespoons chopped parsley
1 tablespoon concentrated tomato
  purée
¼ pint (150ml) red wine or beef
  stock

Topping
2 eggs
2 level tablespoons plain flour
¼ pint (150ml) natural yoghurt

Stuffed marrow

Serves 4

1 medium-sized marrow
salt and freshly milled pepper
½ oz (15g) butter
2 oz (50g) grated hard cheese

Stuffing
1 medium-sized onion
1 oz (25g) butter
1 slice white bread
2 tablespoons milk
1 lb (450g) lean minced beef
1 egg
salt and freshly milled pepper
1 teaspoon concentrated tomato
    purée

Cut the marrow in half lengthways. Scoop out the centre seeds, season the hollow with salt and pepper and add a few flakes of butter. Place both halves cut side up in a roasting tin and spoon in just enough water to cover the base of the tin. Cover the marrow with kitchen foil and cook in an oven heated to 350°F (180°C) or Gas no. 4 for 30 minutes until tender. Test by piercing the thickest part with a knife.

Peel and finely chop the onion. Melt the butter in a large frying pan over low heat, add the onion and fry gently for 5 minutes to soften but not brown. Soak the bread in the milk for a few minutes and squeeze out the liquid. Combine the lean minced beef and egg in a mixing bowl and season with salt and pepper. Add the bread to the meat along with the tomato purée and mix together. Add the meat mixture to the onions and cook gently, stirring occasionally, for 20 minutes.

When marrow halves are ready remove from the oven and tip out the liquid that will have collected in each half. Spoon the stuffing mixture into the cooked marrow halves, heaping it down the centre. Sprinkle with grated cheese and return to the oven, uncovered, for about 15–20 minutes. Serve cut in slices. Any leftover is delicious cold – the marrow tastes so moist and juicy.

Beef and ham mould

Serves 6

1 lb (450g) rump steak
½ lb (225g) lean bacon
1 onion
4 tomatoes
2 oz (50g) soft white breadcrumbs
2 large eggs
1 level teaspoon salt
freshly milled pepper

Trim the steak and bacon and cut in pieces. Peel the onion and cut in quarters. Pass the steak, bacon and onion through a mincer two or three times and put into a mixing bowl. Or chop ingredients in a food processor. Scald the tomatoes and peel away the skins. Cut the tomatoes in half and press through a sieve to make a purée. Add to the meat mixture along with the breadcrumbs, eggs, salt and a seasoning of pepper. Mix together well.

Spoon into a greased 2 pint (1.1 litres) pudding basin. Cover with a double thickness of greased greaseproof paper and tie tightly with string. Steam gently for 4 hours in a steamer, or place the pudding basin on an upturned saucer in a saucepan one-third filled with boiling water. Either way keep the pan topped up with extra boiling water during the cooking time so that it does not boil dry. Remove damp paper coverings and cover with a circle of fresh greaseproof paper and a weighted plate. Leave overnight until completely cool. Turn out on to a serving plate and serve the mould cut in slices.

Serve with new potatoes and tender young beans or a green salad. Any leftover makes a delicious sandwich filling. This is one of the nicest cold meat loaves you could wish for. Steaming rather than baking keeps the mixture deliciously moist.

Ox tongue in jelly

Soak the tongue overnight in a saucepan of cold water. Bring slowly to the boil, draw off the heat and drain. (This helps to get rid of the excess salt.) Pour over fresh cold water to cover. Peel the onion and push the cloves into the onion. Peel and slice the carrots. Add onion and carrots to the pan along with the bay leaf. Bring to the boil, then lower the heat, cover with a pan lid, and simmer gently for 3–4 hours. Skim occasionally and top up with extra boiling water, if necessary. Pierce a skewer or sharp knife into the tip of the tongue; if it feels tender, then tongue is cooked.

Plunge the tongue at once into a large bowl of cold water. When cool enough to handle, peel off the skin with your fingers, and remove ducts, gristle and any bones from the back of the tongue.

Fit tightly into a deep 6 inch (15cm) round cake tin – for best results tongue should be squeezed into the tin. Cover with a plate and press down with a heavy weight. Leave overnight until completely cool, then chill. Loosen the sides with a palette knife and turn out on to a serving plate. There will be sufficient natural jelly on the tongue to glaze it. Serve cut in slices with mustard pickles or Cumberland sauce. This ox tongue is much nicer than the ones you can buy and very economical. It makes an excellent addition to a cold-table along with other cold sliced meats.

Serves 8

cured ox tongue, weighing about
   3½–4 lb (1.6–1.8kg)
1 onion
2 cloves
2 carrots
1 bay leaf

Pork terrine

Trim and cut the belly of pork in pieces. Trim and cut pig liver in pieces. Pass liver and pork through a mincer into a mixing bowl or chop ingredients in a food processor. Peel and finely chop the onion. Melt the butter in a saucepan over low heat, add the onion and fry gently for 5 minutes to soften but not brown. Add the onion and butter to the bowl or food processor along with the eggs, mixed herbs, sherry and salt. Season with plenty of pepper and mix together well.

Trim the bacon rashers and flatten and stretch them by running a knife back and forth over the bacon. Reserve 2 rashers and use those remaining to line the base and sides of a 2 pint (1.1 litre) terrine. Spoon the meat mixture into the terrine and spread level. Top with the reserved bacon rashers and bay leaves. Cover with a lid or buttered kitchen foil and place terrine in a roasting tin. Fill tin to a depth of 1 inch (2.5cm) with water. Cook in an oven heated to 325°F (160°C) or Gas no. 3 for 2½ hours. Leave to cool overnight pressed with a heavy weight. Serve from the dish cut in slices.

Serves 6–8

2 lb (900g) belly of pork
1 lb (450g) pig liver
1 large onion
1 oz (25g) butter
2 eggs
1 teaspoon dried mixed herbs
2 tablespoons medium sherry
3 level teaspoons salt
freshly milled pepper
8 oz (225g) streaky bacon rashers
2 bay leaves

Barbecuing from start to finish

● A marinade gives flavour and also tenderizes food before cooking. Allow between 1–3 hours for foods to marinate.

● Frozen steaks, chops, chicken joints, hamburgers and any other meats must be allowed to thaw completely before grilling.

● Score fat on chops and steaks to keep meat from curling up, but do not trim completely. Fat helps to keep meat moist and any drips on hot coals help give food its lovely charcoal flavour.

● Light the fire at least 1 hour before cooking and avoid disturbing it. Keep a reserve supply of charcoals round the edge of the fire so that they warm up. Then move them to the centre of the fire to build it up, if necessary. Adding cold fuel reduces temperature and slows down the fire.

● Do not grill over too fierce a heat; if fire is too hot meat dries and juices are lost. When fire is ready coals will look ash-grey by day and have a red glow after dark. Test for correct temperature before you start: hold your hand over the grill at the height you intend to cook the food. If you have to take your hand away before you count past one, then the fire is too hot; you should be able to count to three with your hand held comfortably above the fire.

● Control the intensity of heat by adjusting the distance between the food and the fire. Most barbecue grids can be raised or lowered. A distance of 2 inches (5cm) above the hot coals is about right for most foods.

● Lay out items for cooking on a large plate or board ready for action – it looks good. Have equipment required near at hand. You will need oven gloves, long-handled tongs, a fish slice, a long-handled fork and a brush for basting. Water for dousing flames may also be useful.

● It's a good idea to have two tables: one for food to be cooked along with the baste, oil, butter, seasoning and serving plates required by you, the chef; the other table with cutlery, salads, bread and desserts for the guests. Remember the condiments: include sea salt and a pepper mill, a choice of sweet pickles, mustards and various table sauces you may wish to include.

● A baste is a sauce that is brushed on to the food while it is cooking to add flavour and keep foods moist. Most are quite strong in flavour and usually have honey or sugar added. Use a baste towards the end of cooking time to help prevent meats from scorching.

● A good baste for chicken is to mix 2 tablespoons soy sauce with 1 level tablespoon clear honey. Brush over chicken joints and let stand for 1 hour. Baste again during cooking. For sausages and hamburgers, mix equal quantities of tomato ketchup and oil.

● While fire is getting hot, let guests help themselves to crunchy relishes. Fill a bowl with crushed ice, poke in spring onions, carrot sticks and celery stalks porcupine style. Provide radishes with salt for dipping, olives and a platter of thinly sliced salami and garlic sausage for guests to nibble with drinks.

● Spear some fat trimmings or a chunk of bacon fat on a long-handled fork and rub over the hot grill to grease it, then foods will not stick. Don't brush foods with too much oil – it causes the fire to smoke.

● Seal *steaks* on both sides, then cook for 8–10 minutes depending on how you like them cooked. Wait until you turn steaks before seasoning with salt and pepper. Season the other side after you take them from the fire.

● *Lamb* is delicious cooked over charcoal. The easiest chops to eat are best-end cutlets with a long rib bone as they can be held and eaten in the fingers. Cook lamb cutlets or chops for 10–15 minutes until lamb is well browned on the outside and pink in the centre.

● *Pork* must be well cooked. Do not have pork chops thicker than 1 inch (2.5cm). Cook for a total of 15–20 minutes, and turn them frequently so they are well cooked and brown on both sides. Baste with marinade or barbecue sauce towards end of cooking time.

● It takes time to cook food over a charcoal grill even for a small number of people. It's a good idea to go for foods that are not bulky – *chicken* drumsticks and leg portions cut in half are excellent. You can crowd these on to a barbecue grill. Allow 15–20 minutes, turning fairly often. Brush with marinade or melted butter.

● Larger chicken joints or small chickens cut in half should be placed on the grill bone side down – the bone acts as a heat conductor and speeds up cooking. Allow 20–25 minutes, turning often, but allow chicken to cook slightly longer on the bone side. Salt chicken joints before grilling to make a crisp skin. Baste with marinade or melted butter and barbecue sauce towards end of cooking time.

● *Lamb liver* cut in thick slices like steak is very tasty. Brush with melted butter and cook quickly, turning pieces frequently. Allow 10–12 minutes cooking time until well browned on outside and pink in the centre. Serve with herb butter melting on top or béarnaise sauce (page 118).

● *Hamburgers* are popular. Make your own hamburgers using lean minced beef, seasoning and minced onion. Pat into a fairly thick round shape as hamburgers shrink on cooking. Brush with melted butter or oil and cook for 8–10 minutes, turning once. A hinged double-sided wire grill is good for cooking hamburgers – you can turn them all at once. Serve in soft rolls which have been split and toasted cut side down on the grill. For a special treat place a thin slice of mild cheese on hamburgers after each one is turned.

● *Pork or beef sausages* grill well. No need to prick them nor do they require basting. Allow 15–20 minutes cooking time, turning fairly often. Chipolatas only need 10–12 minutes but watch that they do not slip through the grill bars. Cumberland sausage is coarse and spicy and comes in one long line. Cut in pieces for serving. A hinged double-sided wire grill is very useful for sausages, too.

● For *kebabs* choose skewers that are long and flat; food will slip on round skewers when turned over. For uniform cooking string each type of food on separate skewers, then you can start to grill foods that need longest cooking first and add other skewers of food later.

● Good kebab meats are beef steak cut in cubes, pork fillet trimmed and cut in pieces or shoulder or leg of lamb cut in pieces. Make smaller chipolata sausages by holding the ends, and twisting in opposite directions, then snipping to cut them in half. Bacon rolls made from trimmed rashers are nice wrapped around pineapple chunks or chicken livers.

● To make beef kebabs for cooking rare, push meat close together on skewer; for medium or well done leave a little space between them.

● Skewer meat kebabs with vegetables. Use onion cut in quarters and separated into layers, small tomatoes, button mushrooms (placed on skewer ends as they break if pushed too far up skewer) and green peppers deseeded and cut in chunky pieces. Try threading apricot halves on to lamb kebabs and tinned chunks of pineapple on to pork kebabs.

● *Fish* cooked over a barbecue grill must be turned fairly frequently and a hinged double-sided wire grill is excellent for small whole fish like trout and mackerel. Have fish cleaned and slash the sides of mackerel to prevent curling up. Brush with melted butter or oil and allow 10–15 minutes for mackerel and 8–10 minutes for trout. Baste frequently. Serve fish with lemon quarters.

● Trout or fish steaks are good cooked in individual loose foil parcels. Brush the inside of the parcel with oil or melted butter and season the fish with salt and pepper. Or dot the fish with herb butter (page 117) such as parsley and tarragon. Allow 15-20 minutes cooking time.

● For extra flavour arrange items for cooking close together to trap smoke taste from fire. Or you can burn something aromatic in the coals. Try a few split cloves of garlic, thin spirals of orange peel thrown on fire towards the end of cooking time or some thyme, rosemary or bay leaves added during the last few minutes.

● *Toasted sandwiches* are very tasty when grilled on the barbecue. Use ordinary white bread slices and make ham or cheese sandwiches. Spread the outside of bread slices with soft butter then place on hot grill. Use a long-handled fish slice for turning. Or arrange sandwiches inside hinged double-sided wire grill. Turn when brown on underside and serve as soon as cooked when they will be hot, crisp and delicious.

● Don't attempt to cook everything over the barbecue fire. Stick to the main course only and combine with other foods prepared in the kitchen. Baked potatoes to serve with herb butter and rice can be oven cooked. Salads are a must. Refrigerate salad greens so they are cool and crunchy and add tomato and cucumber just before serving. Potato salads are always favourites.

● Cheese is a natural for outdoor eating. Arrange a sumptuous cheese board and present with fresh fruits. Wedges of well chilled watermelon are lovely, so are grapes on ice.

● Barbecue foods are often spicy and thirst mak-ing. Provide plenty of refreshments in the way of chilled beer, lager and soft drinks. Or make up a cooling wine cup like sangria (page 332).

● Use the last of the glowing embers to bake bananas in their skins. They take about 20–30 minutes and the skins will turn black. Peel open and serve with brown sugar and lemon for a wonderful and easy dessert.

When the barbecue is over, rake out coals and cool for use again. Place barbecue grill in water while still warm and give a quick scrub with wire wool to banish all pieces of burnt food. Then your grill will be ready for use next time.

Marinades

● A marinade can do great things for meat or fish by way of flavouring and tenderizing.

● Wine vinegar, lemon juice and wine are all acid ingredients that are used as tenderizers; add flavourings such as chopped shallot, garlic, onion rings, lemon rind, herbs, peppercorns, allspice and juniper berries.

● Your own favourite oil and vinegar dressing will do very well for steaks, chops and kebabs.

● No need to submerge foods in a marinade: use a shallow dish and turn items at regular intervals.

● Meat pieces that have been soaked in a wine marinade are best dried with absorbent kitchen paper before being browned in butter for using in a casserole. Remember wet foods don't brown.

● Marinating times usually range from 2 hours to overnight. Sometimes it's a good idea to thaw frozen meat in a marinade – it needs the thawing time so you might as well get the flavour.

All-purpose marinade: Use for chicken, steaks, pork chops or escalopes that are to be grilled, fried or barbecued. Place meat in a shallow dish. Add a crushed clove of garlic or a few crushed parsley stalks, a bay leaf and seasoning of freshly milled pepper. Pour over 1 teaspoon French mustard blended with 4 tablespoons oil.

Marinade for fish: Use for kebabs, cod cutlets, salmon or halibut steaks. Place fish in a shallow dish. Sprinkle over a little finely chopped onion or shallot. Add a crushed clove of garlic, a bay leaf and a seasoning of freshly milled pepper. Pour over the grated rind and juice of 1 lemon mixed with 4 tablespoons oil.

Marinade for kebabs: Use for beef, pork or lamb kebabs. Place cut-up meat in a shallow dish (best to skewer afterwards). Mix together 3 table-spoons oil, 1 tablespoon Worcestershire sauce or soy sauce, 1 teaspoon soft light brown sugar and a seasoning of freshly milled pepper. Pour this over meat and add 1 bay leaf. Use as a baste while cooking as well.

Wine marinade for meat: Use for cut-up braising steak or game that is to be casseroled or braised. The strained marinade can be added with the recipe liquid for cooking. Place cut-up meat or game in a deep bowl. Add 2–3 onion rings, 1 bay leaf or sprig of thyme, and 4–6 crushed black peppercorns, allspice or juniper berries (for veni-son). Pour over ¼ pint (150ml) red wine blended with 2 tablespoons oil.

6

Sauces

Often smooth and subtle, either piquant or mild,
a sauce will enhance simple grills, roasts
and vegetables and will make cold meats twice as
nice. Give sauces your undivided attention
for the few minutes it takes to make them and
you should have success every time.

Sauces

How to make better sauces

● Use a heavy-based saucepan that stands steady and will allow sauces to cook gently without scorching.

● Stir a sauce all the time as it is brought to the boil so it thickens evenly. If a smooth sauce goes lumpy before boiling, a vigorous beating with a whisk will correct it, but if it's lumpy after boiling, you'll need to strain it.

● Infuse milk with a bay leaf or onion when making a white sauce. It not only gives the sauce a subtle flavour but warm milk is also easier to mix into the roux.

● For vegetables such as cauliflower or leeks that are to be served with a sauce, use half vegetable cooking water and half milk to make the sauce. The cooking liquid from fish baked in milk or white wine is also good to use. The sauce will have a flavour that complements the dish.

● Where both a hot and cold liquid are used in a roux sauce, stir in the hot liquid first to keep the roux soft and prevent it from going lumpy.

● A home-made stock used in a rich brown sauce will give it a flavour and gloss that's infinitely superior to a brown sauce made with water and a stock cube.

● A stainless steel conical strainer called a chinois is the best to use for straining most sauces. It's strong enough for vegetable purées to be pushed through and there's no danger of a metallic taste. The V-shape point means you can easily direct sauces into small saucepans or bowls without any spills.

● Check seasoning often. Cream added to a sauce will mellow the flavour so always re-check seasoning after adding the cream.

● I have a pepper mill just for white peppercorns and use it for white sauces. This way there are no dark speckles of black pepper in the sauce.

About keeping and holding sauces

● You can make a white roux sauce in advance and keep it hot without a skin forming on the surface by stirring in just over half the recipe milk during preparation and bringing through to the boil so sauce thickens. Then add rest of milk, pouring it over the surface. Keep on lowest heat and stir again only when you want to use the sauce.

● Keep prepared sauces hot without scorching by setting the saucepan in a larger one of hot (not boiling) water so the base of the pan is away from direct heat.

● More delicate egg-based hollandaise or béarnaise sauces can be held for a short time if you turn the sauce into a warmed jug and set in a saucepan of warm water away from the heat, to hold the correct temperature.

● Sauces to be prepared and used later in a recipe – white sauce for mousse, curry or brown sauce for casseroles or tomato sauce for pasta – should be poured into a bowl, then covered with a circle of wetted greaseproof paper (wet side against the sauce) to prevent a skin forming as sauce cools. Refrigerate as soon as cold. Keep roux-based sauces and ragù sauce with meat no more than 24 hours.

● Acid sauces such as Cumberland, apple, barbecue, cranberry and tomato can be made in advance and refrigerated for up to 48 hours. Soured cream sauces also keep for up to 48 hours.

● Home-made mayonnaise will keep 3 weeks in the refrigerator. Once mayonnaise is mixed with other ingredients – herb mayonnaise, curry or seafood dressing – the keeping time cuts to 1 week.

Roux mix

A roux is a cooked butter and flour mixture and the first stage in the preparation of a white sauce. Preparing a roux can be the most time consuming part of making a sauce. But you can save time by making a roux mix in advance and storing it in the refrigerator. The mix keeps for several months and has plenty of uses.

Melt 8 oz (225g) butter in a large saucepan. Stir in 8 oz (225g) plain flour and blend well. Cook very gently for about 15 minutes, stirring frequently. As the roux cooks it will become lighter in colour and sandy in texture. Draw off the heat and allow to cool. The mixture sets quite hard. I like to break it up with a wooden spoon and press it through a coarse sieve or grate the lumps so the mix maintains a crumbly texture for easy measuring. Tip into a polythene bag and store in the refrigerator.

To use: For every ½ pint (300ml) heated milk add 2 rounded tablespoons roux mix off the heat and stir to blend. When the mix has blended in the milk, return the pan to the heat and bring to the boil, stirring all the time to make a smooth sauce. Simmer gently for 2–3 minutes to thicken. Season with salt and pepper and it's ready to use. If your sauce is not thick enough, add more mix and if it's too thick, add more liquid.

White sauce (*roux method*)

Makes ½ pint (300ml)

1½ oz (40g) butter
1 oz (25g) plain flour
½ pint (300ml) milk or part
   cooking liquid and part milk
salt and freshly milled pepper

A sauce made from a roux is less likely to go lumpy if you use a little extra butter. It's easier to blend in the liquid because the roux is softer. The resulting sauce will be rich and glossy.

Melt the butter in a saucepan over low heat and stir in the flour to make a smooth paste, or roux. Cook gently for 1 minute until it lightens in colour and takes on a sandy texture. Gradually pour in the liquid, stirring well all the time. Make sure you stir round the edges of the saucepan where unmixed roux may collect.

If you are using a mixture of liquids such as part hot stock or vegetable water and part cold milk always add the hot liquid first to keep the roux soft, then stir in the cold liquid. When all the liquid has been added, bring to the boil, stirring all the time. Lower the heat and simmer gently for 2–3 minutes to thoroughly cook the flour. Season to taste with salt and pepper.

Variations of white sauce

Parsley sauce: Stir 2 tablespoons finely chopped parsley into the cooked sauce. Check seasoning and serve with boiled gammon or bacon. Or add a squeeze of lemon to the parsley sauce and serve with fish.

Egg sauce: Gently stir 2 coarsely chopped hard-boiled eggs into the cooked sauce and season with extra salt and pepper. Serve with poached white fish.

Lemon sauce: Add a squeeze of lemon juice to the cooked sauce, then stir in 1 egg yolk. Check seasoning and serve with chicken or baked fish.

Onion sauce: Boil 2 medium-sized onions until tender. Finely chop or purée onions in a blender or food processor. Add to the cooked sauce along with 2 tablespoons cream and a pinch of nutmeg. This sauce is traditionally served with boiled mutton or lamb cutlets.

Prawn sauce: Add 4 oz (100g) chopped peeled prawns, a squeeze of lemon juice and ½–1 teaspoon anchovy essence or 1 tablespoon tomato ketchup (which gives a pink colour) to the cooked sauce. Alternatively, add 1 carton potted shrimps (with butter). Serve with fish.

White sauce (*blending method*)

This is a quick method to use if the liquid used is cold milk. The flour and milk are first blended to a smooth thin cream or 'blend'. With this method you may cut down on the amount of butter that you use.

The secret of making a smooth blend of the milk and flour is to pour the milk into a wide bowl, sift over the flour and quickly whisk together. Do not stir with a spoon or trickle the liquid slowly into the flour because either method is likely to produce an uneven blend and a lumpy sauce. If you want to use part cold milk and part hot stock or vegetable liquid make sure you blend the flour with the cold milk first, then stir in the hot liquid.

Melt the butter in a saucepan over low heat. Pour in the blended liquid and slowly bring to the boil, stirring all the time. Lower the heat and simmer gently for 2–3 minutes. Season to taste with salt and pepper.

Makes ½ pint (300ml)

1 oz (25g) plain flour
½ pint (300ml) milk
1 oz (25g) butter
salt and freshly milled pepper

Velouté sauce

Makes ½ pint (300ml)

1 oz (25g) butter
1 oz (25g) plain flour
½ pint (300ml) hot stock
salt and freshly milled pepper
squeeze of lemon juice
1 egg yolk
3 tablespoons single cream

This is a white sauce made with hot stock and enriched with egg yolk and cream. It has a delicious, subtle flavour and is used for coating cooked fish or chicken that has been poached or simmered; in each case the hot stock used in the sauce is taken from the cooking liquid.

Melt the butter in a saucepan over low heat. Stir in the flour and cook gently for 1 minute until mixture lightens in colour and takes on a sandy texture. Gradually pour in the hot stock, stirring well all the time to make a smooth sauce. Bring to the boil, stirring all the time, then lower the heat and simmer gently for 2–3 minutes. Season to taste with salt and pepper, add a squeeze of lemon juice and draw off the heat.

Blend the egg yolk and cream in a bowl and stir in a little of the sauce. Add the mixture to the sauce, return the pan to the heat and cook gently for 1 minute, but do not allow to boil. Check seasoning again because the cream mellows the flavour.

Variations: Add sautéed mushrooms, cooked asparagus tips or peeled prawns to the cooked sauce.

Cheese sauce

Serves 4

½ pint (300ml) milk
1½ oz (40g) butter
1 oz (25g) plain flour
2 oz (50g) grated Cheddar cheese
½ teaspoon made English mustard
salt and freshly milled pepper

Warm the milk in a saucepan over low heat and melt the butter in a separate saucepan over low heat. Stir the flour into the butter and cook gently for 1 minute, then gradually pour in the warm milk, stirring well all the time to make a smooth sauce. Bring to the boil, stirring all the time, then lower the heat and simmer gently for 2–3 minutes. Draw off the heat and add the cheese and mustard. (The heat of the pan will be sufficient to melt the cheese.) Season to taste with salt and pepper.

Variation: Combine 1 egg yolk with 3 tablespoons single cream (to make a liaison) and stir into the sauce last of all. Reheat for 1 minute, stirring, but do not allow to boil. The result is a smooth, golden mixture which browns beautifully under the grill – use for fish or vegetable dishes.

Cheeses for cheese sauce

Of our traditional English cheeses, Cheddar is the most popular for cheese sauce, but you should try Lancashire which can be crumbled into the sauce and melts almost immediately. For good browning qualities (where sauce is poured over food and grilled) Gruyère is the best, but expensive. Swiss Sbrinz and Dutch Gouda are both excellent alternatives. Use a blue cheese and you get a different flavour. Stilton and Danish blue are delicious. Pour Stilton sauce over cooked cauliflower for a rare treat. In fact, you can use any cheese of your choice, remembering the stronger the flavour the less you'll need to get the right taste. Hard cheese should be finely grated; for soft or processed cheese use a coarse grater or dice cheese.

Illustrated: Cumberland sauce, page 115, with cold sliced gammon

Brown sauce

Finely chop the bacon. Melt the cooking fat in a saucepan over low heat, add the bacon and fry gently until bacon fat runs. Meanwhile, peel the onion and carrot, trim the celery and cut the vegetables in small dice (extracts more flavour). Add the vegetables to the saucepan and cook gently for about 10 minutes until the onion is tender and golden. Stir in the flour and cook gently for a further 20 minutes – this is a slowly-made sauce – stirring occasionally, until the flour is a rich nutty brown colour.

Stir in the tomato purée and draw the pan off the heat. Stir in the stock and add the bay leaf and chopped mushroom stalks, if using them. Bring to the boil, stirring all the time to make a smooth sauce, then cover with a pan lid and simmer gently for 40 minutes. Strain the sauce, stir in the sherry and season with salt and pepper. Reheat if necessary. This sauce is delicious served over fried chicken, steak or liver.

Variation: Add 2–3 oz (50–75g) sliced mushroom caps which have been lightly fried in butter.

Makes ½ pint (300 ml)

2 streaky bacon rashers or bacon trimmings
1 oz (25g) white cooking fat
1 medium-sized onion
1 carrot
1 stalk celery
1 oz (25g) plain flour
1 teaspoon concentrated tomato purée
1 pint (600ml) beef stock
1 bay leaf
few chopped mushroom stalks (optional)
2 tablespoons dry sherry
salt and freshly milled pepper

Tomato sauce

Scald the fresh tomatoes if using them, and peel the skins. Halve, then remove seeds and chop the flesh. Peel and finely chop the onion and garlic.

Heat the oil in a saucepan over low heat, add the onion and cook gently for about 10 minutes until tender and golden. Stir in the garlic and tomato purée. Add the fresh chopped tomatoes and cook for 2–3 minutes to soften and draw juices. Or add the tinned tomatoes with juices but omit the cooking. Add the sugar, bay leaf and stock and season with salt and pepper. Cover with a pan lid and cook gently for about 20 minutes.

Press tomato mixture through a sieve and return to the rinsed saucepan. Blend the cornflour with the cold water and stir into the mixture. Simmer gently stirring all the time, to make a thick sauce. Serve with pasta, chicken or fish.

Makes ¾ pint (400ml)

1 lb (450g) ripe tomatoes or
    1 × 14 oz (400g) tin chopped tomatoes
1 small onion
1 clove garlic
2 tablespoons oil
1 tablespoon concentrated tomato purée
1 level teaspoon castor sugar
1 bay leaf
¼ pint (150ml) chicken stock
salt and freshly milled pepper
1 level tablespoon cornflour
3 tablespoons cold water

Mushroom sauce

Peel and finely chop the onion. Melt half the butter in a frying pan over low heat, add the onion and fry gently for 5 minutes to soften but not brown. Meanwhile, trim and slice the mushrooms.

Add remaining butter to the pan along with the sliced mushrooms. Shake the pan and toss the mushrooms to cook them very gently. Before juices begin to run, stir in the cream and slowly bring just to the boil. Stir in the herbs and season with salt and pepper. Serve at once with steaks, chops or omelettes.

Serves 4

1 small onion
2 oz (50g) butter
8 oz (225g) button mushrooms
¼ pint (150ml) double cream
1 tablespoon finely chopped parsley or chives
salt and freshly milled pepper

Illustrated: Hollandaise sauce, page 118, with broccoli

Ragù sauce

Serves 4

4 oz (100g) chicken livers
2 streaky bacon rashers
1 onion
1 carrot
1 stalk celery
2 tablespoons oil
4 oz (100g) lean minced beef
1 tablespoon concentrated tomato
   purée
¼ pint (150ml) dry white wine
½ pint (300ml) beef stock
pinch of oregano or dried mixed
   herbs
salt and freshly milled pepper

Trim and finely chop the chicken livers. (They are easier to chop if first blanched in boiling water for 2 minutes.) Trim and chop the bacon rashers. Peel the onion and carrot, trim the celery and finely chop the vegetables.

Heat the oil in a saucepan over low heat, add the vegetables and bacon and cook gently for about 10 minutes, until the onion is tender and golden. Add the minced beef and chopped livers and cook, stirring all the time, until the meat loses its pink colour. Stir in the tomato purée and wine. Simmer for 2 minutes, then stir in the stock. Add the herbs and season with salt and pepper. Cover with a pan lid and simmer for 45 minutes. Remove the lid and simmer for a further 10–15 minutes to evaporate some of the liquid and make a thick, rich sauce.

Serve with tagliatelle or spaghetti. You'll find a generous sprinkling of freshly grated Parmesan complements the flavour beautifully, and hot garlic bread is just right for serving with the sauce-topped noodles. This sauce can also be used as a meat sauce for making lasagne.

Curry sauce

Makes ¾ pint (400ml)

1 medium-sized onion
1 small cooking apple
1 oz (25g) butter
2–4 level tablespoons curry powder
1 oz (25g) plain flour
1 small clove garlic
½ level teaspoon caraway seeds
1 small bay leaf
1 teaspoon curry paste (optional)
½ level teaspoon salt
1 tablespoon desiccated coconut
1 pint (600ml) chicken stock
1 teaspoon black treacle
1 tablespoon sweet chutney
squeeze of lemon juice

Peel and finely chop the onion. Peel, core and dice the apple. Melt the butter in a saucepan over low heat, add the onion and apple and fry gently for 5 minutes to soften the onion but not brown. Stir in the curry powder and cook for 1 minute to draw out the flavour, then stir in the flour. Crush together the garlic and caraway seeds with the back of a wooden spoon. Add to the pan, along with the bay leaf, curry paste, if using it, salt and desiccated coconut.

Gradually pour in the stock and bring to the boil, stirring all the time. Cover with a pan lid and simmer gently for 1 hour stirring occasionally. Stir in the treacle, chutney and a squeeze of lemon juice. Strain the sauce into a bowl. This delicious sauce is greatly improved in flavour if made up the day before it is to be used – the sauce mellows on standing. Reheat and serve with cooked meats or egg dishes or use as a 'cook-in' sauce to casserole a chicken.

Ready-mixed seasoning

Seasoning salt: Make up your own mixed seasoning salt and keep it handy in a jar. This is a perfect blend for seasoning sauces, casseroles and soups.

Sift together three times 8 oz (225g) kitchen salt, 1 level tablespoon freshly milled black pepper and 1 level teaspoon ground mace.

Seasoned flour: As useful is a ready-mixed seasoned flour which you can use to coat fish, chicken and meat for frying or casseroles; it's also useful for thickening gravies.

Sift together three times 8 oz (225g) plain flour and 1 level tablespoon seasoning salt.

Orange and lemon barbecue sauce

Peel and finely chop the onion. Melt the butter in a saucepan over low heat, add the onion and cook gently for 10 minutes until tender and golden.

Put the soft brown sugar, cornflour, mustard and Worcestershire sauce into a mixing bowl. Add the finely grated orange rind, orange juice, lemon juice, tomato purée and water and season with salt and pepper. Mix together and add to the pan. Bring to the boil, stirring all the time, then lower the heat and simmer gently for 5 minutes to make a smooth sauce. Draw off the heat and check seasoning. This sauce is delicious served with grilled or fried chicken or beef kebabs.

Variation: Add 1 finely chopped green pepper along with the onion and serve with pork chops.

Makes ¾ pint (400ml)

1 medium-sized onion
1 oz (25g) butter
2 oz (50g) soft light brown sugar
1 level tablespoon cornflour
2 teaspoons made English mustard
1 teaspoon Worcestershire sauce
finely grated rind and juice of 1 orange
juice of ½ lemon
1 tablespoon concentrated tomato purée
½ pint (300ml) water
salt and freshly milled pepper

Apple sauce

Halve, core and coarsely chop the apples (leaving on the skins which will add flavour and colour to the sauce). Put into a saucepan along with the pared lemon rind and water. Cover with a pan lid and cook gently for about 10 minutes, or until apples are soft. Draw off the heat.

Add the sugar and stir until dissolved. (The heat of the pan will be sufficient.) Press apples through a nylon sieve to make a purée and add the butter. Serve hot or cold with roast pork, duck, grilled or fried chops or black pudding.

Serves 4

1 lb (450g) cooking apples
large piece of pared lemon rind
2–3 tablespoons water
1 oz (25g) castor sugar
½ oz (15g) butter

Cumberland sauce

Thinly pare the rind of 1 orange using a vegetable peeler, then with a sharp knife cut the rind in narrow julienne strips. Place in a saucepan, pour over cold water to cover and bring to the boil, then lower the heat and simmer for 15 minutes until tender. Drain and set aside.

Squeeze the juice from both oranges and the lemon and put into the rinsed saucepan along with the redcurrant jelly. Stir over low heat until the jelly has melted (using a whisk helps jelly to disperse). Add the port or red wine and mustard and bring to the boil. Draw off the heat. Blend the arrowroot with the water in a bowl, stir in a little of the hot sauce and pour mixture into the saucepan. Return to the heat. Bring back to the boil, stirring all the time, and cook until sauce is clear and slightly thick. Draw off the heat and add the cooked orange peel. Allow sauce to cool to room temperature, stirring occasionally to prevent a skin forming. Do not refrigerate. Serve with either hot or cold meats, especially baked gammon, roast venison or turkey.

Serves 4

2 oranges
1 lemon
8 oz (225g) redcurrant jelly
¼ pint (150ml) ruby port or red wine
1 rounded teaspoon French mustard
2 rounded teaspoons arrowroot
1 tablespoon cold water

illustrated facing page 112

Stroganoff sauce

Serves 4

1 medium-sized onion
1 oz (25g) butter
4 oz (100g) button mushrooms
1 teaspoon concentrated tomato
   purée
½ pint (300ml) soured cream
salt and freshly milled pepper

Peel and finely chop the onion. Melt the butter in a frying pan over low heat, add the onion and fry gently for about 5 minutes to soften but not brown. Meanwhile, trim and slice the mushrooms.

Add the mushrooms to the pan and toss them over the heat for a few minutes. Stir in the tomato purée and soured cream. Bring just to the boil (soured cream does not separate) and season with salt and pepper. Serve at once with steaks, hamburgers or chicken or spoon over baked jacket potatoes.

Bread sauce

Serves 4

1 medium-sized onion
½ pint (300ml) milk
1 small bay leaf
1 blade of mace (optional)
2 oz (50g) soft white breadcrumbs
½ oz (15g) butter
salt and freshly milled pepper
1 tablespoon single cream

Peel the onion and put into a saucepan along with the milk, bay leaf and mace, if using it. Bring just to the boiling point, then draw off the heat, cover, and allow flavours to infuse for 15 minutes. Discard onion, bay leaf and mace.

Add the breadcrumbs and set the pan in a warm place (on the corner of the cooker) for at least 15 minutes, until breadcrumbs soak up milk. Add the butter, season with salt and pepper and stir until smooth. It is best to keep bread sauce away from direct heat but if your sauce is on the thin side, simmer it gently for about 5 minutes, stirring frequently. Just before serving stir in the cream. Serve with roast chicken or turkey.

Cranberry sauce

Serves 4–6

1 lb (450g) fresh cranberries
6 oz (175g) castor sugar
¼ pint (150ml) water
finely grated rind of 1 orange

Pick over the cranberries. Put the sugar, water and grated orange rind into a saucepan and stir over low heat until the sugar has dissolved.

Add the cranberries and bring to the boil, then simmer, uncovered, for about 5 minutes, or until cranberry skins pop. Allow to cool slightly, then turn into a small serving bowl and leave until completely cool. Don't reserve this delicious sauce for turkey alone, serve it with roast pork or venison as well.

Fresh mint sauce

Serves 6

1 large handful of fresh mint leaves
1 level tablespoon castor sugar
2 tablespoons boiling water
4 tablespoons wine vinegar

Strip the leaves from the stems of the mint and, using a stainless steel knife (to prevent discoloration), chop the mint with the sugar on a board. (Sugar acts as an abrasive and starts to draw juices.) Transfer mint leaves to a mixing bowl along with the sugar and crush with the back of a wooden spoon until mushy. Add the water to dissolve the sugar, then add the vinegar. Leave to stand for at least 1 hour. This thick fresh sauce is traditionally served with roast lamb.

Flavoured butters

Parsley butter: Cream 4 oz (100g) unsalted butter until soft. Beat in 2 tablespoons finely chopped fresh parsley, a seasoning of salt and pepper and a squeeze of lemon juice. Mix together well and chill. *To use:* Spoon parsley butter on to hot vegetables; use to enrich vegetable soup before serving or for scrambled eggs. Pots of parsley butter can be served with crusty rolls as an accompaniment to soups. Use instead of ordinary butter for making ham, chicken and other cold meat sandwiches. Dot the butter over grilled gammon or fish. Make **tarragon butter** the same way and spread it over chicken joints before grilling or baking them.

Garlic butter: Cream 4 oz (100g) unsalted butter until soft. Crush 2–3 cloves of garlic and remove papery coating, then mash to a purée with a little salt. Add garlic purée, 2 tablespoons finely chopped parsley, a squeeze of lemon juice and a seasoning of freshly milled pepper to the butter. Mix together well and chill. *To use:* Serve over steaks, or use for frying mushrooms or for making hot garlic bread.

Blue cheese butter: Cream 4 oz (100g) unsalted butter and 3 oz (75g) Roquefort cheese (or similar blue cheese like Danish Blue), until soft and blended. Add a squeeze of lemon juice and a seasoning of salt and pepper. Mix together well and chill. *To use:* Serve over steaks.

Mustard butter: Cream 4 oz (100g) unsalted butter until soft. Beat in 2 tablespoons French mustard, a seasoning of salt and pepper and a squeeze of lemon juice. Mix together well and chill. *To use:* Serve over steaks or with roast fillet of beef. Use to spread over chicken joints before grilling or baking them.

For flavoured butters to slice: Spoon the softened flavoured butter on to a square of kitchen foil, then roll up and twist ends in opposite directions like a Christmas cracker to make a fat roll. Chill until firm. When required, unwrap and slice chilled butter using a hot knife blade. Neat rounds of flavoured butter slowly melting over grilled meats and fish make these simple dishes look especially appetizing.

Clarified butter

Clarified butter is butter with the salt, moisture and curd extracted. It is marvellous for frying omelettes or vegetables. It is also excellent to use for sealing potted meats, pâtés and terrines.

Melt the butter over gentle heat until the foaming subsides. Pour into a bowl and leave until cold and firm. Carefully scrape away the top white layer which contains the salt. Loosen the sides and lift out the cake of butter, discarding any liquid or curd at the bottom of the bowl. Gently melt the butter again until oily. Store in the refrigerator.

To clarify dripping: This is the traditional method of clarifying dripping left over from a roast joint, roast duck or goose. Place dripping in a saucepan with boiling water to cover and heat until dripping has melted. Pour into a bowl and leave until cold. Then loosen the sides and lift out the cake of dripping, discarding liquid and sediment at the bottom of the bowl. Melt the dripping again and pour into a container. Store in the refrigerator.

Beurre manié

This is a blended butter and flour mixture used to thicken hot soups, sauces and gravies. To make beurre manié, use a table knife to blend 1½ oz (40g) butter with 1 oz (25g) plain flour on a plate. Always add the beurre manié in very small lumps to the liquid off the heat, a few at a time. I always place a few lumps on the tip of a knife and scrape them off against the hot saucepan side. The beurre manié melts as it runs down into the hot liquid – a good way to ensure that the beurre manié is slowly added without it going lumpy.

Stir the hot liquid until the beurre manié is completely blended. Return the saucepan to the heat and slowly bring to the boil, stirring all the time, until thickened. The amount of beurre manié given above is sufficient to thicken ½ pint (300ml) liquid for a sauce, 1 pint (600ml) liquid for sauces of pouring consistency like gravy and 2 pints (1.1 litres) liquid for soups.

How to make better hollandaise and béarnaise sauces

Hollandaise and béarnaise sauces are the kind you only make occasionally – but they are worth it and take only a few minutes to make in a saucepan over direct heat, which may surprise you, but follow my instructions and see for yourself.

● Both sauces rely on a reduction of vinegar to give them their special flavours – of course you must do this in a saucepan over direct heat.

● Add 1 tablespoon cold water to the hot pan, off the heat, to reduce the heat of the pan before you add the egg yolks – a hotel chef taught me this trick and it works every time. The cold water prevents the yolks from over-cooking.

● When you whisk in the melted butter the sauce will thicken. Remember it's very important not to have the butter too hot or the egg yolks will just scramble when butter is added.

● These sauces barely reach more than a warm temperature and should be served warm. To hold these sauces for a short period see page 110.

Hollandaise

Serves 4

4 oz (100g) butter
2 tablespoons white wine vinegar
1 tablespoon cold water
2 egg yolks
juice of ½ lemon
salt and freshly milled pepper

illustrated facing page 113

Melt the butter in a saucepan over low heat and allow to cool slightly. Boil the vinegar in a separate saucepan until reduced to a scant tablespoon. Draw off the heat and add the cold water, then add the egg yolks. Whisk over low heat for several minutes until thick and frothy. Draw off the heat again and slowly whisk in the warm (not hot) butter, then whisk in the lemon juice and season with salt and pepper. Serve with tender asparagus, broccoli, summer vegetables or poached salmon.

Variation **Blender hollandaise:** Though it lacks the bite of hollandaise made by hand, this is a good, quick method. Put 3 egg yolks and 2 tablespoons lemon juice into the goblet of a blender or food processor and season with salt and pepper. Cover and blend a few seconds. Have the butter bubbling hot and gradually pour it on to the egg yolks while the blender or food processor is at high speed. Blend for a few seconds until thick and light.

Béarnaise sauce

Serves 4

4 oz (100g) butter
1 teaspoon chopped fresh tarragon
1 teaspoon finely chopped shallot
2 tablespoons white wine vinegar
freshly milled pepper
1 tablespoon cold water
2 egg yolks
juice of ½ lemon
1 teaspoon chopped fresh parsley
pinch of salt

Melt the butter in a saucepan over low heat and allow to cool slightly. Put the chopped tarragon, chopped shallot and wine vinegar into a separate saucepan and season with the pepper. Boil until vinegar has reduced to a scant tablespoon. Draw off the heat and add the cold water, then add the egg yolks. Whisk over low heat for several minutes until thick and frothy. Draw off the heat again and slowly whisk in the warm (not hot) butter. Whisk in the lemon juice, add the chopped parsley and season with salt. Serve with grilled steaks.

Variation: If you can't get fresh tarragon use tarragon vinegar in place of the wine vinegar.

Lemon aspic jelly

Put the water into a saucepan, sprinkle in the gelatine and leave to soak for 5 minutes. Add the lemon juice, wine vinegar, sugar and salt. Stir over low heat to dissolve the gelatine (do not boil).

Allow to cool until the mixture begins to thicken and shows signs of setting. (You can speed this up by setting the pan in a bowl of iced water.) If aspic sets firm simply warm until completely dissolved and allow to cool again.

To use: Spoon cooled jelly over the surface of a mousse or pâté. If decorating mousses or pâtés, it's a good idea to spoon a little of the jelly into a saucer and use this for dipping and fixing the decorations. If decorations are positioned and chilled then they will remain in place when the glaze is added. Sometimes it looks pretty if you spread a little aspic over the base of a serving plate – the sliced pâté will be reflected in the plate. Any leftover jelly can be chopped with a wet knife and spooned around cold foods. Lemon aspic jelly gives a glorious finish to a cold poached salmon.

Makes ¼ pint (150ml)

¼ pint (150ml) cold water
2 level teaspoons powdered gelatine
1 tablespoon lemon juice
1 tablespoon wine vinegar
1 level tablespoon castor sugar
¼ level teaspoon salt

How to make better mayonnaise

Mayonnaise is a delicious cold sauce and is used in so many dishes that it is really worthwhile making it yourself. There is no secret to getting mayonnaise to thicken: it works on the simple basis that as the oil is whisked into the egg yolk, a creamy emulsion is formed. If you add the oil too quickly or the eggs are too cold the emulsion breaks down and the oil separates out. It doesn't spoil the flavour but it looks unappetizing. Start again with a clean bowl and a fresh egg yolk and slowly whisk the separated mixture into the egg yolk and it will thicken perfectly.

Oil – olive oil or corn oil is best – and egg yolk are the basic ingredients. White wine vinegar, cider vinegar or a herb-flavoured vinegar (especially tarragon) or lemon juice is added to thin the mixture. Salt and freshly milled pepper are the basic seasonings, and a little prepared French or English mustard is added which encourages the mixture to form an emulsion. You can also add herbs, garlic, tomato and other flavours to suit your tastes.

● Have the ingredients at room temperature.

● Use a heavy small mixing bowl and stand it on a folded damp cloth or sponge so it stays firmly in place. Use a coil-rimmed hand whisk or fork for beating the oil. Your other hand is then free for adding the oil.

● Whisk together the egg yolk, seasoning, a little mustard and some of the vinegar or lemon juice before adding any oil.

● Measure the oil into a jug, and then you can pour it slowly. Add the oil a few drops at a time initially. Then as soon as the mayonnaise begins to thicken, you can pour the oil in a thin steady stream by holding the jug high above the bowl.

● Halfway through whisking, add the rest of the vinegar to thin the mayonnaise.

● A little boiling water added at the very end makes mayonnaise lighter in texture.

● If making mayonnaise in a blender and you have a choice of speeds, keep the speed set at low as a high speed will result in a thin mayonnaise. With a blender you can make mayonnaise more economically by using 1 whole egg but the best results still come from using 2 egg yolks. Make large quantities when making mayonnaise in an electric blender.

Mayonnaise

Makes ¼ pint (150ml)

¼ pint (150ml) oil
1 egg yolk
¼ teaspoon made English mustard
2 teaspoons wine vinegar or lemon juice
salt and freshly milled pepper
1 teaspoon boiling water

Put the oil into a jug. Put the egg yolk, mustard and half the vinegar or lemon juice into a mixing bowl and season with salt and pepper. Whisk ingredients together to blend. Whisk in about half the oil, a few drops at a time, until the mayonnaise begins to thicken. Whisk in the remaining vinegar or lemon juice which will thin the mayonnaise a little, then hold the jug well above the bowl and pour the remaining oil on to the mayonnaise in a thin steady stream, whisking all the time until thick. Whisk in the boiling water to make a soft, light consistency. Spoon into a container, cover, and store in the lowest section of the refrigerator where it will keep for up to 3 weeks.

Blender mayonnaise

Makes ½ pint (300ml)

½ pint (300ml) oil
2 egg yolks or 1 whole egg and 1 egg yolk
½ level teaspoon made English mustard
2 tablespoons wine vinegar or lemon juice
¼ level teaspoon salt
freshly milled pepper
1 tablespoon boiling water

Put the oil into a jug. Put the eggs, mustard, 1 tablespoon of the vinegar or lemon juice and salt into the goblet of a blender or food processor. Season with pepper. Cover and blend on low speed for a few seconds.

Remove centre cap from the lid and slowly pour the oil on to the revolving blades. The mayonnaise will begin to thicken when the blades are covered. Add the remaining vinegar or lemon juice which will thin the mayonnaise a little, then pour in the remaining oil and lastly the boiling water. Spoon into a screw-topped jar and store in the lowest section of the refrigerator where it will keep for up to 3 weeks.

Green mayonnaise

Makes ½ pint (300ml)

1 whole egg and 1 egg yolk
1 tablespoon wine vinegar
1 level teaspoon castor sugar
½ level teaspoon made English mustard
1 tablespoon chopped parsley
1 tablespoon chopped chives
salt and freshly milled pepper
½ pint (300ml) oil

Put the whole egg and egg yolk into the goblet of a blender or food processor. Add the wine vinegar, sugar, mustard and herbs and season with salt and pepper. Cover and blend for a few seconds. Remove the centre cap from the lid and add the oil in drops at first, blending on lowest speed, until an emulsion has been formed, then add in a slow steady stream.

The mayonnaise will become beautifully thick and pale green in colour. Taste and check seasoning. Spoon into a screw-topped jar and store in the lowest section of the refrigerator where it will keep for up to 1 week. This mayonnaise is especially delicious with cold salmon.

Mayonnaise variations

The very simplicity of mayonnaise makes it enormously versatile – you can add a variety of flavours.

Light mayonnaise: If you find mayonnaise too rich, combine mayonnaise and natural yoghurt in equal parts and use as for ordinary mayonnaise.

Mayonnaise for coating: Add 3 tablespoons single cream to ½ pint (150ml) mayonnaise to thin it to a coating consistency for salad vegetables.

Tartare sauce: Rub the inside of a mixing bowl with a crushed clove of garlic. Spoon 3 tablespoons mayonnaise into the bowl along with 1 teaspoon finely chopped gherkins, 1 teaspoon finely chopped parsley and a squeeze of lemon juice. Mix together and serve with fried fish.

Mayonnaise for seafood: Combine 2 tablespoons mayonnaise with 2 tablespoons tomato ketchup and 2 tablespoons double cream. Add 1 teaspoon Worcestershire sauce, a squeeze of lemon juice and a dash of Tabasco (optional). Serve with prawns or use to make egg mayonnaise.

Curry mayonnaise: Mix together 4 tablespoons mayonnaise, 2 tablespoons soured cream, 1 teaspoon concentrated tomato purée, 1 level teaspoon curry powder and a squeeze of lemon juice. Chill for at least 1 hour and use as a dressing for cold chicken or to make egg mayonnaise.

Garlic mayonnaise: Crush 1 clove garlic (or more) to a purée with salt and stir into ¼ pint (150ml) mayonnaise along with 2 tablespoons of single cream. Use as a dressing for cold chicken.

Cucumber mayonnaise: Peel and dice ½ cucumber and sprinkle with salt. Leave in a colander for 30 minutes to draw juices, then rinse and press dry in absorbent paper. Stir into ½ pint (300ml) mayonnaise along with 2 tablespoons single cream. Serve with cold salmon.

Herb mayonnaise: Add 2 tablespoons finely chopped chives, 1 tablespoon finely chopped parsley and 2 tablespoons cream to ½ pint (300ml) mayonnaise. Or use 2 tablespoons chopped fresh dill in place of the parsley and chives. Serve with cold salmon, salmon trout or crabmeat.

Aspic mayonnaise: Sprinkle ½ level teaspoon powdered gelatine into 1 tablespoon cold water and leave to soak for 5 minutes. Dissolve the soaked gelatine in 1 tablespoon boiling water, then strain into ¼ pint (150ml) mayonnaise. Leave until at setting point. Use to decorate canapés and open sandwiches by piping the mixture through a star nozzle on to them.

Oil and vinegar dressing

dash of French mustard
1 tablespoon wine vinegar
salt and freshly milled pepper
3 tablespoons oil

Mix the mustard, vinegar and a good seasoning of salt and pepper with a fork until blended. Add the oil and beat vigorously until an emulsion is formed. (The oil separates on standing so beat again before using.)

Variations

Mixed herb dressing: Add 2 teaspoons finely chopped parsley and 1 teaspoon chopped chives. Use as a dressing for green salads or vegetable salad.

Garlic dressing: Add ½ finely chopped garlic clove and 1 teaspoon chopped parsley. Or rub bowl with crushed garlic (impaled on a fork) before mixing the dressing. Use as a dressing for chicory or endive salads.

Mint dressing: Add 1 teaspoon finely chopped mint. Use as a dressing for new potato salad or a salad of fresh pears.

Blue cheese dressing: Add 1 oz (25g) crumbled Roquefort cheese. Use as a dressing for a green salad to be served with steak.

Chive dressing: Add 1 tablespoon finely chopped chives and 3 tablespoons soured cream. Beat well to make a creamy emulsion. Spoon on to avocado halves or use as a dressing for avocado or cucumber salads.

Tomato cream dressing: Add 1 tablespoon tomato ketchup and 3 tablespoons double cream. Beat well to make a pale pink dressing. Serve with fish salads or hard-boiled eggs.

Easy soured cream sauces

Commercial soured cream is made from fresh cream which has been treated with a culture (like yoghurt) to give it a sharp flavour and thick texture. It is ideal for using to make delicious, quick sauces.

Soured cream horseradish sauce: Combine 4 tablespoons prepared horseradish relish (not sauce) and ¼ pint (150ml) soured cream. Season with salt and freshly milled pepper and add a dash of Worcestershire sauce. Leave to stand for 1 hour so flavours develop. This is a delicate mixture that is not so biting as horseradish on its own. Serve with roast beef, smoked mackerel or smoked trout.

Soured cream chive sauce: Combine ¼ pint (150ml) soured cream, a seasoning of salt and freshly milled pepper and 2 tablespoons finely chopped chives. Use as a topping for baked jacket potatoes or as a dressing for herring salad.

Soured cream avocado sauce: Scoop out the flesh from 1 ripe avocado and mash with a fork. Stir in 3 tablespoons oil and vinegar dressing and ¼ pint

(150ml) soured cream. Season with salt and freshly milled pepper and mix together well. This makes a pretty pale green sauce that is good served with salmon.

Soured cream curry sauce: Combine ¼ pint (150ml) soured cream, 3 tablespoons mayonnaise, 1 teaspoon concentrated tomato purée and 1 level teaspoon curry powder. Leave to stand for 1 hour, then mix again. Serve with cold chicken or hard-boiled eggs.

Soured cream mustard sauce: Combine ¼ pint (150ml) soured cream, 3 tablespoons mayonnaise, 1 teaspoon made English mustard, 1 teaspoon finely chopped onion and 1 tablespoon finely chopped parsley. Serve with cold chicken or ham salad.

Soured cream cucumber sauce: Combine 1 teaspoon castor sugar, 1 tablespoon wine vinegar, ½ teaspoon made English mustard and a seasoning of salt and pepper. Stir in ¼ pint (150ml) soured cream and ¼ finely diced cucumber. Serve with cold salmon or salmon trout.

7

Vegetables and Salads

Careful selection and simple cooking are usually
all that is needed to appreciate the lovely flavours
and textures of vegetables. Sometimes a glaze, a
few herbs or the lightest of dressings will help to
bring out or enhance their natural flavours.

Vegetables and Salads

How to cook better vegetables

● Use a sharp knife to cut vegetables. A small vegetable knife is the one for slicing and paring and a large kitchen knife is the one for chopping.

● Most vegetables have a better flavour, appearance and texture when cooked until just tender.

● Timing, although a guide, is no substitute for testing thicker stalky stems with a knife tip or removing a piece from the pan and biting into it.

● Use as little water as possible to cook vegetables. Usually only about 1 inch (2.5cm) boiling water in the saucepan is enough. Add vegetables and cook over moderate heat covered with a pan lid to hold in steam. Vegetables, especially green ones, produce a lot of water and need only a little water to start them cooking.

● Some of the nutrients are removed when vegetables are peeled, so cook vegetables in skins whenever possible, especially potatoes.

● Some vegetables have a natural sweetness, particularly root vegetables like carrots, onions and turnips. Emphasize their natural sweetness by adding a little sugar to the cooking water – it will make all the difference to the flavour.

● Tomatoes are improved with a pinch of sugar to counteract their natural acidity, and if you add sugar to the boiling water for cauliflower it makes the curds whiter.

● For tying bunches of celery stalks or celery hearts for boiling or braising, use a 1 inch (2.5cm) wide gauze bandage. The celery won't slip out and the gauze won't cut into the celery the way string would. Use for leeks and asparagus, too.

● Many cooked vegetables are delicious served cold or at room temperature. Add a seasoning of salt and pepper, some herbs, lemon juice or vinegar and oil to the vegetables while warm and they will absorb the flavour as they cool.

● If you plan to serve green vegetables such as broccoli, French beans and asparagus cold, then immerse them in cold water for a few minutes as soon as they are cooked to retain their colour.

● Tomatoes, aubergines, courgettes, onion, marrow and green peppers all make decorative and delicious vegetable cases for stuffings. With few exceptions, stuffings are made using tender meats or cooked vegetables flavoured with herbs and spices that require short cooking times.

● Serve vegetables immediately after cooking. Don't let them stand for long periods, though in some exceptions they reheat well, red cabbage for example.

Asparagus

Buds should be tightly closed and a good green colour, stems firm and with some bleached or white part showing; fat asparagus stalks will be too fibrous.

Carefully wash asparagus, then scrape with a sharp knife along the lower part of the stem to the base – this encourages quicker cooking of the stalks. If the base is at all tough and woody it should be cut away and all stalks should be trimmed to the same length. Tie asparagus in single or double portions with tape or a 1 inch (2.5cm) wide bandage and wind it several times around the bundle so stalks will not slip. Asparagus boiled loose would move around and the delicate heads might break.

Asparagus stems require a thorough boil while the tips need only a gentle simmer. Ideally, bundles should be placed upright in a deep pan with sufficient simmering salted water to come to within 1 inch (2.5cm) of the tips when the stems are standing upright. There are special tall asparagus pans for this or you could use one of those fine mesh blanching baskets (the stiff, non-collapsible kind), and the bottom half of a pressure cooker provides a good deep pan. On the other hand, you can get away with simmering bundles of asparagus immersed completely in water – a cast iron flameproof casserole is roomier than a conventional saucepan.

Cover pan with a lid or kitchen foil so that the steam will cook the tips. Asparagus will take about 15–20 minutes – test by piercing the tip of the stalks with a knife tip: they should be just tender. When ready hook a fork under the tape or gauze and lift asparagus from the pan. Drain by placing on a clean tea-towel so that no water will dilute sauces or dressing. Loosen tapes and asparagus is ready to serve.

Serve with melted butter seasoned with salt and pepper and a squeeze of lemon juice. If you have the plates tilted by placing a fork underneath them, the butter will run into a pool on the far side of the plate – handy for dipping heads and keeping stalks grease free for holding with your fingers.

● Asparagus can be cooked, then cut and served cold in a salad.

● Roll cooked asparagus in ham and serve in a light cheese sauce.

● Allow approximately 6–8 stems per person for a first course. Thinner sticks are often sold loose rather than in bundles – it's easier to be more generous with these.

● Asparagus wilts quickly so store in a cool place. Stand stems in cold water to revive them.

Aubergines

Look for firm, shiny deep purple skins with no wrinkles or soft parts. Wipe, then remove stem and small leaves that surround it. The skin adds flavour so don't peel aubergines. Sprinkle cut aubergines with salt and leave to stand in a colander with a weighted plate on top for 30 minutes to draw some of the bitter juices. Rinse in cold water, then press dry with absorbent paper.

Fried aubergines: either shallow fry aubergines in butter or oil, or dust with seasoned flour and deep fry for 2–3 minutes until crisp and tender.

● Allow 1½ lb (700g) for 4 servings. An average aubergine weighs about 8 oz (225g). Store for up to 1 week in a cool place or in the salad drawer in the refrigerator.

Avocados

Avocados are picked unripe and shipped under refrigeration. If bought firm they will ripen in 3–4 days at room temperature. You can speed the ripening by putting them in a paper or polythene bag or kitchen drawer. To test for ripeness, cradle the fruit in the palm of your hand and press gently – it will give to gentle pressure. Store ripe avocados in the salad drawer of the refrigerator for up to 4 days. Don't cut into them until serving time.

● Cut avocado lengthways and separate halves by twisting gently. Lightly pierce the stone with the sharp edge of the knife and the stone can then be lifted out leaving avocado flesh without a mark. Brush the surface with lemon juice or cover with cling film to avoid discoloration.

● For salads, place halved avocados cut side down on work surface. Then with a sharp knife lightly score skin along the centre back. Peel back and remove each section of skin, then slice crossways.

● Allow ½–1 avocado per person.

Beans

Broad beans are soft kidney-shaped beans in a furry lined pod. Pods should snap easily, then you can squeeze out the beans. Look for small, plump pods, which indicate that the beans will be tender.

● Add to boiling salted water and cook for about 10 minutes. Drain and slip beans from their outer skins while hot – extra work but worth it for improved taste and appearance. Serve tossed in butter. Beans tossed in oil are good served cold in tossed salads.

● Allow 2 lb (900g) in the pod for 4 servings.

French beans should be thin, crisp and firm. They are stringless so top and tail only.

● Cook beans either whole or cut in boiling salted water for about 5 minutes until just tender. Serve tossed in butter.

● Toss the beans in butter along with toasted flaked almonds.

● Drain cooked beans, add a seasoning of freshly milled pepper, a nut of butter and a pinch of herbs – try dried marjoram, rosemary, dillweed or snipped fresh mint.

● Newly cooked beans dressed with oil and vinegar dressing and left until cold are delicious added to salads.

● Allow 1–1½ lb (450–700g) for 4 servings.

Runner beans should have fresh crisp pods that are not too large; small developing beans inside are a good sign. Older beans will need the strings from both sides removed with a sharp knife, otherwise they are simply topped and tailed. Shred the beans diagonally as finely as possible or use a bean shredder.

● Add to boiling salted water and cook for about 10–15 minutes. Drain and serve with butter.

● Allow 1–1½ lb (450–700g) for 4 servings.

Green beans with onion: Put 1 oz (25g) butter in the hot pan in which 1–1½ lb (450–700g) beans were cooked. Add 1 finely chopped onion and fry for 5 minutes until the onion is softened and beginning to brown. Return the hot beans to the pan and toss to blend with the butter and onion.

● This method of preparation can be used for all types of green beans and is especially good for adding interest to frozen beans.

Beetroot

Though beetroots are more often bought ready-cooked, it's well worth the time to cook them yourself. Raw beetroots should be firm with a good dark colour and fresh unbroken skins. Any leaves attached should be fresh. Cut or twist off leafy tops about 1 inch (2.5cm) above the root so skin remains unbroken, or beetroot will bleed when boiled, then scrub clean.

● Bring beetroots to the boil in salted water and cook for up to 2 hours, depending on size, then drain. Hold beetroots under cold water and slip off skins. Slice or dice the beetroot and serve coated with a white sauce.

● Grate cooked beetroot into a saucepan with hot melted butter. Season with plenty of freshly milled pepper, toss and serve – this is delicious.

Beetroot with orange: Remove skins from 1 lb (450g) cooked beetroot and cut beetroot into dice. Put 1 oz (25g) butter, 1 rounded tablespoon orange marmalade and the juice of ½ orange into a saucepan. Heat until the butter melts, then add beetroot. Simmer gently, stirring occasionally, for about 6–8 minutes until beetroot is heated through and glazed. Serve hot beetroot with roast chicken or turkey.

● Cooked and skinned beetroot can be grated and served in an oil and vinegar dressing for salads. The bright red juice of beetroot, which can so annoyingly stain other ingredients in the same dish, can be used to advantage in salads. Try mixing sliced celery and diced apple with diced beetroot. The apple and celery will take on a delicate pink colour. Add a garnish of watercress sprigs to make a pretty colour contrast.

● Traditionally, cooked beetroot is sliced or diced into vinegar for passing round with cold meats. Try a soured cream dressing for a change (page 159).

● Allow 1–1½ lb (450–750g) for 4 servings.

Broccoli

Purple sprouting broccoli should be firm, with tightly closed buds tinged with purple and no wilted or yellow leaves. Remove outer leaves and trim stalks. Soak for 30 minutes in salted water to remove any grubs. Purple sprouting broccoli turns green when cooked.

● Add to boiling salted water and cook for 10 minutes. Test stalks for tenderness with a knife tip. Drain and serve with melted butter or hollandaise.

● Allow 1½–2 lb (700–900g) for 4 servings.

Calabrese is a much fuller and larger variety of broccoli with bluish-green heads. Avoid those with any signs of yellowing. Trim the stalks.

● Add to boiling salted water and cook for 10 minutes until tender but still firm, then drain. Serve with butter.

● Serve calabrese broccoli cold in an oil and vinegar dressing.

● Allow 1–1½ lb (450–700g) for 4 servings.

Brussels sprouts

Look for small, firm Brussels sprouts with a fresh green colour and no yellow or wilting leaves. They are best after the first frosts; if weather stays warm sprouts are inclined to become 'blown' and open. Trim the base and remove outer loose leaves, then slash base stalks with a knife to speed up cooking. Rinse in cold water.

● Add to boiling salted water and cook for about 10–15 minutes. Drain and serve with butter.

● Toss equal parts cooked chestnuts (page 130) with cooked sprouts in hot butter and serve.

Puréed Brussels sprouts: Purée sprouts by putting cooked vegetables through a food mill. Then return the purée to the saucepan and heat through with a knob of butter, a seasoning of salt and freshly milled pepper and a few tablespoons double cream added. This is a good way to use leafy open sprouts.

● Allow 1½–2 lb (700–900g) for 4 servings.

Cabbage

Green or *white cabbage* should look fresh and crisp with no signs of wilting. It should have a firm head with closely packed leaves. Remove outer coarse leaves. Halve, then quarter the head and cut away centre core. With cut side down on a chopping board, finely shred across the leaves.

● Cook in 1 inch (2.5cm) boiling salted water, with pan covered for 15 minutes. Turn cabbage once or twice to cook evenly, then drain in a colander and press well to remove moisture. Return to hot pan and toss cabbage with butter, freshly milled black pepper and just a little grated nutmeg if you like.

● Drain cooked cabbage, season with freshly milled pepper, add a nut of butter and crumbled crisp fried bacon or finely grated hard cheese.

● Shred white cabbage and use in salads with an oil and vinegar dressing.

● Allow 1 lb (450g) cabbage for 4 servings.

Spring greens are cabbages that do not form a head. Separate leaves and cut any thick stems from the base. Wash in cold water, then roll up leaves in bundles and shred crossways.

● Cook as for cabbage allowing only 10 minutes.

● Allow 1 lb (450g) for 4 servings.

Red cabbage is usually sold with outer leaves removed, so look for a firm head with a good fresh colour – it will be more moist. Cut in half, then quarters and cut away the core. With cut side down on a chopping board, finely shred across the cabbage leaves.

● Red cabbage is best cooked in a covered pan with apples, vinegar and sugar for about 1–2 hours. Serve with rich meats like duck and pork.

● Use red cabbage in winter salads. It's very pretty mixed with bean sprouts, grated carrots and snipped watercress. Toss in an oil and vinegar dressing.

● Allow 1–1½ lb (450–700g) for 4 servings. A red cabbage will stay fresh for 5–6 days stored in a cool place.

Illustrated: Macédoine of vegetables, page 146

Carrots

Look for a bright colour – maincrop carrots should be tender with no woody core. New carrots should snap cleanly and have no sign of green on the tops. Scrub clean, then cut away the tops. Peel maincrop and scrape new carrots, then slice or dice; small new carrots can be left whole.

● Bring carrots to the boil in 1 inch (2.5cm) salted water with a bay leaf added and cook in a covered pan for about 15–20 minutes. Drain and toss in butter with a pinch of sugar added. A sprinkling of chopped parsley is pretty.

● Carrots have a natural sweetness which should be emphasized; they are delicious glazed.

● Coarsely grated new carrots are good as a salad tossed in an oil and vinegar dressing with grated apples added.

● Cook whole new carrots until just tender, allow to cool and toss them in mayonnaise.

● Allow 1–1½ lb (450–900g) for 4 servings.

● Remove newly purchased carrots from any plastic bags or covering before storing.

Cauliflower

Compact creamy coloured curds that are firm and closely packed are the freshest. Trim the stalk and remove all but the small green leaves. Using a sharp knife, cut out the centre core to help speed up cooking.

● Add a whole cauliflower head, stalk end up, to boiling salted water, and cook for 15–20 minutes. Drain and serve with a white or cheese sauce.

● Break into even-sized florets and boil in salted water for about 10–12 minutes until just tender.

● Add a bay leaf to simmering cauliflower to help take away the cauliflower smell.

● Small florets of cauliflower are delicious served cold with an oil and vinegar dressing. Add to salads or serve with a little chopped onion and parsley for a first course.

● Allow 1 large head for 4 servings.

Celeriac

Rough skinned and brown, celeriac can be anything from the size of an apple to a coconut and has a mild, pleasant celery flavour. Scrub, then peel the thick skin with a knife. Slice and cut into chips or dice.

● Add to boiling salted water and cook for 10 minutes until tender. Drain well and serve with a lemon sauce (page 142).

Celeriac purée: Cook with an equal quantity of peeled potatoes until tender. Drain and mash both to a purée, season with salt and pepper and add butter. Serve with game.

Celeriac salad: Cut celeriac in matchstick strips. Blanch in boiling water for 2 minutes. Chill, then toss in an oil and vinegar dressing or mustard-flavoured mayonnaise.

● Allow 1–1½ lb (450–700g) for 4 servings.

Celery

Look for crisp stalks with no discoloration at the base. Unwashed celery keeps best. To revive limp celery, stand stalks in a jug of iced water for 30 minutes. Trim off root and leafy tops, then separate stalks and scrub well.

● Use coarse outer stalks for soups and stock; leafy tops add a good flavour to soups.

● Crisp inner stalks are nice served with cheese. If you chill stalks in the refrigerator for a few hours beforehand they will be crunchy.

● Snap stalks and pull apart to draw the strings before you shred celery for salads.

● Celery will curl up in iced water if you cut the inner stalks to 2 inch (5cm) lengths, then cut along the length to within ½ inch (1cm) of one end to make a fringed effect. Leave in iced water for 1–2 hours and fringes will roll back. They make a nice garnish for salads.

● 1 head should be sufficient for 4–6 servings.

● Store celery unwashed for up to 3 days in the salad drawer of the refrigerator or loosely wrapped in the lowest section of refrigerator.

Illustrated: Bacon stuffed onions, page 146

Chestnuts

The ones we eat are the fruit of the sweet chestnut tree. The reddish brown skin is peeled off and the kernel when cooked is sweet and floury.

● Chestnuts must first be cooked if they are going to be served as a snack in the same way as other nuts. Traditionally, they are roasted in the hot ashes of a fire (page 337).

● To peel chestnuts for cooking, make a cut in the brown outer skin with a knife. Immerse in a saucepan of boiling water for 2 minutes. Lift out and peel off the outer and inner skin. Boil only a few at a time, otherwise chestnuts will cool and harden again and be difficult to peel.

● If kernels are to be used in a savoury dish, simmer peeled chestnuts in chicken stock for about 35–40 minutes until tender. Test for tenderness with a knife tip. They can be served as a vegetable, used in stuffings, or made into soups.

● Cooked chestnuts tossed with hot Brussels sprouts are delicious served with any roast meat or poultry. They are traditionally served with roast turkey, but try serving with boiled or baked ham.

● Purée cooked chestnuts (page 145) and serve with roast game. Whole chestnuts will add interest to a game stew.

● For dessert recipes either to use whole or as a purée, simmer in milk and water as above (page 220), then make into a sweet purée.

● Dried chestnuts are very good. Let them soak covered with cold water for 4–6 hours and they are ready to cook and serve as for fresh.

● 1 lb (450g) fresh chestnuts yields about 12 oz (350g) peeled chestnuts.

● Allow 1–1½ lb (450–700g) for 4 servings.

Chicory

Heads of chicory must be fresh with closely packed white leaves having edges of faintest yellow; if there are any tinges of green, chicory will taste bitter. Chicory must be stored in a dark place and any green on the leaves indicates that it has been exposed to light for too long in the shop. Cut a sliver from the base, and with a pointed knife, cut out the core. Remove outer damaged leaves.

● Add to boiling salted water and cook for about 20 minutes until tender. Drain and serve with melted butter or a cheese sauce.

● Wrap cooked chicory in slices of ham and coat with a cheese sauce.

● Serve chicory in salads by cutting the heads crossways in 1 inch (2.5cm) slices, then separate the layers. For an extra crunchy texture, refrigerate chicory or chill in iced water for 30 minutes before mixing into salads.

● Allow 1 head per person.

Chinese leaves

This unusual vegetable looks like a cross between a pale cos lettuce and a head of celery, though it is larger and considerably heavier. It tastes like a delicately flavoured cabbage with just a hint of celery. Chinese leaves make a lovely vegetable for salads during winter months. Rinse the head under the cold tap and drain.

● Hold the head tightly together and shred with a sharp knife by cutting the leaves crossways in about 8 thin slices starting from the green open end. Shake shreds loose and use in the same way as cabbage to make salads with an oil and vinegar dressing. Or use shredded leaves as a garnish in the same way as you would use lettuce.

● Good additions to Chinese leaves for salad are red or green pepper strips, grated carrot, seedless raisins, orange segments, tinned pineapple cubes, or sliced raw mushrooms.

● Shred Chinese leaves and cook in 1 inch (2.5cm) boiling salted water for 5 minutes until just tender. Drain, add a knob of butter, salt and pepper and chopped parsley.

● Allow 1 head for 4 servings for salad.

● Chinese leaves will keep for at least 10 days in the refrigerator placed in a plastic bag or the salad drawer. It's a good buy for a single person as it can be shredded and used for salad over several days.

Courgettes

Smooth firm small courgettes not more than 6 inches (15cm) long have the most tender skins and the best flavour. No need to peel or remove the seeds. Just wash courgettes and trim ends.

● Whole small courgettes are good steamed for about 5 minutes and served tossed in butter. Or cut larger courgettes in diagonal slices before steaming them.

● Salt slices and leave in a colander for 30 minutes to draw juices. Rinse under the cold tap and press dry in absorbent paper to remove excess water, then use for frying.

● Fry gently for about 20 minutes in a covered pan with melted butter until tender – use about 1 oz (25g) butter per 1 lb (450g) courgettes. Then sprinkle with chopped herbs or toss courgettes in herb butter.

● Alternatively, shake courgettes in seasoned flour and deep fry until golden and crisp. Drain on absorbent paper and sprinkle with vinegar. Serve with grilled meats.

● For salads, blanch courgette slices in boiling water for 2 minutes, then toss in an oil and vinegar dressing. Combine them with tomato slices and chopped parsley.

● Allow 1 lb (450g) courgettes for 4 servings.

● Store courgettes in salad drawer of refrigerator and use within 3–4 days.

Cucumber

Avoid soft, shrivelled cucumbers or extremely large cucumbers, which tend to be full of seeds. Look instead for small, smooth-skinned ones.

● Do not peel cucumbers for salads; just slice them thinly. For decorative slices, score cucumber lengthways with the prongs of a fork before slicing it.

● Cut cucumbers in half lengthways and scoop out seeds with a teaspoon. Slice diagonally or cut in chunks. Mix with oil and vinegar dressing, mayonnaise or yoghurt. To keep slices crisp do not add the dressing until just before serving.

● To remove the bitter juices, slice or chop the cucumber, sprinkle with salt and leave to stand in a colander for about 30 minutes. Rinse in cold water, then drain and pat dry in absorbent paper.

● Thinly sliced unpeeled cucumber makes an attractive garnish for salads. Use slices to line the inside of a glass serving bowl before filling it with salad.

● Allow ½ cucumber for 4 servings.

● If cucumber is purchased in a polythene skin, leave it on until ready to use, or wrap uncovered cucumbers in newspaper and leave in a cool place – not in the refrigerator as extreme cold spoils the flavour. Once cut, cover the end with a piece of kitchen foil kept in place with a rubber band.

Fennel

Look for fresh bulbs with evenly trimmed tops. This is the Florence fennel that is widely cultivated in southern Europe for its thick and fleshy leaf stalk, as distinct from the common fennel which is a perennial that can be grown in any country garden and of which only the delicate leaves are used in the kitchen. Florence fennel has a distinct aniseed flavour which is fresh and pleasant and becomes milder when cooked. Trim the base and green tops and remove any damaged stalk.

Fennel au gratin: Cut whole fennel in half lengthways. Add to boiling salted water and simmer for about 20 minutes until tender. Drain and arrange in a buttered flameproof dish, then sprinkle with grated cheese and breadcrumbs. Put under the grill or in the oven until cheese has melted.

● Cook until tender and serve in a cheese or white sauce made using the cooking liquid.

● Shred the bulbs across so fennel falls into slivers and dress with oil and vinegar. It makes a good salad on its own or add to other salad mixtures in the way you would celery.

● Shred the fennel and cook in boiling salted water for 10 minutes. Drain and serve tossed in butter, especially with fish.

● Allow ½–1 head per person.

Globe artichokes

Globe artichokes should be a good green colour with tight clinging fleshy leaves and about 6 inches (15cm) of stem attached. Remove the 4 lower leaves, then hold firmly and snap off stem close to base. Rub the cut part with lemon to prevent discoloration. Trim the leafy top by cutting off about ½ inch (1cm) with a sharp knife. Soak globe artichokes in cold water with a squeeze of lemon juice added until ready to cook.

● Add to boiling salted water – use about 2 teaspoons salt per 1 pint (600ml) water – in a large pan and cook, uncovered, for about 20 minutes, or until a base leaf pulls out easily. Drain the artichokes upside down. Pull out the hairy choke and scrape out excess hairs with a teaspoon.

● Serve warm with melted butter, vinaigrette or herb mayonnaise (page 121) for dipping the fleshy base of each leaf. For the base, or *fond*, you will need a knife and fork.

● Allow 1 per person.

Jerusalem artichokes

Jerusalem artichokes are pale buff-coloured tubers which grow underground; modern varieties are less knobbly than they used to be. Scrub well, peel and plunge into cold water with a squeeze of lemon juice to prevent discoloration – a saucer on top will keep them submerged.

● Bring the artichokes to the boil in salted water to which a little lemon juice or vinegar has been added and cook for about 30 minutes, then drain. Serve with melted butter or in a white sauce or cheese sauce.

Roasted artichokes: Blanch in boiling water for 5 minutes, then drain and roast artichokes around a joint or in a baking tin with hot drippings. Set above centre in an oven heated to 375°F (190°C) or Gas no. 5 and cook for 30–40 minutes.

● One raw artichoke peeled and thinly sliced or grated into a winter salad will add a delicious crunchy texture.

● Allow 1½–2 lb (700–900g) for 4 servings.

Leeks

Look for leeks with lots of white stem; avoid any with withering yellow tops. Old leeks have a thick core running up the stem and are not recommended even for soups. Trim roots and cut green tops from about 2 inches (5cm) above where they start to separate. Slice leeks in half lengthways, leaving them hinged on one side, and to within 1 inch (2.5cm) of the base. Wash well under cold running water, opening the layers with your fingers to remove all dirt. If leeks are to be simmered and served whole it's a good idea to tie the washed leeks in bundles of 2 or 3 with a 1 inch (2.5cm) wide gauze bandage.

● Cook in boiling salted water for about 15 minutes, then drain. Serve with melted butter or a white sauce or cheese sauce made using half cooking liquid and half milk.

● Allow cooked leeks to cool and serve in an oil and vinegar dressing. Sprinkle with chopped parsley and chopped hard-boiled egg.

● Raw leeks can be shredded crossways and the layers separated for use in winter salads but use sparingly.

● Allow about 1½–2 lb (700–900g) leeks for 4 servings.

Lettuce

Hothouse varieties are soft-leaved and tender; outdoor varieties are crisp with a firm heart. Trim outer leaves.

Round or *cabbage lettuce* has loosely packed, dark green leaves. Wash lettuce by dunking it up and down in a bowl of cold water so the suction draws out grit; keep changing the water until it remains clear. Separate into leaves, then shake leaves dry in a tea-towel or use one of those salad spinners.

● Tear leaves for salad or roll leaves up in bundles and shred across to use for prawn cocktails or as a garnish.

● This variety of lettuce makes the best soup – the colour will be a lovely shade of green.

● To store washed lettuce, put it in a polythene bag and tie closed – the important thing is to exclude the air. Lettuce will become crisp and crunchy after a few hours in the refrigerator and will keep for several days, but make sure lettuce is completely dry or drops of water will turn leaves brown.

Cos lettuce is an elongated variety, very firm and crisp. Separate the leaves, rinse and shake dry. Replace leaves in a bundle and shred across for use in salads.

Iceberg lettuce has a firm crisp heart and crisp outer leaves which are often removed before lettuce is sold. Keep the head whole and remove the centre core with a knife. Hold whole lettuce, core end up, under cold running water to clean, then turn upside down and drain thoroughly.

● Using a stainless steel knife, cut the lettuce lengthways into slices about 1 inch (2.5cm) thick. Then cut slices crossways into crisp chunks.

● To shred, cut the head in half lengthways, then place halves cut side down on a board and slice across.

● Store in the salad drawer of the refrigerator for up to 1 week – it keeps longer than other varieties.

Marrow

Choose tender young marrows about 9–12 inches (22.5–30cm) long. No need to peel young marrows but older ones have tough skins and are best if peeled. Cut marrow in half lengthways and remove seeds, then cut flesh in chunky cubes.

● Boil in salted water for 5–7 minutes, then drain well and serve with butter.

● Marrow is very watery and is better if cooked in the oven. Blanch pieces in boiling water for 1 minute, then drain and place in a casserole. Top with flakes of butter and cook in an oven heated to 350°F (180°C) or Gas no. 4 for 30 minutes. Serve sprinkled with plenty of seasoning and chopped parsley.

● Allow 1½ lb (700g) for 4 servings.

Mushrooms

Buy firm fresh mushrooms and choose the right type for your dish. *Button mushrooms* are tightly closed with a mild flavour and do not colour sauces or soups. *Cup mushrooms* have pink gills just showing and are for general purpose. Large *flat mushrooms* are completely open and have the most flavour; they are best for grilling or frying.

● Do not wash mushrooms before storing, just leave in the supermarket pack, or if bought loose, place in a covered container in the lowest section of the refrigerator – buttons keep best.

● Mushrooms absorb water like a sponge so just wipe with a damp cloth to remove the dirt or rinse quickly under cold running water, then quickly pat dry in absorbent paper. Do not peel but trim stalks where necessary.

● Leave buttons or cups whole or slice thickly with a stainless steel knife and fry in hot butter. Allow 1 oz (25g) butter per 8 oz (225g) mushrooms and toss over moderate heat for 2–3 minutes only. Place flats in hot butter gill side down and cook for about 4 minutes, turning once.

● Try rubbing a crushed clove of garlic over the base of the frying pan before adding the butter to fry mushrooms.

● Grill only flats. Leave flat mushrooms whole and brush all over with melted butter or oil. Place under the grill for 3–4 minutes and serve with steaks, omelettes or as part of a mixed grill.

● Season mushrooms with salt and freshly milled pepper after cooking to avoid drawing juices. A squeeze of lemon juice over mushrooms adds to the flavour.

● Small buttons can be sliced and served in your favourite oil and vinegar dressing as a salad. They look pretty with chopped parsley added.

● For kebabs use buttons or cups and blanch mushrooms in boiling water for 1 minute to prevent them from splitting when you push them on to the skewers.

● Allow 8–12 oz (225–350g) for 4 servings.

Onions

Good onions should be firm with dry skins and thin wispy necks; reject any that are sprouting. Flavourwise you'll find English onions are strong and those from warmer climates such as Spain are milder in flavour. Take a slice from the top and base and peel away brown outer skin only. Hold onions under cold water when doing this if they make you cry. Small button onions can be peeled more quickly by putting them together in a bowl and pouring over boiling water to cover, then leaving for 5 minutes and draining. You'll find skins slip off easily.

● Choose onions of similar size and add to salted cold water and bring to the boil, then simmer gently, uncovered, to prevent the centres from coming out. Medium-sized onions take 25–30 minutes to cook, less for button onions. Test with a knife tip for tenderness. Drain and toss in hot butter with a little English made mustard added or toss them in a white sauce.

● Thinly slice or finely chop onions and add to hot butter or oil in a frying pan. Onions take time to completely soften so cook over low heat for about 10 minutes, though 5 minutes is usually enough if the onions are going to be cooked longer in a casserole or soup. A pinch of sugar added towards the end of cooking encourages browning. To 'sweat', or soften, onions without taking colour, cover the pan with a lid.

● Blanch onions for 5 minutes in boiling water, then drain. Place in hot drippings round a joint and roast for about 45 minutes, basting occasionally.

Deep-fried onion rings: Peel 2 large onions and cut into thin slices. Separate into rings and chill in iced water for about 20 minutes so that they are nice and crisp. Then drain onion rings and pat dry. Beat 1 egg white with a fork, just enough to break up the white but not to make it frothy. Dip the onion rings (spear them on a fork) first in the egg white and then in seasoned flour. Shake away any excess coating and deep fry the rings in hot fat for 1–2 minutes, or until crisp and pale golden. They make a marvellous garnish for grilled steaks and liver.

● Add a whole peeled onion stuck with a clove to chicken or beef stock, or infuse in milk for about 15 minutes when making white or bread sauce to give extra flavour.

● For a hint of onion flavour in mousses or milk and cheese mixtures, twist an onion half cut crossways on a lemon squeezer to extract the juice.

● Onions to be stuffed should be baked unskinned in an oven heated to 400°F (200°C) or Gas no. 6 until they feel tender when pressed. Allow to cool and peel off skins. Spanish onions, which are larger and flatter than other onions, are particularly suitable for stuffing.

● For meatball or terrine recipes where onion is mixed with minced meat, put the onion through the mincer or into the food processor together with the meat ingredients so texture is even.

● Rinse hands, knife and chopping board in cold water to remove onion smells.

● Allow 1½ lb (900g) for 4 servings.

● Onions are sold dry. In other words, they have been uprooted and hung to get rid of the moisture in the surface skin; this way they keep for longer. Store onions in a dry place.

Shallots are small with violet tinted skins and are sweeter and more delicate in flavour than onions, which make them useful for flavouring delicate sauces. They are also good added to fish dishes. Cut a slice from top and bottom and peel as for onions.

● Finely chop and sauté in butter to soften, then add chopped parsley and serve over steaks or grilled fish.

Spring onions are usually used raw. The stems should be crisp and the bulbs almost unnoticeable – more a thickening at the stem than a distinct bulb shape. Trim roots and pull away any coarse outer leaves and thin membrane-like covering, then trim green tops.

● Finely chop both the green tops and white bottoms of spring onions and add to salads. The tender part of the green stems makes a good substitute for chives. Try adding chopped spring onion tops to omelettes, or mix with soured cream and use as a topping for baked potatoes.

Parsnips

Parsnips should be firm and free from blemishes. Avoid very large or soft ones that look shrivelled; they should snap easily. Brush off dirt and scrub clean. Peel and cut in half lengthways and remove woody core, then cut across in quarters or in half.

● Cover with salted cold water and bring to the boil. Simmer for 30 minutes, then drain and dry for a moment over the heat. Toss with butter.

Roast parsnips: Blanch for 5 minutes. Drain and dry for a moment over the heat, then roll in seasoned flour. Add to a roasting tin with hot drippings and baste. Roast in an oven heated to 375°F (190°C) or Gas no. 5 for 45 minutes. They will become deliciously crisp and brown and make an excellent vegetable on their own or combined with roast potatoes round a joint.

● Allow 1½ lb (700g) for 4 servings.

● Remove from plastic bag, if they were bought that way, and store in a cool place.

Peas

Peas in pods should look fresh and rustle when the greengrocer picks them up. Look for pods that are not too fat: the peas inside should be tender and sweet. Shell the peas before cooking.

● Add to boiling salted water with a pinch of sugar and a sprig of fresh mint added. Cook for 10 minutes, then drain and toss in butter.

● Cook peas the French way on a bed of lettuce with a little butter and finely chopped spring onion added (page 148). This is a marvellous way to perk up frozen peas.

● Allow 2 lb (900g) unshelled peas for 4.

Mange-tout, which means 'eat all', are deluxe peas in the pod. They are delicious – you eat pods and tiny peas inside. Rinse mange-tout, then top and tail.

● Add to boiling salted water and cook for 6–8 minutes, then drain and serve tossed in butter with a pinch of sugar.

● Allow 1 lb (450g) for 4 servings.

Peppers

Peppers should be firm and bright coloured with smooth and shiny skins. Different colour peppers come from the same plant. They start off green and gradually turn from yellow to red as they mature; the red ones being more mature are sweeter. Peppers are crisp and crunchy and so are good in salads. When cooked they soften and have a sweeter taste. The inner seeds are always removed: for whole peppers cut around stalk end and pull out seeds with white membrane. Otherwise, cut peppers in half and remove seeds and white membrane.

● Cut peppers into rings, strips or dice and add to salads for crunchiness and colour. Green peppers look good in rice salad or coleslaw and can be used to decorate potato salad.

Green pepper salad: Some people find peppers more digestible if the skin is removed for salads. Place peppers under a hot grill for about 5 minutes, turning them as the skin blisters and blackens. Wrap in a tea-towel for 10 minutes and skins will peel off easily. The colour is a much brighter green after this treatment too and peppers soften slightly. Halve, deseed and cut the peppers into ½ inch (1cm) strips and toss them in an oil and vinegar dressing.

● Chunks of peeled pepper are nice pushed on to kebab skewers. They make a pretty contrast of colour with chunks of white fish or chicken, but peppers are a favourite kebab ingredient with any meat.

● Use finely chopped pepper as a pretty garnish for soups. Use red pepper to garnish pale green soups and green pepper to sprinkle over tomato soup. Chopped pepper is also a nice garnish for party dips.

● Try slicing and frying green peppers with an equal quantity of sliced onion in hot butter and oil – both take about 10 minutes to soften. Season to taste with salt and freshly milled pepper and add a dash of lemon juice. Serve with steak or use as a filling for omelettes.

● Allow 1 pepper per person, or less for salads.

● Peppers will keep for 1 week in the salad drawer of the refrigerator.

Potatoes

Maincrop potatoes

Maincrop varieties are wonderfully versatile. They can be baked, boiled, roasted and mashed. Choose potatoes with shallow eyes. Avoid sprouts, cuts and soft or green spots. Scrub potatoes well and as they are peeled place them in a bowl of salted cold water until ready for cooking to prevent discoloration. Peel them thinly and cut potatoes in even-sized chunks.

● Add to salted cold water and bring to the boil, then lower the heat and simmer gently for 20 minutes until tender. Drain and dry for a moment in the pan over the heat. Then toss with butter.

● Maincrop potatoes are the ones to use for thickening vegetable soup.

● Remember that boiling potatoes for roasting is not to partially cook them, but to heat potatoes through to speed up their roasting time. Potatoes that are overcooked become soft at the edges and do not roast well. Bring cut-up potatoes slowly to the boil, then draw off the heat. Always drain potatoes well, return to the hot pan and dry for a few minutes over the heat – then they won't spit when you add them to the hot fat. You can further speed up cooking time by adding a good lump of dripping to the hot pan and tossing the potatoes to coat them, before turning them into the roasting tin.

Roast potatoes: Cut potatoes in half or in quarters for roasting. Bring them just to the boil, then drain and dry in the pan over the heat. For crisp roast potatoes, roll the potatoes in seasoned flour. Add to hot dripping in a separate tin from the roast and cook in an oven heated to 425°F (220°C) or Gas no. 7 for 1 hour.

● Buy potatoes for baking where they are sold loose so you can choose even sized ones; King Edwards are one of the best varieties for this method of cooking.

Baked potatoes with toppings: Select potatoes of even size, scrub them clean, then while still damp roll them in kitchen salt for a crisp skin or rub with buttered paper for a soft skin. Arrange potatoes on a baking tray so they don't touch and bake in an oven heated to 425°F (220°C) or Gas no. 7 for 1–1½ hours, or until they feel soft when gently pressed at the sides. When cooked make a criss-cross slit on top of each potato and squeeze the potato gently in a cloth to open. Good toppings include:

cubes of butter: cut chilled butter into ½ inch (1cm) cubes and pile in a dish.

soured cream: serve plain or with chopped chives, or a spoonful of lumpfish caviar added.

chopped spring onions: include white and green parts of spring onion stems and finely chop.

crisp bacon bits: trimmed and grilled bacon rashers cooked until crisp and then crumbled in pieces when cold.

chopped mushrooms: small button mushrooms sliced or chopped and lightly fried in butter, with chopped parsley added.

Sauté potatoes: Slice peeled potatoes about ¼ inch (5mm) thick. Add slices to boiling salted water. Bring back to the boil, then simmer for exactly 5 minutes and drain. Add slices to hot butter with 1 tablespoon oil added and fry quickly for about 5 minutes, turning potato slices until they are golden and crisp. Sprinkle with salt and a little chopped parsley or dried rosemary.

Creamed potatoes: Press cooked potatoes through a sieve into a warmed mixing bowl. Add a good seasoning of salt and pepper, 1 oz (25g) butter and a little hot milk. Beat with a wooden spoon, adding more milk as required, to produce a smooth, creamy consistency. Creamed potatoes can be prepared ready for serving and kept hot, if you cover the bowl with a plate and set the bowl over a saucepan of simmering water until ready to serve. For a special occasion, finely chopped chives, chopped parsley or spring onions may be added and a little grated orange rind added to the potatoes is especially nice when served along with a beef casserole.

Duchesse potatoes: These are prepared in the same way as creamed potatoes except that they are mixed with beaten egg instead of hot milk. Mix to a smooth piping consistency and spoon mixture into a large nylon piping bag fitted with a rosette nozzle. Pipe whirls of potato on a buttered baking tray and brush each one with melted butter. They can be prepared to this stage which makes them useful for a dinner party. Place potatoes above centre in an oven heated to 400°F (200°C) or Gas no. 6 for about 10 minutes, or until golden. This same mixture can be used for piped potato borders.

Potato chips: To cook chips that are crisp on the outside and tender in the middle you must fry them twice. The first frying cooks the chips and the second makes them brown and crisp. Use maincrop potatoes and cut into thin chips. Rinse chips in cold water and pat dry in a clean tea-towel. Heat sufficient oil to cover potatoes in a deep frying pan. Add the chipped potatoes and cook until they are tender but not browned. Drain from the hot fat. Return the chips to the pan and fry quickly to a golden brown. Drain well, sprinkle with salt and serve immediately.

● Allow 1–1½ lb (450–700g) for 4 servings.

● Store maincrop potatoes in a cool dark place but not in the refrigerator.

New potatoes

New potatoes are as different from maincrop potatoes as chalk from cheese. They have quite a different flavour and texture. The British varieties have very flaky skins. If skins rub-off easily, then this usually means that the potato has come on the market within 24 hours of harvesting.

● Choose small new potatoes if you have a choice. Larger ones that have to be cut in half spoil the effect. You don't even need to scrub or scrape the small ones if you wash them well in cold water. After cooking the skins peel off easily, if you really want to remove them, but new potatoes with the skins on are the most delicious of all.

● Add new potatoes to boiling salted water that barely covers them. When they come back to the boil, cover with pan lid and simmer for about 15 minutes. Drain and dry for a moment in the pan, then toss in butter with snipped chives.

● Toss boiled new potatoes in butter with a little garlic that has been crushed to a purée with salt, then pour over a little double cream. Serve with grills and steak.

Baked new potatoes: Scrub or scrape even-sized new potatoes and place on a large square of kitchen foil. Add a good lump of butter and a seasoning of salt and freshly milled pepper. Draw foil edges up over potatoes and secure to make a baggy parcel. Place on a baking sheet. Set in an oven heated to 375°F (190°C) or Gas no. 5 and bake for 1 hour. Open foil parcel and serve the hot, tender new potatoes in the buttery juices.

Buttercrisp new potatoes: These are cooked in butter only in a covered pan so they come out crisp and brown, but soft inside. A lidded frying pan is best so the potatoes cook evenly in one layer. Scrub 1½ lb (700g) new potatoes and dry them well. Melt 2 oz (50g) butter in a frying pan over low heat. Add the potatoes and stir to coat them in the butter. Cover the pan with a lid and cook gently for 20–30 minutes. Shake pan occasionally so potatoes brown and cook evenly. Sprinkle with coarse salt from a mill before serving. These are marvellous served with hot or cold salmon or salmon trout.

Crunchy new potatoes: Boil 1½ lb (700g) new potatoes until tender, then drain. Add 1 tablespoon coarse oatmeal to the hot cooking pan and toast over the heat just long enough for it to crisp and brown. Return the cooked potatoes along with a good lump of butter to the pan and toss until well coated. The potatoes will have a delicious crunchy texture that goes well with bacon or ham.

● New potatoes are the very best for salads. Toss them in mayonnaise or an oil and vinegar dressing while still warm or coat them in mayonnaise.

● Allow 1½ lb (700g) for 4 servings.

● With new potatoes freshness is very important: buy little and often.

Radishes

Varieties of radishes differ in their degree of pungency; some are all red and others, often more mildly flavoured, are red and white. Just wash in cold water and trim roots if necessary.

● Leave on stems and serve whole with a bowl of salt for dipping.

● Trim and slice radishes to add a lovely red and white colour to a green salad, or sprinkle them over the top of a potato salad.

Radish roses: Trim root end and stalk neatly, then make 4–8 small, deep cuts across the centre at the stalk end. Leave in iced water for 2 hours until the cuts open to form petals. Use to garnish plates of sandwiches. If you make about 12 roses and pile them in a clear glass brandy balloon, they will look stunning on a cheese tray.

● Radishes will keep crisp in the salad drawer of the refrigerator for 2–3 days.

Salsify

Known as the vegetable oyster, salsify has long tapering roots with brown skin and white flesh. Salsify turns brown on exposure to the air so handle carefully. To prepare, scrub well, then scrape or peel the roots and plunge into cold water with a squeeze of lemon juice added to prevent discoloration; place a saucer on top to keep them submerged in the water.

● Add to boiling salted water to which a little lemon juice has been added. Simmer for about 30 minutes until tender, then slice and toss in butter.

● An old-fashioned method that is very good is to cut scraped roots into short lengths and soak overnight in milk and water to whiten, then cook in the soaking liquid for about 30 minutes until tender. Drain and serve in a white sauce made using the cooking liquid with a dash of lemon juice added, or serve with a cheese sauce.

● For salads, slice or dice scraped roots and squeeze over lemon juice or mix immediately with an oil and vinegar dressing.

● Allow 1½–2 lb (700–900g) for 4 servings.

Spinach

Spinach must be fresh and crisp with large green leaves. Discard any yellow or wilted leaves. Wash leaves well in several changes of cold water and pull away the midribs. When water is free of sand or grit, spinach is ready to cook.

● Lift straight from the water to the pan and cook, covered with a pan lid, for 10–15 minutes. There will be enough water clinging to the leaves for cooking. Drain and press well to extract water. Return spinach to saucepan and dry over the heat. Toss with butter for serving.

Creamed spinach purée: Cook as above, then finely chop to make a purée. Reheat in the saucepan with butter, 2–3 tablespoons double cream and a seasoning of salt, pepper and grated nutmeg.

● Tender young summer spinach makes a good salad vegetable.

● Allow 2 lb (900g) for 4 servings.

Swedes

Swedes have tough outer skins that should first be scrubbed and then thickly peeled with a vegetable knife. Then cut in even-sized chunks.

Mashed swedes: Cover with salted cold water and bring to the boil. Simmer for 20 minutes, then drain and dry in the saucepan over the heat. Mash well with salt, plenty of freshly milled pepper and a knob of butter. A little fresh cream can also be added for extra smoothness.

● Allow 1½ lb (700g) per 4 servings.

Sweetcorn

Corn on the cob deteriorates more quickly after picking than any other vegetable, which explains why corn from your garden tastes so good. Check that the corn you buy has good green husks and silks – they should not have been removed by the greengrocer. A cob with shrivelled kernels indicates it is old. Strip off the outer leaves, husks and silks just before cooking.

● Plunge corn into boiling unsalted water to which a little sugar has been added. Simmer for

15–20 minutes until kernels are tender. Lift cobs out with tongs and transfer to a serving platter lined with a folded napkin. Serve with plenty of melted butter for pouring over and salt for sprinkling. Hold with fingers or special corn skewers, or pierce a fork into each end.

● Allow 1 corn on the cob per person for a first course or 1–2 as a vegetable accompaniment.

Tomatoes

The perfect ripe tomato is red all over; it is also red throughout the inside. If seeds are a pink colour and not green, then the tomato will be deliciously sweet. Green tomatoes can be ripened in a drawer or paper bag. Add an apple to speed up ripening.

● **Stuffed tomatoes:** Cut a slice off the tops and scoop out the inside with a teaspoon. Season with salt and turn tomatoes upside down on a plate to drain for 30 minutes. Use the larger beefsteak tomatoes for this when you can find them. Fill tomatoes with prawns in mayonnaise (page 64), mashed avocado well seasoned with salt and pepper and a good squeeze of lemon juice, or tuna fish in mayonnaise. Replace slice of tomato as a lid and serve on crisp lettuce.

● Remove skins for salads: nick the skin at stalk end with knife tip. Place tomatoes in a bowl and cover with boiling water – as soon as skin curls back, drain and run under cold water, so tomatoes don't soften, then peel the skins.

● Decorative tomato quarters look more interesting if the cut length of each wedge is dipped in finely chopped parsley or Parmesan cheese to make a line of contrasting colour.

● If tomatoes are sour or acid sprinkle them with a little castor sugar and add a little sugar to tomato soups and sauces.

Grilled tomatoes: Slice unpeeled tomatoes in half and sprinkle with salt and pepper, a pinch of sugar and some dried herbs – basil is best. Then flake butter or drizzle oil over the tops and place under a moderate grill for 6–8 minutes.

● Allow 1–2 tomatoes per person.

Turnips

Maincrop turnips should be firm and feel heavy for their size with no scars. Reject any with yellow or wilted tops. Maincrop turnips are more yellow in colour than new turnips. Scrub them well and thickly peel with a knife.

● Cut in even-sized chunks and bring to the boil in salted water to cover. Simmer for 20 minutes until tender. Drain, then dry in the pan over the heat for a moment. Serve with butter.

● Cook until tender, then mash with butter and a good seasoning of freshly milled pepper.

● Allow 1½ lb (700g) for 4 servings.

New turnips are sometimes sold in bunches. They have a sweet flavour and white flesh. Scrub clean and take a slice from the top and base but leave whole; skins are removed after cooking.

● Add to boiling salted water and simmer for about 25 minutes until tender, then drain and remove the skins – they will slip off easily. Toss in butter to serve.

● Cut turnips in even-sized pieces and cook, covered, with just a little water and sugar and butter to glaze them. Serve as a garnish for roasts.

● Allow 1½–2 lb (700–900g) for 4 servings.

Watercress

Fresh watercress has a delicious peppery flavour. Just pick over and rinse quickly in cold water; long stalks can be trimmed a little.

● Use as a garnish or add to sandwiches. Toss with oil and vinegar or lemon juice for a salad.

● At its best watercress makes a delicious soup that can be served hot or cold (page 30). Add to soup during last minute of cooking for best flavour.

● Watercress will keep for 1–2 days if rinsed and shaken dry of all water drops and stored in a closed polythene bag (gently press out air) in the lowest section of the refrigerator. To revive watercress, treat it like cut flowers: trim off roots and place stems in a jar of cold water.

Using pulses

● Dried peas, beans and lentils, collectively known as pulses, are the edible seeds of leguminous plants. They are cheap, nourishing and handy for the storecupboard since they keep for up to 1 year. A health food store is a good source for more unusual varieties.

● *Butter beans* are in any supermarket. This flat, white bean keeps a good shape on cooking. I always take the trouble to pop cooked butter beans out of their skins; it makes all the difference to the taste and appearance. Butter beans make an excellent vegetable and are traditionally served with boiled bacon when they are tossed with butter, freshly milled pepper and chopped parsley. You can also toss cooked butter beans in butter with lightly fried onions and a teaspoon concentrated tomato purée. Serve them with pork.

● *Lentils* come in a range of colours but the small red split lentils are the most popular. Split lentils are inclined to break up on cooking but they do tenderize very quickly and are best used in soups or purées. Lentil soup has a lovely flavour if you have the cooking liquid from a bacon joint to use as the soup stock or a bundle of trimmed bacon rinds to add to the pot.

● *Haricot beans* are the aristocrat of the pulse family. These small white beans are traditionally used in casserole dishes. Although small in size they are nice as a vegetable, especially if you cook them, then toss in butter and add a little fried onion and chopped peeled tomato.

● *Kidney beans* are a good buy for salads because the red colour is pretty. Bear in mind that beans have a mealy texture and they make the best salads when mixed with crunchy vegetables. A mixture of cooked kidney beans, chopped green peppers, shredded celery and chopped parsley in an oil and vinegar dressing makes a nice salad. There is a white variety of kidney beans called *cannellini* which is also good for salads.

● *Green split peas* are not so easy to find as the yellow variety but they are one of my favourites and make a wonderful green soup with leeks. The soup will taste even better if you simmer a small bacon joint in the soup and then return the cooked and diced bacon meat to the soup before serving.

● *Mung beans* are the prettiest of the pulses. They are tiny and a deep green. These are popular for sprouting when they can be used raw in salads. To do this, soak mung beans overnight in cold water to cover, then drain and spread on a plate covered with absorbent paper. Add a sprinkling of water to keep them moist and put beans and plate inside a polythene bag. Set in a dark place for 3 days and they will sprout; they are ready to use when the shoots are about 1 inch (2.5 cm) long. To use, snip off root ends and add to salads.

To cook pulses

● With the exception of lentils, all pulses require soaking before use. An overnight soak is best as it makes them more digestible and ensures they will cook in the required time.

● Rinse in cold water, then place in a bowl and cover generously with cold water. Soft water is best; in hard water areas use water that has been boiled and allowed to cool.

● Always strain pulses from the soaking liquid. Put them in a saucepan with fresh cold water to cover and bring slowly to the boil for cooking.

● You can add a peeled onion, a carrot or bouquet garni to the water for flavour. Cover with a lid, simmer and avoid stirring or pulses will break up. Add salt towards the end of the cooking time.

● Cooking methods are the same but times vary with different pulses. You will find split ones like lentils and split peas take about 40 minutes; whole beans such as butter beans, kidney beans and haricot beans will need about 1–1½ hours. Kidney beans should be first boiled for about 10 minutes, then simmered for rest of cooking time.

● Test beans for tenderness by pressing one between the fingers; there should be no hard core. In the case of the larger varieties, try biting a bean – they can be deceptive and feel soft on the outside while still hard in the centre.

● If you toss cooked beans while still hot in an oil and vinegar dressing you will find they take the flavour as they cool. Make dressing sharper than usual by using equal parts oil and vinegar.

Aubergine and tomato ragout

Cut the aubergines in bite-sized pieces, place in a colander, sprinkle with salt and leave to stand for 30 minutes to draw some of the juices. Rinse and pat dry in absorbent paper. Peel and slice the onions. Scald the tomatoes, peel the skins and cut in quarters.

Melt the butter in a saucepan over low heat, add the onions and fry gently for 5 minutes to soften but not brown. Mash the garlic to a purée with salt and add to the pan along with the aubergines, tomatoes, sugar, bay leaves and mixed herbs. Toss together and season with freshly milled pepper. Cover with a pan lid and simmer, stirring occasionally, for 40–45 minutes. Remove the pan lid towards the end of cooking time to allow some of the juices to evaporate. When ready the ragout should be quite thick. Serve with steaks or chops.

Serves 6

3 medium-sized aubergines
salt
2 large onions
1 lb (450g) tomatoes
1 oz (25g) butter
1 clove garlic
1 teaspoon castor sugar
2 bay leaves
good pinch of dried mixed herbs
freshly milled pepper

Stuffed aubergines

Cut the aubergines in half lengthways. Using a sharp knife, criss-cross the cut surfaces, sprinkle with salt and leave, cut surface down, for 30 minutes to draw some of the juices. Rinse and pat dry in absorbent paper. Heat the oil in a large frying pan, add the aubergines (cut surface down) and fry gently for 5–10 minutes, or until the flesh is soft. Scoop out aubergine flesh with a spoon and place shells in a greased ovenproof dish. Coarsely chop the aubergine flesh.

Peel and finely chop the onions and garlic. Trim and chop the mushrooms. Heat extra oil in the frying pan, add the onions and fry gently for 5 minutes to soften but not brown, then add the garlic and chopped aubergine flesh. Cook over moderate heat for 2–3 minutes, stirring to prevent mixture sticking to the pan. Add the chopped mushrooms, parsley and breadcrumbs. Season well with salt and pepper. Fill each aubergine shell with the mixture and sprinkle the tops with the grated cheese. Bake in an oven heated to 375°F (190°C) or Gas no. 5 for 30–40 minutes.

Serves 4

2 large aubergines
salt
oil, for frying
1–2 tablespoons grated hard cheese

Stuffing
2 onions
1 clove garlic
4 oz (100g) button mushrooms
3 tablespoons chopped parsley
3 oz (75g) soft white breadcrumbs
salt and freshly milled pepper

Corn fritters

Sift the flour into a mixing bowl. Add the egg and milk and whisk to a smooth batter. Thoroughly drain the sweetcorn and add to the mixture. Season with salt and pepper.

Heat the oil in a frying pan. Carefully spoon 4 tablespoons of the corn batter into the hot oil, allowing space for the fritters to spread. Fry for 2 minutes until golden, then turn and cook the second side for about 2 minutes until golden. Remove from the pan with a perforated spoon and drain fritters on absorbent paper. Keep warm (uncovered) while frying the rest of the batter to make 12 fritters. Serve with fried chicken or grilled bacon.

Serves 4

4 oz (100g) self-raising flour
1 egg
¼ pint (150ml) milk
1 × 7 oz (198g) tin whole kernel
   sweetcorn
salt and freshly milled pepper
2–3 tablespoons oil

Celeriac in lemon sauce

Serves 4

1–1½ lb (450g–700g) celeriac

Sauce
1½ oz (40g) butter
1 oz (25g) plain flour
½ pint (300ml) milk
salt and freshly milled pepper
squeeze of lemon juice
1 egg yolk
1–2 tablespoons single cream

Remove the thick outer peel of the celeriac and cut celeriac in thick slices, then cut each slice into strips like large chips. Add to a pan of boiling salted water and simmer gently for about 10 minutes until just tender. (Test with a knife tip; if overcooked, celeriac will be soggy.)

Meanwhile, make the sauce. Melt the butter in a saucepan over low heat and stir in the flour. Cook gently for 1 minute, then gradually stir in the milk. Bring to the boil, stirring all the time to make a smooth sauce, then lower the heat and simmer gently for 2–3 minutes. Season to taste with salt and pepper. Draw off the heat and stir in the lemon juice.

Blend the egg yolk and cream in a bowl and stir into the sauce. Return the pan to the heat and cook gently for 1 minute, but do not allow to boil. Thoroughly drain the celeriac, place in a buttered serving dish and pour over the sauce.

Glazed carrots

Serves 4

1 lb (450g) new carrots
½ small onion
1 bay leaf
1 teaspoon castor sugar
½ oz (15g) butter

Scrape the carrots and cut in slices or in dice. Peel and finely chop the onion. Put carrots and chopped onion into a saucepan, add the bay leaf, sugar, butter and sufficient water to just cover the vegetables. Cover with a pan lid and simmer gently for about 15–20 minutes until carrots are tender.

Remove the pan lid and continue to simmer carrots until the cooking liquid evaporates. When carrots begin to fry in the butter and are glazed, draw off the heat. Discard the bay leaf and serve.

Variation: Glazed carrots look pretty mixed with peas, but add peas towards the end of the cooking time because they take less time to cook.

Courgettes with herbs

Serves 4

1 lb (450g) small courgettes
1 small onion
1 oz (25g) butter
1 tablespoon finely chopped parsley
    or chives
salt and freshly milled pepper

Trim the courgettes and cut diagonally in slices. (If courgettes are large, add slices to a pan of boiling salted water and simmer for 2 minutes to blanch, then drain.)

Peel and finely chop the onion. Melt the butter in a frying pan over low heat. Add the onion, courgettes, parsley or chives and a seasoning of salt and pepper. Cover with a pan lid and cook gently for about 20 minutes. Serve with lasagne, pasta or steak.

Variation: Use oil instead of butter and serve these courgettes cold.

Stuffed green peppers

Using a sharp knife, carefully cut around the stem of each green pepper and pull out the white membrane with seeds. Rinse peppers to remove loose seeds and set aside while preparing the stuffing.

Peel and finely chop the onions for the stuffing. Heat the oil in a saucepan, add the onions and fry gently for 5 minutes to soften but not brown. Stir in the rice and mix with the onions and oil. Then stir in the hot stock, tomato purée and sultanas. Bring to the boil, cover with a pan lid, then simmer gently for about 20 minutes, or until rice has absorbed the liquid and the grains are tender. Draw off the heat and fluff the rice with a fork. Season with salt and pepper. Allow to cool.

Fill each green pepper case with stuffing and arrange peppers close together in a greased casserole dish. Blend together the oil, water, tomato purée and sugar. Pour mixture over the peppers. Cover with a lid or kitchen foil and bake in an oven heated to 350°F (180°C) or Gas no. 4 for 30–40 minutes. Allow to cool completely in the cooking liquid. Arrange cold stuffed peppers in a serving dish with the liquid spooned over. Serve at a buffet supper or cold table.

Serves 6

6 medium-sized green peppers
2 tablespoons oil
¼ pint (150ml) water
2 teaspoons concentrated tomato purée
1 teaspoon castor sugar

Rice stuffing
2 medium-sized onions
4 tablespoons oil
8 oz (225g) long-grain rice
1 pint (600ml) hot chicken stock
1 tablespoon concentrated tomato purée
4 oz (100g) sultanas
salt and freshly milled pepper

Hot spinach mould

Tear away the coarse stems and thoroughly wash spinach in cold water. Set aside 6 leaves. Pack wet spinach into a saucepan, cover with a pan lid, and cook over moderate heat for 10 minutes until spinach is quite soft. (The water clinging to the leaves will provide sufficient cooking liquid.) Drain well and purée in a blender or food processor or pass through a food mill.

Melt the butter in a saucepan over low heat. Stir in the flour and cook gently for 1 minute, then gradually stir in the milk. Bring to the boil, stirring all the time to make a smooth sauce, then lower the heat and simmer for 2–3 minutes. Draw off the heat and stir in the spinach purée, eggs, cream and a grating of nutmeg. Season with salt and pepper.

Immerse reserved spinach leaves in boiling water for a moment to soften and press dry in absorbent paper. Use to line a buttered 6 inch (15cm) soufflé dish. Pour in the creamed spinach mixture and turn any extending spinach leaves over the filling.

Place the soufflé dish in a large roasting tin and pour boiling water into the roasting tin to a depth of 1 inch (2.5cm). Bake in an oven heated to 350°F (180°C) or Gas no. 4 for 1 hour until set firm. Allow to cool for 5 minutes, then turn out and serve. This is delicious served with pork.

Serves 6

2 lb (900g) fresh spinach
1 oz (25g) butter
1 oz (25g) plain flour
½ pint (300ml) milk
2 eggs
1 tablespoon single cream
grated nutmeg
salt and freshly milled pepper

Marrow in parsley sauce

Serves 4

1 medium-sized marrow
salt and freshly milled pepper
1 oz (25g) butter

Sauce
1½ oz (40g) butter
1 oz (25g) flour
½ pint (300ml) milk
1 tablespoon chopped parsley
salt and freshly milled pepper

Peel, halve and remove the seeds from the marrow. Cut the flesh in bite-sized pieces and put into a pan. Cover with salted cold water and bring to the boil. Draw off the heat and drain – this blanching improves the colour of the flesh. Tip the marrow into a casserole dish, season with plenty of salt and pepper and add the butter. Cover with a lid, and cook in an oven heated to 350°F (180°C) or Gas no. 4 for 30 minutes until tender.

Meanwhile, melt the butter for the sauce in a saucepan over low heat and stir in the flour. Cook gently for 1 minute, then gradually stir in the milk. Bring to the boil, stirring all the time, to make a smooth sauce, then lower the heat and simmer gently for 2–3 minutes. Pour the liquid from the cooked marrow into the sauce and stir in the parsley. Season to taste with salt and pepper. Pour the sauce over the marrow and serve.

Red cabbage with apple

Serves 4–6

1 small or ½ large red cabbage
1 medium-sized onion
1 oz (25g) butter
2 large cooking apples
¼ pint (150ml) boiling water
1 oz (25g) castor sugar
juice of ½ lemon
salt and freshly milled pepper

Red cabbage retains its deep vibrant colour when cooked with acid cooking apples. Cut the cabbage in quarters, cut away the core and finely shred crossways. Peel and finely chop the onion. Melt the butter in a large saucepan over low heat, add the onion and fry gently for 5 minutes to soften but not brown.

Meanwhile, peel, core and coarsely chop the apples. Pack the red cabbage in the pan together with the chopped apples. Pour in the boiling water, add the sugar and lemon juice and season with salt and pepper. Mix ingredients together, cover with the pan lid, and cook gently for 1½–2 hours, stirring occasionally to prevent the cabbage from sticking to the pan. As the apple cooks it turns to a pulp and provides the moisture necessary for cooking the cabbage so you most likely will not need to add extra water. Red cabbage goes very well with fatty or rich meats such as hamburgers, sausages, pork or roast duck. This is a good vegetable dish to make in advance and reheat just before serving.

Fried chicory

Serves 4–6

4–6 heads of chicory
seasoned flour
2 oz (50g) butter

Remove outer damaged leaves and trim each head of chicory. Add to a pan of boiling salted water and cook for about 15 minutes until just tender. Drain and leave until completely cool. Then, lightly roll the heads of chicory in seasoned flour to completely coat them.

Melt the butter in a large frying pan over low heat and when hot and foaming, add the chicory. Fry gently for about 5 minutes, turning them once or twice, until chicory is golden brown and heated through. This makes a marvellous vegetable to serve with pork chops, lamb chops or roast beef.

Chestnut purée

Slit the flat sides of the chestnuts, add to a pan of boiling water and boil for 2 minutes. Drain and peel away the outer shells and inner skins. Return the peeled chestnuts to the pan and pour over sufficient mixed milk and stock to cover. Bring to the boil, then lower the heat and simmer gently for about 35–40 minutes, or until chestnuts are tender. Drain and set aside.

Peel and finely chop the onion. Melt 1 oz (25g) of the butter in a saucepan, add the onion and fry gently for 5 minutes to soften but not brown, then draw off the heat. Toss the cooked chestnuts in the onion and butter and mash to break them up. Press the mixture through a sieve to make a purée. Melt the remaining butter, add to the chestnut purée and season with salt and plenty of pepper. Beat in sufficient cream to make a smooth, soft purée. Serve hot or cold with roast pheasant, venison or roast turkey.

Serves 4–6

1 lb (450g) chestnuts
milk and chicken stock (see recipe)
1 medium-sized onion
1½ oz (40g) butter
salt and freshly milled pepper
4–6 tablespoons single cream

Caramelized onions

Choose small onions so you can serve two or more per person. Peel and leave them whole. Melt the butter in a pan large enough for the onions to stand in one layer, add the onions and turn them in the hot butter. Season with salt and pepper and sprinkle over the sugar. Fry gently for 5 minutes, turning the onions frequently and shaking the pan so that they are lightly browned all over.

Pour water into the pan to a depth of about ½ inch (1 cm). Add the lemon juice or vinegar and the bay leaf, cover with a pan lid, and simmer onions for about 30 minutes. Turn the onions occasionally so they become golden all over. By the time the onions are tender, they should be in a syrupy glaze. Serve them with the syrup poured over. They are good with roast pork, roast duck, chops or steaks.

Serves 4

1 lb (450g) small onions
1 oz (25g) butter
salt and freshly milled pepper
2 teaspoons castor sugar
1 teaspoon lemon juice or wine
   vinegar
1 bay leaf

Tomatoes with garlic stuffing

Slice off the tops of the tomatoes and scoop out the seeds. Sprinkle with salt and turn cut side down to drain. Peel and finely chop the garlic. Combine garlic, breadcrumbs and chopped parsley in a mixing bowl and season to taste with salt and pepper.

Generously fill hollowed-out tomatoes with the stuffing and place close together in a greased ovenproof dish. Drizzle the oil over the tops. Bake in an oven heated to 400°F (200°C) or Gas no. 6 for 15 minutes until heated through and golden brown on top. Serve with grilled meats.

Serves 4

8 large tomatoes
salt
2 tablespoons oil

Stuffing
2–3 cloves garlic
3 oz (75g) soft white breadcrumbs
4 tablespoons chopped parsley
salt and freshly milled pepper

Bacon stuffed onions

Serves 4

4 large onions
2–3 tablespoons stock or water

Stuffing
4 oz (100g) rashers streaky bacon
2 oz (50g) butter
2 oz (50g) soft white breadcrumbs
salt and freshly milled pepper
½ teaspoon dried sage or
  1 tablespoon chopped parsley

illustrated facing page 129

Heat the oven to 400°F or Gas no. 6. Place the unskinned onions in a roasting tin and bake in an oven heated to 400°F (200°C) or Gas no. 6 for about 30 minutes, or until tender. Remove from the oven and allow to cool. Peel away the outer skin and cut onions in half horizontally. Pull out the onion centres to make a hollow for the stuffing and chop the onion centres. Arrange onion shells in a greased flameproof dish. Trim and chop the bacon.

Melt the butter in a frying pan. Add the chopped onion centres and bacon and fry gently for 10 minutes to soften and brown the onion. Draw off the heat and add the breadcrumbs, a good seasoning of salt and pepper and the sage or parsley. Spoon the mixture into the onion shells filling them to the tops. Add the stock or water to the baking dish and return the onions to the oven for about 20 minutes to heat through and brown. These look good arranged around a roast joint of pork or they can be served on their own for a snack supper.

Macédoine of vegetables

Serves 6

1 lb (450g) carrots
1 small swede
2 medium-sized new turnips
2 oz (50g) butter
1 level teaspoon castor sugar
salt and freshly milled pepper

illustrated facing page 128

A macédoine of vegetables is a mixture of cooked vegetables of similar size and shape. Root vegetables are particularly good for this since they offer a contrast of colours. You'll find there's a lot of vegetable trimmings which you can use in a vegetable soup. A macédoine is well worth the trouble for a special dinner party.

Peel the carrots and with a vegetable knife, cut away the peel from the swede and turnips. Then cut the vegetables to a similar size: they can be diced or cut in ½ inch (1cm) oblongs and trimmed to a barrel shape. Cook the carrots in boiling salted water for about 20 minutes. In separate saucepans, cook the swedes and turnips for about 10 minutes each, until tender.

Place cooked vegetables together in a rinsed saucepan. Add the butter, sugar and a seasoning of salt and freshly milled pepper. Set over low heat for 2–3 minutes until butter has melted, then toss to glaze and serve.

Stir-fried asparagus

Serves 4

2 lb (900g) fresh asparagus stalks
2 tablespoons oil
salt and freshly milled pepper

Snap off and discard the woody end of asparagus stalks. Line up several stalks at a time on a cutting board, and using a sharp knife cut across the asparagus on the extreme bias making slices about ¼ inch (5mm) thick. This should give thin slanting slices about 1 inch (2.5cm) long, taking in the heads and tender stalks.

Heat the oil in a large saucepan or frying pan over moderate heat. When hot, add the asparagus and cover with a lid. Cook for 5 minutes, shaking pan as if you were popping corn. Draw off the heat and test: the asparagus pieces should be tender but crisp. Season with salt and pepper and serve at once. You'll find cooking asparagus this way preserves all the lovely flavour and you can serve it as a vegetable with omelettes, chops or steaks.

Stir-fried asparagus with mushrooms: Reduce quantity of asparagus used to 1 lb (450g) and include 8 oz (225g) thinly sliced button mushrooms.

Croquette potatoes

Peel the potatoes, add to a pan of boiling salted water and simmer for 15–20 minutes until tender. Drain well, return to the pan and allow potatoes to dry for a minute over the heat. Press the potatoes through a sieve into a mixing bowl to make a smooth purée. Melt the butter in a saucepan and stir it into the sieved potatoes. Separate the egg. Beat the egg yolk into the potato and season with salt and pepper. Break up the egg white with a fork and reserve for coating.

Turn potato mixture on to a lightly floured work surface, shape into a fat roll and cut in 12 portions, then roll each one into a ball. Coat croquettes first in lightly mixed egg white and then roll in toasted breadcrumbs. Chill for at least 30 minutes until coating is firm.

Deep fry about half the croquettes in hot oil for 2–3 minutes until crisp and golden brown. Drain on absorbent paper and keep hot (uncovered) while frying the remaining croquettes. Serve with fried or grilled meats or fish – especially dishes with a tasty sauce.

Serves 4

1 lb (450g) potatoes
1 oz (25g) butter
1 egg
salt and freshly milled pepper
toasted breadcrumbs, for coating
oil, for deep frying

Potato pancakes

Peel the potatoes and onion and coarsely grate them into a mixing bowl. Add the eggs, flour and salt and season with pepper. Mix together with a wooden spoon.

Heat about 2 tablespoons oil in a frying pan over moderate heat. Carefully spoon 3–4 heaped tablespoons of the potato mixture into the hot oil and flatten them slightly. Fry for about 5 minutes until brown, then turn them over and fry for a further 2–3 minutes. Remove from the pan with a fish slice and drain on absorbent paper. Add more oil as necessary and fry remaining batter to make a total of 12 pancakes. Serve with grilled bacon.

Serves 4

1 lb (450g) potatoes
1 medium-sized onion
2 eggs
2 oz (50g) plain flour
1 level teaspoon salt
freshly milled pepper
3–4 tablespoons oil

Peas with lettuce

Serves 6

3 lb (1.4kg) fresh peas in pods
    or 1 lb (450g) frozen peas
4–6 leaves of cos lettuce
10–12 spring onions
1 oz (25g) butter
4 tablespoons water
salt and freshly milled pepper
1 level teaspoon castor sugar
beurre manié (page 117)

Shell the peas. If using frozen peas they can be added while still frozen. Rinse and shred the lettuce. Trim the spring onions and cut off green tops right down to the bulbs. Put the butter and water into a roomy saucepan. If using frozen peas use only 2 tablespoons water. Add the shredded lettuce, a seasoning of salt and pepper and sprinkle over the sugar. Scatter the spring onions on top and put in the peas.

Bring to the boil, then lower the heat and simmer gently, covered with a pan lid, for 30 minutes by which time there will not be much liquid left. Draw off the heat and add the beurre manié in small pieces. Stir to blend, then return pan to the heat and stir gently until mixture is thickened slightly. Serve the peas together with the lettuce and spring onion. This is very good with lamb or chicken dishes. Though this dish is traditionally made with fresh peas, it's a marvellous way of adding interest to tender frozen peas.

Scalloped potatoes

Serves 4–6

¾ pint (400ml) milk
bay leaf
1½–2 lb (700–900g) potatoes
1 large onion
salt and freshly milled pepper
2 oz (50g) butter
1 oz (25g) plain flour

Heat the milk with the bay leaf in a saucepan over low heat. Draw off the heat, cover, and allow flavours to infuse for 10 minutes. Meanwhile, peel the potatoes and cut in ¼ inch (5mm) thick slices. Add to a saucepan of boiling salted water, and simmer for 5 minutes, then drain. Peel and finely chop the onion. Place alternate layers of potato and onion in a well greased 2 pint (1.1 litre) baking dish, seasoning each layer with salt and pepper and adding ½ oz (15g) of the butter in flakes. Finish with a layer of potatoes.

Melt the remaining butter in a saucepan over low heat. Stir in the flour and cook gently for 1 minute. Gradually pour in infused milk (discarding bay leaf), stirring well all the time to make a smooth sauce. Bring to the boil, stirring all the time. Season with salt and pepper. Pour the sauce over the potatoes. Cover with a buttered paper and a lid or kitchen foil and bake in an oven heated to 300°F (150°C) or Gas no. 2 for 1½–2 hours. Scalloped potatoes are filling and go best with plain meats such as slices of turkey, chicken or roast pork.

Variation: Add 2 oz (50g) grated hard cheese to the sauce. Sprinkle cooked potatoes with extra cheese and brown them under the grill.

Rice

Rice is so versatile. Not only does it combine well with other ingredients with which it is cooked but it makes the perfect accompaniment to dishes with a tasty sauce.

Types of rice

Polished rice is milled to remove the husk and layers of bran that enclose the grain so that it cooks up beautifully white. Rice grains vary in size and you should choose rice according to the dish you are making.

Short-grain rice or **pudding rice** is plump and has a chalky appearance. This rice has good absorbing qualities and when cooked becomes soft and creamy – the one traditionally used for puddings.

Medium-grain rice or **risotto rice** is plump but the grains are not so chalky and in some varieties are quite golden. When cooked the rice is a little sticky. Italians use this rice for risottos because it absorbs the flavour of stock perfectly.

Long-grain rice cooks up light and fluffy with grains that stay separate. A good quality long-grain rice is opaque and not chalky. This is the one to use in most savoury dishes especially for plain boiled rice. *Basmati* is a fine quality long-grain rice with slim grains and has a distinctive fragrance and flavour; it is ideal for serving with curries. For best results, soak basmati rice 1 hour before cooking.

Parboiled rice or **easy-cook rice** has undergone a special treatment so grains retain natural vitamin and mineral content. The resulting grains are a translucent yellow colour but when cooked turn white. The grains are harder, so parboiled rice takes longer to tenderize and absorbs more water than ordinary long-grain rice, but grains remain beautifully separate.

Brown rice is whole grain rice, milled only to remove the outer husk. The layers of bran are retained so rice is brown in appearance. It has a nutty flavour and should be chewy, not soft, when cooked. Brown rice can be prepared following the method for polished rice but takes about 35–40 minutes to cook. Cooking time is reduced slightly if you let brown rice soak in tepid water for 1 hour.

How to cook better rice

● The quality of rice is important; however carefully you cook cheap rice the result can be very disappointing.

● Give polished rice grains a thorough wash in cold water (except parboiled) to remove loose starch which makes grains sticky; swirl rice grains in a bowl of cold water and refresh the water until it remains clear.

● Grease the inside of the pan and grains won't stick. Or add a flake of butter to rice as it cooks and grains will stay separate and shiny.

● Use chicken stock or water plus a chicken stock cube for boiling rice, and if you also add a peeled onion, long-grain rice will have a flavour similar to wild rice.

● Test rice by biting a grain, or squeeze a grain between forefinger and thumb – there should be no hard or chalky core. Fluff up cooked rice for serving with an oiled fork and use a lightly oiled spoon for serving so hot rice grains stay separate.

● A rice mould looks pretty for serving, particularly with dishes that have a lot of sauce. Drain and rinse the cooked rice, return it to the hot saucepan and fork through a few knobs of butter. Spoon rice into a buttered ring mould and press down gently. Keep it hot before serving by setting the mould in a shallow tin with a little boiling water. Place a serving plate over the top of the mould and invert plate and mould, then gently lift away the mould.

● Rice is also nice pressed into a teacup and unmoulded for individual servings. Toasted nuts, chopped parsley or onion, sautéed mushrooms, cooked peas or grated cheese are just a few of the foods which could be combined with rice when it's served as a mould.

Boiled rice

Serves 4

8 oz (225g) long-grain rice
4 pints (2.4 litres) water
4 level teaspoons salt
½ oz (15g) butter

Bring the water to the boil in a saucepan, add the salt and slowly sprinkle in the rice, keeping the water boiling all the time. Boil rapidly, uncovered, for about 8–10 minutes until rice is just tender. Test by pressing a cooked grain between forefinger and thumb – there should be no hard core. Draw off the heat and drain at once in a sieve or colander, then pour over boiling water (from the kettle) to separate the grains.

Turn into a greased casserole, top with a few flakes of butter and cover with a lid or kitchen foil. Place rice in an oven heated to 325°F (160°C) or Gas no. 3 for about 30 minutes, or until ready to serve. Fluff the rice with a fork and serve. Cooked rice can be stored in the refrigerator for up to 1 week in an airtight container. Reheat by adding the rice to boiling salted water and simmering for just 2–4 minutes.

Variations

Buttered lemon rice: Add a slice of lemon to the boiling water (remove for serving). Then add 1–2 oz (25–50g) butter to the hot cooked rice just before serving. Serve with shellfish dishes, especially scampi.

Herb rice: Add 1–2 oz (25–50g) butter, 1 tablespoon finely chopped parsley and 1 tablespoon chopped chives or spring onions to the hot cooked rice. Serve with chicken or fish dishes.

Onion rice: Lightly fry 1 medium-sized peeled and finely chopped onion in 1 oz (25g) butter until tender and just beginning to brown. Add to the hot cooked rice and toss together. Serve with steak or braised beef.

Easy saffron rice: Warm a good pinch of saffron in a small bowl in the oven until crisp. Add a pinch of granulated sugar to the saffron and crush to a fine powder with the back of a wooden spoon. Add 1 tablespoon boiling water (from the kettle) to the saffron and allow to infuse for 1–2 minutes. Stir saffron liquid into the hot cooked rice. Add 1 oz (25g) butter and 2 oz (50g) coarsely chopped walnuts or toasted almonds, if liked. Serve with fish or chicken.

Golden rice: Drain the cooked rice, return to the pan and add 1 oz (25g) butter and ½ level teaspoon turmeric powder. Stir with a fork until rice is an even yellow colour.

Oven-cooked rice

Put the rice into a well greased casserole. Add the salt and boiling water and stir well. Cover dish with a tight-fitting lid or kitchen foil and cook for 35–40 minutes in an oven heated to 350°F (180°C) or Gas no. 4 until rice grains are soft and cooking liquid has been absorbed. Add the butter, fluff grains with a fork and serve.

Variations: Garnish with colourful strips of green pepper that have been blanched for 1 minute in boiling water or sprinkle with chopped parsley. Cook the rice in chicken stock in place of the water but omit the salt. Add lightly fried mushrooms to the cooked rice. Fry a little bacon or chopped onion in the casserole before adding the rice and water.

Serves 4

8 oz (225g) long-grain rice
1 level teaspoon salt
1 pint (600ml) boiling water
½–1 oz (15–25g) butter

Rice pilaff

Peel and finely chop the onion. Melt the butter in a medium-sized saucepan over low heat, add the onion, cover with a pan lid, and cook gently for 5 minutes until soft but not brown. Add the rice and toss to coat in the butter and onion. Pour in the hot stock and bring to the boil, then simmer, covered with a lid, for about 20 minutes until stock is absorbed and rice is tender. Fluff the rice with a fork and serve with steak, kebabs, grilled sausages, braised beef or chicken casserole dishes.

Variation **Brown rice pilaff:** Use twice the quantity of stock and extend the cooking time to 40 minutes.

Serves 4

1 medium-sized onion
1 oz (25g) butter
8 oz (225g) long-grain rice
1 pint (600ml) hot chicken stock

Spanish rice

Peel and slice the onion. Halve, deseed and finely shred the pepper. Melt the butter in a saucepan over low heat, add the onion and pepper, cover with a pan lid, and fry gently for about 5 minutes until onion is soft but not brown. Stir in the tomatoes with juice and add the sugar, bay leaf and salt. Cover and simmer for 15 minutes, stirring occasionally.

Meanwhile, add the rice to a saucepan of boiling salted water. Bring back to the boil, then simmer for 8–10 minutes, or until tender. Drain well. Add the cooked rice to the tomato mixture and mix together. Turn into a greased casserole and cook, uncovered, in an oven heated to 350°F (180°C) or Gas no. 4 for about 15 minutes, so that any excess liquid evaporates. Fluff the rice with a fork, check seasoning and sprinkle with grated Parmesan cheese. Serve with fried chicken, chops, steaks, hamburgers or sausages.

Serves 4

1 medium-sized onion
1 green pepper
1 oz (25g) butter
1 × 14 oz (396g) tin peeled
   tomatoes
2 level teaspoons castor sugar
1 bay leaf
½ level teaspoon salt
6 oz (175g) long-grain rice
1–2 oz (25–50g) grated Parmesan
   cheese

Salads

How to make better salads

● Salads will be good to look at and even better to eat if ingredients are crisp, fresh and colourful and you can make wonderful salads all year round, using seasonal ingredients.

● Don't wash salad vegetables until just before you are ready to use them. Rinse vegetables under cold running water. Wash vegetables like spinach which are full of grit in several changes of cold water. But never leave leafy vegetables to soak or they will become soggy.

● Thoroughly dry leafy vegetables. Loosely wrap vegetables in a clean tea-towel and shake until dry – I do this outdoors. Salad spinners, which you can buy at kitchen supply shops, also work well.

● Shake oil and vinegar dressing each time before using. Don't dress a green salad in advance or the vinegar will cause the leaves to wilt.

● Add nuts for crunchiness; salted peanuts are good in cabbage salads. Salted and toasted flaked almonds make all the difference in a rice salad.

● Choose unusual salad greens to add different colours, textures and flavours. *Radicchio* has deep red-coloured leaves marbled with white and a distinctive bitter taste. *Endive* also has a bitter taste but the curly, ragged leaves will make salads look pretty. *Sorrel* is perhaps more of an acquired taste. Use in small quantities as it has a sharp and sour flavour; cultivated varieties are milder than wild sorrel.

● Make winter salads interesting by adding finely shredded Brussels sprouts or grated raw Jerusalem artichokes to them. Shredded raw leeks are also good, but use sparingly as their flavour when raw tends to be strong.

● Include fruits like seedless raisins, apple slices, grapes, melon balls, citrus fruit segments or tinned mandarins and even a sliced banana. They add colour and combine perfectly with the sweet-sharp flavour of an oil and vinegar dressing.

● Slice avocado and apple or other fruits that discolour directly into the oil and vinegar dressing or into lemon juice to retain colour.

● Herbs give a lift to salads. Use parsley, chives or mint generously. Hold a bunch over your salad mixture and snip with kitchen scissors or push them through a Mouli herb mill.

● Plunge boiled eggs into cold water immediately to arrest cooking and avoid dark rings round the yolks. Remember eggs for salads will not be dry if they are cooked until the yolk is set but still slightly moist.

● Add oil and vinegar dressing to hot vegetables and serve them cold. Allow sufficient time for vegetables to absorb the flavour – about 30 minutes at room temperature.

● Pickled onions are popular with cold meats. Try this quick idea: cut thin slices of onion and separate into rings, then cover with malt vinegar and leave for 24 hours – they are delicious.

● For salad dressings use wine vinegar, cider vinegar or herb-flavoured wine vinegar – tarragon is my favourite; lemon juice can be used instead for a milder flavour. Malt vinegar is too harsh.

● Oil and vinegar dressings have the best flavour when olive oil is used, but it's expensive. Use corn oil or ground nut oil as a good alternative. I have a bottle of ground nut oil with a few black olives steeping in it – the oil takes on the flavour of the olives and makes an inexpensive alternative to olive oil.

● Before unmoulding a gelatine salad, dampen the centre of the serving plate and sprinkle surface of salad with cold water, then if salad unmoulds a little off centre you can move it into position without marring its shape.

● Never soak a wooden salad bowl in water. After each use either rinse it quickly in lukewarm water and promptly wipe dry or simply wipe it out with absorbent paper. Garlic and other salad flavours will season a wooden bowl.

Tomato and spring onion salad

Scald the tomatoes and peel away the skins. Cut in thick slices and place in a serving bowl. Trim and finely chop the spring onions, including some of the green tops and add to the tomatoes.

Combine the sugar, wine vinegar and a seasoning of salt and pepper in a bowl. Then stir in the oil and pour into the tomato salad. Leave to stand, covered with cling film, for at least 1 hour so dressing draws the juices from the tomatoes and the flavours combine. Sprinkle with chopped parsley and serve. The dressing is delicious and worth mopping up with a slice of crusty bread.

Variations **Tomato and avocado salad:** Arrange 1 thinly sliced avocado that has been dipped in the dressing (to prevent discoloration) around the edge of the serving bowl.

Tomato and orange salad: Oranges look pretty tucked in with the tomato slices. Add 1 peeled and thinly sliced orange to the salad and serve with cold ham.

Serves 6

1 lb (450g) ripe tomatoes
4–6 spring onions
1 tablespoon chopped parsley

Dressing
1 level teaspoon castor sugar
1 tablespoon wine vinegar
salt and freshly milled pepper
3 tablespoons oil

Raw mushroom salad

Cut the mushrooms in thick slices and put into a mixing bowl along with the marjoram and lemon juice. Spoon over the oil and toss together to make the mushrooms shine. Season with salt and pepper and sprinkle with chopped parsley.

This is a popular salad for buffets and it also makes a good, simple dish to serve with grilled fish or roast chicken.

Variation: Add 4 oz (100g) peeled prawns and serve as a first course for 6.

Serves 4

8 oz (225g) button mushrooms
pinch of dried marjoram
2 tablespoons lemon juice
3–4 tablespoons oil
salt and freshly milled pepper
1 tablespoon chopped parsley

Melon, cucumber and tomato salad

Peel and cut the cucumber in thick slices, place in a colander and sprinkle with coarse salt. Leave to stand for 30 minutes to draw some of the juices. Meanwhile, cut the melon in half and remove the seeds. Slice each half across and cut away the rind. Neatly dice the melon and put into a mixing bowl. Scald the tomatoes, peel away the skins and cut in quarters. Thoroughly rinse the cucumber and press dry in absorbent paper. Add the cucumber and tomatoes to the melon.

Pour over the oil and vinegar dressing, add the chopped parsley and toss together. You can do this about 1 hour before serving but no longer because the juices will run from the melon. This salad looks pretty served in a glass bowl and makes a marvellous first course when served with hot herb bread (page 286).

Variation: Add 4 oz (100g) peeled prawns to the salad.

Serves 6

1 cucumber
coarse salt
1 ripe honeydew melon
1 lb (450g) tomatoes
¼ pint (150ml) oil and vinegar
    dressing
1 tablespoon chopped parsley

Niçoise salad

Serves 4

8 oz (225g) French beans
1 medium-sized onion
4 ripe tomatoes
2 hard-boiled eggs
1 firm lettuce heart
1 × 8 oz (225g) tin tuna fish, drained
1 × 1¾ oz (50g) tin anchovy fillets, drained
6–8 stoned black olives
4–6 tablespoons oil and vinegar dressing
1 tablespoon chopped parsley

Cook the beans in boiling salted water for about 6–8 minutes until just tender. Drain and allow to cool. Peel and thinly slice the onion and separate into rings. Cut the tomatoes and eggs in quarters and cut the beans in 1 inch (2.5cm) lengths.

Tear the lettuce in bite-sized pieces and arrange on a serving plate. Attractively arrange the beans, onion, chunky pieces of tuna fish, anchovy fillets and tomato quarters on the lettuce. Garnish the salad with the egg quarters and black olives. Spoon over the oil and vinegar dressing and sprinkle with chopped parsley. Serve with crusty French bread and butter, hot herb bread (page 286) or hot new potatoes in their skins. Niçoise salad makes a good lunch or cold-table dish.

Variation: Used diced cold roast beef in place of the tuna fish.

Tomato coleslaw

Serves 6

½ small white cabbage
2–3 new carrots
4 ripe tomatoes
4–5 tablespoons oil and vinegar dressing
2 tablespoons mayonnaise
1 tablespoon tomato ketchup
3 tablespoons single cream

Remove outer damaged leaves from the cabbage, cut the cabbage in quarters and cut away the hard core. Finely shred the cabbage crossways, rinse and shake dry, then put into a mixing bowl.

Peel and coarsely grate the carrots. Scald the tomatoes and peel the skins. Halve, deseed and coarsely chop the tomato flesh. Add the carrot and tomato to the cabbage along with the oil and vinegar dressing. Toss together and leave cabbage to marinate for at least 15 minutes to soften.

Combine mayonnaise, tomato ketchup and cream in a bowl. Add to the salad and toss together. Turn into a serving bowl and serve with smoked mackerel or cold ham.

Coleslaw vinaigrette

Serves 6

½ small white cabbage
1 green pepper
1 medium-sized onion
1 tablespoon chopped parsley

Dressing
2 tablespoons castor sugar
2 tablespoons hot water
2 tablespoons wine vinegar
salt and freshly milled pepper
3–4 tablespoons oil

Remove the outer damaged leaves from the cabbage, cut the cabbage in quarters and cut away the hard core. Finely shred the cabbage crossways, rinse and shake dry, then put into a mixing bowl. Halve, deseed and finely shred the green pepper. Peel and thinly slice the onion. Add the pepper and onion to the cabbage and toss together the pretty shades of white and green.

Dissolve the castor sugar in the hot water (from the kettle) and add the vinegar and a seasoning of salt and pepper. Beat in the oil and pour the dressing over the salad. Toss together and leave to marinate for at least 2 hours to soften. Just before serving, sprinkle in the parsley and toss the salad again. This salad will keep for 3 days in the refrigerator.

Variation: Use 2 grated carrots in place of the green pepper.

Crunchy cabbage salad

Cut the apricots in fine slivers and soak in the orange juice for 2–3 hours. Remove outer damaged leaves from the cabbage, cut the cabbage in quarters and cut away the hard core. Finely shred the cabbage crossways, rinse and shake dry, then put into a mixing bowl.

Add the oil and vinegar dressing and leave the cabbage to marinate for at least 15 minutes to soften. Add the soaked apricots along with any orange juice. Quarter, core and dice the apples. Quickly add to the salad and toss together. Just before serving, add the salted peanuts and toss the salad again. Serve with cold sliced turkey or chicken.

Serves 6

8 dried apricots
juice of 1 orange
½ small white cabbage
¼ pint (150ml) oil and vinegar
   dressing
2–3 red dessert apples
2 tablespoons salted peanuts

New potato salad

Cook the potatoes in their skins for 15 minutes, or until just tender, then drain and return to the pan. Shake the pan over the heat for a moment to dry the potatoes. Spread them out on a cloth and when cool enough to handle, cut in thick slices and put into a mixing bowl. Trim and chop the spring onions and add to the warm potatoes along with the oil and vinegar dressing and a seasoning of salt and pepper. Toss together, cover and chill for at least 1 hour so the potatoes can absorb the flavours of the dressing and spring onions.

About 30 minutes before serving, remove from the refrigerator and allow the salad to come to room temperature. Mix in the chopped parsley or chives and turn into a salad bowl.

Variation: Omit the spring onions and parsley and sprinkle the salad with about 1 tablespoon dillweed.

Serves 6

1½ lb (700g) new potatoes
4–6 spring onions
¼ pint (150ml) oil and vinegar
   dressing
salt and freshly milled pepper
1 tablespoon chopped parsley or
   chives

Traditional potato salad

Cook the potatoes in their skins for 15 minutes, or until just tender, then drain and return to the pan. Shake the pan over the heat for a moment to dry the potatoes. Spread them out on a cloth and when cool enough to handle, peel off the skins. Cut in thick slices and put into a mixing bowl. Trim and chop the spring onions or peel and finely chop the shallots. Add to the warm potatoes along with the oil and vinegar dressing and a seasoning of salt and pepper. Cover and chill for at least 1 hour.

About 30 minutes before serving, remove from the refrigerator and allow the salad to come to room temperature. Thin the mayonnaise with the cream and mix into the salad. Turn into a salad bowl and sprinkle with chopped chives.

Variation: Sprinkle the salad with crumbled fried bacon along with the chopped chives.

Serves 6

1½ lb (700g) new potatoes
4–6 spring onions or shallots
2 tablespoons oil and vinegar
   dressing
salt and freshly milled pepper
¼ pint (150ml) mayonnaise
2–3 tablespoons single cream
1 tablespoon chopped chives

Party potato salad

Serves 6

1½ lb (700g) new potatoes
1 small clove garlic (optional)
1 tablespoon wine vinegar
salt and freshly milled pepper
1 green pepper
¼ pint (150ml) double cream
2 tablespoons mayonnaise
squeeze of lemon juice
1 level teaspoon curry powder

Cook the potatoes in their skins for 15 minutes, or until just tender, then drain and return to the pan. Shake the pan over the heat for a moment to dry the potatoes. Spread them out on a cloth and when cool enough to handle, peel the skins and cut the potatoes in thick slices.

Crush the garlic, if using it, and use to rub the inside of a mixing bowl, then add the warm sliced potatoes. Sprinkle over the vinegar and season with plenty of salt and pepper. Halve, deseed and finely chop the green pepper, add to the potatoes and toss together. Cover and chill for at least 1 hour.

About 30 minutes before serving, remove from the refrigerator and allow the salad to come to room temperature. Whip the cream and combine with the mayonnaise, lemon juice and curry powder in a bowl. Pour the dressing over the salad and mix together well. Turn into a salad bowl. Serve at barbecues or summer parties.

Greek summer salad

Serves 6

4 tomatoes
1 cucumber
2 green peppers
4 oz (100g) black olives
1 tablespoon chopped parsley
¼ pint (150ml) oil and vinegar
    dressing
3 oz (75g) fetta cheese

illustrated facing page 97

Scald the tomatoes, peel away the skins and cut the tomatoes in quarters. Thinly slice the unpeeled cucumber. Halve, deseed and finely shred the green peppers.

Put the tomatoes, cucumber and green peppers into a shallow serving bowl along with the olives and parsley. Pour over the oil and vinegar dressing. Coarsely crumble the fetta cheese into the bowl. Toss the salad ingredients together. Serve this colourful, crunchy salad with kebabs at outdoor barbecues.

Variation: Use 1 teaspoon dried marjoram in place of the parsley.

Chef's salad

Serves 4

8 oz (225g) sliced ham or tongue
4 oz (100g) Gruyère or Gouda
    cheese
2 hard-boiled eggs
4 tomatoes
1 firm lettuce heart
1 bunch watercress
oil and vinegar dressing, for serving

Cut the ham or tongue and the cheese in julienne strips and cut the eggs and tomatoes in quarters. Tear the lettuce in bite-sized pieces and place on a serving plate. Arrange alternate small bunches of meat and cheese (cartwheel fashion) on the lettuce. Arrange tomato and egg quarters on the border of the plate and place a bunch of watercress in the centre. Serve with a jug of oil and vinegar dressing passed round separately. This salad looks fresh and appetizing on a hot summer day and is good served with crusty French bread, poppy seed rolls or rye bread and butter.

Variations: The ingredients in a chef's salad really depend on the tastes of the chef. Choose firm, non-crumbly cheeses that can be easily sliced. White turkey or chicken meat and ham is a tasty combination. Other garnishes could include trimmed spring onions, cooked asparagus or French beans and sliced radishes or grated carrot.

Rice salad

Cook the rice in boiling salted water for about 8–10 minutes until just tender. Drain well and turn into a mixing bowl. Add 2–3 tablespoons of the oil and vinegar dressing, toss to coat rice and set aside until completely cool.

Halve, deseed and finely chop the green pepper. Trim and finely chop the spring onions. Add the pepper and spring onions to the rice along with the raisins and the remaining oil and vinegar dressing. Toss together. Just before serving, grill the flaked almonds to a golden brown and sprinkle with salt. Stir into the rice salad to make a crunchy contrast. Serve with cold chicken or ham and salads that have a mayonnaise dressing.

Variations: Any number of additions are delicious in rice salad. Add tinned pineapple pieces, orange segments, diced avocado, finely chopped fried bacon, cold cooked peas, diced cucumber, sliced radishes or chopped parsley. Combine contrasting colours and use foods with a good crunch.

Serves 6

4 oz (100g) long-grain rice
¼ pint (150ml) oil and vinegar
  dressing
1 medium-sized green pepper
1 bunch spring onions
2 tablespoons seedless raisins
1–2 oz (25–50g) flaked almonds
salt

Pickled peaches

Drain the peach halves, reserving the juice, and put peaches into a mixing bowl. Pour the syrup – approximately 8 fl oz (225ml) – into a saucepan. Add the cloves, sugar, wine vinegar and stick cinnamon to the pan of juice and stir over low heat until the sugar has dissolved. Bring to the boil, add the peaches, then simmer for 4 minutes.

Pour into a mixing bowl and allow to cool. Cover and chill for at least 24 hours or put peaches with syrup into a screw-topped jar and store for up to 1 week. Lift peach halves from the syrup and put into a shallow serving bowl. Or serve from the jar with a long pickle fork to spear the fruit. Pickled peaches make a pretty garnish arranged on a serving platter of cold meats, especially gammon, ham or chicken.

Serves 8–10

1 × 1 lb 13 oz (822g) tin peach
  halves
6 cloves
3 oz (75g) castor sugar
4 fl oz (125ml) wine vinegar
1 piece stick cinnamon

Celery, apple and walnut salad

Trim the celery base and leaves. Separate the stalks, snap each one in half and pull apart to remove the strings, then finely slice the celery. Quarter, core and dice the apples – do not peel if they are a pretty red colour. Put the celery and apple into a mixing bowl, pour over the oil and vinegar dressing and quickly toss together (to prevent the apples from discolouring). Chill until ready to serve, then turn into a serving bowl and add the chopped walnuts.

Variation: Add 2–3 oz (50–75g) sultanas that have been soaked in hot water for 10 minutes. Or use 2 oranges cut in segments in place of the diced apples.

Serves 4–6

1 head celery
2–3 red dessert apples
3–4 tablespoons oil and vinegar
  dressing
2 tablespoons chopped walnuts

Swedish cucumber salad

Serves 4

½ cucumber
coarse salt
2 level tablespoons castor sugar
2 tablespoons white wine vinegar
4 tablespoons water
salt and freshly milled pepper
1 tablespoon chopped fresh dill or 1
    teaspoon dillweed

Thinly slice the cucumber, place in a colander and sprinkle with coarse salt. Cover with a weighted plate and leave to stand for 30 minutes to draw the juices, then thoroughly rinse and press cucumber dry in absorbent paper.

Combine the sugar, wine vinegar and water in a mixing bowl and season with salt and pepper. Add the cucumber slices and chopped dill or dillweed. Leave to marinate for several hours. Turn into a serving bowl and use a pickle fork for spearing the slices. This has a sweet and sour flavour and is lovely with cold roast chicken.

Carrot and raisin salad

Serves 4

4 large carrots
4 tablespoons seedless raisins
1 oz (25g) salted peanuts
¼ pint (150ml) soured cream
2 level teaspoons castor sugar
finely grated rind and juice of ½
    lemon
salt and freshly milled pepper
lettuce leaves

Peel the carrots, then refrigerate them for about 30 minutes until they are really crisp. Coarsely grate the chilled carrots into a mixing bowl. Add the seedless raisins and salted peanuts.

Blend the soured cream, sugar, grated lemon rind and juice in a small mixing bowl. Add to the salad and toss ingredients together. Season with salt and pepper. Arrange lettuce leaves on individual salad plates and divide the salad mixture between them. This combination of crisp, sweet carrots and a sharp flavoured, fresh dressing is delicious served with cold chicken.

Waldorf salad

Serves 4

3 celery stalks
4 dessert apples
2 tablespoons double cream
2 tablespoons mayonnaise
squeeze of lemon juice
2 oz (50g) chopped walnuts

Snap each celery stalk in half and pull apart to remove the strings, then finely slice the celery. Quarter, core and dice the apples – do not peel if they are a pretty red colour.

Lightly whip the cream in a mixing bowl and add the mayonnaise and a squeeze of lemon juice. Quickly add the apples and the celery and toss together well. Chill until ready to serve, then turn into a serving bowl and add the chopped walnuts.

Chicory salad

Serves 4

2 heads chicory
1 carrot
2–3 spring onions
1 medium-sized cooking apple
1 teaspoon castor sugar
2–3 tablespoons oil and vinegar
    dressing
1 tablespoon chopped parsley

Trim the base of each chicory head and using a pointed knife, cut out the core. Slice the chicory very finely crossways, separate out the layers and put into a mixing bowl. Peel and grate the carrot into the bowl. Trim and chop the spring onions and add to the bowl. Peel, core and grate the apple into the bowl.

Sprinkle with castor sugar to counteract the sharpness of the apple, add the oil and vinegar dressing and toss together. Turn into a salad bowl and sprinkle with chopped parsley. Serve at once with smoked mackerel, ham or cold chicken.

Devilled-egg salad

Boil the eggs for 8 minutes from cold. Drain and plunge into cold water to arrest cooking. Shell the eggs and submerge in a bowl of water until cold.

Using a wet knife blade cut each egg in half lengthways. Carefully remove each egg yolk and put into a mixing bowl. Reserve the egg whites. Mash yolks with a fork and beat in the mayonnaise. Add the mustard and curry powder and season with salt and pepper. Place the lettuce leaves on a serving plate. Fill each egg white with a heaped teaspoon of the egg yolk mixture and arrange them on the lettuce leaves. Sprinkle with chopped parsley and serve with thinly sliced brown bread and butter. Devilled eggs also may be used to garnish a salad of cold meats.

Serves 6

6 eggs
2 tablespoons mayonnaise
½–1 level teaspoon made English mustard
pinch of curry powder
salt and freshly milled pepper
few crisp lettuce leaves
chopped parsley, to garnish

Onions in soured cream

Peel and slice the onions and separate into rings. Put into a mixing bowl, pour over boiling water to cover and leave to soak for 2 minutes. Drain and chill for at least 1 hour.

Combine soured cream, a seasoning of salt and pepper and a squeeze of lemon juice in a serving bowl. Add the onion rings and mix together. This onion salad is very mild in flavour and goes well with cold rare roast beef, beef and ham mould or cold ham.

Variation **Beetroot in soured cream:** Peel and dice 1 lb (450g) cooked beetroot but do not soak or chill. Add 2 tablespoons mayonnaise to the soured cream dressing. Add the beetroot and mix together to make a pink salad which will brighten a cold table or buffet.

Serves 4

2 medium-sized onions
¼ pint (150ml) soured cream
salt and freshly milled pepper
squeeze of lemon juice

Pasta salad with tuna

Add pasta shells to a saucepan of boiling salted water, bring back to the boil, then lower the heat and simmer for 8 minutes, or until pasta shells are just tender. Drain pasta and turn into a mixing bowl. Add the oil and vinegar dressing and turn pasta shells to coat them. Set aside for 30 minutes.

Halve, deseed and finely chop the green pepper. Snap celery stalks in half and pull apart to remove the strings, then finely shred the celery. Add the green pepper and celery to the pasta. Combine the mayonnaise and soured cream, add to the bowl and season with salt and pepper. Turn ingredients to coat them in the dressing. Drain tuna fish and break into chunky pieces, then gently fold into the salad. Turn into a serving bowl and sprinkle with the chives. This makes a good lunch dish.

Serves 4

4 oz (100g) pasta shells
2 tablespoons oil and vinegar dressing
1 green pepper
1–2 stalks celery
3 tablespoons mayonnaise
2 tablespoons soured cream
salt and freshly milled pepper
1 × 7 oz (198g) tin tuna fish
1 tablespoon chopped chives

Cottage cheese and fruit salad

Serves 4

1 firm lettuce heart
2 oranges
4 pineapple rings
oil and vinegar dressing
2 × 8 oz (227g) cartons cottage
    cheese
salt and freshly milled pepper
2 tablespoons chopped walnuts
salad cress, to garnish

Arrange the lettuce leaves on a salad plate. Slice the top and base off each orange and cut round each orange to remove peel and white pith, then thinly slice the oranges. Arrange the orange slices and pineapple rings on the lettuce and pour over the oil and vinegar dressing.

Turn cottage cheese into a mixing bowl. Season with salt and plenty of pepper. Spoon the cottage cheese on to the centre of the salad. Sprinkle with chopped walnuts to make a crunchy texture and then generously garnish with snipped, washed cress which gives a light summery touch. Serve with slices of wholemeal bread or crispbread.

Variations: Pep up the flavour of seasoned cottage cheese by adding chopped spring onion or chives. Or mix cottage cheese with stewed prunes, seedless raisins, chopped dates, apples or grated carrot. A little horseradish relish added gives a nice sharp flavour. Something crunchy makes a difference, too: sprinkle toasted flaked almonds or crisply fried and crumbled bacon rashers on top of the salad. Other garnishes could include tinned peach or pear halves, sliced tomatoes, fresh cucumber, radishes or a wedge of blue cheese crumbled over the top.

Cauliflower salad with yoghurt dressing

Serves 4

1 medium-sized cauliflower
¼ pint (150ml) natural yoghurt
1 level teaspoon castor sugar
1 level teaspoon curry powder
squeeze of lemon juice
1 tablespoon finely chopped parsley

Break the cauliflower into even-sized florets. Using a vegetable knife, peel away as much of the skin from the stalks as possible – this will help the cauliflower cook more quickly. Add florets to boiling salted water with just a little lemon juice added and cook for about 6 minutes, or until just tender. Drain and place in a serving dish.

In a mixing bowl, combine the yoghurt, sugar and curry powder with lemon juice to taste. Pour dressing over cauliflower while still warm and leave for at least 30 minutes. Toss salad together and sprinkle with chopped parsley. This is excellent with cold ham and slices of wholemeal bread and butter.

Variation **Cauliflower vinaigrette:** Add 2 tablespoons finely chopped onion or spring onion to the warm cauliflower and pour over ¼ pint (150ml) oil and vinegar dressing. Allow to cool and cauliflower will absorb the flavour of the dressing, then chill. Sprinkle over 1 tablespoon chopped parsley and toss salad.

Using herbs

● Go easy when flavouring with herbs at first and use just enough to complement the food.

● If you substitute dried herbs for fresh, use less as dried flavours are more concentrated. Substitute about 1 teaspoon dried herbs for every 1 tablespoon fresh herbs.

● More robust herbs like bay leaf, marjoram and thyme can take a longer cooking time than delicate ones like basil and tarragon, which should be added towards the end of cooking time. If colour is important, then add herbs such as parsley and chives just before the dish has finished cooking.

● Leaves are usually chopped or pounded to release flavouring oils. Use a stainless steel knife to retain the colour, especially with mint; the finer you chop herbs the more their flavours will be released.

● A **bouquet garni** is a small bundle of aromatic herbs. Usually thyme, parsley stalks and a bay leaf are tied together or placed in a muslin bag and added to the cooking pot, but there is no set combination of herbs – use what suits.

● Use **basil** sparingly. Its hot clove-like flavour has an affinity with tomatoes. Sprinkle basil over salads or on tomato halves for grilling.

● **Chives** impart a delicate onion flavour to dishes. Use lavishly in egg dishes, mix with cream cheese or add to potato salads. Snip chives finely with scissors for best flavour and use as a garnish instead of parsley.

● Dried **bay leaves** are often used but it's well worth looking out for fresh bay leaves as they have a wonderful aroma. They give a distinctive background flavour to a number of dishes. Infuse a bay leaf in milk when making white sauces or add to a pan of simmering potatoes when making salads. Fresh bay leaves make a pretty decoration on pâtés and terrines.

● **Dill** is quite unique as a pickling herb and has a subtle caraway flavour. Use in cucumber and potato salads.

● Graceful feathery sprays of **fennel** are pretty as a garnish for fish dishes and good sprinkled over rich fish like salmon or mackerel. Add chopped fennel to a white sauce for fish.

● **Garlic** is worth a mention here, it's used so much. Lightly crush a garlic clove to loosen and remove outer papery coating. For the strongest flavour of all, mash garlic to a purée with salt, and for the mildest, just rub a peeled clove round the inside of the cooking dish. A garlic press is useful.

● **Marjoram** is warm and sweet-flavoured and a good herb for meat; use in terrines and especially with beef and pork dishes. Or sprinkle marjoram over grilled mushrooms.

● For a refreshing taste you can't beat **mint**. It goes well with salad vegetables and fruits; add a bouquet of mint to cucumber soup. Chop mint and add to oil and vinegar dressing for pears. Use sprigs to garnish cold drinks; add to salads in hot weather. When chopping mint leaves add a pinch of sugar to draw out the flavouring oils.

● **Parsley** must be very fresh. Wash curly tops and dry by twisting in a corner of a tea-towel. When chopped it looks extra green. Use parsley lavishly – it's mild-flavoured and full of nutrients.

● Every cottage garden usually has a **rosemary** bush. This pungent herb is best used with discretion and goes well with gammon, bacon and lamb. Try sprinkling rosemary over hot sauté potatoes.

● **Sage** is very aromatic; the finely chopped leaves are slightly bitter and go well with rich, fatty foods when it helps redress the balance. Use cautiously when flavouring duck or goose; add to pork, pork sausage meat mixtures and mix into potted cheese.

● A good way to keep precious **tarragon** is to strip the leaves and use to make tarragon butter for freezing, then use it for spreading on oven-cooked chicken portions. The soft green leaves of tarragon impart a distinctive aniseed flavour and are especially good with chicken.

● Versatile **thyme** is warm and pungent and can be added to flavour almost any food; it's good with vegetables and enlivens soups, especially carrot soup. Use in stuffings.

Using spices

● Store spices in tightly closed jars; take a sniff from time to time: when aroma has gone it's time to replace them.

● Whole spices are added at the start of a recipe. Tie spices in a muslin bag and suspend it in the cooking pot on a long string.

● Ground spices are used in baking. Sift with the flour when making cakes or mix with the sugar when using in pies. Both ensure even distribution.

● For uncooked dishes, mix spice and ingredients together well before serving to allow time for flavours to develop.

● Remove whole spices from the pan when the flavour is right, otherwise they may overpower the flavour of the dish.

● **Allspice** seems to combine the flavour of cinnamon, clove and nutmeg; the berries look like peppercorns and can be ground in a mill and used to flavour pork or beef dishes.

● **Caraway seeds** are what give seed cake its lovely flavour. They are often added to breads and also go nicely with mild-flavoured cheeses – you can buy caraway studded cheeses which are nice with ham. Use caraway seeds to flavour stews, especially a traditional beef goulash.

● **Cardamom** belongs to the ginger family and has a similar spicy flavour. If used with discretion, the crushed seeds taken from the pods will perk up the flavour of cooked fruit desserts. A few crushed seeds added to black coffee makes a nice change for after-dinner coffee.

● Go easy with **cayenne** because it's hot and fiery. Add a pinch to pep up the flavour of cheese or seafood dishes.

● **Cinnamon** is sweet, fragrant and wonderful with fruit. Use stick cinnamon, the elegant curled inner bark of the cinnamon tree, to infuse with the syrup for cooking pears and plums and for making mulled wine.

● You only need a few whole **cloves** to add to a dish as they are pungent and spicy; press one or two into a peeled onion so you can easily remove them and use for flavouring sauces and stocks. Add a pinch of ground cloves to fruit cakes for added flavour.

● Aromatic seeds of **coriander** are a favourite of mine; crush them and they have an aroma of sandalwood; use to flavour orange marmalade and the soaking syrup for savarin or add to fruit salads.

● **Cumin seeds** are the favourite curry spice; they taste much like caraway seeds and add a powerful but warm flavour.

● I like to use the dried **ginger** (sold at chemists') for adding a sharp but subtle flavour to cooked fruits. Give dried ginger a hearty whack with a rolling pin to crack it before adding it to the pot. Ground ginger is used in cakes and biscuits.

● **Juniper berries** should be crushed to release their resinous flavour. Add a few crushed berries to marinades, especially for venison, or add to game terrines.

● Pretty blades of **mace**, the outer coating of nutmeg, have a similar, but more delicate flavour, to nutmeg; infuse it in milk for sauces or fish dishes. Ground mace makes a marvellous mixed seasoning (page 114).

● For best flavour, **nutmeg** should be freshly grated. I keep a mini-grater specially for grating whole nutmegs. Nutmeg is warm and aromatic; grate it over green vegetables, especially spinach, and use to flavour cheese dishes and meat loaf.

● Don't confuse **paprika** with cayenne. They look alike but paprika is milder and gives a rich colour and mild flavour to stews and sauces.

● **Poppy seeds** are steely grey seeds that are used to decorate plaited milk breads and buns. Besides looking pretty, they add a contrasting texture and give a warm pleasant flavour to the bread.

● **Saffron** not only adds colour but it gives a superb flavour. Saffron strands must be infused before using.

● The yellow in curry powder comes from **turmeric**; use it to colour rice and, surprisingly, pickles and chutneys.

8

Pastry
and Dessert Pies

There's no special magic about making good
pastry. It's merely a matter of understanding how
the ingredients work and following easy
directions. Then you can make tempting pies
and luxurious filled pastries.

Pastry
and Dessert Pies

Pastry

Ingredients

Flour: Plain flour is best for shortcrust pastry, but heavy-handed beginners will find self-raising flour good to use as it gives a lighter crust because of the chemical raising agents in the flour. For a sweet shortcrust pastry or biscuit pastry, plain flour should be used to make a crisp result. Strong white flour is best for puff pastry as it counteracts the softening effect of fat; it also improves the volume of choux pastry.

Fat: The fat in pastry is very important. Generally the type of pastry made depends on the proportion of fat to flour. With richer pastries methods change in order to accommodate higher proportions of fat and you need more expertise to handle them. For shortcrust pastry the proportion used is usually half fat to flour so it's a pastry that is quite easy to handle. Pastry only becomes difficult to handle when the fat becomes too soft.

Use fats that are solid at room temperature like butter, block margarine (in preference to soft spreading) and white cooking fat or lard. Butter is best for flavour – important when proportion in recipe is high. Margarine is good too and is less expensive. I keep block margarine specially for pastry. White cooking fat does not add flavour but has excellent shortening properties. A mixture of cooking fat and margarine is popular for short-crust pastry – you get the best of both.

Liquid: Pastry is usually mixed with cold water and you'll find the higher the proportion of fat used, the less water is needed. Water for mixing pastry should be fresh and cold from the tap. Lemon juice is added in puff pastry because the acid modifies the gluten in strong white flour and makes the dough easier to roll out. In some recipes a pinch of cream of tartar is sifted with the flour which works the same way. Where egg is used for mixing pastry, the pastry bakes to a crisp finish.

Working with pastry

● Work on a very cool surface – marble is best and wood is good, too. Both are poor conductors of heat and remain reasonably cool even in a hot kitchen. I sometimes run a few ice cubes over a marble surface before making rich pastries. A wooden pastry board is much better to use than a formica surface.

● Handle all pastry lightly and work quickly. Touch your cheeks with your fingertips, which are cool, then with palms, which are warm. A good pastry cook has flour on fingers only – never on the palms of the hands. If you have hot hands, hold your wrists under a running cold tap for a few minutes before starting. Or you can cut fat into flour (instead of rubbing in) by using two table knives in a scissor-like movement.

Shortcrust pastry

Plain shortcrust is probably the most frequently used of all pastries. It is quick and easy to make and very versatile. Use it for everyday pies and flans, jam tarts and for most of our traditional pastry dishes; it's not an expensive pastry to make either.

Shortcrust gets its name from the method used to make it. The fat is rubbed into the flour until the mixture looks like fine breadcrumbs. Flour particles are coated with fat, which results in 'short' and crisp pastry – one that easily crumbs if broken in pieces.

How to make better shortcrust pastry

● To increase or decrease quantities used in a shortcrust pastry, take the amount of flour as your guide and increase other ingredients in the same proportion to it.

● Fat at room temperature is easier to rub in. Remove it from refrigerator 30 minutes before starting to make pastry.

● Use a little extra fat, which makes pastry 'shorter', when you want to serve the pastry cold.

● Do the rubbing in and chill the mix. Then ingredients are really cold for making the dough.

● Allow a newly mixed pastry dough to rest for 15–30 minutes to relax; a relaxed pastry is easier to roll out.

● Unprotected, your pastry will form a dry skin on the surface which cracks. For short resting periods leave dough under the upturned mixing bowl on the work surface.

● For longer periods of resting, place dough in a polythene bag and refrigerate, but allow pastry to stand at room temperature for at least 10 minutes before rolling out.

● Use self-raising flour for shortcrust pastry when making a quiche. I always bake filling and pastry together and get a dry pastry underneath every time.

● No need to grease tins for plain shortcrust pastry – only grease tins for pastry where fat is less than half the weight of the flour.

● Pastry likes a hot oven – the richer the pastry the hotter the oven is the general rule; a hard pastry is often the result of too low an oven temperature.

● Use a baking tray under a quiche, flan or pie plate. Metal is a good conductor of heat and helps spread the heat evenly and cook the bottom crust; place baking tray in the heating oven.

Basic shortcrust pastry

Sift the flour and salt into a mixing bowl. Using a palette knife, blend the butter and white cooking fat on a plate and add in pieces to the sifted flour. Pick up mixture in small handfuls and rub fat into the flour with the fingertips, allowing the ingredients to fall back into the bowl between the fingers. Continue until fat is evenly blended and mixture looks like fine breadcrumbs. There should be no loose flour in the bowl.

Sprinkle the water evenly over the mixture and stir with a table knife or fork, cutting through the mixture, until the dough clings together and leaves the sides of the bowl clean. Turn on to a lightly floured surface and knead once or twice to remove the cracks. Allow dough to rest for 15–20 minutes. Bake in an oven heated to 400°F (200°C) or Gas no. 6 unless otherwise indicated.

Variations: For an extra short shortcrust pastry increase the fat used to 2½ oz (65g) and reduce water for mixing to 1 tablespoon. To make pastry with 6 oz (175g) plain flour, increase fat used to 3 oz (75g).

Quiche pastry: When making quiches use self-raising flour instead of plain flour.

Wheatmeal pastry: Use 2 oz (50g) self-raising flour and 2 oz (50g) wholemeal flour. This makes a delicious mealy shortcrust pastry. Because brown flour absorbs more water than plain flour you may have to increase the amount of water a little.

4 oz (100g) plain flour
pinch of salt
1 oz (25g) butter
1 oz (25g) white cooking fat
2 tablespoons cold water

Sweet shortcrust pastry

Sift the flour and salt into a mixing bowl. Using a palette knife, blend the butter and white cooking fat on a plate and add in pieces to the sifted flour. Pick up mixture in small handfuls and rub fat into the flour with the fingertips, allowing the ingredients to fall back into the bowl between the fingers. Continue until fat is evenly blended and mixture looks like fine breadcrumbs. There should be no loose flour in the bowl.

Stir the sugar into the cold milk and sprinkle evenly over the mixture. Stir with a table knife or fork, cutting through the mixture until the dough clings together and leaves the sides of the bowl clean. Turn on to a lightly floured surface and knead once or twice to remove the cracks. Allow dough to rest for 15–20 minutes before rolling out. Bake in an oven heated to 400°F (200°C) or Gas no. 6 unless otherwise indicated in the recipe. Use for making dessert pies and flans.

Variation: For a smaller quantity of pastry, use 4 oz (100g) plain flour, 1½ oz (40g) butter and ½ oz (15g) white cooking fat and combine 1 level tablespoon castor sugar with 1½ tablespoons cold milk. Sufficient for one 8 inch (20cm) flan.

8 oz (225g) plain flour
pinch of salt
4 oz (100g) butter
½ oz (15g) white cooking fat
1 oz (25g) castor sugar
3 tablespoons cold milk

Cheese shortcrust pastry

4 oz (100g) plain flour
pinch of salt
pinch of cayenne pepper
1½ oz (40g) butter
1 oz (25g) white cooking fat
2 oz (50g) grated hard cheese
2 tablespoons lightly mixed egg

Sift the flour, salt and cayenne pepper into a mixing bowl. Using a palette knife, blend the butter and white cooking fat on a plate and add in pieces to the sifted flour. Pick up mixture in small handfuls and rub into the flour with the fingertips, allowing the ingredients to fall back into the bowl between fingertips. Continue until fat is evenly blended and mixture looks like breadcrumbs. There should be no loose flour in the bowl. Stir in the grated cheese.

Pour the lightly mixed egg evenly over the mixture and stir with a table knife or fork, cutting through the mixture, until the dough clings together and leaves the sides of the bowl clean. Turn on to a lightly floured work surface and knead once or twice to remove the cracks. Allow dough to rest for 15–20 minutes before rolling out. Bake in an oven heated to 375°F (190°C) or Gas no. 5 unless otherwise indicated in the recipe. Use for savoury flans or quiches or for cheese straws.

Variation **Cheese straws:** Roll out cheese shortcrust pastry to a thickness of ¼ inch (5mm). Cut in 3 inch (7.5cm) wide strips, then cut across to make straws. Transfer to a greased baking sheet and bake for 8 minutes. Makes 48.

German (or biscuit) pastry

Makes 4 × 8 inch (20cm) flan cases

1 lb (450g) plain flour
10 oz (275g) butter
5 oz (150g) castor sugar
1 egg

Sift the flour on to a wood or marble work surface and using the hand, sweep the flour out and around to form a circle with a large space in the centre.

Put the butter and sugar on to the centre of the circle and, using the fingertips, cream the mixture until smooth and light. Break up the egg with a fork and blend with creamed ingredients. Then draw in the flour with the fingertips (or use a pastry scraper) and mix to a smooth dough. Divide in four equal pieces, cover and chill for at least 30 minutes.

To make flan cases: Take one portion of dough from the refrigerator at a time and leave to stand for 10 minutes before rolling out. Roll out the dough on a floured work surface to a circle slightly larger than an 8 inch (20cm) flan ring set on a baking tray and use to line the flan ring. Trim edges and prick the base with a fork. Line with a circle of greaseproof paper and weight down with some baking beans.

Bake flan in an oven heated to 400°F (200°C) or Gas no. 6 for 15–20 minutes. Repeat procedure with remaining dough. Allow to cool completely before storing or freezing. These will taste newly baked if you crisp them in an oven heated to 325°F (160°C) or Gas no. 3 for 5 minutes before using.

Serve filled with confectioner's custard (page 204) and fresh strawberries with a jam glaze (page 183). Or fill with other fresh fruits and a jelly glaze (page 183).

Home pastry mix

Sift the flour and salt into a large mixing bowl. Using a palette knife, blend the butter and cooking fat on a plate and add in pieces to the sifted flour. Rub in with the fingertips and cut through the mixture several times with a table knife. Spoon into a polythene bag and tie tightly. Store in the refrigerator for up to 2 months.

2 lb (900g) plain flour
2 level teaspoons salt
8 oz (225g) white cooking fat
8 oz (225g) butter or margarine

To use: Remember shortcrust pastry has half as much fat as flour. If your recipe calls for shortcrust pastry made with 4 oz (100g) flour, measure out 6 oz (175g) mix; for shortcrust pastry made with 6 oz (175g) flour, measure out 9 oz (250g) mix, and for shortcrust pastry made with 8 oz (225g) flour, measure out 12 oz (350g) mix. Stir in sufficient cold water (anything from 1–3 tablespoons) and mix to a dough with a fork.

Crumble topping: Add 2 oz (50g) castor sugar to 10 oz (275g) pastry mix. Rub in lightly until mixture clings in coarse crumbs. Sprinkle the crumble in a thick layer over fruit and press it gently.

Finishing touches for pies

● The top crust is either slashed or a hole is cut in the centre to allow steam to escape, otherwise the pastry may burst during baking.

● With a double crust pie, a good seal around the rim is essential to hold in pie juices. Dampen only the bottom crust – two wet surfaces will not stick together – and place the pie cover on top. Trim the edge by cutting with a sharp knife held upright and at a slight slant inwards.

● *Knock up* pie edges by holding the knife horizontally and placing the forefinger just behind the pastry rim to keep the pastry in place. Seal by 'knocking' the pie edges using the flat of the knife blade.

● *Flute* pie edges by pressing the pastry edges at intervals. To do this, place two fingers on the rim facing outwards from pie centre and draw in the pastry that is between the fingers with a knife. Traditionally a savoury pie is fluted at wide intervals and a dessert pie at narrow intervals.

● Pies can be glazed with milk or beaten egg to give the crusts a golden finish. Alternatively, a dessert pie can be brushed with lightly beaten egg white and sprinkled with castor sugar. Brush pie with glaze just before baking so pastry does not get soggy.

● Glazes are also used to fix on decorations to pie crusts. Brush the pie crust, arrange decorations, then brush the decorations.

● To make pastry leaf decorations, roll pastry trimmings thinly and cut in 1 inch (2.5cm) wide strips. Then cut diagonally into diamond-shaped pieces. Mark veins on leaf with the back of the knife, and pinch one end to form a leaf shape.

● To make a pastry rose for steak and kidney pie, roll pastry trimmings thinly and cut 3 pastry circles in decreasing sizes. Place one on top of the other with the smallest circle on top. Draw circles together into a ball and pinch to seal. Turn with rounded side uppermost and cut a cross on top with a sharp knife. Open out pastry layers to make the petals.

● To position the rose on a covered pie, set a small square of greaseproof paper with a cross cut in the centre (to allow steam to escape) over pie hole and under the decoration so that the rose can be lifted from the baked pie to allow for the addition of hot gravy and then be replaced.

Flaky and puff pastry

Pastry that rises in flakes or layers is made in a special way. The method of preparation and high proportion of fat to flour mean these have a crisp, golden, flaky texture that is quite unlike any other pastry. To achieve this the flour is made into a dough with the water, and the fat is incorporated at a second stage in either small lumps or in a single layer. The subsequent rolling and folding builds up layers of dough and fat.

A common mistake is to roll the pastry dough too thinly during the preparation. The size to roll the dough each time (for folding and turning) is not difficult to judge if you remember that the length is determined by the width – the dough piece should be about three times as long as it is wide. This way you can fold the pastry in three and end up with a neat square to start off with again. Start each rolling by giving the pastry a half-turn clockwise so the open ends are facing towards and away from you, then pastry will roll out easily.

These pastries take time to prepare because they need a certain amount of resting and chilling so the dough remains easy to handle. But they can be made in advance and will stand up well for 2–3 days in the refrigerator. It is also worth freezing these pastries. Chill the finished dough thoroughly and then overwrap with polythene.

What actually makes the pastry rise in flaky layers is the steam which comes from the water in the dough and, to a lesser extent, the air trapped by the rolls and folds. A very hot oven is essential and forces the pastry to rise in layers; the heat also enables the flour to absorb the fat as it melts – too cool an oven and you'll find the fat runs all over the baking sheet.

How to make better flaky and puff pastry

● Butter that is to be rolled for puff pastry should be taken from the refrigerator about 30 minutes in advance so that it is not as hard as a brick. Shape it neatly by rolling it between two sheets of greaseproof paper.

● Don't roll the pastry too thinly during preparation or you risk blending the layers of fat and dough and there will be no flaky texture. ,

● Brush surplus flour off at every stage so it doesn't get into the dough. Too much extra flour makes pastry blister.

● Rest pastry between rollings; wrap in a damp cloth or put dough in a polythene bag to prevent a dry crust forming on the surface.

● Chill pastry before cutting or shaping and again before baking; the fat firms so you'll cut better shapes and there will be less shrinkage in the oven.

● After rolling out flaky pastry, you must free the layers by cutting all edges neatly with a sharp knife; a cutter used for vol-au-vents should be dipped in flour; press the dough firmly – don't twist – for a clean edge. Metal cutters are best.

● Wet baking sheets with cold water to help prevent pastry burning on the underside in the very hot oven.

● When you cut out shapes for pie tops or vol-au-vents turn the pastry over; the underside (next to table) is smooth and pastry will rise evenly.

● Brush dough with beaten egg to make a golden glaze, but don't let glaze run down sides. It will set in the oven and seal pastry layers together.

● For any of the recipes using puff pastry you can use frozen or ready-made puff pastry. Be careful, however, of the amount you buy. Remember that ready-made pastry is sold by *weight*. A home-made pastry recipe indicates only the amount of flour and since puff pastry is made with equal parts flour and fat your home-made pastry actually weighs twice as much. To replace pastry made with 8 oz (225g) flour you will need to buy about 1 lb (450g) or a 13½ oz (370g) packet frozen or ready-made pastry.

Quick flaky pastry

Sift the flour and salt into a mixing bowl. Cut butter or margarine in ½ inch (1cm) cubes and add to the flour. Alternatively, have fat thoroughly chilled and grate on a coarse grater directly on to flour. Dip fat in the flour as you grate to keep the pieces separate. Mix flour and pieces of fat with the fingertips to separate lumps of fat but do *not* rub it into the flour.

Add the water and lemon juice and lightly mix to a soft dough with a table knife, keeping pieces of fat whole. Turn on to a floured surface (do not knead) and roll out to a rectangle three times as long as it is wide. Fold the bottom third of the pastry over the centre, then fold the top third down. Gently press the open ends to seal and give the dough a half turn to bring sealed ends to the top and bottom. Repeat the rolling, folding and sealing. Wrap in cling film and chill for 30 minutes. Repeat rolling, folding and sealing twice more to make a total of four times. Bake in an oven heated to 425°F (220°C) or Gas no. 7 unless otherwise indicated. This pastry will keep for 2 days in the refrigerator.

8 oz (225g) plain flour
pinch of salt
6 oz (175g) butter or margarine
6–8 tablespoons cold water
squeeze of lemon juice

Puff pastry

Sift the flour, cream of tartar and salt into a mixing bowl. Add the cooking fat in pieces and rub in with the fingertips. Add the water and mix to a rough dough with a fork. Turn on to a floured work surface and knead dough lightly once or twice to remove the cracks. Wrap in cling film and chill for 30 minutes.

Sprinkle the butter with flour and roll out or shape into a neat rectangle about ½ inch (1cm) thick. Roll out the chilled dough to a rectangle about ½ inch (1cm) wider than the butter and slightly more than three times as long. Place butter in centre and fold the pastry over to enclose it completely. Gently press the open edges with the rolling pin to seal. (This is the first roll and fold.)

Give the dough a half turn to bring sealed ends to the top and bottom. Press dough gently with rolling pin, moving it from centre to top, then from centre to bottom to distribute the air. With quick light strokes roll out dough to a rectangle three times as long as it is wide. Fold the bottom third up over the centre and the top third down. Seal edges again. Wrap and chill the pastry for 30 minutes. Repeat the rolling, folding and sealing twice, then chill for 30 minutes and repeat rolling, folding and sealing twice again to make a total of six times. (A useful trick of the trade among pastry cooks is to impress the fingertips in the dough to indicate how many rolls and folds it has had – it's so easy to forget. Chill pastry for 30 minutes before rolling out. Bake in an oven heated to 450°F (230°C) or Gas no. 8 unless otherwise indicated in the recipe. Prepared puff pastry will keep in the refrigerator for 2–3 days. Wrap in kitchen foil or polythene to prevent drying out.

8 oz (225g) strong white flour
¼ teaspoon cream of tartar
pinch of salt
1 oz (25g) white cooking fat
6–8 tablespoons cold water
7 oz (200g) butter

Choux pastry

The method for choux pastry is quite different from other pastries. For one thing it's made in a saucepan. You start by bringing the water and fat to the boil, then the flour is quickly added all at once. This is an important stage because the heat will immediately cook the flour and with a bit of stirring, the mixture cooks to a kind of roux in the saucepan. It's terribly important to tip the flour into the boiling water and not the other way round or the water stops boiling.

Once the mixture has cooled a little, the eggs are beaten in. This is where the hard work begins. It's best to beat the eggs directly into the contents of the pan using a wooden spoon. Or, you can use an electric hand mixer. The eggs must be beaten in gradually and very thoroughly until you get the right texture. It must be smooth, shiny and just firm enough to hold its shape, like softly whipped cream. Up to this stage choux pastry can be set aside and baked later. In fact, a short rest in a cool place actually improves choux pastry – it becomes firm and easier to use for piping.

Choux pastry will collapse on cooling if it's not baked until very crisp and dry. Test by pinching the sides – they should not feel the slightest bit soft. I stab a little hole in the sides of baked choux pastry with the tip of a vegetable knife to let the steam out and then return it to the oven to dry out completely.

How to make better choux pastry

● Sift the flour and salt on to a square of grease-proof paper so you can tip it quickly into the boiling liquid; it's a good idea to set the flour in a warm place while getting everything else ready.

● Make pastry with butter for flavour and use strong white bread flour (the kind you use for bread making); you will get beautifully puffed up choux pastry with an excellent volume.

● It's very important to cook the 'paste' for about 1 minute over the heat, until it leaves the side of the pan clean.

● Beat the egg in gradually and make sure the pastry has cooled sufficiently. If eggs are beaten in when mixture is hot they will scramble and lose much of their aerating power.

● Choux pastry is piped or spooned out; use a teaspoon for cocktail snippets or profiteroles and a dessertspoon for a larger bun size. Otherwise, you will need a large piping bag.

● Baking sheets must be greased; if you require guidelines for piping, dust greased sheet with flour and tap sharply to knock out excess, then mark lines on sheet with fingertips.

● Choux pastry likes a steamy atmosphere for baking to help expansion; don't open oven door until baking time is up.

● You must bake pastry until absolutely dry (like cardboard) or it will collapse when you take it from the oven.

● Choux pastry has very little flavour on its own. Delicious sweet or savoury fillings and toppings are what make choux pastry taste so nice.

● Don't fill choux pastry too far ahead of serving or the dry pastry will absorb moisture from the filling and soften.

● You can make choux pastry ahead and re-frigerate until required – 24 hours at the most. Or, baked but unfilled choux puff buns or eclairs will keep firm and dry for a day in an airtight tin. Store when quite cold.

● Sweetened whipped cream or confectioner's custard (page 204) are the most popular fillings for choux buns or eclairs. Or you can fill tiny profiteroles with flavoured cream cheese and serve them with drinks.

Choux pastry (recipe)

Sift the flour on to a square of greaseproof paper. Put the butter into a medium-sized saucepan, along with the water, salt and sugar (if making pastry for sweet fillings). Heat gently until butter has completely melted, then bring to a fast boil and immediately tip in all the flour.

Beat with a wooden spoon for 1 minute over the heat, until the mixture forms a ball and leaves the side of the pan clean. Allow to cool until the hand can be comfortably held against the side of the pan.

Lightly beat the eggs and add to the pastry a little at a time, beating well after each addition. (You may have to add an extra egg yolk to get the right consistency.) When ready choux pastry will appear smooth and glossy and just stiff enough to hold its own shape. Chill until ready to use. Bake in an oven heated to 425°F (220°C) or Gas no. 7 unless otherwise indicated in the recipe.

Makes 12 buns or eclairs

2½ oz (65g) strong white flour
2 oz (50g) butter
¼ pint (150ml) cold water
pinch of salt
1 level teaspoon castor sugar
   (optional)
2 eggs
1 egg yolk (optional)

How to make better pies and flans

● Make pastry in advance and chill for at least 30 minutes; a relaxed pastry will shrink less when baked in the oven.

● To get maximum use and little waste, first shape pastry dough with your knuckles to a small version of the shape you intend to roll it.

● Sprinkle flour on your work surface from a dredger to minimize the amount used; dust the work surface and the rolling pin but never the pastry; too much extra flour used will only make the pastry hard.

● A wooden rolling pin is the best kind to use – preferably one with no handles. Place palms of the hand on the pin for even pressure and roll with short, light movements.

● Lift rolled out pastry on the rolling pin (reduces handling) by placing the rolling pin at far end of pastry and rolling it towards you, lifting pastry loosely around rolling pin; then unroll over the pie plate or flan ring.

● Or fold pastry circle in half and lay it across centre of pie plate or tin, then open it out so it covers the whole area.

● Ease pastry into baking tin; start pressing with fingertips from centre to outer edge to expel air underneath.

● Roll the rolling pin over the top of flan ring to cut off surplus pastry; if you've judged it right there should be very little left over.

● Start and end with layers of fruit in a covered pie – sugar directly under the crust makes pastry soggy underneath.

● Keep quantity of liquid in a covered fruit pie to a minimum to avoid contents bubbling out. Only 2–3 tablespoons of water are needed–fruits will supply extra juices.

● To avoid spilled fillings such as those with custard, have prepared pie case on a baking tray and set tray on oven rack, then slowly pour in filling from a jug.

● Pastry crusts, whether pie is hot or cold, always taste best if pie is warmed in the oven for a few moments before serving. Exceptions are custard and cream filled pies or those with whipped cream. Refrigerate these as soon as possible.

Deep dish plum pie

Serves 4–6

shortcrust pastry, made using 6 oz
   (175g) plain flour (page 167)
milk or beaten egg, for glazing
castor sugar, for dusting

Filling
1½–2 lb (700–900g) plums
3–4 oz (75–100g) castor sugar
2–3 tablespoons water

Heat the oven to 400°F (200°C) or Gas no. 6. Halve and stone the plums for the filling. Place half the fruit in a 1½ pint (900ml) pie dish, add the sugar and cover with remaining fruit. Sprinkle over the water and set aside.

Roll out prepared pastry on a lightly floured work surface about 1 inch (2.5cm) larger than the pie dish rim. Using pie dish as a guide, cut out a lid ½ inch (1cm) larger than the rim. Fold dough in half and make several slits across fold. Line greased pie dish rim with the pastry trimmings – place cut edge inwards and they will fit rim perfectly. Damp pastry rim and cover with pie top. Press rim to seal, trim, knock up and flute pie edge attractively. Brush pie with milk or beaten egg.

Set pie dish on a baking tray, and place in the centre of preheated oven to bake for 15 minutes. Then lower oven temperature to 350°F (180°C) or Gas no. 4 and bake for a further 15–20 minutes, or until pastry is crisp and brown and fruit is tender. (Test by pushing a knife through pastry vent.) Dust pie with sugar. Serve with a jug of cream or vanilla ice cream.

Variations **Deep dish apple pie:** Peel, core and thinly slice 1½–2 lb (700–900g) apples. A little pared lemon rind is nice with apple and a mixture of apples and plums is delicious.

Deep dish rhubarb pie: Trim off leafy tops and base of stems and cut stalks in 1 inch (2.5cm) lengths. Sprinkle rhubarb with 1 teaspoon grated orange rind.

Deep dish apricot pie: Halve and stone 1½–2 lb (700–900g) apricots. Use soft light brown sugar in place of the castor sugar.

Double crust apple pie

Serves 6

sweet shortcrust pastry, made using
   8 oz (225g) plain flour (page 167)
milk, for glazing
icing sugar, for dusting

Filling
1½ lb (700g) cooking apples
3 oz (75g) castor sugar
1–2 oz (25–50g) sultanas
nut of butter or 1 tablespoon water

Heat the oven to 400°F (200°C) or Gas no. 6. Roll out one-third of the pastry on a lightly floured work surface to a circle and use to line a 9 inch (22.5cm) pie plate. Peel, core and slice the apples. Arrange half the apples in the pie plate. Sprinkle with the castor sugar and sultanas and add a few flakes of butter or 1 tablespoon water. Arrange the rest of the apples neatly on top.

Roll out remaining pastry to a circle about 1 inch (2.5cm) larger than the pie plate rim and cut a few slits for air vents. Damp pastry rim and cover with pie top. Press rim to seal, trim, knock up and flute pie edges attractively. Brush pie with milk. Place above centre in preheated oven and bake for 30–35 minutes, or until pastry is crisp and brown and fruit is tender. Dust the top with icing sugar. Serve hot or cold.

Variations: Use chopped dates in place of the sultanas; a sliver of lemon peel will delicately flavour the pie as will the grated rind and juice of an orange. Add a sliced quince along with the apple, a few cloves or a pinch of ground cinnamon – the variations are numerous.

Raspberry plate pie

Heat the oven to 400°F (200°C) or Gas no. 6. Roll out half the prepared pastry on a lightly floured work surface to a circle and use to line a 9 inch (22.5cm) pie plate.

Pick over the raspberries and arrange them level in pie plate. Mix together the sugar and cornflour and sprinkle mixture over the raspberries. Damp pastry rim. Roll out remaining pastry to a circle about 1 inch (2.5cm) larger than pie plate rim and make a few slits in the dough. Cover the pie, press rim gently to seal and trim edges. Knock up and flute pie rim attractively and brush the top with milk. Place above centre in preheated oven and bake for 15 minutes. Then lower oven temperature to 375°F (190°C) or Gas no. 5 and bake for a further 15–20 minutes. Dust with icing sugar and serve hot or cold.

Variations: Use 8 oz (225g) trimmed blackcurrants, gooseberries or rhubarb (cut in short lengths) in place of the raspberries.

Serves 4–6

shortcrust pastry, made using 6 oz (175g) plain flour (page 167)
milk, for glazing
icing sugar, for dusting

Filling
8 oz (225g) raspberries
2 oz (50g) castor sugar
1 level tablespoon cornflour

Custard pie

Heat the oven to 400°F (200°C) or Gas no. 6. Roll out the prepared pastry on a lightly floured work surface to a circle and use to line an 8 inch (20cm) tart tin or flan ring set on a baking tray. Chill while preparing the filling.

Crack two whole eggs and one egg yolk into a mixing bowl. Reserve the remaining egg white. Whisk in the sugar, milk and vanilla essence. Strain the custard into a jug. Lightly beat the egg white with a fork and brush it over the pastry, then sprinkle over the raisins.

Pour the prepared custard into the pie shell and grate a little nutmeg on top. Place in the centre of preheated oven and bake for 15 minutes. Then lower oven temperature to 350°F (180°C) or Gas no. 4 and bake for a further 15 minutes, or until custard filling is set. Shake gently – if centre quivers like a jelly it's done. Serve warm or cold.

Serves 6

shortcrust pastry, made using 4 oz (100g) plain flour (page 167)
little grated nutmeg

Filling
3 large eggs
1 oz (25g) castor sugar
½ pint (300ml) milk
few drops of vanilla essence
1 oz (25g) seedless raisins

Lemon pie

Serves 6

sweet shortcrust pastry, made using
    4 oz (100g) plain flour (page 167)

Filling
3 large eggs
6 oz (175g) castor sugar
finely grated rind and juice of 2
    lemons
2 oz (50g) ground almonds
2 oz (50g) butter

Heat the oven to 400°F (200°C) or Gas no. 6. Roll out the prepared pastry on a lightly floured work surface to a circle and use to line an 8 inch (20cm) round tart tin or flan ring set on a baking tray. Prick the base, line the pastry with a circle of greaseproof paper and weight down with some baking beans. Place above centre in preheated oven and bake blind for 15 minutes. Remove beans and paper and bake for a further 5 minutes, or until pie shell is crisp and brown. Remove from oven. Lower oven temperature to 350°F (180°C) or Gas no. 4.

Crack the eggs into a mixing bowl and add the sugar, finely grated lemon rind, ground almonds and butter cut in pieces. Set over a saucepan one-quarter filled with hot (not boiling) water and stir until the butter has melted and sugar has dissolved. Draw off the heat, and stir in the lemon juice.

Pour the filling into the baked pastry case. Place in centre of oven and bake for 20 minutes, or until filling has set. Allow to cool completely. Serve cold with pouring cream.

Apple and cream pie

Serves 6

sweet shortcrust pastry, made using
    4 oz (100g) plain flour (page 167)
icing sugar, for dusting

Filling
1–2 oz (25–50g) ground hazelnuts
3 tart dessert apples
2 egg yolks
1 oz (25g) castor sugar
¼ pint (150ml) double cream
finely grated rind of 1 small lemon

Heat the oven to 400°F (200°C) or Gas no. 6. Roll out the prepared pastry on a lightly floured work surface to a circle and use to line an 8 inch (20cm) round tart tin or flan ring set on a baking tray. Prick the base, line the pastry with a circle of greaseproof paper and weight down with some baking beans. Place above centre in preheated oven and bake blind for 15 minutes. Remove beans and paper and bake for a further 5 minutes, or until pie shell is crisp and brown. Remove from oven and lower oven temperature to 350°F (180°C) or Gas no. 4.

Sprinkle the ground hazelnuts evenly over the pie base. Peel, core and thinly slice the apples and arrange slices over the hazelnuts. Combine egg yolks, sugar, cream and finely grated lemon rind in a mixing bowl and pour mixture over the apple slices. Place pie in centre of oven and bake for 15–20 minutes, or until custard filling has set and pastry is golden brown. Dust with icing sugar. For an attractive finish put the pie under a hot grill to caramelize apple slices.

For a crisp pie crust

Fruit tends to make a pie crust soft. The way to prevent this is to use something which will absorb the fruit juices while the pie is baking. Sprinkle a thin layer of crumbled trifle sponge over the pastry base before adding the fruit. What I like to do is sprinkle ground almonds or hazelnuts on the pastry base because nuts add such a nice flavour to a fruit pie. Try using almonds for an apricot pie and hazelnuts with apples or plums.

Illustrated: Plum slice, page 177

Plum slice

On a lightly floured work surface, roll out pastry to a 12 × 14 inch (30 × 35cm) rectangle. Trim pastry edges straight and cut pastry in half lengthways. Then cut 2 × ½ inch (1cm) strips from the long side of each half to use for borders.

Transfer each pastry half to a wetted baking tray and prick them all over with a fork. Brush the longer pastry edges with beaten egg and place pastry borders on top. Press gently to seal, then flute the edges. Chill while preparing the filling.

Heat the oven to 425°F (220°C) or Gas no. 7. Halve and stone the plums. Cream the butter and sugar in a mixing bowl until soft and light. Add the egg, ground almonds, flour and almond essence and mix to a smooth paste. Spread the centre of each pastry slice with the almond filling. Arrange plums close together, rounded sides up, over the almond filling. Brush pastry borders with egg. Place both slices in preheated oven and bake for 20 minutes. Then lower oven temperature to 400°F (200°C) or Gas no. 6 and bake for a further 10 minutes, or until pastry is golden and filling is cooked through. Transfer to a wire rack. Brush the hot fruit topping with hot jam glaze. Allow to cool and serve cut in slices.

Variations **Apricot slice:** Use 2 lb (900g) fresh apricots instead of plums. If you prefer you can use 1 lb (450g) of each fruit and make two different slices. Use hot jam glaze made with apricot jam.

Strawberry slice: Omit almond filling. Bake pastry slices without any filling for 20–25 minutes at 400°F (200°C) or Gas no. 6. Allow to cool completely, then fill with 2 lb (900g) fresh strawberries and glaze with hot jam glaze made using strawberry jam.

Serves 12

puff pastry, made using 8 oz (225g) strong white flour (page 171)
beaten egg, for glazing
jam glaze made using apricot jam (page 183)

Filling
2 lb (900g) fresh plums
2 oz (50g) butter
2 oz (50g) castor sugar
1 egg
2 oz (50g) ground almonds
1 level tablespoon plain flour
few drops of almond essence

illustrated facing page 176

Strawberry tartlets

Heat the oven to 400°F (200°C) or Gas no. 6. Roll out the prepared pastry on a lightly floured work surface. Using a plain or fluted 2½ inch (6cm) round cutter, cut 12 circles of pastry, using all the trimmings for the last few. Use to line 12 patty tins. Prick the base of each pastry case with a fork. Chill for 10 minutes. Then place in the centre of preheated oven and bake for 12 minutes. Allow pastry cases to cool.

Pick over and hull the strawberries. Slice any large ones in half. Blend the cream cheese with the sugar in a mixing bowl, then work in the cream or milk to make a soft consistency. Spoon a little cream cheese mixture into the base of each baked pastry tartlet and top with strawberries.

Bring the jelly and lemon juice to the boil in a saucepan and stir to blend. Spoon the jelly over the strawberry tartlets to glaze. Chill for 30 minutes before serving.

Makes 12

sweet shortcrust pastry, made using 4 oz (100g) plain flour (page 167)

Filling
1 lb (450g) fresh strawberries
4 oz (100g) soft cream cheese
1 level tablespoon castor sugar
1–2 tablespoons cream or milk

Glaze
2 tablespoons redcurrant jelly
juice of ½ lemon

Illustrated: Strawberry tartlets, see above

Lemon meringue pie

Serves 6

shortcrust pastry, made using 4 oz (100g) plain flour (page 167)

Filling
2 oz (50g) cornflour
6 oz (175g) castor sugar
½ pint (300ml) water
finely grated rind and juice of 2 lemons
2 egg yolks
½ oz (15g) butter

Meringue topping
2 egg whites
3 oz (75g) castor sugar

Heat the oven to 400°F (200°C) or Gas no. 6. Roll out the prepared pastry to a circle on a lightly floured work surface and use to line an 8 inch (20cm) tart tin or flan ring set on a baking tray. Prick the base, line the pastry with a circle of greaseproof paper and weight down with some baking beans. Place above centre in preheated oven and bake for 15 minutes. Remove beans and paper and bake for a further 5 minutes, or until the pie is crisp and brown.

Put the cornflour and sugar into a saucepan. Stir in the water and mix well to blend the cornflour. Add the finely grated lemon rind. Bring to the boil, stirring all the time as mixture thickens. Lower the heat and cook gently for 1 minute, then draw off the heat. Stir in the lemon juice, then beat in the egg yolks one at a time. Stir in the butter. Pour the lemon filling into the baked pie shell and spread level.

Lower oven temperature to 300°F (150°C) or Gas no. 2. Beat the egg whites until stiff peaks form. Add half the sugar, 1 tablespoon at a time, whisking well after each addition. Then fold the remaining sugar into the eggs with a metal spoon. Spoon the meringue over the lemon filling. Place pie in the centre of preheated oven and bake for about 20 minutes, or until meringue is golden. Serve with cream.

Apple amber

Serves 6

shortcrust pastry made using 4 oz (100g) self-raising flour (page 167)

Filling
1½ lb (700g) cooking apples
2 oz (50g) butter
3 oz (75g) castor sugar
2–3 pieces thinly pared lemon rind
2 egg yolks

Topping
2 egg whites
3 oz (75g) castor sugar

Roll out the prepared pastry on a lightly floured work surface to a circle and use to line an 8 inch (20cm) tart tin or flan ring set on a baking tray. Chill while preparing the filling.

Heat the oven to 375°F (190°C) or Gas no. 5. Peel, core and slice the apples. Melt the butter in a saucepan over low heat. Add the apples, sugar and thinly pared lemon rind and stir until sugar has dissolved. Cover the pan and cook gently until apples are tender. Beat apple mixture to a purée with a wooden spoon, then press through a sieve into a mixing bowl. Add the egg yolks and mix together well. Pour the mixture into the prepared pastry case and spread level. Place above centre in preheated oven and bake for 25–30 minutes, or until filling has set. Remove from oven and lower oven temperature to 300°F (150°C) or Gas no. 2.

Beat the egg whites for the topping until stiff peaks form. Add half the sugar 1 tablespoon at a time, whisking well after each addition. Then fold in the remaining sugar with a metal spoon. Spoon the whisked eggs over the apple filling. Place pie in centre of oven and bake for a further 20 minutes, or until meringue is golden. Serve warm or cold with cream.

Treacle tart

Roll out the prepared pastry on a lightly floured work surface to a circle and use to line an 8 inch (20cm) tart tin or flan ring set on a baking tray. Reserve any pastry trimmings. Chill while preparing the filling.

Heat the oven to 400°F (200°C) or Gas no. 6. Warm the syrup in a saucepan until thin and runny. (If you heat the tablespoon for measuring in boiling water you will find it easier to measure out the syrup.) Stir in the breadcrumbs and leave to stand for 10 minutes until the crumbs have absorbed the syrup. Check the consistency at this stage: if the mixture looks stodgy add more syrup and if it looks thin and runny stir in a few more breadcrumbs – the mixture should have the consistency of thick honey. Stir in the finely grated lemon rind and lemon juice.

Spread the mixture evenly in the prepared pastry case. Roll out pastry trimmings and cut in narrow strips. Use to make a lattice pattern across the top of the pie. Place above centre in preheated oven and bake for 10 minutes. Then lower oven temperature to 375°F (190°C) or Gas no. 5 and bake for a further 15 minutes. Serve warm or cold.

Serves 6

shortcrust pastry, made using 4 oz (100g) plain flour (page 167)

Filling
4 rounded tablespoons golden syrup
4 rounded tablespoons soft white breadcrumbs
finely grated rind and juice of ½ lemon

Mincemeat jalousie

Roll out the puff pastry on a lightly floured work surface to a 12 inch (30cm) square. Trim the edges with a sharp knife and cut the pastry square in half.

Lightly flour one pastry strip and fold in half lengthways. Using a sharp knife, cut a series of slits along the folded edge to within ½ inch (1cm) of the trimmed edge. Place the other strip of pastry on a wetted baking sheet. Spread with the mincemeat to within 1 inch (2.5cm) of the border. Sprinkle with brandy, if using it. Open out slashed strip of pastry and carefully place over the filling to cover and match the edges. Seal edges and knock up and flute as you would for a pie. Chill for at least 20 minutes.

Heat the oven to 425°F (220°C) or Gas no. 7. Brush pastry with beaten egg. Place above centre in preheated oven and bake for 30–35 minutes. Lower the oven temperature to 400°F (200°C) or Gas no. 6 after 20 minutes if pastry browns too much. Dust with icing sugar and return to the oven until the sugar has caramelized to a beautiful brown – watch baking as top will easily burn. Serve hot cut in slices with whipped cream or hard sauce (page 228).

If you dislike fiddling with individual tartlets, a jalousie is a novel way of presenting mince pie. Serve at a buffet when you could bake 2 or more by doubling the quantities.

Serves 6

1 × 13 oz (370g) frozen puff pastry, thawed, or puff pastry made using 8 oz (225g) strong white flour (page 171)
4 tablespoons mincemeat
2 teaspoons brandy (optional)
beaten egg, for glazing
icing sugar, for dusting

Mince pies

Makes 24

10 oz (275g) plain flour
1 oz (25g) ground almonds
6 oz (175g) butter
3 oz (75g) icing sugar
finely grated rind of ½ lemon
1 egg yolk
3 tablespoons milk
icing sugar, for dusting

Filling
1 tablespoon brandy (optional)
8 oz (225g) mincemeat

Sift the flour into a mixing bowl and add the ground almonds. Add the butter in pieces and rub in with the fingertips. Sift over the icing sugar and add the grated lemon rind. Lightly mix the egg yolk with the milk and stir into the flour mixture. Mix to a rough dough in the bowl, then turn out and knead just long enough to remove the cracks. Cover with upturned mixing bowl and leave to rest for 30 minutes.

Heat the oven to 400°F (200°C) or Gas no. 6. Roll out pastry thinly on a lightly floured work surface. Using a 2½ inch (6cm) round cutter, cut 24 circles of pastry and use to line 24 patty tins. Then with a smaller 2 inch (5cm) round cutter cut 24 circles for the tops, using all the trimmings for the last few.

Combine brandy, if using it, with mincemeat and place 1 teaspoon of mincemeat in the centre of each pie. Damp edges, press on pastry tops and snip a small hole in each top. Place in the centre of preheated oven and bake for 15–20 minutes, or until lightly browned. Dust the tops with icing sugar. Serve hot with hard sauce (page 228).

Macaroon tarts

Makes 12

sweet shortcrust pastry, made using
    4 oz (100g) plain flour (page 167)
raspberry jam

Filling
2 egg whites
4 oz (100g) castor sugar
4 oz (100g) ground almonds
few drops of almond essence

Heat the oven to 350°F (180°C) or Gas no. 4. Roll out prepared pastry thinly on a lightly floured work surface. Using a floured 2½ inch (6cm) round cutter, cut 12 circles of pastry using all the trimmings to make the last few. Use to line 12 tartlet tins. Spoon a tiny blob of raspberry jam in the base of each tartlet and set aside while preparing the filling.

Whisk the egg whites until stiff peaks form. Add half the sugar, 1 tablespoon at a time, whisking well after each addition. Then fold the remaining sugar and ground almonds into the egg whites with a metal spoon. Flavour with almond essence. Place 1 rounded dessertspoon of the mixture into each tartlet case. Place in the centre of preheated oven and bake for 25 minutes. Transfer to a wire rack and leave until completely cool.

Apple dumplings

Serves 4

sweet shortcrust pastry, made using
    8 oz (225g) plain flour (page 167)
4 even-sized cooking apples
2 oz (50g) castor sugar
milk and extra castor sugar, for
    glazing

Divide prepared pastry in quarters and shape each one to a round. On a floured surface, roll out each portion to a circle about 8 inches (20cm) in diameter. Set aside to rest for 10 minutes.

Heat the oven to 400°F (200°C) or Gas no. 6. Peel and core the apples leaving them whole. Place an apple on each round of pastry and fill the centre with castor sugar. Bring edge of pastry circle up over apple, trim any uneven pieces and press together to seal. Place apples seam side down on a greased baking tray. Make a hole in the centre of each dumpling so steam escapes. Roll out trimmings and cut diamond-shaped pieces to make leaves and 4 strips to make stalks.

Brush apple pastry with milk to glaze. Attach pastry leaves and brush them with milk. Place in centre of preheated oven and bake for 30 minutes. Brush apples with extra milk and sprinkle with sugar, then place pastry stalks on tray and return dumplings to oven for a further 5–10 minutes until tender. Test apples by piercing with a sharp knife. Insert a pastry stalk in the hole of each dumpling.

Bakewell tart

Heat the oven to 400°F (200°C) or Gas no 6. Roll out prepared pastry on a lightly floured work surface to a circle and use to line an 8 inch (20cm) tart tin or flan ring set on a baking tray. Spread pastry base with the jam and chill until required.

Sift the flour and baking powder for the filling on to a plate and add the ground almonds. Cream the butter and sugar in a mixing bowl until soft and light. Lightly mix the egg and almond essence and beat in to the creamed mixture a little at a time. Fold the flour and ground almonds into the mixture with a metal spoon, then spread mixture over the jam.

Decorate pie with pastry leaves cut from pastry trimmings or sprinkle with flaked almonds. Place in the centre of preheated oven and bake for 30 minutes, or until well risen and firm to the touch. Allow to cool completely.

Serves 6

shortcrust pastry, made using 4 oz
   (100g) plain flour (page 167)
1 tablespoon raspberry jam
flaked almonds, for sprinkling
   (optional)

Filling
1 oz (25g) plain flour
½ level teaspoon baking powder
2 oz (50g) ground almonds
2 oz (50g) butter
2 oz (50g) castor sugar
1 egg
few drops of almond essence

Apple squares

Sift the flour into a mixing bowl. Add the butter in pieces and rub in with the fingertips until the mixture looks like fine breadcrumbs. Stir in the sugar. Lightly beat the egg, add to the mixture and lightly mix to a rough dough with a fork. Turn on to a floured work surface and knead just long enough to remove the cracks. Cover the pastry with upturned mixing bowl and leave to rest.

Heat the oven to 350°F (180°C) or Gas no. 4. Roll out half the dough and use to line the base of an 8 × 11 inch (20 × 27.5cm) baking tin. Peel, core and coarsely grate the apples for the filling. Mix together the sugar, cinnamon and sultanas, if using them. Arrange alternate layers of the grated apple and sugar mixture over the pastry base. Roll out the remaining dough to an 8 × 11 inch (20 × 27.5cm) rectangle, trim the edges straight, and use to cover the apple mixture.

Place in the centre of preheated oven and bake for 1 hour. Sprinkle an even layer of icing sugar over the warm pastry and leave until completely cool. Cut in 12 squares and lift out of the tin.

Makes 12

8 oz (225g) self-raising flour
4 oz (100g) butter
2 oz (50g) castor sugar
1 large egg
icing sugar, for sprinkling

Filling
1 lb (450g) cooking apples
4 oz (100g) castor sugar
½ level teaspoon ground cinnamon
1 tablespoon sultanas (optional)

Cream slices

Makes 16 slices

quick flaky pastry, made using 8 oz (225g) plain flour (page 171)
beaten egg, for glazing
icing sugar, for dusting

Filling
½ pint (300ml) double cream
3 tablespoons raspberry jam

Divide prepared pastry in half. Roll out each piece on a lightly floured work surface to a 9 × 6 inch (22.5 × 15cm) rectangle. Trim the edges straight with a sharp knife, then cut each rectangle in half lengthways and in quarters crossways to make a total of 16 slices. Place on two wetted baking sheets and chill for 20 minutes.

Heat the oven to 450°F (230°C) or Gas no. 8. Brush pastry slices with beaten egg to glaze. Place in preheated oven and bake for 10 minutes. Then lower the oven temperature to 425°F (220°C) or Gas no. 7 and bake for a further 5 minutes until risen and brown. Transfer to a wire rack and leave until completely cool and crisp.

Whip the cream until soft peaks form. Carefully split each pastry slice horizontally with a sharp knife and sandwich with a little raspberry jam and whipped cream. Dust the tops with icing sugar. These are nice to serve at buffet suppers.

Variations: Sandwich slices with fresh raspberries or strawberries and confectioner's custard flavoured with kirsch (page 204).

Eccles cakes

Makes 12

quick flaky pastry, made using 8 oz (225g) plain flour (page 171)
milk, for glazing
granulated sugar, for sprinkling

Filling
1 oz (25g) butter
1 oz (25g) soft light brown sugar
1 oz (25g) chopped candied peel
4 oz (100g) currants
½ level teaspoon mixed spice

Roll out the prepared pastry very thinly on a lightly floured work surface. Leave pastry to rest for a few minutes while preparing the filling. Melt the butter in a saucepan over low heat. Draw off the heat and stir in the brown sugar, candied peel, currants and mixed spice.

Using a 4 inch (10cm) round cutter, cut 12 rounds of the pastry. Alternatively, using a saucer as a guide, cut rounds with a sharp knife. Place 1 teaspoon of the filling in the centre of each circle. Brush pastry edges with water and draw the pastry edges up over the filling with the fingers and pinch pastry together. Turn each pastry over, flatten with the hand, then gently roll each one to a circle about 3 inches (7.5cm) in diameter – until the filling breaks the surface a little. Make three slashes across the tops with a sharp knife and place on a wetted baking sheet.

Heat the oven to 425°F (220°C) or Gas no. 7. Brush each eccles cake with milk and sprinkle with a little granulated sugar. Chill for 10 minutes. Then place in preheated oven and bake for 15–20 minutes, or until crisp and golden.

Variation: Eccles cakes are an excellent way to use up the trimmings from making vol-au-vents. Trimmings from puff pastry should never be formed into a ball before rolling out or the delicate layering will be lost. Just place the trimmings on top of each other in order to roll them out.

Vol-au-vents

Roll out the prepared pastry on a lightly floured work surface to a thickness of ¼ inch (5mm). Lightly flour a baking sheet and slide the pastry on to it. Chill for 20 minutes until firm which makes cutting easier.

Heat the oven to 450°F (230°C) or Gas no. 8. Using a 3 inch (7.5cm) round cutter, cut 12 circles of pastry. Using a palette knife (so they are not pulled out of shape) transfer 6 rounds on to a wetted baking sheet. Prick them with a fork and brush lightly with beaten egg. Using a 2 inch (5cm) round cutter, cut the centre from the remaining circles of pastry to make 6 pastry rings. Carefully lift these rings and turn them over on to the pastry circles. Press edges gently to seal. (Chill remaining centre circles of dough and bake them for 10 minutes after the cases have been baked to make lids, if liked.)

Lightly brush the top of each vol-au-vent case with beaten egg. Place in the centre of preheated oven and bake for 15–20 minutes, or until well risen. Then lower the oven temperature to 400°F (200°C) or Gas no. 6 and bake for a further 10 minutes, or until crisp and brown. Remove any soft pastry from the centre of each vol-au-vent with a fork. These are very handy to have (unbaked) in the freezer. Place straight in a hot oven and up they come in beautiful even layers.

Makes 6 cases

puff pastry, made using 8 oz (225g) strong white flour (page 171)
beaten egg, for glazing

Glazes for fruit flans

A glaze is a shiny covering for fruit flans, tarts or sponges which protects fruit from drying out or discolouring. There are three kinds of glazes:

Arrowroot glaze: A clear glaze which shows fruit off best – arrowroot has the edge on cornflour for this. Use arrowroot with tinned fruit juices. Measure out ¼ pint (150ml) fruit juice, then put 1 rounded teaspoon arrowroot into a saucepan and dilute with a little of the fruit juice. Stir in rest of fruit juice. Bring to the boil, stirring all the time, so mixture thickens evenly. Draw off the heat and spoon glaze over tart or flan while hot. An arrowroot glaze thickens and clears immediately, so quickly draw off the heat as soon as it comes to the boil or air bubbles in the liquid will be impossible to get rid of.

Jelly glaze: Another clear glaze but one that is used as a layer over a fresh fruit filling. Use the same flavoured jelly as that of the fruit, or use complementary flavours such as lemon jelly with bananas. Unless the flan is very large you will find ½ packet jelly tablet made up to ½ pint (300ml) with water is enough. Once jelly has completely dissolved, stir over a pan of iced water until it begins to thicken and shows signs of setting. Spoon glaze over tart or flan to cover fruit. Chill until set firm. Always take care to have everything ready beforehand – there is no time to waste once jelly starts to set.

Jam glaze: Choose a jam with a flavour that goes well with the fruit filling – strawberry, raspberry or apricot are the most frequently used. Allow about 2 rounded tablespoons jam for an 8 inch (20cm) fruit tart or flan. Sieve the jam into a saucepan and add the juice of ½ lemon. Stir over the heat until ingredients are blended, then bring to the boil. Simmer for a moment before spooning over the fruit tart. Allow to cool before serving. If jelly such as redcurrant jelly is used for the glaze, as in tartlets, there is no need to sieve it; but a light whisk in the pan as it comes to the boil will help it melt and blend.

Profiteroles with chocolate sauce

Serves 8

choux pastry (page 173)
beaten egg, for glazing
chocolate sauce (page 227)
1 oz (25g) chopped walnuts

Filling
½ pint (300ml) double cream
1 level tablespoon vanilla sugar

Heat the oven to 425°F (220°C) or Gas no. 7. Spoon prepared choux pastry into a large nylon or cotton piping bag fitted with a ½ inch (1cm) plain nozzle and pipe small mounds about 1 inch (2.5cm) in diameter on to two greased baking sheets. Alternatively, place rounded teaspoons of choux pastry on to prepared sheets – no more than 12 per sheet – to make a total of 24 profiteroles. Brush the egg over tops. Place in preheated oven and bake (undisturbed) for 15 minutes, until crisp and golden brown. Stab the side of each one with the tip of a knife and return to the oven for a further 3 minutes. Allow to cool completely before filling, or store overnight in an airtight tin.

Lightly whip the cream, add the vanilla sugar and whip until soft peaks form. Make a small slit in the side of each profiterole and spoon in cream. Alternatively, pipe cream through stabbed openings – this is the way confectioners fill profiteroles. Pile into a serving dish making a pyramid shape, if liked. Pour over cold chocolate sauce and sprinkle with chopped walnuts.

Cream puffs

Makes 12

choux pastry (page 173)
beaten egg, for glazing
coffee fondant icing (page 249)

Filling
½ pint (300ml) double cream
1 oz (25g) castor sugar
few drops of vanilla essence

Heat the oven to 425°F (220°C) or Gas no. 7. Spoon prepared choux pastry into a large nylon or cotton piping bag fitted with a ½ inch (1cm) plain nozzle. Pipe 12 mounds about 2 inches (5cm) in diameter on to two greased baking sheets, spacing them well apart. Alternatively, place rounded dessertspoonsful of choux pastry on to the baking sheets. Brush each pastry with a little beaten egg, then mark each one with the back of a fork. Place in preheated oven and bake (undisturbed) for 20 minutes, until crisp and golden brown. Stab the side of each pastry with the tip of a knife and return to the oven for a further 5 minutes. Allow to cool completely before filling.

Make a small slit in the side of each choux bun. Lightly whip the cream, add the sugar and vanilla and whip until soft peaks form. Spoon into a piping bag fitted with a ¼ inch (5mm) plain nozzle (or use a heavy paper piping bag) and pipe the cream into each bun. Then dip the rounded side of each filled bun into coffee fondant icing (page 249). Drain for a moment, then turn right side up. Allow icing to set before serving.

Variations: Fill choux buns with coffee-flavoured confectioner's custard (page 204) in place of the whipped cream.

Chocolate eclairs: Using the piping bag fitted with the ½ inch (1cm) plain nozzle, pipe choux pastry in 3 inch (7.5cm) lengths on to two greased baking sheets, spacing them about 2 inches (5cm) apart. Bake as directed above and when cool, fill them, then dip the smoothest side – often the bottom is best – in chocolate fondant icing (page 249). Allow icing to set before serving.

9

Desserts

The impressive finish to a meal need be no more
than simple combinations of fruits or it can be a
refreshing sorbet, rich ice cream, an unusual hot
pudding or an elegant dessert cake.

Desserts

Fruit

Apples are our most versatile fruit. Use acid cooking varieties that quickly cook to a pulp for dishes that require purées. Dessert apples retain their shape when cooked and are the ones to use for poaching and in flans, pies or fruit salads. Sliced apples should be dipped in lemon juice to prevent discoloration.

Apricots are especially good poached in a vanilla-flavoured sugar syrup. Crack the stones, remove the kernels and use a few to add a subtle almond flavour to apricot dishes.

Bananas: The skins of ripe bananas are yellow and flecked with brown. For cooking or storing bananas, skins should be yellow only or tinged with green at the tip. You can hurry the ripening if you put them in a polythene bag. Sliced bananas should be dipped in lemon juice to keep them white. Never store bananas in the refrigerator.

Blackberries picked off the hedgerow on a warm summer day will be sweet enough to eat raw. Otherwise, it's best to cook them. Cultivated blackberries are large, juicy and also delicious eaten raw. Blackberries are wonderful in mousses and pies and make delicious fruit fools.

Blackcurrants and redcurrants grow in pretty little clusters like grapes. They are very acid and need to be cooked. Use in compotes and to make lovely sorbets. For decoration you can coat tiny clusters with sugar which counteracts the acid flavours. Arrange them on puddings. Redcurrants are delicious mixed with raspberries in pies and puddings.

Cape gooseberries, also called Chinese lanterns, are small pale orange fruits about the size of a marble that are covered with a lantern-shaped papery husk. The berries can be eaten raw and have a perfumed sweet-sour taste. Chefs often fold back the husk, dip the fruit in melted fondant and serve in petits fours cases.

Cherries: Sweet dessert cherries are delicious eaten raw out of the hand. They also make a colourful addition to a fruit salad. A cherry stoner is a handy gadget to have for removing the stones.

Cranberries are crimson and about the size of a raspberry. Even when ripe, they are too acid to be eaten uncooked. Use in tarts, pies and to make sauces. They have an affinity with apples and oranges and make lovely preserves.

Custard apples are about the size of a large apple and have a greenish grey scaly skin – not a pretty fruit. The flesh is sweetly scented and has a custard texture. Cut the fruit in half and eat the flesh by scooping it out with a spoon.

Damsons are a type of plum that is very astringent. They have a beautiful colour which they retain on cooking. Stewed damsons are delicious.

Dates: Fresh dates are not so sweet as the dried sticky ones sold in boxes. If you pinch off the stalk end and squeeze the opposite end, the stones will slide out. Eat them whole or slice the dates and add to a fruit salad. Or slice them open and stuff with cream cheese for a cocktail snack or with marzipan for an after-dinner sweetmeat.

Figs: The flesh is usually a pretty pink but a number of varieties are grown. When ripe, figs are soft and very perishable. The nicest way I've had them is sliced opened like a flower and served with Parma ham.

Gooseberries: Early varieties are green and hard and very sour so use them in puddings, pies and preserves. Large dessert gooseberries are a yellowish green and are good for eating. You need to top and tail gooseberries.

Grapefruits: Peel and break open the grapefruit into segments and eat as you would an orange. The pink tinged varieties are the best as they are sweet and very juicy. Pink grapefruits are good for slimmers – you won't want to add any sugar.

Grapes are usually sweet and juicy but some have sharp-tasting tough skins. They range in colour from a pale green to a deep purple. Remove the seeds and leave the grapes whole by pushing a cocktail stick in at the stalk end and twisting. To skin grapes, immerse them in boiling water for about 30 seconds, then peel away the skins. Grapes make pretty garnishes for meat and fish dishes, especially if you paint small clusters with egg white and dip them in sugar. Wash grapes just before serving and serve them well chilled on ice.

Guavas are a pear-shaped fruit with a pink flesh and lots of seeds. They are juicy and aromatic and fresh ones are well worth looking out for. However, they are more likely to be found tinned and make an unusual addition to fruit salads.

Kiwi fruits: When you peel away the brown hairy skin, underneath you will find a juicy green flesh pitted with tiny black seeds. Green is an unusual colour for fruit so if you slice just one kiwi fruit into a fruit salad the colour contrast is stunning.

Or arrange slices on cheesecakes, mousses or pavlova. Don't try to set kiwi fruit in jelly. Like fresh pineapple, they contain an enzyme that makes jellies soften and run.

Kumquats are a type of orange about the size of a cherry. They are bright yellow, pungent and can be eaten rind and all. Kumquats poached in a sugar syrup are delicious as an ice cream topping. They are often sold bottled in a sugar syrup – the little kumquats look very pretty suspended in the sugar syrup.

Lemons: No good cook should be without fresh lemons. They add a zest and sharpness to both sweet and savoury dishes. When buying, look for lemons with a waxy yellow skin; they should also feel heavy for their size. Roll a lemon between the palms of the hand, pressing lightly to get the juices running – this helps to warm the fruit which makes squeezing easier. Lemon flavouring oils are in the outer yellow rind and when grating, be careful to avoid grating the bitter white pith. To make thinly pared rinds a vegetable peeler is the tool to use. Store lemons in the lowest section of the refrigerator where they will keep for 2 weeks.

Limes are a thin-skinned citrus fruit with a greenish yellow skin. The juice is very acid but has a clean sharp flavour. Slices of lime are good in iced tea as well as in many cocktail drinks; they are also very good squeezed over fresh melon.

Lychees have a thin brown, scaly skin that is quite brittle. Crack the skin and peel them to reveal the translucent white flesh. Discard the stone and serve lychees chilled either fresh or poached in a syrup. Tinned lychees are readily available and are often served in Chinese restaurants.

Mangoes: If the flesh yields to gentle pressure a mango is ripe. Look for mangoes with a blush of yellow or red as those that are all green do not ripen properly. The sweet flesh is bright orange and has a flavour reminiscent of apricots and pineapples. And they are so juicy you should eat them in the bath! Try cutting them in half lengthways, remove the stone and serve mangoes well chilled for eating with a spoon. Alternatively, peel the skin and slice the flesh lengthways, then cut in bite-sized pieces. Add to a fresh fruit salad and the whole dish will take on the wonderful fragrant flavour.

Medlars are dark brown pear-shaped fruits. They can be eaten raw, but must be picked and stored until they are almost overripe, or 'bletted'. To eat a medlar, hold it between your finger and thumb and squeeze until the skin splits, then put split end to your mouth and squeeze again. They are traditionally served with port.

Melons are refreshing, sweet and juicy. They are surprisingly versatile and as happy with sugar as they are with an oil and vinegar dressing. A melon is ripe if the flesh gives when pressed at the stem end. Some varieties have a lovely perfume fragrance too. If you chill a whole melon for at least an hour it will taste very fresh. Store whole melons in a polythene bag or other foods will take on the fragrance. They will keep perfectly for 4–5 days in a cool larder and are useful standbys for long weekends.

Nectarines are similar to peaches but have a smooth rather than fuzzy skin, a rich colour and smoother texture. Use as for peaches.

Oranges: Small oranges are usually the best. Select those with a glossy skin and feel the weight in your hand – the heavier the fruit the more juice it contains. Don't worry about the colour; an orange with a slight green tinge is usually just as ripe as a bright orange one. Oranges that are warm peel more easily. To peel, mark the skins in quarters as you would for eating, then put oranges in a bowl and cover with boiling water. Leave to stand for 5 minutes, then drain and the peel should come away with most of the white pith. Scrape off remaining white pith with a knife. Cut the oranges in slices or in segments and add to salads. Remember to grate the rind before you squeeze fruit juice. Bitter oranges are used for preserves only; they have lots of pips which contain pectin and a very sour juice which gives marmalade its excellent flavour.

Passion fruit has a brown, wrinkled skin and looks like a shrivelled plum but don't let that put you off – they are delicious. Cut the fruit in half and scoop out the flesh with a spoon – you can eat the seeds too.

Peaches: The blush on a peach is no guarantee of ripeness – look for a change in colour from pale green to yellow around the stalk. Cut peaches in half following the natural line of the fruit; separate by gently twisting halves in opposite directions. If you want to remove the skin, scald peaches in boiling water for about 10 seconds only. Peel and slice a ripe peach into a wine glass, top up with chilled wine or champagne and the wine will take on the flavour of the peach. You sip the wine and eat the peach.

Pears are ripened off the tree. They are picked when full size but not yet ready to eat and are usually sold when they are not quite ripe. Ripe pears bruise easily so it's best to buy them to ripen at home. Keep at room temperature for 1–2 days until pears yield to gentle pressure at the neck. Serve fully ripe soft pears for eating and use firm ripe pears for cooking. You'll find pears discolour immediately they are peeled and should be dipped in water with lemon juice added.

Pineapples always look good and are especially refreshing. You can slice off the leafy top and cut pineapple into wedges as you would a melon. Alternatively, cut away the outer rind and remove the tiny brown 'eyes' with a sharp knife, then cut in rings and remove the tough central core with a pastry cutter. Remember fresh pineapple contains an enzyme that makes jelly soften and run; use tinned pineapple pieces for setting in jelly.

Plums are delicious to eat raw or cooked. The best all-round plum is Victoria, good for cooking and eating. Purple plum varieties are better for cooking in pies and flans. Greengages, which are amber when ripe, are the sweetest and most delicate member of the plum family. Plums should be halved and stoned in the same way as peaches. Crack a few plum stones, remove the kernels and add to stewed plums to give a delicate almond flavour.

Pomegranates are about the size of a large apple and have a hard pinkish skin. Cut the fruit in half: the inside has pockets of red fleshy seeds which you spoon out and eat. I've served the seeds sprinkled over a winter fruit salad and the effect was very pretty.

Quinces are good for cooking and preserving but not for eating. They are as hard as wood, even when ripe, but quickly turn to a pulp when cooked. They make wonderful jams and jellies and are especially good for mixing with apples in pies. Peel and slice or chop and use 1 quince for every

1 lb (450g) apples. Quinces have a strong scent which quickly penetrates other foods so store them separately.

Raspberries are a wonderful fruit to eat raw but if picked in wet weather they will quickly go mouldy. Purée raspberries and use to make mousses and sorbets. They are also marvellous served plain with sugar and cream or soft cream cheese. Pile raspberries in melon halves – use the round Ogen or Galia melons – for a refreshing dessert.

Rhubarb: Only the stalk of this leafy plant is used – on no account use the leaves. Pale pink forced rhubarb is available in winter and is deliciously tender. Garden rhubarb follows in spring and summer. Washed stalks are trimmed and cut in pieces and used to make pies or puddings. The flavour is sharp and refreshing but very acid. If rhubarb is scalded in boiling water just before cooking, you can get away with using considerably less sugar in the recipe. Remember gentle cooking – never fierce boiling – is the rule with rhubarb.

Sharon fruit is a type of persimmon and looks like a large tomato. Unlike a persimmon this fruit is not astringent to eat. The sharon fruit is seedless, has a delicate sweet taste and you can eat the orangy flesh skin and all. Slice into fruit salads for added colour.

Strawberries are best served simply with sugar and cream. Try squeezing a little orange juice over a bowl of fresh strawberries.

Tangerines, satsumas and *clementines:* These close cousins of oranges make charming additions to winter fruit bowls. They are all easily peeled and separated into segments and satsumas and clementines are seedless, which is an added bonus. They have a delicious honey-like orange flavour and are best eaten raw or added to fruit salads.

Ugli fruits are a cross between a grapefruit and a tangerine. They look like a very large misshapen grapefruit and have a sweet pink flesh. Use in the same way as you would grapefruit; they make a nice addition to a fruit salad.

Poached or stewed fruits

Firm fruits like apricots, peaches, plums and pears make some of the loveliest desserts when gently poached in a delicately flavoured syrup. All fruits should be first washed well and then prepared according to type.

● Use a pan wide enough for the fruit to lie in a single layer so they cook gently and retain their attractive shapes.

● Water and sugar used to cook the fruit should be made into a syrup before the fruit is added. Unless the fruit is very sour use 4 oz (100g) castor sugar and ½ pint (300ml) water for each 1 lb (450g) fruit; when sugar has dissolved bring syrup to the boil, then lower the heat, simmer for 1 minute and add the fruit.

● The syrup can be flavoured with thinly pared orange or lemon rind, elderflowers, a vanilla pod or vanilla sugar and it can be spiced with cloves or cinnamon stick. Or you can use brown sugar in place of castor sugar to add colour and flavour.

● Draw the pan off the heat before the fruit is completely cooked. Leave to stand, covered, until the fruit is tender. Cooking times vary but are usually between 3–5 minutes or a little longer if the fruit is hard and not completely ripe.

● Chilled poached fruits are nice served simply on their own with soft sponge fingers or crisp shortbread. Or you can accompany them with pouring cream or vanilla ice cream and they go well with baked custard or with something simple like muesli.

Poached fresh fruit

Trim fruit according to type. Put the water and sugar into a large pan and stir over low heat until the sugar has dissolved. Bring to the boil, then lower the heat and simmer for 1 minute. Add the trimmed fruit and bring the syrup back to the boil. Then lower the heat, cover with a pan lid, and cook gently for 3–5 minutes, or until tender. Turn fruit with a perforated spoon, if necessary. Serve warm with cream or leave until cold.

Serves 4

1 lb (450g) fruit
½ pint (300ml) water
4–6 oz (100–175g) castor sugar

Pears in ginger syrup: Put 4 oz (100g) castor sugar, ½ pint (300ml) water, ½ level teaspoon ground ginger and the finely grated rind and juice of 1 lemon into the pan and stir over low heat until the sugar has dissolved, then bring to the boil. Add 4 peeled, halved and cored dessert pears. Poach for 3–5 minutes, turning the fruit occasionally with a perforated spoon.

Apricots in vanilla syrup: Put 4 oz (100g) castor sugar and ½ pint (300ml) water into a pan. Add a vanilla pod. Stir over low heat until the sugar has dissolved, then bring to the boil. Add 1 lb (450g) halved and stoned apricots. Crack a few of the stones to remove the kernels and add to the pan. Poach for 2–3 minutes, turning the fruit occasionally with a perforated spoon. Draw off the heat and leave until tender. Use vanilla sugar in place of the castor sugar and vanilla pod if you like.

Peaches in brandy syrup: Halve 4 large peaches and remove stones. Pour boiling water over them to cover, then peel off skins. Put 4 oz (100g) castor sugar and ½ pint (300ml) water into a pan. Stir over low heat until the sugar has dissolved, then bring to the boil. Add the peaches. Poach for 3–4 minutes, turning the fruit occasionally with a perforated spoon. Transfer to a serving dish. Add 3–4 tablespoons brandy and chill.

Plums in spiced syrup: Put 4 oz (100g) soft light brown sugar, ½ pint (300ml) water, a piece of stick cinnamon, 3 cloves and the thinly pared rind of 1 lemon into a pan. Stir over low heat until the sugar has dissolved, then bring to the boil. Add 1 lb (450g) plums and poach for 3–5 minutes until tender, turning the fruit occasionally with a perforated spoon. Add the juice of 1 lemon and allow to cool. Serve chilled spiced plums with vanilla ice cream.

Apple slices in lemon syrup: Put 4 oz (100g) castor sugar, ½ pint (300ml) water, the finely grated rind and juice of 1 lemon and a piece of stick cinnamon into a pan. Stir over low heat until sugar has dissolved, then bring to the boil. Add 1 lb (450g) dessert apples that have been peeled, quartered, cored and sliced in thick wedges. Poach for 3–4 minutes until just tender, turning the fruit occasionally with a perforated spoon to distribute apple slices evenly in the syrup. Apple slices hold their shape when poached this way.

Oranges with candied peel

Serves 6

6–8 oranges
6 oz (175g) castor sugar
¼ pint (150ml) water
juice of 1 lemon

Mark the orange skins in quarters and put oranges in a bowl. Pour over boiling water to cover and leave to stand for 5 minutes, then drain. Peel the oranges in neat quarters and scrape them clean of white pith with a knife. Cut the oranges crossways in thin slices and arrange in a serving dish.

Select the 4 best-looking pieces of orange peel and cut away all the white pith. Then shred the peel into very fine strips and put into a saucepan. Pour over cold water to cover and bring to the boil, then drain. This blanching removes all bitter taste. Return to the pan, pour over cold water to cover and simmer for 15 minutes, or until peel is tender. Squeeze between forefinger and thumb to test. Drain and reserve the peel.

Put the sugar and water into a saucepan and stir over low heat until the sugar has dissolved. Bring to the boil, add the cooked peel and simmer in the syrup for about 5 minutes, or until the peel is glazed and candied. Draw off the heat, add the lemon juice and pour syrup over the orange slices. Allow to cool, then chill for several hours or overnight. Serve the well chilled oranges with scoops of vanilla ice cream or orange sorbet.

Variation **Oranges in Cointreau:** Add 1 tablespoon of Cointreau to the cooled syrup before chilling.

Pears in grenadine

Serves 6

6 firm dessert pears
6 oz (175g) castor sugar
1 pint (600ml) water
1–2 large pieces thinly pared lemon
   rind
juice of ½ lemon
1 small piece stick cinnamon
3 tablespoons grenadine syrup
1 level tablespoon cornflour
2 tablespoons cold water

Peel the pears leaving them whole and with the stalks intact. Put the sugar, water, lemon rind and juice, stick cinnamon and grenadine into a pan large enough to hold the pears lying flat. Stir over low heat until the sugar has dissolved. Bring to the boil and add the pears. Lower the heat, cover with a pan lid, and simmer gently for about 20 minutes, or until pears are tender but firm. Turn fruit occasionally during cooking so they colour evenly. Draw the pan off the heat.

Lift the pears from the pan with a perforated spoon and place in a serving dish. Blend the cornflour with the cold water and stir into the hot syrup remaining in the pan. Return to the heat and stir until syrup has thickened and is clear. Remove the stick cinnamon and lemon rind and pour the syrup over the fruit. Leave for several hours or overnight until cold – do not chill. Serve with fresh pouring cream.

Variation **Pears in red wine:** Use ½ pint (300ml) red wine mixed with ½ pint (300ml) water, the sugar, pared lemon rind and cinnamon. Omit the lemon juice and grenadine. The pears cook to a pretty wine colour and the flavour is particularly good using this method.

Illustrated: Pears in grenadine, see above

Rhubarb with orange

Trim the rhubarb and cut in 1 inch (2.5cm) lengths. Put the sugar and water into a large saucepan and stir over low heat until the sugar has dissolved. Bring to the boil and add the prepared rhubarb, then bring back to the boil. Lower the heat, cover with a pan lid, and simmer gently for 2 minutes. Draw off the heat.

Leave to stand, covered, for 10 minutes to soften the rhubarb. Add the finely grated rind and juice of the orange. Transfer to a serving bowl, leave until completely cool, then chill for at least several hours. The flavour is especially delicious when served after 24 hours chilling.

Serves 6

2 lb (900g) rhubarb
6 oz (225g) castor sugar
½ pint (300ml) water
finely grated rind of 1 orange
juice of 1 orange

Summer fruit compote

Trim the fresh fruits. Put the sugar and water into a saucepan and stir over low heat until the sugar has dissolved. Add the dessert gooseberries and bring to the boil. Then add the remaining fruits and bring back to the boil. Draw the pan off the heat.

Using a perforated spoon, lift the fruits from the pan and put into a serving bowl. Return the pan of juices to the heat. Blend the cornflour with a little water to make a thin paste and stir into the fruit juice. Bring to the boil, stirring all the time, and simmer until thickened and clear, then pour the syrup over the fruit. Allow to cool for several hours or overnight. Do not chill. Serve with cream or vanilla ice cream.

Serves 6

2 lb (900g) mixed fresh or frozen
  dessert gooseberries, redcurrants,
  raspberries and strawberries
6 oz (175g) castor sugar
1 pint (600ml) water
1 level tablespoon cornflour

Fresh fruit salad

Put the sugar and water for the syrup into a saucepan and stir over low heat until the sugar has dissolved. Bring to the boil, then lower the heat and simmer for 1 minute. Draw the pan off the heat and add the lemon juice. (It will keep the colour of the apples and bananas.) Pour into a serving bowl and leave until cold.

Trim fruits according to kind and add to the syrup as they are prepared: Core and slice the apples (leave on any red skins). Remove peel and membrane from the oranges and cut in segments. Seed the grapes. Hull and slice the strawberries. Chill for several hours so fruit juices and syrup blend, then slice in the bananas. A fruit salad is delicious served with cream or vanilla ice cream and crisp shortbread biscuits, especially petticoat tails.

Variations: Add a tablespoon of kirsch, brandy or sherry to the syrup if liked. Other fruits to include are slices of a peeled kiwi fruit, pink seeds of a pomegranate, fresh dates, plums, peaches, and a ripe mango – the wonderful fragrance of the mango will keep everybody guessing. Allow about 2 lb (900g) fruit for 6 servings.

Serves 6

2 dessert apples
3 oranges
4 oz (100g) black or green grapes
8 oz (225g) strawberries
2 bananas

Syrup
4 oz (100g) castor sugar
¼ pint (150ml) water
juice of ½ lemon

Illustrated: Summer fruit compote, see above

Strawberry and orange compote

Serves 6

3 oranges
1 lb (450g) strawberries

Syrup
6 oz (175g) sugar
¼ pint (150ml) water
juice of 1 lemon
2 tablespoons grenadine syrup or
  orange-flavoured liqueur

Mark the orange skins in quarters and put the oranges into a bowl. Pour over boiling water to cover and leave to stand for 5 minutes. Meanwhile, hull the strawberries and slice them into a glass serving bowl. Drain the oranges and peel them in neat quarters, then scrape them clean of white pith with a knife. Cut crossways in thin slices and add to the strawberries.

Put the sugar and water into a saucepan and stir over low heat until the sugar has dissolved. Bring to the boil, then lower the heat and simmer for 1 minute. Draw off the heat and add the lemon juice and grenadine or orange-flavoured liqueur. Pour the syrup over the fruits. Allow to cool, then chill for several hours or overnight. You will find the hot syrup draws out the fruit juices.

Strawberries in raspberry sauce

Serves 6

2 lb (900g) strawberries

Sauce
1 lb (450g) raspberries
4 oz (100g) castor sugar
squeeze of lemon juice

Hull the strawberries. Put them in a pretty glass serving bowl and chill. Put the raspberries into a saucepan, add the sugar, and crush a few of the raspberries with the back of a wooden spoon to make the juices run. Cook over low heat to soften the fruit and dissolve the sugar, then press fruit and juices through a nylon sieve. Add a squeeze of lemon juice to sharpen the flavour and chill.

Pour the raspberry sauce over the strawberries to coat them – a perfect combination of flavours and a spectacular look of red sauce on red fruit. An alternative serving method is to place a block of vanilla ice cream on a serving plate, top with the strawberries and pour over the sauce. Serve with *langues de chat* or crisp dessert biscuits.

Variation **Strawberries with orange:** Use only 1 lb (450g) fresh strawberries and place in a serving bowl. Sprinkle over 2 oz (50g) castor sugar and leave to stand for 10 minutes. Then add the juice of 1 orange and toss strawberries in the juice. Omit the raspberry sauce. Serves 4.

Apple snow

Serves 6

1½ lb (700g) cooking apples
1 tablespoon water
2 large pieces thinly pared lemon
  rind
3 egg whites
3 oz (75g) castor sugar

Peel, core and thinly slice the apples. Put them into a wetted saucepan and add the water and pared lemon rind. Cover with a tight-fitting lid and cook gently for 15 minutes, or until apples are quite soft.

Press the apples through a nylon sieve to make a smooth, thick purée and allow to cool. Whisk the egg whites until stiff peaks form. Sprinkle in the castor sugar and whisk again until glossy. Fold the egg whites into the apple purée. Spoon into six individual serving glasses and chill for several hours.

Summer pudding

Rinse a 1½ pint (900ml) pudding basin with cold water. Trim the crusts from the bread slices. Cut a circle from 1 slice to fit the bottom of the basin. Cut enough wedge-shaped pieces to fit round the sides. Press bread in firmly to line the basin making sure there are no gaps. Reserve a few pieces of bread to cover the top.

Trim the fruits and put them into a saucepan. Add the sugar, cover with a pan lid, and cook gently for 5 minutes, or until fruit is softened. Turn hot fruits into the lined pudding basin. Cover the top with the remaining pieces of bread and put a weighted plate on top. Allow to stand overnight.

Remove the weighted plate and place a serving plate over the pudding. Invert pudding on to the plate and serve with cream.

Serves 6

8–10 slices day-old white bread
1 lb (450g) redcurrants
8 oz (225g) raspberries
8 oz (225g) strawberries
4–6 oz (100–175g) castor sugar

Gooseberry fool

Put the gooseberries and water into a saucepan, cover with a pan lid, and simmer gently for 10 minutes, or until the fruit is quite soft. Draw the pan off the heat and stir in the sugar – it will dissolve in the hot fruit.

Press the fruit and juices through a nylon sieve into a mixing bowl and allow the purée to cool. Whip the cream and egg white, if using it, together until thick and light. (The egg white increases the volume and lightness of the cream.) Fold the whipped cream into the fruit purée. Spoon into six individual serving glasses or ramekins. Chill for several hours or overnight. Serve chilled.

Variations: Blackcurrants, blackberries, apricots and raspberries all make good fruit fools – these fruits have a good colour and flavour. With the exception of raspberries, the fruits are gently cooked and then pressed through a sieve. (Press uncooked raspberries through the sieve.) The fruit purée is then combined with an equal amount of whipped cream.

Serves 6

1 lb (450g) green gooseberries
2 tablespoons water
4 oz (100g) castor sugar
½ pint (300ml) double cream
1 egg white (optional)

Raspberries with soft cheese

Press the cottage cheese through a sieve into a mixing bowl to make a fine texture. Add the cream, mix together well and stir in the sugar. Whisk the egg whites until stiff peaks form and fold into the cheese mixture. Turn into a muslin-lined nylon sieve and leave to drain overnight in the refrigerator.

Place the raspberries in a serving bowl. Turn the cheese out on to a serving plate. Pass both round separately along with a bowl of castor sugar. If you've never tasted fresh raspberries with a lavish sprinkling of sugar and those delicious *petit suisse* cheeses, you've missed a treat. This cheese is similar.

Serves 6

1 × 8 oz (227g) carton cottage cheese
¼ pint (150ml) double cream
2 tablespoons castor sugar
2 egg whites
1 lb (450g) raspberries
extra castor sugar, for serving

Baked bananas with rum

Serves 6

6 firm ripe bananas
juice of ½ lemon
3 oz (75g) soft light brown sugar
pinch of ground cinnamon
1 oz (25g) butter
2–3 tablespoons rum

Heat the oven to 400°F (200°C) or Gas no. 6. Peel the bananas and cut in half lengthways. Arrange close together in a well-buttered baking dish and sprinkle over the lemon juice, brown sugar and cinnamon. Top with the butter in flakes.

Place in the centre of preheated oven and bake for 15 minutes. Remove from the oven and spoon over the rum. Bake for a further 5 minutes, until bananas are soft and glazed. Serve from the dish with chilled whipped cream.

Pears with brown sugar and cream

Serves 6

6 firm dessert pears
3 tablespoons soft light brown
    sugar
1 oz (25g) butter
¼ pint (150ml) double cream

Heat the oven to 400°F (200°C) or Gas no. 6. Peel the pears, cut in half lengthways and scoop out the cores with a teaspoon. Arrange pear halves in a buttered baking dish cut side down. Sprinkle over the sugar and top with the butter in flakes. Cover with buttered greaseproof paper or kitchen foil.

Place above centre in preheated oven and bake for 20 minutes, or until pears are tender. Remove buttered paper, pour the cream over the hot pears and serve. The contrasting flavours of cold cream and hot fruit is delicious.

Baked apples

Serves 4

4 even-sized cooking apples
castor sugar (see recipe)
1 oz (25g) butter
2–3 tablespoons water

Plan the cooking so you can serve baked apples straightaway – they collapse if left to stand. Heat the oven to 350°F (180°C) or Gas no. 4. Remove the cores from the apples keeping apples whole. Run the tip of a sharp knife round the middle of each one to cut the skin. If you take care to make the cut meet neatly as you bring the knife around, the apples will rise beautifully when baked and the skins will separate into two halves. Place the apples in a baking dish or small roasting tin.

Spoon castor sugar into each centre, filling the hole from where the core was taken. Place a good flake of butter on top of each one and spoon the water into the baking dish. Place apples in pre-heated oven and bake for 45 minutes, or until well risen and soft through to the centre when pierced with a knife tip. Serve with the syrup formed in the baking dish and top with scoops of vanilla ice cream.

Variations: Add grated orange or lemon rind to the sugar and put a little orange juice in the baking dish. Add a good pinch of ground cinnamon to the sugar before filling the apples. Fill the holes with hard sauce (page 228) in place of the butter.

Hot fruit salad

Heat the oven to 350°F (180°C) or Gas no. 4. Place apricot halves with juice in a large shallow ovenproof dish. Add the brown sugar and rum and stir to mix. Peel and thickly slice the bananas and add them to the dish.

Place in preheated oven for 25 minutes, or until fruit is hot and beginning to bubble round the edges. Take straight to the table and serve with scoops of vanilla ice cream.

Variation **Hot spiced peaches:** Drain a 1 × 1 lb 13 oz (822g) tin of peach halves and reserve the juice. Arrange peach halves cut side up in the dish and pour over the reserved juice. Mix the brown sugar with 1 level teaspoon ground cinnamon and sprinkle this over the peaches. Omit the rum. Heat through for 20 minutes.

Serves 6
2 × 14½ oz (411g) tin apricot halves
2 oz (50g) soft light brown sugar
2–4 tablespoons rum
4 large bananas

Plum crumble

Halve and stone the plums. Put them into a saucepan and add the water, butter and sugar. Bring to the boil, cover with a pan lid, then cook gently for 5 minutes, or until plums are tender. Spoon the fruit mixture into a buttered 1½ pint (900ml) baking dish. Choose one that is shallow rather than deep so you get a good area of crumble. Set aside while preparing the topping.

Heat the oven to 350°F (180°C) or Gas no. 4. Sift the flour into a mixing bowl. Add the butter in pieces and rub in with the fingertips, then add the sugar and continue to rub in until mixture forms large crumbs that cling together – this is the secret to a crunchy texture. Spoon crumble evenly over the fruit and press gently. Place above centre in preheated oven and bake for 40 minutes. Serve with cream or vanilla ice cream.

Variation **Raspberry crumble:** Put 1 lb (450g) fresh raspberries in the greased baking dish. Sprinkle over 3 oz (75g) castor sugar and add 1 tablespoon water. Omit the butter.

Serves 4

1½ lb (700g) plums
1 tablespoon water
1 oz (25g) butter
2–3 oz (50–75g) castor sugar

Crumble topping
6 oz (175g) plain flour
3–4 oz (75–100g) butter
2 oz (50g) castor sugar

Apple pancakes

Peel, core and slice the apples. Put the apples, sugar and butter into a saucepan, cover with a lid, and cook gently until the apples are reduced to a purée, then add the cinnamon and seedless raisins. Stir the mixture just long enough for the raisins to soften and plump up.

Have the pancakes hot by having them stacked on a soup plate set over a pan of simmering water. Keep them covered with a second plate. Spoon a little hot apple filling down the centre of each pancake and roll up carefully. Dust the rolled pancakes with icing sugar and serve them with whipped cream or vanilla ice cream.

Serves 6

12 pancakes (page 268)
icing sugar, for dusting

Apple filling
2 lb (900g) cooking apples
4 oz (100g) castor sugar
1½ oz (40g) butter
pinch of ground cinnamon
2 oz (50g) seedless raisins

Apple brown betty

Serves 4–6

4 oz (100g) butter
4 oz (100g) soft white breadcrumbs
4 oz (100g) soft light brown sugar
½ level teaspoon ground cinnamon
finely grated rind of 1 lemon
1½ lb (700g) cooking apples
3 tablespoons water
juice of 1 lemon

Heat the oven to 350°F (180°C) or Gas no. 4. Generously grease a 2 pint (1.1 litre) baking dish. Melt the butter in a saucepan over low heat. Draw off the heat and stir in the white breadcrumbs with a fork. Mix the brown sugar, ground cinnamon and grated lemon rind in a small mixing bowl. Peel, core and slice the apples.

Sprinkle a third of the buttered crumbs over the base of the prepared baking dish. Cover with half the apple slices and sprinkle over half the sugar mixture. Add another layer of the buttered crumbs, then the remaining apples. Sprinkle over the remaining sugar mixture and cover with the remaining buttered crumbs. Spoon the water and lemon juice over the top.

Cover the pudding with buttered greaseproof paper or kitchen foil. Place in the centre of preheated oven and bake for 30 minutes. Remove the greaseproof paper or kitchen foil and bake for a further 30 minutes, or until apples are tender and top is golden brown and crisp. Serve hot or cold with cream.

Eve's pudding

Serves 4

2 cooking apples
2 tablespoons castor sugar
finely grated lemon rind
1 tablespoon water
icing sugar, for dusting

Topping
3 oz (75g) self-raising flour
2 oz (50g) soft creaming margarine
2 oz (50g) castor sugar
1 egg
1 tablespoon milk

Heat the oven to 375°F (190°C) or Gas no. 5. Generously grease a 1½ pint (900ml) baking dish or pie dish. Peel, core and slice the apples and place in the prepared dish. Sprinkle over the sugar and grated lemon rind. Spoon over the water and set aside while preparing the topping.

Sift the flour into a mixing bowl. Add the margarine, sugar, egg and milk. Using a wooden spoon, stir to blend, then beat thoroughly for 1 minute to make a smooth cake batter. Spoon the cake mixture over the apple slices and spread evenly with a knife, making sure that the cake batter touches the sides of the dish.

Place in the centre of preheated oven and bake for 35–40 minutes, or until the top feels springy when gently pressed. Test the apples by pushing a sharp knife through the baked topping – they should feel quite tender. Dust the pudding with icing sugar and serve.

Baked rice pudding

Serves 4

1 pint (600ml) milk
1½ oz (40g) pudding rice
1 oz (25g) castor sugar
few drops of vanilla essence
½ oz (15g) butter
2–3 tablespoons single cream
   or top of milk

The secret of a successful rice pudding is slow cooking when the starchy rice grains cook without too much evaporation of the milk. The best way to get a delicious creamy consistency is to stir in the first three skins when they form on the pudding, but before they have time to brown.

Heat the oven to 300°F (150°C) or Gas no. 2. Generously grease a 1½ pint (900ml) baking dish or pie dish. Heat the milk just to the boiling point in a saucepan. While the milk is heating, sprinkle the rice over the base of the prepared dish and add the sugar, vanilla essence and butter cut in small pieces. Pour the hot milk over the rice and mix together.

Place the dish below centre in preheated oven and bake for about 2 hours, or until the rice is tender and creamy and the top is brown. Stir the pudding every 15 minutes during the first hour of baking (3 times) to mix in the skin that will have formed. Then stir in the cream and leave the pudding undisturbed until baked.

Lemon pudding

Heat the oven to 375°F (190°C) or Gas no. 5. Generously grease a 2 pint (1.1 litre) baking dish or pie dish. Sift the flour and salt on to a plate. Cream the butter or margarine, sugar and grated lemon rind in a mixing bowl until soft and light. Break up the eggs with a fork and gradually beat them into the creamed mixture. Add a little of the sifted flour along with the last addition of egg, then fold the remaining flour into the mixture and add sufficient milk to make a medium-soft consistency. Spoon the mixture into the prepared baking dish and spread level. Set aside while making the sauce.

Blend the cornflour with the sugar in a small bowl. Make the lemon juice up to ½ pint (300ml) with hot water and stir into the cornflour mixture. Pour lemon sauce over the cake mixture. Place the pudding above centre in preheated oven and bake for 40 minutes. During baking the sauce will sink to the bottom and thicken. Serve hot. Lemon pudding is very good with ice cream.

Serves 4

4 oz (100g) self-raising flour
pinch of salt
4 oz (100g) butter or margarine
4 oz (100g) castor sugar
finely grated rind of 1 lemon
2 eggs
about 1–2 tablespoons milk

Sauce
2 level tablespoons cornflour
4 oz (100g) castor sugar
juice of 1 lemon

Guard's pudding

Butter a 2 pint (1.1 litre) pudding basin and set aside. Sift the flour and bicarbonate of soda on to a plate. Cream the butter and sugar in a mixing bowl until soft and light. Lightly mix the eggs and beat into the creamed mixture, a little at a time, adding a little of the flour along with the last addition of egg, if necessary. Beat in the raspberry jam. Then fold in the flour and milk and mix to a medium-soft consistency.

Turn the mixture into the prepared pudding basin and spread level. Cover with a double-thickness greased greaseproof paper or a single layer of greased kitchen foil and secure with string. Steam briskly for 2 hours, topping up the pan with extra boiling water as necessary. The mixture for this pudding is flavoured and coloured pink by the addition of raspberry jam, but turns a rich brown after steaming due to the bicarbonate of soda in the recipe – so don't leave it out.

Meanwhile, prepare the jam sauce. Blend the cornflour and water in a saucepan. Add the lemon juice and raspberry jam. Slowly bring to the boil, stirring as sauce thickens. Unmould the pudding on to a warmed serving plate and serve with the jam sauce.

Serves 6

6 oz (175g) self-raising flour
½ level teaspoon bicarbonate of
  soda
4 oz (100g) butter
4 oz (100g) castor sugar
2 eggs
2 tablespoons raspberry jam
2 tablespoons milk

Jam sauce
1 level tablespoon cornflour
¼ pint (150ml) water
juice of ½ lemon
2 rounded tablespoons raspberry jam

Notes on a Christmas pudding

● Ingredients must be well mixed so spices blend, which may explain the tradition of each member of the family taking a turn to stir the pudding and making a wish.

● You will get the best flavour in your pudding if ale or stout, particularly Guinness, is used.

● Any tiny charms, especially silver, should be tightly wrapped in greaseproof paper and added just before spooning the mixture into pudding basins. Then stir the charms into the pudding.

● Puddings need 6–8 hours total steaming to bring out the full flavour and produce a rich, dark colour. Steam gently the first time and briskly the second time. The pudding will be darker after second steaming.

● Pour a spoonful of rum or brandy over the pudding after cooking instead of adding it to the mixture if a stronger flavour is liked. The same applies to Christmas cake.

● Remove wet paper after steaming and cover pudding with fresh ungreased paper, then store in a cool but *not* airtight place. Re-cover with greased paper before reheating.

Christmas pudding

Makes 2 puddings, each to serve 6

4 oz (100g) self-raising flour
pinch of salt
1 level teaspoon mixed spice
1 level teaspoon ground cinnamon
¼ level teaspoon ground nutmeg
8 oz (225g) shredded beef suet
8 oz (225g) soft white breadcrumbs
12 oz (350g) soft dark brown sugar
1 lb (450g) currants
8 oz (225g) sultanas
8 oz (225g) seedless raisins
4 oz (100g) chopped candied peel
2 oz (50g) chopped blanched
   almonds
finely grated rind of 1 lemon
2 tablespoons black treacle
juice of 1 lemon
2 tablespoons rum or brandy
3 large eggs
½ pint (300ml) brown ale or stout

Sift the flour, salt and spices into a large mixing bowl. Add the suet, breadcrumbs, brown sugar, currants, sultanas, raisins, chopped peel, chopped almonds and grated lemon rind. Mix together well.

Warm the treacle in a saucepan just to make it runny, but not hot. Draw off the heat and stir in the lemon juice and rum or brandy. Break up the eggs with a fork and stir into the treacle mixture. Add to the fruit mixture along with the brown ale or stout and mix together well with a wooden spoon. Cover with a cloth and leave to stand overnight.

Generously butter two 2 pint (1.1 litre) pudding basins. Stir the pudding mixture and divide equally between the prepared basins. Cover with a double thickness of greased greaseproof paper or kitchen foil and tie tightly. Gently steam the puddings for 5–6 hours. Top up the pan with extra boiling water as necessary. Allow the puddings to cool, then re-cover with fresh ungreased paper. Store in a cool but airy place for up to a year.

To serve: Re-cover with greased greaseproof paper or kitchen foil and steam briskly for 2 hours. Keep the Christmas pudding hot in the basin, then turn on to a serving plate and take it to the table. Serve the pudding with hard sauce (page 228).

To flame the pudding: Measure about 2 tablespoons brandy into a ladle – a pretty silver one if possible – and warm it over the flame of a candle at the serving table. Tilt the ladle a little and allow the candle flame to lick over the rim. When the brandy is hot it will burn with a blue flame. As you pour the brandy over the hot Christmas pudding it will burn even more brightly and last for at least 1 minute.

Custards

A custard is the basis of many dishes – some you don't think of like ice cream and quite a few of our traditional puddings; a quiche is a savoury custard. It's worth knowing how to make them perfectly – we use them so much.

Too much heat or overcooking, which amounts to the same thing, make custards curdle and weep. Custards cannot be hurried, but must be cooked gently. This is why they are stirred in a double saucepan with hot water underneath or baked in dishes set in larger tins of water – both serve to maintain a steady cooking temperature. But even if you cook them gently, if they are overcooked, they will be ruined.

Baked custard

● Egg yolks provide the creaminess in a baked custard and the whites help the mixture to set. Most baked custards are made with whole eggs, but for a really delicious flavour and soft texture, use a higher proportion of egg yolks to egg whites.

● A baked custard is richer if you substitute single cream for some of the milk – a good example is the richest baked custard, *crème brûlée*.

● A slow oven of about 325°F (160°C) or Gas no. 3 is a good temperature for baking custards. Set the oven timer so you don't forget about it.

● If a baked custard is to be turned out of the baking dish as in caramel custard, more eggs are used so the custard will hold its shape.

Custard sauce

A custard with a pouring consistency made with egg yolks has a smooth texture and a shine that is superior to any of its imitations. The big plus for a real egg custard is the creamy texture it takes on when cold. A properly made custard sauce is as delicious as cream for serving with stewed fruit, pies or Christmas pudding. For flavouring, a little vanilla essence can be added, or better still, use vanilla sugar.

● A custard made with egg yolks is easier to cook. If whole eggs are used, add a little cornflour because egg whites thicken into tiny threads making it more difficult to get a smooth texture.

● When cornflour or flour, as in confectioner's custard, is included you must bring the sauce to the boil. Use about 1 level teaspoon cornflour per ½ pint (300ml) milk and mix with the eggs and sugar for a custard sauce.

How to make better custards

● Gently introduce the eggs to the heat. With a stirred custard do this by beating the egg yolks and sugar together and heating the milk separately, then stir the hot milk into the eggs and sugar.

● Rinse out the milk saucepan with cold water before returning the custard mixture to the heat and it's less likely to catch over the heat.

● Turn the custard sauce into a chilled bowl as soon as it is cooked or dip the base of the saucepan in cold water to arrest the cooking. Stir hot custard sauce over a bowl of iced water to cool it if you want a smooth shiny texture.

● Cook baked custard the day before serving and it will turn out more easily.

How to tell when a custard is cooked

A custard sauce, which is made by stirring egg yolks and milk over direct heat, doesn't thicken too noticeably when cooked – it thickens as it cools. One reliable guide is to dip your little finger in the custard and if it's as hot as your finger can comfortably bear, the egg mixture is cooked because the temperature is high enough for the egg to coagulate. Or, you can dip a cold metal spoon into the custard to see if it coats the spoon; run your finger across the back of the spoon and it should show a clean line. With a baked custard, made by cooking a whole egg and milk mixture in the oven, pierce the centre, which is the last part to set, with the tip of a knife and it should come out clean. The best way to test, however, is to simply shake the dish gently and the centre of the custard should wobble like a jelly.

Custard sauce

Makes about ½ pint (300ml)

½ pint (300ml) milk or single
  cream
3 egg yolks
½ oz (15g) castor sugar
few drops of vanilla essence

Heat the milk or cream to just below the boiling point in a saucepan. While milk or cream is heating, blend the egg yolks and sugar in a mixing bowl. Gradually stir in the hot milk or cream and blend well.

Place bowl of custard over a saucepan a quarter filled with simmering water – the water must not touch the base of the bowl. Cook gently for 8–10 minutes, stirring all the time, until custard has thickened. Draw off the heat and stir in vanilla essence.

To serve warm, pour into a jug and set in a pan of warm water until required. (You cannot keep a custard sauce hot since there would be a danger of overcooking it.) For a cold sauce, pour the custard into a bowl and leave until completely cool, stirring occasionally to prevent a skin forming. If you set the bowl in a larger one containing iced water, the sauce will cool more quickly.

Baked custard

Serves 4

1 pint (600ml) milk
4 eggs or 3 whole eggs and 1 egg
  yolk
1 oz (25g) castor sugar
few drops of vanilla essence

Heat the oven to 325°F (160°C) or Gas no. 3 and lightly grease a 1½ pint (900ml) baking dish. Heat the milk in a saucepan until just below the boiling point. While milk is heating, lightly beat the eggs, sugar and vanilla essence in a mixing bowl. Gradually stir in the hot milk and blend well. Strain the custard into a jug.

Set the baking dish in a roasting tin or shallow baking tin and pour the custard into the baking dish. Fill the tin to a depth of about 1 inch (2.5cm) with cold water. Place in the centre of preheated oven and bake for 40–45 minutes, or until custard has set. Serve warm or cold. This is delicious with poached apples or plums.

Caramel custard

Serves 6

3 oz (75g) granulated sugar
1 tablespoon cold water
1 pint (600ml) milk
6 eggs or 4 eggs and 2 egg yolks
3 oz (75g) castor sugar
few drops of vanilla essence

Heat the oven to 325°F (160°C) or Gas no. 3. Put the granulated sugar into a dry saucepan and stir over moderate heat until the sugar dissolves and turns to a golden caramel syrup. Draw off the heat and add the water. (Take care: the mixture will bubble up with the addition of a cold liquid.) Return to the heat and stir to make a smooth caramel syrup. Pour the hot caramel syrup into an ungreased 6 inch (15cm) round cake tin or 1½ pint (900ml) baking dish. Hold the hot dish in a cloth and tilt gently to coat the base and sides evenly. Set the dish in a shallow baking tin or roasting tin.

Heat the milk in a saucepan until just below the boiling point. While milk is heating, lightly beat the eggs, sugar and vanilla in a mixing bowl. Gradually stir in the hot milk and blend well. Strain the custard into a jug and pour into the prepared dish. Fill the baking tin or roasting tin to a depth of about 1 inch (2.5cm) with cold water. Place in the centre of preheated oven and bake for 1–1½ hours, or until custard has set. Allow to cool, then chill.

Loosen round the top edge of custard with a knife and tilt the dish so custard draws away from the sides. Place a serving dish over the dish and invert. Take care to use a dish with a shallow rim that will contain the caramel syrup that flows out as you lift the dish away.

Crème brûlée

Heat the oven to 325°F (160°C) or Gas no. 3. Grease a 1½ pint (900ml) ovenproof serving dish – a soufflé dish is pretty. Set the dish in a shallow baking tin or roasting tin. Heat the cream in a saucepan until just below the boiling point. While cream is heating, blend the egg yolks and sugar in a mixing bowl using a wooden spoon. Slowly stir in the hot cream and blend well. Strain custard into a jug. Pour custard into prepared dish. Cover with a lid, kitchen foil or a plate to prevent a skin forming. Fill the tin to a depth of about 1 inch (2.5cm) with cold water. Place in centre of preheated oven and bake for 50–60 minutes, or until custard has set. Allow to cool, then chill thoroughly for at least 12 hours.

About 1 hour before serving, sprinkle the top generously with demerara sugar to evenly cover the surface. Place under a hot grill to caramelize the sugar. Turn the dish while grilling to brown the surface evenly. Chill until sugar topping becomes hard and crunchy. The contrasting texture of smooth custard and crunchy topping is what makes this custard so special.

Serves 6

1 pint (600ml) single cream
6 egg yolks
3 oz (75g) castor sugar
demerara sugar, for topping

Snow eggs

Heat the milk in a saucepan to just below the boiling point. While heating, lightly beat together the egg yolks and sugar in a mixing bowl. Gradually stir in the hot milk and blend well. Strain custard back into the rinsed saucepan and stir over low heat until custard thickens. Do not allow to boil. Turn hot custard immediately into a mixing bowl, add a few drops of vanilla essence and leave until completely cool, stirring occasionally to prevent a skin forming.

Whisk the egg whites until stiff peaks form. Add half the sugar, 1 tablespoon at a time, whisking well after each addition, then fold in remaining sugar with a metal spoon. Bring a shallow pan (frying pan is excellent) of water to a simmer. Scoop out rounded tablespoons of meringue and drop on to the surface of the simmering water – cook no more than 4 at a time. Simmer for 3–4 minutes, then turn meringues over with a perforated spoon and simmer for a further 2–3 minutes. Lift from the pan with a perforated spoon and drain on absorbent paper. Continue until the meringue mixture is used up – you should make 18 meringues. Spoon chilled custard into individual serving bowls and float 2 or 3 meringue mounds on top. Sprinkle with crushed praline.

Serves 6

4 egg whites
5 oz (150g) castor sugar
2 tablespoons praline (page 322)

Custard
¾ pint (400ml) milk or single cream
4 egg yolks
2 oz (50g) castor sugar
few drops of vanilla essence

illustrated facing page 208

Confectioner's custard

Makes about ½ pint (300ml)

½ pint (300ml) milk
1 vanilla pod (optional)
3 egg yolks or 1 whole egg and 1
    egg yolk
2 oz (50g) castor sugar
1 oz (25g) plain flour
pinch of salt
½ oz (15g) butter
1–2 tablespoons double cream
1 tablespoon kirsch, sherry or rum

Put the milk and vanilla pod, if using it, into a saucepan and heat gently until milk is hot and infused with the vanilla flavour. In a mixing bowl, beat the eggs, sugar, flour and salt with a wooden spoon until creamy and light. Stir in the hot milk, blend well and strain back into the rinsed saucepan.

Place over low heat and whisk constantly until custard boils. (The presence of flour will prevent custard separating.) Draw off the heat and stir in the butter. Pour the custard into a chilled bowl and allow to cool, stirring frequently while it cools to prevent a skin forming. Chill for several hours or overnight.

Whip the cream until soft peaks form and fold into the chilled custard along with the kirsch, sherry or rum. Use the custard in place of whipped cream to fill cakes, choux buns or fruit flans.

Variation **Coffee-flavoured confectioner's custard:** Use 1 teaspoon coffee essence in place of the kirsch to make a delicious filling for choux buns.

Sherry trifle

Serves 6

1 trifle sponge (page 243)
1 tablespoon strawberry jam
2 oz (50g) ratafia biscuits
4 tablespoons sherry
¼ pint (150ml) double cream
glacé cherries and angelica, to
    decorate

Custard
½ pint (300ml) milk
½ pint (300ml) single cream
4 eggs
1 oz (25g) castor sugar
few drops of almond essence

Heat the milk and cream for the custard in a saucepan to just below the boiling point. While heating, lightly beat together the eggs and sugar. Gradually whisk the milk and cream into the eggs and sugar. Strain the custard back into the rinsed pan and stir over low heat until the custard thickens. Do not allow to boil. Turn custard into a mixing bowl and leave until completely cool, stirring occasionally to prevent a skin forming, then add the almond essence.

Split the trifle sponge and spread with strawberry jam. Break in pieces and place in a glass serving bowl. Coarsely crush the ratafia biscuits and sprinkle them over the cake. Spoon over the sherry, then pour over the custard. Chill for several hours to give the sponge cake a chance to thoroughly soak. Whip the cream until soft peaks form and swirl over the custard. Decorate with a few glacé cherries and chopped angelica. Chill until ready to serve.

Variation **Summer trifle:** When soft summer fruits are in season this trifle makes a lovely change from the traditional sherry trifle. Omit the strawberry jam and sherry. Strip 8 oz (225g) redcurrants from their stems with a fork and pick over 1 lb (450g) raspberries. In a saucepan over low heat, gently stew the fruits with 2 tablespoons water and 4 oz (100g) sugar for about 10 minutes until tender. Spoon the fruit mixture over the trifle sponge pieces and proceed as above.

Cream crowdie

Toast the oatmeal in a dry frying pan until lightly browned. Turn on to a plate and allow to cool. Whip the cream until soft peaks form in a mixing bowl, then whisk in the sugar and rum. Fold the toasted oatmeal and fresh raspberries into the cream. Spoon into six individual serving glasses and chill for several hours. This is best served on the day of making so the oatmeal retains its wonderful crunchy texture.

Variation: Flavour with Drambuie in place of the rum.

Serves 6

2 oz (50g) coarse oatmeal
½ pint (300ml) double cream
2 oz (50g) castor sugar
1 tablespoon rum
8 oz (225g) fresh raspberries

Syllabub with strawberries

Put the cream, sugar, finely grated lemon rind, lemon juice and sherry into a mixing bowl. Beat together for about 2–3 minutes until thick and light. Hull the strawberries and slice into the base of six individual serving glasses, reserving 3 strawberries for decoration. Spoon the syllabub mixture into the glasses and chill for several hours.

Decorate the top of each serving with half a strawberry. The syllabub mixture can be served on its own but the contrast of colours makes a beautiful summer dessert. Serve with sponge fingers.

Serves 6

½ pint (300ml) double cream
4 oz (100g) castor sugar
finely grated rind of 1 large lemon
juice of 1 large lemon
4 tablespoons medium dry sherry
8 oz (225g) fresh strawberries

Wine syllabub

Put the wine and thinly pared lemon rind into a mixing bowl and leave to stand overnight so the wine takes the flavour of the lemon, then remove the peel.

Add the lemon juice, sugar and double cream. Whisk until thick and light. Spoon into eight individual serving glasses and chill for several hours. This syllabub is rich so portions should be small. Serve with sponge fingers or *langues de chat*.

Serves 8

4 fl oz (100ml) dry white wine
thinly pared rind of 1 lemon
juice of 1 lemon
4 oz (100g) castor sugar
½ pint (300ml) double cream

Highland flummery

Blend the whisky, lemon juice and honey together to thin the honey. Add the double cream and whisk until thick and light. Spoon into six individual serving glasses. If you have whisked it really well the mixture should mound softly in each glass. Chill for several hours.

Lightly toast the oatmeal (as you would nuts) for a few minutes under a hot grill or in a dry frying pan. Sprinkle a little over each serving to give a contrasting crunchy texture.

Serves 6

3 tablespoons whisky
1 tablespoon lemon juice
2 tablespoons clear honey
½ pint (300ml) double cream
medium oatmeal, for sprinkling

illustrated facing page 209

Jellies and mousses

About using gelatine

● Too much gelatine will make jellies and mousses rubbery and unpalatable so measure gelatine accurately. Correct proportions are approximately ½ oz (15g) gelatine to 1 pint (300ml) liquid, or according to packet instructions. In soufflés and mousses part of the liquid may consist of eggs and cream.

● Sprinkle powdered gelatine over a measured amount of cold liquid, usually about 3 tablespoons, in a teacup or small bowl and leave for about 5 minutes until the granules have absorbed the liquid. In some recipes this 'cake' of soaked gelatine can be added directly to a hot mixture when it will dissolve quickly and easily.

● The bowl of soaked gelatine can be placed in a saucepan that has about 1 inch (2.5cm) of hot water in it. Gently stir until the gelatine has dissolved and there are no granules visible. Allow to cool slightly and when lukewarm add to the main mixture.

● Do not allow gelatine to boil or its setting power will be reduced.

● Metal moulds conduct heat efficiently; desserts quickly set and will always turn out well. China moulds are best reserved for cornflour or blancmange mixtures. Scald metal moulds with hot water to make sure they are clean and free from grease. For quick reference mark the capacity on the base of your moulds as sizes can be deceptive.

● Setting times for gelatine desserts can vary from 2–4 hours and depend on the mixture, the size of the mould and the chilling temperature. The more acid the mixture the longer the gelatine takes to set.

Fresh fruits in jelly

Serves 6

1 tablet lemon jelly
½–1 lb (225–450g) fresh fruits

Scald a 1½ pint (900ml) decorative mould in boiling water. Make jelly up to ½ pint (300ml) with boiling water and stir to dissolve, then make jelly up to 1 pint (600ml) with iced water.

Trim fruits according to type. Do not use fresh pineapple or kiwi fruit – both contain an enzyme which acts on gelatine to prevent proper setting. Cut fruits in pretty pieces such as thinly sliced peaches, orange segments, halved seeded grapes or cubes of apple. Allow jelly to cool until slightly thickened, then fold the fruits into the jelly. Turn at once into the mould and chill until set firm. Alternatively, you can set the fruit and jelly in layers – this takes longer but is more attractive as the fruit is evenly distributed throughout the mould. Except for the first layer, the jelly used must be cool so that it does not soften preceding layers. Unmould on to a serving plate.

Variation **Frozen fruits in jelly:** Frozen soft fruits look like fresh fruits in a jelly. Put 8 oz (225g) frozen strawberries in a serving bowl and pour over 1 pint (600ml) hot prepared strawberry jelly; the jelly will set fast (frozen berries act like ice cubes) but the berries will thaw slowly so they stay suspended in the jelly and look like fresh fruit. Equally spectacular is a combination of frozen raspberries in a raspberry jelly. Chill for at least 2 hours before serving as berries need that long to thaw.

Unmoulding a jelly or mousse

● To unmould a jelly or mousse dessert, start by loosening the edge of a plain mould with the tip of a knife blade dipped in warm water. Or loosen the edge with wetted fingers on a decorative one – don't forget the centre of a ring mould. Fill a bowl with hand-hot water, then with the mould held level, dip it into the water up to the rim. Hold for a few seconds only, then place a serving plate over the top, invert plate and mould together and give a sharp shake. The dessert should slip out easily and the mould can be lifted off.

● Long periods in hot water may melt the outside of a pretty dessert mould, so two quick dips in hot water rather than one long one is best if the mould did not come out the first time.

● If you first wet the serving plate with cold water, you can slide the dessert into the correct position if it happens to fall out of the mould a little off centre.

Wine jelly

Put 3 tablespoons of the water into a teacup, sprinkle in the gelatine and leave to soak for 5 minutes. Pour the remaining water into a saucepan and add the thinly pared orange and lemon rinds and sugar. Stir over low heat until the sugar has dissolved. Simmer gently for about 5 minutes to infuse the flavours. Draw the pan off the heat, add the soaked gelatine and stir until dissolved. (The heat of the pan will be sufficient.)

Stir the wine into the liquid and strain into a bowl. Leave to stand until the jelly thickens and shows signs of setting. Seed the grapes and stir into the thickened jelly. Pour into a 1½ pint (900ml) mould and chill until set firm. Unmould and serve with cream. For a buffet supper wine jelly looks pretty decorated with sugared grapes (page 321).

Serves 6

½ pint (300ml) water
½ oz (15g) powdered gelatine
thinly pared rind of 1 orange
thinly pared rind of ½ lemon
6 oz (175g) castor sugar
½ pint (300ml) red wine
8 oz (225g) green or black grapes

How to make better mousses

● If gelatine is first soaked and then added to a hot mixture, the heat of the contents of the pan is sufficient to dissolve it; there is no need to stir it over direct heat.

● If the dissolved gelatine is being added to a slightly cooled mixture the procedure is different: hold the pan of dissolved gelatine well above the mixing bowl and pour it in a slow, steady stream directly over the part of the mixture where whisking. Slowly pouring gelatine from a height helps to cool it and pouring while whisking all the time will incorporate it immediately.

● Maximum volume and best texture are obtained when mixtures for creams, mousses or soufflés are allowed to cool before the beaten egg whites or cream are folded in. A basic rule in cookery dictates that to combine ingredients together successfully, they must be of a similar texture and temperature. Gelatine mixtures are allowed to cool until they show signs of thickening and setting – then ingredients won't separate.

● Have cream well chilled to obtain best volume. Double cream should be beaten to soft peaks when it will fold in evenly and easily. Whisk egg whites at the last minute to stiff peaks and reserve 1 teaspoon of the recipe sugar to whisk into the egg white – this helps to retain a good volume when whites are blended with other ingredients.

● The flavour of most mousses is best if they are allowed to stand at room temperature for about 1 hour before serving, rather than serving them straight from the refrigerator.

Blackberry and apple mousse

Serves 6

1 lb (450g) cooking apples
1 lb (450g) blackberries
¼ pint (150ml) water
4 oz (100g) castor sugar
juice of 1 lemon
½ oz (15g) powdered gelatine
2 egg whites

Peel, core and slice the apples and put them into a saucepan. Add the blackberries, water and 3 oz (75g) of the sugar. Cover with a lid and cook gently for about 15 minutes, or until fruit is tender. Strain the lemon juice into a small bowl, sprinkle in the gelatine and leave to soak for 5 minutes.

When fruit is cooked draw the pan off the heat. Add the soaked gelatine and stir until dissolved. (The heat of the pan will be sufficient.) Press the fruit and juices through a nylon sieve into a mixing bowl. Leave to stand until mixture thickens and shows signs of setting. Whisk the egg whites until stiff peaks form. Sprinkle in the remaining sugar and whisk again until glossy. Fold beaten whites gently and evenly into the fruit mixture. Pour into a serving dish and chill until set firm. Serve with cream.

Raspberry mousse

Serves 6

1 lb (450g) raspberries
4 tablespoons water
½ oz (15g) powdered gelatine
4 oz (100g) cream cheese
2 oz (50g) castor sugar
¼ pint (150ml) double cream
2 egg whites

Press the fruit through a nylon sieve to make a purée and set aside. Put the water into a saucepan, sprinkle in the gelatine and leave to soak for 5 minutes. Then, stir over low heat until the gelatine has dissolved. Do not boil. Draw the pan off the heat.

Beat the cream cheese and sugar in a mixing bowl until soft and blended. Stir in the raspberry purée. Pour the gelatine in a thin stream on to the raspberry mixture whisking all the time. Leave to stand until mixture thickens and shows signs of setting. Whip the cream until soft peaks form and whisk the egg whites until stiff peaks form. Lightly fold first the cream, then the egg whites into the raspberry mixture. Pour into a serving bowl and chill until set firm. In summer decorate with fresh raspberries. This mousse has a vivid colour and the addition of fresh cream cheese gives it richness and a most pleasing texture.

Gooseberry mousse

Serves 6

1 lb (450g) green gooseberries
4 oz (100g) castor sugar
5 tablespoons cold water
½ oz (15g) powdered gelatine
few drops of green food colouring
   (optional)
juice of ½ lemon
¼ pint (150ml) double cream
2 egg whites

Put the gooseberries (no need to top and tail), 3 oz (75g) of the sugar and 2 tablespoons of the water into a saucepan. Cover with a pan lid and cook gently for 10 minutes, or until fruit is quite soft. Put remaining 3 tablespoons of water into a teacup, sprinkle in the gelatine and leave to soak for 5 minutes.

Draw the pan of cooked fruit off the heat, add the soaked gelatine and stir until dissolved. (The heat of the pan will be sufficient.) Press fruit and juice through a nylon sieve into a large mixing bowl. Add a few drops of green food colouring, if using it, and the lemon juice. Leave to stand until mixture thickens and shows

Illustrated: Snow eggs, page 203

signs of setting. Whip the cream until soft peaks form. Whisk the egg whites until stiff peaks form, sprinkle in remaining sugar and whisk again until glossy. Lightly fold first the cream, then the egg whites into the fruit mixture. Pour into a serving dish and chill until set firm. This tastes delicious with fresh strawberry sauce (page 227).

Strawberry liqueur mousse

Hull the strawberries. Reserve 4 for decoration and press remaining strawberries through a nylon sieve to make a purée. Put half the purée into a medium-sized saucepan and the remainder into a mixing bowl. Put the water into a teacup, sprinkle in the gelatine and leave to soak for 5 minutes.

Add 3 oz (75g) of the sugar, the lemon juice and soaked gelatine to the saucepan of strawberry purée. Stir over low heat until the sugar and gelatine have dissolved. Do not allow to boil. Draw off the heat and add to the remaining strawberry purée. Leave for about 15 minutes until mixture begins to thicken and shows signs of setting. Whip the cream until soft peaks form. Whisk the egg whites until stiff peaks form, sprinkle in remaining sugar and whisk again until glossy. Fold first the whipped cream and liqueur then the egg whites into the strawberry mixture with a metal spoon. Turn strawberry mousse into a serving bowl and chill until set firm. Decorate with reserved sliced strawberries and serve with pouring cream.

Serves 6

1 lb (450g) fresh strawberries
3 tablespoons cold water
½ oz (15g) powdered gelatine
4 oz (100g) castor sugar
juice of 1 lemon
¼ pint (150ml) double cream
2 egg whites
1 tablespoon orange-flavoured
    liqueur

Sharp lemon mousse

Separate the eggs, cracking the yolks into a medium-sized mixing bowl and the whites into a separate larger mixing bowl. Add 3 oz (75g) of the sugar to the yolks and blend well with a wooden spoon. Add the grated lemon rind and juice and mix together well.

Pour the water into a small saucepan, sprinkle in the gelatine and leave to soak for 5 minutes, then stir over low heat just long enough for gelatine to dissolve. Do not allow to boil. Holding the pan well above the mixing bowl, slowly pour the gelatine into the lemon mixture, whisking all the time so gelatine is immediately incorporated. Set aside for about 10 minutes until mixture begins to thicken and shows signs of setting. Whisk the egg whites until stiff peaks form, sprinkle in remaining sugar and whisk again until glossy. Fold the egg whites into the lemon mixture with a metal spoon. Turn the lemon mixture into a serving bowl and chill until set firm.

Whip the cream until soft peaks form and swirl it over the top of the lemon mousse. Chill until ready to serve. This mousse looks pretty with grated lemon rind (reserved from 1 of the lemons) sprinkled on top.

Serves 6

3 eggs
4 oz (100g) castor sugar
finely grated rind of 1 lemon
juice of 3 lemons
¼ pint (150ml) water
½ oz (15g) powdered gelatine
¼ pint (150ml) double cream

Illustrated: Highland flummery, page 205

Ratafia cream

1 × 4 oz (113g) packet ratafias
3 tablespoons cold water
½ oz (15g) powdered gelatine
½ pint (300ml) milk
3 egg yolks
1 oz (25g) castor sugar
½ pint (300ml) double cream
2 egg whites
1 tablespoon kirsch
strawberry sauce (page 227)

Crush the ratafias with a rolling pin and spread on a baking tray. Set under a moderate grill to brown them lightly, then allow to cool. Put the cold water into a teacup, sprinkle in the gelatine and leave to soak for 5 minutes.

Gently heat the milk in a saucepan. In a mixing bowl, blend the egg yolks and sugar together with a wooden spoon. Stir in the hot milk and blend well. Return the custard to the rinsed saucepan, add the soaked gelatine and stir over low heat just long enough for the gelatine to dissolve. Do not allow to boil. Pour into a medium-sized mixing bowl and set aside until mixture begins to thicken and show signs of setting. Whip the cream until soft peaks form and whisk the egg whites until stiff peaks form. Fold first the cream, then the egg whites, ratafias and kirsch into the mixture and turn into a wetted 2 pint (1.1 litre) mould. Chill until set firm, preferably overnight so ratafias soften. Unmould on to a serving plate and serve with strawberry sauce, which provides a lovely contrast in colour.

Apricot bavarois

8 oz (225g) dried apricots
¾ pint (400ml) boiling water
4 oz (100g) castor sugar
juice of 1 lemon
3 tablespoons cold water
½ oz (15g) powdered gelatine
½ pint (300ml) milk
3 egg yolks
¼ pint (150ml) double cream
1 egg white

Rinse the apricots and place them in a saucepan. Pour over the boiling water, cover with pan lid and leave to soak for 2 hours. Then simmer gently, covered, for about 40 minutes until apricots are quite soft. Stir occasionally to break up the fruit. Draw off the heat and add 2 oz (50g) of the sugar and the lemon juice. Press apricots and juices from the pan through a nylon sieve into a mixing bowl.

Put the cold water into a teacup, sprinkle in the gelatine and leave to soak for 5 minutes. Gently heat the milk in a saucepan. In a mixing bowl, blend the egg yolks and remaining sugar together with a wooden spoon. Stir in the hot milk and blend well. Return the custard to the rinsed saucepan, add the soaked gelatine and stir over low heat just long enough for the gelatine to dissolve.

Combine the custard with the apricot purée and set aside until the mixture begins to thicken and shows signs of setting. Whip the cream until soft peaks form and whisk the egg white until stiff peaks form. Fold first the cream then the egg white into the apricot mixture. Turn mixture into a wetted 2 pint (1.1 litre) mould and chill until set firm. Unmould on to a serving plate. This is especially nice served with oranges with candied peel (page 192).

Lemon snow

Put 3 tablespoons of the measured water into a teacup, sprinkle in the gelatine and leave to soak for 5 minutes. Put the remaining water, sugar and lemon rind into a saucepan and stir over low heat until the sugar has dissolved. Bring to the boil and draw off the heat. Add the soaked gelatine and stir until dissolved. (The heat of the pan will be sufficient.) Set aside for about 15 minutes so lemon flavour can infuse, then strain into a large mixing bowl, add the squeezed lemon juice and leave until completely cold.

Add the unbeaten egg whites and leave to stand a little longer until the mixture begins to thicken and shows signs of setting. Whisk the mixture until very light and fluffy – the more the mixture is whisked as it comes up to setting point the better the volume. When thick, light and snowy pour into a glass serving dish (it should mound up) and chill until set firm. Decorate with slivers of glacé cherry and angelica. Serve with single cream.

Serves 6

½ pint (300ml) cold water
½ oz (15g) powdered gelatine
4 oz (100g) castor sugar
thinly pared rind and juice of 2
    lemons
3 egg whites
glacé cherries and angelica
    to decorate

Pineapple cheesecake

Line an 8 inch (20cm) round cake tin with a circle of greaseproof paper. Press the cottage cheese through a sieve into a large mixing bowl and add the grated lemon rind. Drain the crushed pineapple, reserving the juice. Add the crushed pineapple to the cottage cheese. Put the cold water into a teacup, sprinkle in the gelatine and leave to soak for 5 minutes.

Separate the eggs, cracking the yolks into a small bowl and the whites into a larger bowl. Add the sugar to the yolks and, using a wooden spoon, beat until creamy. Make the reserved pineapple juice up to ¼ pint (150ml) with water. Pour into a saucepan and bring just to the boiling point, then add the juice to the creamed egg yolk mixture and blend well. Turn into the rinsed saucepan, add the soaked gelatine and stir over low heat until the gelatine has dissolved. Do not allow to boil.

Stir gelatine mixture into the cottage cheese and pineapple and set aside until the mixture thickens and shows signs of setting. Whisk the egg whites until stiff peaks form and whip the cream until soft peaks form. Fold first the cream, then the egg whites into the cheese mixture. Pour into the prepared tin and spread level.

Finely crush the biscuits for the crumb base. Melt the butter in a saucepan over low heat and stir in the crumbs with a fork. Spoon biscuit mixture evenly over top of the cheesecake and press gently. Chill for several hours or overnight until firm. Loosen sides of cheesecake with a knife. Invert on to a serving plate and peel off the paper.

Serves 6

12 oz (350g) cottage cheese
finely grated rind of ½ lemon
1 × 13 oz (376g) tin of crushed
    pineapple
3 tablespoons cold water
½ oz (15g) powdered gelatine
2 eggs
4 oz (100g) castor sugar
¼ pint (150ml) double cream

Crumb base
8 digestive biscuits
2 oz (50g) butter

211

Orange chiffon

4 tablespoons cold water
½ oz (15g) powdered gelatine
3 eggs
finely grated rind of 1 orange
3 oz (75g) castor sugar
juice of 3 oranges
juice of 1 lemon

Put the water into a saucepan, sprinkle in the gelatine and leave to soak for 5 minutes. Then stir over low heat until the gelatine has dissolved. Do not boil. Draw the pan off the heat and set aside until required.

Separate the eggs, cracking the whites into a medium-sized mixing bowl and putting the yolks into a large bowl. Add the grated orange rind and 2 oz (50g) of the sugar to the yolks and stir with a wooden spoon until pale in colour, then add the orange and lemon juice. Pour the gelatine on to the mixture in a thin stream, whisking all the time. Leave to stand until the mixture thickens and shows signs of setting. Whisk the egg whites until stiff peaks form. Sprinkle over the remaining sugar and whisk again until glossy. Using a metal spoon, fold beaten whites into the orange mixture. Pour into a serving bowl and chill. This looks pretty decorated with orange segments. Serve with chilled single cream or fresh raspberries.

Lemon cheesecake

Serves 8

4 tablespoons cold water
½ oz (15g) powdered gelatine
3 large eggs
4 oz (100g) castor sugar
finely grated rind of 2 lemons
juice of 2 lemons
2 × 8 oz (227g) cartons cottage cheese
¼ pint (150ml) double cream

Crumb base
8 digestive biscuits
2 oz (50g) butter

Line the base of an 8 inch (20cm) round cake tin with a circle of greaseproof paper. Put the water into a saucepan, sprinkle in the gelatine and leave to soak for 5 minutes. Stir over low heat until gelatine has dissolved, then draw off the heat and keep warm.

Separate the eggs. Set aside the whites. Put the egg yolks, sugar, grated lemon rind and lemon juice into a mixing bowl set over a saucepan one quarter filled with hot (not boiling) water. Whisk until mixture is frothy and light in colour. Draw off the heat and whisk in dissolved gelatine.

Press cottage cheese through a sieve into a mixing bowl. Stir in the egg and gelatine mixture and blend well. Leave to stand for about 10 minutes until mixture thickens and shows signs of setting. Whip the cream until soft peaks form and whisk the egg whites until stiff peaks form. Lightly fold first the cream, then the egg whites into the cheese mixture. Pour into prepared tin and spread level.

Finely crush the biscuits for the crumb base. Melt the butter in a saucepan over low heat and stir in the crumbs with a fork. Spoon biscuit mixture evenly over the cheesecake and press gently. Chill for several hours or overnight until firm. Loosen sides of cheese-cake with a knife. Invert on to a serving plate and peel off the paper – the biscuit base is now underneath. Serve with cream or strawberry sauce (page 227).

Ice creams and sorbets

● Use the best ingredients – sorbets are marvellous made using citrus fruits or juicy soft fruits from the garden or freezer.

● Freshest soft fruit flavours come from using uncooked fruits which have been pressed through a nylon sieve to make a purée; if fruit is puréed in a blender it must be sieved afterwards.

● A little gelatine added to a sorbet made with juicy fruits acts as a stabilizer and produces a smooth texture; it also helps sorbets retain the air beaten in so they are never hard as a brick when taken out of the freezer.

● The smoother ice creams and sorbets need to be stirred or whisked during the freezing process to break up large ice crystals and form their smooth consistency.

● Pour ice cream or sorbet mixture into a roomy 1½–2 pint (600–900ml) freezer container with lid (large margarine catering containers are good). Freeze, uncovered, until frozen, then cover with the lid for storage.

● Freeze mixtures for about 2–3 hours until slushy, then in some cases all that is necessary is to turn the sides of the mixture to the centre with a fork. This is done two or three times during freezing. Turn sorbet mixtures into a chilled bowl and whisk quickly until mixture is light and snowy and return it to container.

● The flavour of ice cream is best when it is allowed to soften slightly. Transfer container of ice cream from freezer to refrigerator about 30 minutes before serving. Sorbets are served straight from the freezer.

French vanilla ice cream

Heat the single cream in a saucepan until just below the boiling point. In a mixing bowl, lightly beat the egg yolks, vanilla sugar and salt with a wooden spoon. Gradually pour in the hot cream and blend well. Set the mixing bowl over a saucepan a quarter filled with simmering water and stir for about 10 minutes until custard thickens. Allow to cool, stirring occasionally to prevent a skin forming.

Pour cooled mixture into a freezer container. Freeze, uncovered, until mixture is icy at the edges and slushy. Turn into a chilled mixing bowl and whisk until smooth. Whip the double cream until soft peaks form and fold into the mixture. Return to freezer container and freeze for several hours (without stirring) until firm, then cover with container lid until required. Transfer ice cream from freezer to the refrigerator for 30 minutes to soften slightly before serving.

Variations **Praline ice cream:** Fold in 2 oz (50g) praline (page 322) along with the whipped cram.

Chocolate ripple ice cream: Stir 2–3 tablespoons cold chocolate sauce (page 227) into the ice cream along with the whipped cream. Do not overmix or the rippled effect will be spoiled.

Serves 6

½ pint (300ml) single cream
3 egg yolks
4 oz (100g) vanilla sugar
pinch of salt
½ pint (300ml) double cream

213

Dark chocolate ice cream

Serves 6

2 oz (50g) castor sugar
4 tablespoons water
6 oz (175g) plain chocolate
3 egg yolks
½ pint (300ml) double cream

Put the sugar and water into a saucepan and stir over low heat until the sugar has dissolved. Bring to the boil, then lower the heat and simmer for 2–3 minutes. Meanwhile, break the chocolate into the goblet of an electric blender or food processor. Add the hot sugar syrup and blend until chocolate is smooth. Add the egg yolks and blend again.

Whip the cream until soft peaks form. Gently fold the chocolate mixture into the whipped cream. Pour into a freezer container and freeze, uncovered, for several hours until firm. This rich chocolate ice cream does not form any ice crystals and needs no stirring while freezing. Cover with container lid until required. Transfer ice cream from freezer to refrigerator for 30 minutes to soften slightly before serving. Then scoop into serving glasses. Serve the ice cream sprinkled with roasted chopped hazelnuts or pour over single cream.

Biscuit tortoni

Serves 8

1 × 4 oz (113g) packet macaroons
3 oz (75g) icing sugar
2 egg whites
¼ pint (150ml) single cream
½ pint (300ml) double cream
4 tablespoons medium sherry

Crush the macaroons to crumbs with a rolling pin. Sift the icing sugar on to a plate. Put the egg whites into a large mixing bowl and add the single cream, double cream and sherry. Whip the mixture until soft peaks form – takes about 5 minutes. Whisk in the icing sugar, then, using a metal spoon, fold in the crushed macaroons, reserving 2 tablespoons for decoration.

Pour the mixture into a 1½ pint (900ml) freezer container. (An oblong one will give you the best shape for serving.) Freeze, uncovered, until mixture is icy at the edges and slushy. Turn sides to centre with a fork and stir to a creamy consistency. Freeze for several hours (without stirring) until firm, then cover with container lid until required. Transfer ice cream from freezer to refrigerator for 30 minutes to soften slightly before serving. Then turn on to a serving plate and sprinkle with remaining macaroon crumbs. Cut in slices for serving. Biscuit tortoni is delicious served with a fresh fruit salad.

Blackcurrant ice cream

Serves 6

1 lb (450g) blackcurrants
8 oz (225g) icing sugar
juice of ½ lemon
½ pint (300ml) double cream

Strip the blackcurrants from their stems with a fork. Purée the fruit in a blender or food processor, then press through a nylon sieve into a mixing bowl to make a smooth mixture. Sift the icing sugar into the bowl, add the lemon juice and mix together well.

Whip the cream until soft peaks form. Lightly fold the cream into the blackcurrant purée. Pour into a freezer container. Freeze, uncovered, until icy at the edges and slushy. Turn sides to centre with a fork and stir to a creamy consistency. Freeze for several hours (without stirring) until firm. Cover with container lid until required. Transfer ice cream from freezer to refrigerator for 30 minutes to soften slightly before serving.

Variation **Redcurrant ice cream:** Follow the same recipe but use 1 lb (450g) redcurrants.

Glacé fruit ice cream

Soak the seedless raisins in the rum overnight. Whip the cream until soft peaks form and whisk in the icing sugar and vanilla essence. Whisk the egg whites until stiff peaks form. Add the beaten whites, rum soaked raisins (and any rum not soaked up) and chopped glacé fruits to the whipped cream and fold in gently and evenly.

Pour the mixture into a freezer container. Freeze, uncovered, until mixture is icy at the edges and slushy. Turn sides to centre with a fork and stir to a creamy consistency. Freeze for several hours (without stirring) until firm, then cover with container lid until required. Transfer ice cream from freezer to refrigerator for 30 minutes to soften slightly before serving. Glacé fruit ice cream is rich so portions should be small.

Serves 4–6

1 tablespoon seedless raisins
1 tablespoon dark rum
¼ pint (150ml) double cream
1½ oz (40g) icing sugar
few drops of vanilla essence
2 egg whites
1 tablespoon finely chopped glacé cherries
1 tablespoon finely chopped angelica

Ways to serve home-made ices

● A delicious blend of flavours that never fails to be popular is vanilla ice cream and ginger. Serve scoops of vanilla ice cream topped with slivers of whole stem ginger along with a spoonful of the ginger syrup.

● Heat through your favourite liqueur-flavoured jam mixed with a spoonful of the same liqueur. Hot mincemeat is a good topping, too.

● Anything crunchy provides a contrast in texture which is always appealing. A sprinkling of chopped, toasted hazelnuts (you can buy them in packets) is lovely over chocolate or coffee ice cream. Crumbled macaroons, or better still, those delicately flavoured Italian ones called *amaretti* make wonderful toppings for strawberry and vanilla ice creams.

● Peanut brittle lightly crushed with a rolling pin will delight the children. Or you can improvise by heating granulated sugar in a dry saucepan until it turns to a caramel, then add a few chopped walnuts. Pour this over vanilla ice cream and the caramel will harden into crisp, crunchy flakes when it touches the cold ice cream.

● You may not have thought of double cream poured over ice cream but it's very good. Alternatively, press sweetened soft fruits such as raspberries or strawberries through a sieve and fold the purée into whipped double cream. This is marvellous served over vanilla, raspberry and strawberry ice creams.

● A little Cointreau, crème de menthe or vodka spooned over lemon sorbet makes a splendid dessert. The icy cold suits the liqueurs or vodka.

● Sorbets look impressive served in crisp tulip biscuits (page 258) for a dinner party. *Illustrated facing page 225.*

Lemon sorbet

Serves 8

1 pint (600ml) water
2 level teaspoons powdered gelatine
10 oz (275g) castor sugar
thinly pared rind of 3 lemons
juice of 3 lemons
2 egg whites

illustrated facing page 225

Put 2 tablespoons of the water into a teacup, sprinkle in the gelatine and leave to soak for 5 minutes. Put the remaining water, the sugar and thinly pared lemon rinds into a saucepan. Stir over low heat until sugar has dissolved. Bring to the boil, then lower the heat and simmer for 5 minutes. Draw off the heat, add the soaked gelatine and stir until dissolved. (The heat of the pan will be sufficient.) Stir in the lemon juice and allow to cool completely.

Strain to remove the lemon peel and pour syrup into a freezer container. Freeze, uncovered, until icy at the edges and slushy. Then whisk the egg whites until stiff peaks form. Turn slushy mixture into a chilled mixing bowl, add the beaten whites and whisk until thick and snowy. Return to freezer container and freeze for several hours (without stirring) until quite firm. Cover with container lid until required. Scoop straight from freezer container into serving glasses. Serve with thin dessert biscuits. Lemon sorbet is also nice served in tulip biscuits (page 258).

Orange sorbet

½ pint (300ml) water
2 level teaspoons powdered gelatine
6 oz (175g) castor sugar
juice of 1 lemon
1 × 6¼ oz (178g) tin frozen
    orange juice concentrate
2 egg whites

Put 2 tablespoons of the water into a teacup, sprinkle in the gelatine and leave to soak for 5 minutes. Put the remaining water and the sugar into a saucepan and stir over low heat until sugar has dissolved. Bring to the boil, then lower the heat and simmer for 1 minute. Draw off the heat, add the soaked gelatine and stir until dissolved. (The heat of the pan will be sufficient.) Stir in the lemon juice and frozen orange juice concentrate. Blend together well and allow to cool completely.

Pour the orange syrup into a freezer container. Freeze, uncovered, until icy at the edges and slushy. Then whisk the egg whites until stiff peaks form. Turn the slushy mixture into a chilled mixing bowl, add the beaten whites and whisk until thick and light. Return to freezer container and freeze for several hours (without stirring) until quite firm. Cover with container lid until required.

Variation **Grapefruit sorbet:** Use 1 × 6¼ oz (178g) tin frozen grapefruit juice concentrate in place of the frozen orange juice and serve topped with a sprig of fresh mint.

Serves 8

1 lb (450g) strawberries
juice of 1 lemon
juice of 1 orange
½ pint (300ml) water
8 oz (225g) castor sugar
2 egg whites

Strawberry sorbet

Crush the strawberries with the back of a wooden spoon or purée in a blender or food processor, then press through a nylon sieve to make a seedless purée. Stir in the lemon and orange juice. Put the water and sugar into a saucepan and stir over low heat until the sugar has dissolved. Bring to the boil, then draw off the heat. Add to the strawberry purée and allow to cool completely.

Pour strawberry mixture into a freezer container. Freeze, uncovered, until icy at the edges and slushy. Then whisk the egg whites until stiff peaks form. Turn the slushy mixture into a chilled mixing bowl, add the beaten egg whites and whisk until thick and light. Return to freezer container and freeze for several hours (without stirring) until quite firm. Cover with container lid until required. Scoop straight from freezer container into serving glasses or serve in tulip biscuits (page 258).

illustrated facing page 225

Redcurrant sorbet

Strip the redcurrants from their stems with a fork. Purée the fruit in a blender or food processor, then press through a nylon sieve into a mixing bowl to make a smooth mixture. Stir in the lemon juice. Put 2 tablespoons of the water into a teacup, sprinkle in the gelatine and leave to soak for 5 minutes. Put the remaining water and the sugar into a saucepan and stir over low heat until the sugar has dissolved. Bring to the boil, then draw off the heat. Add the soaked gelatine and stir until dissolved. (The heat of the pan will be sufficient.) Blend the syrup with the fruit purée and allow to cool completely.

Pour redcurrant mixture into a freezer container. Freeze, uncovered, until icy at the edges and slushy. Then whisk the egg whites until stiff peaks form. Turn the slushy mixture into a chilled bowl, add the beaten whites and whisk until smooth and light. Return to freezer container and freeze for several hours (without stirring) until quite firm. Cover with container lid until needed. Scoop straight from freezer container into serving glasses.

Serves 6

1 lb (450g) redcurrants
juice of 1 lemon
½ pint (300ml) water
2 level teaspoons powdered gelatine
10 oz (275g) castor sugar
2 egg whites

Crème de menthe sorbet

Put 2 tablespoons of the water into a teacup, sprinkle in the gelatine and leave to soak for 5 minutes. Put the remaining water, the sugar and thinly pared lemon rinds into a saucepan. Stir over low heat until sugar has dissolved. Bring to the boil, then lower the heat and simmer for 5 minutes. Draw off the heat, add the soaked gelatine and stir until dissolved. (The heat of the pan will be sufficient.) Stir in the lemon juice and allow to cool completely, then add the crème de menthe.

Strain to remove the lemon peel and pour syrup into a freezer container. Freeze, uncovered, until icy at the edges and slushy. Then whisk the egg whites until stiff peaks form. Turn slushy mixture into a chilled mixing bowl, add the beaten whites and whisk until thick and light. Return to freezer container and freeze for several hours (without stirring) until quite firm. Cover with container lid until required. Scoop straight from freezer container into serving glasses or serve in tulip biscuits (page 258).

Serves 8

1 pint (600ml) water
2 level teaspoons powdered gelatine
6 oz (175g) castor sugar
thinly pared rind of 2 lemons
juice of 2 lemons
2 tablespoons crème de menthe
2 egg whites

illustrated facing page 225

Meringue

How to make better meringue

So many cooks dread preparing meringues. But be aware of the following points – any one could be the reason why you succeed or fail with making meringues.

● Egg whites cracked out the day before are best for meringues. Some of the moisture evaporates resulting in a more concentrated solution of albumen, which helps to give a better volume.

● Egg whites cannot be whisked to stiff peaks if they come into contact with any grease or dirt. Bowls and whisks must be very clean. A trace of egg yolk in the white will prevent egg whites from forming stiff peaks. It's a good idea to scald the mixing bowl and whisk with boiling water, then dry them and add the whites.

● I often wipe out my mixing bowl with a cut lemon before putting in the egg whites. The acid helps to stabilize the beaten foam. A pinch of cream of tartar, which is acid, does the same thing. Remember that older eggs are more acid and whisk up better than new-laid eggs which are alkaline.

● Use either granulated or castor sugar – what's important is that the sugar is dry. Damp sugar is fatal and makes whisked egg whites collapse. I always dry the weighed sugar on a baking tray in the heating oven for about 5–10 minutes. Crush any lumps and press the sugar through a sieve – it's worth the trouble.

● Slowly add the sugar in two parts. The first part should be added 1 tablespoon at a time and whisked after each addition to original stiffness. Very lightly fold in the remaining sugar with a

Meringue shells

Makes 12

2 egg whites
pinch of salt
4 oz (100g) castor sugar
extra castor sugar, for sprinkling
½ pint (300ml) double cream

Heat the oven to 300°F (150°C) or Gas no. 2. Grease two baking sheets with white cooking fat, dust with flour and tap sharply to remove excess. Whisk together the egg whites and salt in a mixing bowl until stiff peaks form. Add half the sugar, 1 tablespoon at a time, whisking after each addition. Fold in the remaining sugar using a metal spoon.

The simplest method of shaping meringue shells is to use two tablespoons. Take a rounded spoonful of the mixture, scoop it out with the second spoon to form an oval shape and let fall on to the prepared sheet. Arrange neatly, remembering shells are used in pairs. Sprinkle the shells with extra castor sugar so they become crisp when baked.

Place sheets of meringue in the oven and immediately lower oven temperature to 200°F (110°C) or Gas no. ¼. Leave to dry for 2 hours, rotating the sheets occasionally for even baking. Slip a palette knife under each one and turn them over. Turn off the oven heat and leave meringues in the oven to dry for a further 1 hour.

Whip the cream until soft peaks form and sandwich the cream between pairs of meringue shells. If you press gently in the centre of meringues when they are almost dry the pairs will hold more cream and won't slip apart. The shells are also nice filled with ice cream and served with a fruit salad.

metal spoon. Use a lifting and cutting movement – do not overmix at this stage or the meringue will just collapse.

● Add vinegar to the meringue if a soft and spongy meringue centre is liked.

● Where meringue is used to decorate a pie or pudding the quantity of sugar is reduced to 1½ oz (40g) per egg white to get a lighter mixture.

● Sometimes nuts are added to meringues, usually ground almonds, roasted hazelnuts or walnuts. Use a Mouli hand grater to grind nuts finely – it does the job beautifully. Use about 1 oz (25g) ground nuts per egg white and fold into the whites when adding the second part of sugar.

● Swirl meringue on puddings or spoon out on to prepared trays to make meringue layers or shells. In either case meringue must be placed in the oven and baked at once.

● Don't bake meringues in the oven with anything else; if there's steam from other foods meringues will not dry out.

● When quite crisp and dry meringues will keep perfectly in an airtight tin; sugar attracts moisture and the meringues will soften if they are not tightly covered.

● Fill meringue shells or layers with whipped cream about 2 hours before serving, then meringue softens and takes on just the right texture for eating.

Hazelnut meringue cake

Toast the hazelnuts in an oven heated to 350°F (180°C) or Gas no. 4 for about 10 minutes. Tip into a teacloth and remove the brown skins by vigorously rubbing them. Finely grind the nuts using a Mouli grater or electric grinder. Increase oven temperature to 375°F (190°C) or Gas no. 5. Grease and line two 8 inch (20cm) layer cake tins.

Whisk the egg whites until stiff peaks form. Add half the sugar, 1 tablespoon at a time, whisking after each addition. Mix together the ground hazelnuts and remaining sugar. Using a metal spoon, gently and evenly fold the nut mixture and vinegar or lemon juice into the meringue.

Divide the mixture evenly between the prepared tins and spread level. Place in the centre of preheated oven and bake for 30–40 minutes. Allow layers to cool in the tins, then loosen sides, turn out and peel away the lining papers. Store until required in an airtight tin.

Whip the cream until soft peaks form and sandwich layers with the cream and raspberries. Dust with icing sugar and chill for several hours so that the filling firms and the meringue layers soften. The meringue will cut easily and will be softer.

Serves 6

5 oz (150g) shelled hazelnuts
5 egg whites
10 oz (275g) castor sugar
1 teaspoon vinegar or lemon juice
icing sugar, for dusting

Filling
½ pint (300ml) double cream
8 oz (225g) raspberries

Chestnut pavlova

Serves 6–8

3 egg whites
6 oz (175g) castor sugar
1 teaspoon vinegar
½ pint (300ml) double cream
icing sugar, for dusting

Chestnut purée
1 lb (450g) chestnuts
milk and water (see recipe)
1 vanilla pod
4 oz (100g) castor sugar
3 tablespoons water
1 tablespoon rum

Heat the oven to 325°F (160°C) or Gas no. 3. Draw a circle 8 inches (20cm) in diameter on a sheet of non-stick parchment paper and place, mark side down, on a baking sheet, smearing a little cooking fat at the corners so paper lies flat.

Beat the egg whites until stiff peaks form. Add half the sugar, 1 tablespoon at a time, whisking after each addition. Fold in remaining sugar and vinegar using a metal spoon. Spoon the meringue mixture on to the paper, shaping it into a nest within the marked outline by heaping the sides. Place in the centre of preheated oven and bake for 45 minutes. Turn off the oven heat and leave the meringue in the oven until completely cool. You'll find it easily slips off the paper.

Meanwhile, peel the chestnuts, place in a saucepan and pour over milk and water to cover. Add the vanilla pod and simmer gently for 20–30 minutes, or until chestnuts are tender. Drain the chestnuts and press through a sieve into a mixing bowl. Dissolve the sugar in the water to make a syrup and stir into the sieved chestnuts, to make a sweetened purée. Add the rum and set aside until cold. Whip the cream until soft peaks form and spoon into the meringue nest. Press the chestnut purée through a coarse sieve on to the cream to make a top layer. Chill for several hours or overnight. Serve well chilled. Dust the top with icing sugar just before you take it to the table.

Variation **Lemon cream pavlova:** This is made using the meringue nest. You can also use the leftover egg yolks for the filling. Combine 3 egg yolks with 3 oz (75g) castor sugar in a mixing bowl and beat with a wooden spoon until creamy. Stir in the finely grated rind and juice of 2 lemons. Set over a saucepan one-quarter filled with simmering water and stir for about 15 minutes until mixture takes on a creamy consistency. Allow lemon filling to cool completely. Spoon into baked pavlova and spread level. Top with softly whipped cream and chill. Sprinkle with toasted flaked almonds before serving.

Meringue layer cake

Serves 8

4 egg whites
8 oz (225g) castor sugar
finely chopped walnuts, for
    sprinkling

Filling
4 oz (100g) plain chocolate
¼ pint (150ml) soured cream
1 tablespoon brandy
¼ pint (150ml) double cream

Heat the oven to 300°F (150°C) or Gas no. 2. Cut three sheets of greaseproof paper to fit three baking sheets. Draw a circle 8 inches (20cm) in diameter on each one. Line the trays, mark side down, smearing a little cooking fat at the corners so papers lie flat.

Whisk the egg whites until stiff peaks form. Add half the sugar, 1 tablespoon at a time, whisking after each addition. Then fold in remaining sugar using a metal spoon. Divide the mixture equally between the sheets and spread level within the outline. Sprinkle 1 circle of meringue with chopped walnuts.

Place sheets of meringue in the oven and immediately lower oven temperature to 200°F (110°C) or Gas no. ¼. Leave meringues for 2 hours, rotating the trays occasionally for even baking. When meringue is dry, slide a palette knife underneath to loosen and turn the layers over. Turn off the oven heat and leave for a further 1 hour to completely dry out.

Melt the chocolate and stir in the soured cream and brandy. Whip the cream until soft peaks form and fold gently and evenly into chocolate mixture. Sandwich the 2 plain meringue layers with half the chocolate cream, then, spread with the remaining chocolate cream. Top with the walnut layer and leave to stand for 2 hours.

Orange and almond cake

Heat the oven to 350°F (180°C) or Gas no. 4. Grease and line an 8 inch (20cm) layer cake tin. Separate the eggs, cracking the yolks into a large mixing bowl and the whites into a medium-sized bowl. Add the sugar to the egg yolks and using a wooden spoon, beat until light and creamy. Add the breadcrumbs, ground almonds, finely grated orange rind and orange juice. Stir to blend the ingredients. Whisk the egg whites until stiff peaks form and, using a metal spoon, fold gently and evenly into the mixture.

Pour mixture into the prepared tin and spread level. Place in the centre of preheated oven and bake for 40 minutes, until cake is golden and centre feels spongy when lightly pressed with the fingertips. Loosen sides of cake and leave in tin to cool completely. Turn on to a serving plate. Whip the cream until soft peaks form and swirl over the top and sides. Sprinkle with toasted flaked almonds and chill for at least 1 hour before serving.

Serves 6

3 eggs
4 oz (100g) castor sugar
2 oz (50g) soft white breadcrumbs
4 oz (100g) ground almonds
finely grated rind of 1 orange
juice of 3 oranges
¼ pint (150ml) double cream
toasted flaked almonds, for
    sprinkling

Strawberry shortcake

Heat the oven to 425°F (220°C) or Gas no. 7. Grease an 8 inch (20cm) layer cake tin. Sift the flour, baking powder and salt into a mixing bowl. Add the butter in pieces and rub in with the fingertips. Lightly mix the egg, milk and sugar and pour into the flour mixture. Mix to a rough dough with a fork. Turn on to a floured surface and knead just long enough to remove the cracks.

Divide dough in half and pat or roll out each piece to a circle slightly smaller than the prepared tin. Using the fingertips, press one circle of dough into the tin and brush the surface liberally with the melted butter. Place the other circle of dough on top and press gently to fit. Place in the centre of preheated oven and bake for 15 minutes. Leave to cool in the tin for 5 minutes, then turn out on to a wire rack. Gently separate the two layers with a knife and allow to cool completely.

Hull the strawberries and slice any large ones. Whip together the cream and sugar until soft peaks form. Sandwich shortcake layers with strawberries and cream and dust top with icing sugar.

Serves 6

8 oz (225g) self-raising flour
2 level teaspoons baking powder
pinch of salt
3 oz (75g) butter
1 large egg
3 tablespoons milk
1½ oz (40g) castor sugar
½ oz (15g) melted butter
icing sugar, for dusting

Filling
8–12 oz (225–350g) strawberries
¼ pint (150ml) double cream
1 oz (25g) castor sugar

Coffee brandy cake

Serves 8

6 oz (175g) plain flour
2 level teaspoons baking powder
½ level teaspoon salt
5 oz (150g) soft light brown sugar
2 eggs
6 tablespoons corn oil
4 tablespoons milk
2 tablespoons coffee essence
½ pint (300ml) double cream
toasted flaked almonds, for
   sprinkling

Syrup
4 oz (100g) granulated sugar
¼ pint (150ml) water
2 teaspoons instant coffee
2 tablespoons brandy

Heat the oven to 350°F (180°C) or Gas no. 4. Grease an 8 inch (20cm) layer cake tin and line with a circle of greaseproof paper, then grease the paper. Sift the flour, baking powder and salt into a large mixing bowl and stir in the brown sugar. Separate the eggs, cracking the yolks into a small bowl and the whites into a separate larger bowl. Add the corn oil, milk and coffee essence to the egg yolks and mix together with a fork. Add to the flour mixture and beat with a wooden spoon to make a smooth batter. Whisk the egg whites until stiff peaks form and, using a metal spoon, gently and evenly fold into the batter. Pour the batter into the prepared cake tin and spread level. Place in the centre of preheated oven and bake for 45 minutes.

Put the sugar and water for the syrup into a saucepan and stir over low heat until the sugar dissolves. Bring to the boil, then lower the heat and simmer for 3 minutes to concentrate the flavour. Draw off the heat and stir in the coffee granules and brandy. Prick the surface of the hot cake with a fork or skewer and spoon over the hot syrup. Leave to soak in the tin overnight.

Whip the cream until soft peaks form. Turn cake on to a serving plate and swirl whipped cream over top and sides. Chill for several hours, then sprinkle with toasted flaked almonds.

Passion cake

Serves 12

10 oz (275g) plain flour
1 level teaspoon bicarbonate of
   soda
2 level teaspoons baking powder
1 level teaspoon salt
6 oz (175g) soft light brown sugar
2 oz (50g) chopped walnuts
3 eggs
2 ripe bananas
6 oz (175g) grated carrots
6 fl oz (175ml) oil

Frosting
3 oz (75g) butter
3 oz (75g) cream cheese
6 oz (175g) icing sugar
½ teaspoon vanilla essence
finely chopped walnuts, for
   sprinkling

Heat the oven to 350°F (180°C) or Gas no. 4. Grease and line a 9 inch (22.5cm) round cake tin. Sift the flour, bicarbonate of soda, baking powder and salt into a medium-sized mixing bowl. Add the brown sugar, chopped walnuts and eggs. Peel and mash the bananas and add to the bowl, then add the grated carrots and oil. Mix ingredients together with a wooden spoon, then beat well for 1 minute to make a soft cake batter.

Pour mixture into prepared cake tin and spread level. Place in centre of preheated oven and bake for 1 hour. Allow to cool in tin for 5 minutes, then turn out on to a wire rack and leave until completely cool.

Put the butter and cream cheese into a mixing bowl, sift in the icing sugar, add the vanilla and beat until soft and creamy. Slice cake horizontally and sandwich layers with a little of the frosting. Spread remainder over top and sides, then sprinkle with finely chopped walnuts. Cut in thin slices – passion cake is rich and will go a long way! It's good for a buffet – this is a carrot cake, but don't let that put you off – you can't taste the carrots and they do make the cake deliciously moist to eat.

Gâteau pavé

Put the sugar and water into a saucepan and stir over low heat until sugar has dissolved. Bring to the boil, then lower the heat and simmer for 3 minutes. Draw off the heat, add the rum and allow to cool.

Sift the icing sugar for the chocolate cream on to a plate. Break the chocolate into a mixing bowl. Set over a saucepan one-quarter filled with hot (not boiling) water and stir until chocolate has melted, then draw off the heat. Cream the butter and icing sugar in a mixing bowl until soft and light. Beat in egg yolks one at a time, then stir in melted chocolate.

Dip 1–2 sponge fingers at a time in the rum syrup and arrange a neat row of 5 sponge fingers on a serving plate. Spread over a layer of chocolate cream. Add a second layer of 5 dipped sponge fingers and spread over a second layer of chocolate cream. Make a top layer with the remaining dipped sponge fingers and sprinkle over any unused syrup. Spread the remaining chocolate cream over the top and sides to cover. Sprinkle with chopped walnuts and chill for several hours or overnight until firm. Serve in slices; each serving will have a pretty striped appearance.

Serves 6

2 oz (50g) granulated sugar
3 tablespoons water
2 tablespoons rum
15 sponge fingers
chopped walnuts, for sprinkling

Chocolate cream
4 oz (100g) icing sugar
4 oz (100g) plain chocolate
4 oz (100g) unsalted butter
4 egg yolks

Biskotten torte

Line the base of an 8 inch (20cm) round cake tin with a circle of greaseproof paper. Finely chop the walnuts and toast them under the grill. Set aside 2 tablespoons for decoration and put remaining toasted nuts into a mixing bowl. Bring half the milk to the boil and add to the nuts. Set aside until cool, when the nuts will absorb the milk.

Cream the butter and sugar in a mixing bowl until soft and light. Beat in the egg yolks one at a time, then stir in the cooled nuts. Pour the remaining cold milk into a soup plate and add the sherry. Dip several sponge fingers at a time in the flavoured milk and use about a third of them to line the base of the tin, trimming to fit where necessary. Spread with half the nut mixture and top with a layer of dipped sponge fingers, then spread with the rest of the nut mixture. Finish by topping with remaining soaked sponge fingers. Cover with a circle of greaseproof paper and a weighted plate. Chill overnight.

Loosen round sides and turn torte out on to a serving plate, then peel off the paper. Whip the cream until soft peaks form and swirl over the top and sides to cover. Sprinkle with reserved toasted nuts and chill for several hours before serving.

Serves 6

4 oz (100g) walnuts
½ pint (300ml) milk
4 oz (100g) unsalted butter
4 oz (100g) icing sugar
2 egg yolks
3 tablespoons medium or sweet
  sherry
18–20 sponge fingers
½ pint (300ml) double cream

Chocolate roulade

Serves 8

6 oz (175g) plain chocolate
5 eggs
6 oz (175g) castor sugar
2 tablespoons hot water
icing sugar, for dusting
½ pint (300ml) double cream

Heat the oven to 350°F (180°C) or Gas no. 4. Brush a 13½ × 9½ inch (34 × 23cm) shallow biscuit tin with oil and line the base and shorter sides with a sheet of greaseproof paper long enough to overlap the shorter ends, then brush paper with oil. Break the chocolate into a small bowl and set over a saucepan a quarter filled with hot (not boiling) water. Stir until melted, then draw off the heat and stir in the hot water and blend until smooth.

Separate the eggs, cracking the yolks into a large mixing bowl and the whites into a separate bowl. Add the castor sugar to the yolks and using a wooden spoon, beat until creamy and light. Stir in the melted chocolate and blend well. Beat the egg whites until stiff peaks form and gently and evenly fold into the mixture with a metal spoon. Pour the mixture into the prepared tin and spread level. Place in preheated oven and bake for 15–20 minutes. Remove from the oven and cover with a tea towel. Leave for several hours or overnight until cold.

About 4 hours before serving, loosen unlined sides and turn roulade out on to a sheet of greaseproof paper dusted with icing sugar, then peel off the paper. Whip the cream until soft peaks form and spread evenly over the surface of the roulade. Starting with the long side furthest away from you and using the paper to help, roll up roulade like a Swiss roll. Chill for several hours.

Blackcurrant bombe

Serves 6–8

½ pint (300ml) double cream
1 tablespoon castor sugar

Blackcurrant filling
5 tablespoons water
1 level tablespoon powdered gelatine
8 oz (225g) blackcurrants
4 oz (100g) castor sugar
¼ pint (150ml) double cream
2 egg whites

Whip the cream with the sugar until soft peaks form, then spoon into a 1½ pint (900ml) pudding basin. Using the back of a tablespoon, spread the cream to thinly cover base and sides. Freeze until set firm. Meanwhile, prepare the filling.

Put 3 tablespoons of the water into a teacup, sprinkle in the gelatine and leave to soak for 5 minutes. Put the remaining water and blackcurrants into a saucepan, cover with a pan lid, and cook gently until fruit is soft. Draw off the heat. Add the sugar and gelatine and stir until they have dissolved. Press fruit and juice through a nylon sieve into a mixing bowl and allow to cool completely.

Whip the cream until soft peaks form and whisk the egg whites until stiff peaks form. Lightly fold first the cream, then the egg whites into the blackcurrant mixture. Turn into the cream-lined basin – the mixture should be enough to fill up to the rim. Freeze for at least 6 hours.

About 2 hours before serving, unmould the dessert on to a serving plate and refrigerate to soften slightly. When you slice into the bombe you will reveal the blackcurrant filling. Serve with strawberry sauce (page 227) and crisp dessert biscuits.

Illustrated: Blackcurrant bombe, see above, with strawberry sauce, page 227

Continental cheesecake

Heat the oven to 325°F (160°C) or Gas no. 3. Finely crush the biscuits. Melt the butter in a saucepan and stir in the crumbs with a fork. Spoon biscuit mixture over the base of a greased 9 inch (22.5cm) spring-clip pan and press the crumb mixture down firmly. Chill until required.

Cream the butter and 2 oz (50g) of the sugar in a mixing bowl until soft and light. Add the curd cheese and beat well. Mix together the flour, salt and a further 2 oz (50g) of the sugar and stir into the cheese mixture. Then beat in the egg yolks, one at a time, placing the whites in a separate mixing bowl. Stir the finely grated lemon rind and soured cream into the cheese mixture. Whisk egg whites until stiff peaks form, then sprinkle in the remaining castor sugar and whisk until glossy. Fold the egg whites into cheese mixture. Pour the mixture into the prepared tin and spread level.

Place in centre of preheated oven and bake for 50 minutes. Turn off oven heat and leave cheesecake undisturbed for a further 15 minutes. Remove from oven and run a knife round the edge to loosen, then leave until completely cool before opening the sides of the tin. Chill for several hours or overnight. This is smooth and quite rich and can be served plain or with an attractive glazed fruit topping.

Serves 12

8 digestive biscuits
2 oz (50g) butter

Filling
2 oz (50g) butter
6 oz (175g) castor sugar
2 × 8 oz (227g) cartons curd cheese
2 level tablespoons plain flour
pinch of salt
3 eggs
finely grated rind of 1 lemon
¼ pint (150ml) soured cream

Strawberry cheesecake topping

Hull the strawberries and crush half the berries in a bowl to make ¼ pint (150ml) strawberry purée. Put the purée and sugar into a saucepan and cook over low heat to draw juices. Blend the cornflour with the water and stir into strawberry mixture. Simmer gently, stirring all the time, until thickened. Add the butter and allow to cool. Arrange whole or sliced strawberries on top of cheesecake and spoon the glaze over the strawberries. Allow to set before serving.

1 lb (450g) fresh strawberries
2 oz (50g) castor sugar
3 tablespoons water
1 level tablespoon cornflour
1½ oz (15g) butter

Pineapple cheesecake topping

Drain the pineapple, reserving ¼ pint (150ml) juice. Put sugar, cornflour and pineapple juice into a saucepan and stir to blend well. Simmer gently, stirring all the time, until thickened, then add the butter and allow to cool. Spoon crushed pineapple over cheesecake and spoon glaze over the pineapple.

1 × 13 oz (376g) tin crushed pineapple
1 oz (25g) castor sugar
1 level tablespoon cornflour
1½ oz (15g) butter

Illustrated: Lemon, crème de menthe and strawberry sorbets in tulip cups, pages 216, 217 and 258.

Yoghurt topped cheesecake

Serves 8

8 digestive biscuits
2 oz (50g) butter
1 × 8 oz (227g) tin pineapple rings

Filling
2 oz (50g) butter
2 oz (50g) castor sugar
2 level tablespoons plain flour
2 × 8 oz (227g) cartons curd cheese
2 eggs
½ teaspoon vanilla essence
¼ pint (150ml) soured cream

Topping
¼ pint (150ml) natural yoghurt
2 oz (50g) castor sugar

Heat the oven to 325°F (160°C) or Gas no. 3. Finely crush the biscuits. Melt the butter in a saucepan over low heat and stir in the crumbs with a fork. Spoon biscuit mixture over the base of a greased 8 inch (20cm) spring-clip pan and press down firmly. Drain pineapple rings and arrange on biscuit base. Chill until required.

Cream the butter, sugar and flour in a large mixing bowl until soft. Add the curd cheese and beat well, then beat in the eggs one at a time. Stir the vanilla essence and soured cream into the cheese mixture. Pour the mixture into the prepared tin and spread level. Place in centre of preheated oven and bake for 50 minutes.

Lower oven temperature to 300°F (150°C) or Gas no. 2. Blend yoghurt and sugar for the topping and carefully spoon it over the cheesecake. Return cheesecake to the oven for a further 15 minutes when the yoghurt topping will set. Remove from oven and run a knife round the edge to loosen, then leave until completely cool before opening sides of tin. Chill for at least several hours or overnight.

Cheesecake with sultanas

Serves 6–8

8 digestive biscuits
2 oz (50g) butter

Filling
3 large eggs
4 oz (100g) castor sugar
2 × 8 oz (227g) cartons curd cheese
1 oz (25g) cornflour
1 oz (25g) sultanas
finely grated rind of ½ lemon
¼ pt (150ml) soured cream

Heat the oven to 325°F (160°C) or Gas no. 3. Finely crush the biscuits. Melt the butter in a saucepan over low heat and stir in the crumbs with a fork. Spoon biscuit mixture over the base of a greased 8 inch (20cm) spring-clip pan and press the crumb mixture down firmly. Chill until required.

Separate the eggs, cracking the whites into a medium-sized mixing bowl and yolks into a large bowl. Add the sugar, reserving 1 tablespoon, to the egg yolks and beat together with a wooden spoon until creamy and light. Add the curd cheese and beat until mixture is smooth. Stir in the cornflour, sultanas, finely grated lemon rind and soured cream. Whisk the egg whites until stiff peaks form, add reserved sugar and whisk again until glossy. Fold into the cheese mixture. Pour into the prepared tin and spread level.

Place in centre of preheated oven and bake for 50 minutes. Turn off oven heat and leave cheesecake for a further 15 minutes. Remove from oven and run a knife round the edge to loosen, then leave until completely cool before opening sides of tin. Chill for several hours or overnight.

Chocolate sauce

Put the sugar and water into a saucepan and stir over low heat until sugar dissolves. Bring to the boil, then lower the heat and simmer for 1 minute. Add the cocoa powder and whisk until the sauce is smooth. Bring back to the boil, draw off the heat and pour into a jug. Allow to cool, stirring occasionally. The sauce will thicken as it cools. Serve warm or cold over vanilla, coffee or chocolate ice cream. Pour the sauce over tinned pears topped with vanilla ice cream or use as a sauce for profiteroles.

Serves 6

4 oz (100g) castor sugar
¼ pint (150ml) water
2 oz (50g) cocoa powder

Butterscotch sauce

Put the sugar into a dry saucepan and stir over moderate heat until the sugar has melted and turned to a light, golden caramel. Draw the pan off the heat at once (or caramel will become too dark) and allow the bubbles to subside. Put the water into a teacup and carefully add all at once to the sugar. (Take care: the mixture bubbles up on the addition of a liquid.)

Add the butter and stir over low heat until the butter has melted and the caramel forms a syrup. Leave to cool slightly, then stir in the double cream. This sauce should be served warm. You can hold the temperature or reheat by pouring sauce into a jug and setting jug in a saucepan of warm (not hot) water. Butterscotch sauce is delicious over vanilla ice cream.

Variation **Butterscotch walnut sauce:** Add a few tablespoons finely chopped walnuts that have been lightly toasted under the grill to the finished sauce.

Serves 6

8 oz (225g) granulated sugar
3 tablespoons water
4 oz (100g) butter
¼ pint (150ml) double cream

Strawberry sauce

Put the strawberries, sugar and lemon juice in a blender or food processor and blend to a purée. Alternatively, press strawberries through a nylon sieve, then stir in the sugar and lemon juice. Serve with vanilla or strawberry ice cream or natural yoghurt. It is also good served over fruit mousses, especially gooseberry mousse – the red colour of the strawberries makes a stunning contrast with the green gooseberries.

Serves 4–6

8 oz (225g) fresh strawberries
3 oz (75g) castor sugar
juice of ½ lemon

illustrated facing page 224

Melba sauce

Serves 4

8 oz (225g) fresh or frozen
    raspberries
2 tablespoons redcurrant jelly
2 level teaspoons cornflour
1 tablespoon water
squeeze of lemon juice

Pick over fresh raspberries, if using them, and mash in a saucepan, or heat frozen raspberries until thawed. Add the redcurrant jelly and stir over low heat until jelly has melted and raspberries are quite soft.

Blend the cornflour with the water and stir into the raspberries. Bring to the boil, stirring all the time, and boil until mixture thickens and is clear. Strain the sauce and add a squeeze of lemon juice to sharpen the flavour. Serve warm or cold with strawberry or raspberry ice cream or pour Melba sauce over peaches topped with scoops of vanilla ice cream.

Blackcurrant sauce

Serves 6

1 lb (450g) blackcurrants
¾ pint (400ml) water
6 oz (175g) castor sugar
1 level teaspoon cornflour

Strip the blackcurrants from their stems with a fork. Put the water and sugar into a saucepan and stir over low heat until the sugar has dissolved. Add the blackcurrants and bring to the boil, then lower the heat and simmer for about 10 minutes, or until the berries are quite soft.

Press the fruit and syrup through a nylon sieve to make a thin purée. Return the purée to the rinsed saucepan. Blend the cornflour with a little water just to moisten and stir into the fruit purée. Cook over moderate heat, stirring all the time, until the sauce thickens and is boiling. Pour into a jug and leave to cool. Serve cold with natural yoghurt or vanilla ice cream. The colour is vivid and the flavour very fresh.

Hard sauce

Serves 8

6 oz (175g) unsalted butter
8 oz (225g) icing sugar
2 tablespoons brandy
finely grated rind of ½ orange
    (optional)

Cream the butter in a mixing bowl until soft and light. Sift the icing sugar and gradually beat it into the butter, then beat in the brandy and finally beat in a little grated orange rind, if using it. Spoon into a serving dish. Cover with cling film and chill until ready to serve.

Variations: Add a little hot water along with the brandy to make a softer version of this old-fashioned hard sauce.

Orange hard sauce: Omit the brandy and use the finely grated rind of 1 orange, 1 tablespoon orange juice and 1 tablespoon orange-flavoured liqueur.

Sherry hard sauce: Use dry sherry in place of the brandy.

10

Cakes and Biscuits

You'll like these up-to-date and easy to make old
favourites such as feather light sponges, pretty
cupcakes and buttery biscuits. All deserve to be
placed on the cake stand for tea.

Cakes and Biscuits

Cakes

Ingredients

Fat makes cakes tender and improves the keeping quality. Use fats at room temperature when creaming them and take care not to let butter or margarine melt because it changes the creaming properties.

Butter gives the best flavour and should be used in recipes where there is a high proportion of fat. In general, a good quality margarine is interchangeable with butter. Soft, easy creaming tub margarine is essential for quick mix cakes. In recipes where flavour is very spicy such as gingerbread, white cooking fat may be used.

When oil is used for making a cake, choose a mild flavoured corn oil or vegetable oil – never olive oil which would impart a strong flavour of its own.

Sugar provides sweetness and makes cakes tender and soft; different sugars suit some recipes better than others; sugar must be dissolved, otherwise spots on the crust form and the cake will have a poor volume.

Castor sugar creams more easily with butter and dissolves more quickly when beaten with eggs. In both cases castor sugar helps the mixture retain air.

In melted fat cakes, granulated or demerara sugar can be used because the sugar is dissolved over the heat in the early stages. Some recipes use brown sugar for flavour and in most cases a soft light brown sugar is best unless a dark colour is also required, then soft dark brown sugar is used.

Eggs aerate a cake and provide richness. Use size 2 or 3 eggs unless recipe says otherwise. Eggs should be at room temperature in order to achieve the best aeration; take eggs out of the refrigerator at least 30 minutes before using. Or, put cold eggs into the mixing bowl and cover with warm water. By the time recipe ingredients are weighed, the eggs will be at the right temperature for cracking and the bowl will be pleasantly warm for mixing the cake.

Flour provides the structure that holds cake ingredients together so use the right kind. Rich cakes can be made with plain flour because the eggs and sugar are what give the cake its volume. For soft textured sponges a mixture of plain flour and cornflour makes a good cake flour that is low in gluten. Make your own by sifting 4 oz (100g) cornflour with 1 lb (450g) plain flour and use also for biscuits when you want a short texture.

Some recipes use self-raising flour. Make your own by sifting 4 level teaspoons baking powder with 1 lb (450g) plain flour.

If you like, you can replace half the plain flour in gingerbread or rich fruit cakes with the same quantity of wheatmeal flour to get a different texture, but do not sift it.

Raising agents produce a light texture in cakes. Measure accurately – it is important to use enough raising agent and just as important not to use too much. Baking powder is a ready-made mixture of bicarbonate of soda (alkali) and cream of tartar (acid) sifted with a filler to keep them dry. When the liquid is added the bicarbonate of soda and cream of tartar react to produce carbon dioxide and the heat of the oven expands the gas bubbles to make the cake's light texture.

In some recipes 1 part bicarbonate of soda is used with 2 parts cream of tartar, which are the correct proportions – too much bicarbonate of soda and you will get an after-taste. If acid liquids such as sour milk, lemon juice and milk, butter-milk or yoghurt are used in the same recipe then the amount of cream of tartar is reduced. Sometimes bicarbonate of soda is used on its own to give heavy mixtures a lift, especially when the mixture has a spicy flavour such as in ginger biscuits or gingerbread.

Dried fruit is usually prewashed and spin dried so there's no need to clean. Dried fruit that needs washing should be well drained and spread on a cloth to dry for 2–3 hours in an oven turned to its lowest setting or another warm place. Remember wet fruit sinks to the bottom of a cake.

Sugared or glacé fruits like glacé cherries, pineapple or citron peel should be rinsed in warm water to remove sugary coating and dried before use. Otherwise sugary coating dissolves during baking and drags fruit down. Mix the fruit with 1 tablespoon of the recipe flour before folding it into the cake mixture.

Preparation of cake tins

If tins are to be greased or floured:

● Apply a thin film of melted fat with a pastry brush or grease the cake tin with soft fat using your fingers.

● If tins are fluted, fingers or a pastry brush will get into all the corners more efficiently than greased paper.

● Sprinkle greased tin with a little flour, then shake to coat evenly. Remove excess flour by gently knocking inverted tin on work surface.

If tins are to be lined:

● Set round layer or sandwich cake tins on a large piece of greaseproof paper. Trace around the bottom with a pencil and cut out the shape. Grease the tin and line base with paper, then grease the paper.

● Deep round or square cake tins should be lined on the base and sides. Use a double thickness folded strip of greaseproof paper about 2 inches (5cm) higher than the depth of the tin and long enough to fit the sides of the tin and overlap about 1 inch (2.5cm). Along the folded edge of the paper, turn up a margin of about 1 inch (2.5cm) wide. Straighten out and snip with scissors in a sloped direction all along the margin. Brush tin with melted fat, then brush lining paper all over with melted fat. Put the long strip inside the tin with the snipped margin round the bottom lying flat. The ends should overlap so that sides are completely covered and the lining should stand up about 1 inch (2.5cm) above the rim of the tin. Then place a circle of greaseproof paper inside on the base to cover the snipped margin.

● For large fruit cakes that need extra protection during a long baking period tie a strip of corrugated paper, double thickness brown paper or newspaper around the outside of the tin and stand the tin on several thicknesses of paper on the baking sheet.

● Loaf-shaped, oblong or Swiss roll tins need only a strip of greaseproof paper cut the width of the base and long enough to overlap the 2 shorter sides of the tin. Grease and line the tin, then grease the paper. When baked the unlined sides can be loosened with a knife and the paper ends used to lift out the baked cake or teabread.

Baking temperatures

● Always turn on the oven before you start mixing a cake. The oven must be at the correct baking temperature before the cake is placed in the oven. Arrange oven shelves so they are suitably spaced apart.

● As a general rule, the smaller or thinner the cake, the hotter the oven so the cake bakes without drying out. And the plainer the cake, the hotter the oven because heat must penetrate the cake quickly.

● Most layer cakes are baked in a moderate oven but richer cakes, particularly fruit cakes, require a lower temperature because they take longer to cook; if the oven is too hot the outside of the cake will dry out before the heat has time to reach the centre of the cake.

● Modern hot air ovens heat up very quickly and baking temperatures can be reduced by 10 per cent of what the recipe indicates, but be guided by the manufacturer. In these ovens and in fan-assisted ovens, food can be cooked on different levels so there is no need to rotate cakes or biscuits during cooking.

How to tell when a cake is baked

● Give cakes the baking times directed in the recipe, then test the cake in the centre, which is the last part to bake.

● Small cakes should be evenly brown, well risen and feel firm to the touch when pressed lightly with the finger.

● Test sandwich layer cakes or sponge cakes by gently touching the centre with your fingertips – if the cake feels springy and no imprints remain the cake is done. It also will have shrunk a little from the sides of the tin.

● For heavy cakes like fruit cakes, warm a skewer by pushing it between the baking paper and the tin, then push warmed skewer into the cake centre and it should come out clean.

● Remember a cake will go mouldy if it's not completely baked, especially Christmas cake.

About cooling cakes

● A newly baked cake is fragile. Leave cakes for at least 2 minutes in the tin before turning out.

● Loosen round sides of a layer cake with a spatula or palette knife, then turn on to a wire rack and immediately invert it on to a second wire rack so cake top is not marked with indentations from the rack. Or, invert cake on to a cloth-covered hand and turn right way up on wire rack.

● Place a baked sponge cake layer while still in the tin on to a damp cloth for a few moments and you will find it turns out more easily. Or, give a series of sharp taps all round the tin to loosen the base before turning out the cake.

● Rich fruit cakes are soft when newly cooked and should be cooled for at least 30 minutes in the tin. Very rich fruit cakes can be left in the tin for 24 hours until cold – this also keeps the crust soft.

● Do not peel baking paper from rich fruit cakes if they are intended for keeping; the paper helps keep the cake moist.

To store cakes

● All cakes must be quite cold before storing, otherwise there will be condensation inside a closed tin.

● Put plain or frosted cake layers in a cake container with a cover. Or, invert a mixing bowl over the cake plate and your cake will keep fresh for days.

● Fruit cake should be wrapped in greaseproof paper and a clean tea-towel or in cling film and stored in a cool place. Or, wrap in kitchen foil and replace in the baking tin.

● Differences in keeping times depend on the type of cake: a fatless sponge will keep fresh for only 1–2 days, but one with added fat will keep for about 3 days. Creamed sandwich or layer cakes will keep for 1 week. Light fruit cakes keep for 2–3 weeks and rich fruit cakes will store well for at least a month.

How to make better cakes

● Have ingredients at room temperature so they blend easily. Remove fat and eggs from the refrigerator at least 30 minutes in advance.

● For accuracy and to avoid a messy scale, weigh the syrup, treacle or honey along with the sugar: weigh the sugar on the scale first and spread it out to make a bed, then weigh the syrup on top. Slide off both sugar and syrup into the saucepan. Or, use a measuring spoon dipped in boiling water and you'll find sticky ingredients slide off easily.

Quick mix cakes: For these all the the ingredients are mixed together in one bowl. You can mix these cakes in less time than it takes to heat the oven.

● The fat must blend quickly and smoothly in these cakes and butter, ideal in other cakes, is too hard. Soft tub margarines, or creaming margarines, are best for these cakes. An extra raising agent is used to ensure the cake rises well.

Creamed cakes: The creaming method is used for cakes where the fat is equal to half or all the weight of the flour; cakes of this type have a close and tender crumb.

● Because of the high fat content use butter to give the best flavour. Use a wooden spoon to cream the butter and sugar together, but for large mixes use your hand – the warmth will help to soften the mixture.

● When making creamed cakes add the beaten egg slowly so it blends with the creamed fat and sugar; if added too quickly or the eggs are too cold the mixture may separate. Adding a little of the flour with the last addition of egg helps to prevent separation. Once the flour has been added, be careful not to over-mix or the gluten in the flour will develop and cause the cake to be too heavy.

● Never let creamed cake mixtures get too stiff or heavy. For small cakes the mixture should just drop from the spoon when given a light shake. Larger cake mixtures will be slightly softer to allow for extra evaporation during the longer baking time.

Whisked sponges are made by beating eggs and sugar together and folding in the flour. Whisked sponges are not intended for keeping and are best eaten within a day or two of baking.

● The light texture depends chiefly on the amount of air beaten in. Use a balloon whisk or coil-rimmed hand whisk, or an electric mixer.

● To get best volume a sponge mix should be warm. The mixing bowl can be set over a saucepan of hot (not boiling) water but the base of the bowl must not touch the water.

● Use the baker's method and place the weighed sugar on a square of kitchen foil or in a foil plate and place in the oven for about 5 minutes until hot. This eliminates the need for a saucepan of hot water and is a good idea if you are using a mixing machine.

● Whisking will take about 8–10 minutes (less with a machine) to do it properly. Eggs and sugar should be whisked until mixture leaves a trail when dropped from the whisk – the mixture is allowed to fall from the whisk and it rests on the mixture in the bowl showing a trail or ribbon before it disappears.

● Tins for sponges are usually dusted with equal parts flour and castor sugar. This gives the baked sponge an attractive golden crust.

● Bake without delay – a whisked sponge mixture will not stand.

Melted fat cakes have a moist close texture and keep very well. They are easy to make as there is no creaming or whisking.

● The thin batter of these cakes must be beaten well with a wooden spoon to develop the gluten in the flour which makes a shiny surface on the top of the baked cake.

● Because of their high sugar content these cakes take longer to set in the oven – do not open the oven door during the first 40 minutes of baking time or they will collapse.

Victoria sandwich cake

Heat the oven to 350°F (180°C) or Gas no. 4. Grease two 7 inch sandwich cake tins and line the bases with greased greaseproof paper. Sift the flour, baking powder and salt into a mixing bowl. Add the sugar, soft creaming margarine, eggs and vanilla essence. Mix together with a wooden spoon, then beat well for 1 minute until batter is smooth.

Divide mixture equally between the prepared tins and spread level. Place in the centre of preheated oven and bake for 20–25 minutes. Allow to cool in tins for 2 minutes, then turn out on to a wire rack and leave until completely cool. Sandwich cake layers with raspberry jam and sprinkle the top with castor sugar.

Variations: To make an 8 inch (20cm) sandwich cake, spoon the mixture into an 8 inch (20cm) cake tin and split for filling. Alternatively, increase the amounts of the flour, margarine and sugar to 6 oz (175g) each and use 3 eggs. Spoon mixture into two 8 inch (20cm) sandwich cake tins and bake for 25–30 minutes.

To make a sponge slab, spread mixture level in a greased and lined 11 × 7 inch (27.5 × 17.5cm) baking tin and bake for 25–30 minutes. Allow to cool in tin for 2 minutes, then turn out. Ice and decorate top with buttercream (page 249). Cut into 18 small cakes.

Orange or **lemon sandwich cake:** Add the finely grated rind of 1 orange or lemon to mixture in place of vanilla essence. Fill with buttercream (page 249) and use the juice of 1 orange or lemon to make glacé icing (page 248) for the top.

Makes one 7 inch (17.5cm) sandwich cake

4 oz (100g) self-raising flour
1 level teaspoon baking powder
pinch of salt
4 oz (100g) castor sugar
4 oz (100g) soft creaming margarine
2 eggs
few drops of vanilla essence
1 tablespoon raspberry jam
extra castor sugar, for sprinkling

Coffee walnut cake

Heat the oven to 350°F (180°C) or Gas no. 4. Grease two 7 inch (17.5cm) sandwich cake tins and line the bases with greased greaseproof paper. Sift the flour and baking powder into a mixing bowl. Add the soft brown sugar, soft creaming margarine, coffee essence, eggs and chopped walnuts. Mix together with a wooden spoon, then beat well for 1 minute until batter is smooth.

Divide mixture equally between the prepared tins and spread level. Place in the centre of preheated oven and bake for 25 minutes. Allow to cool in tins for 2 minutes. Turn out on to a wire rack and leave until completely cool. Sandwich cake layers with half the frosting and spoon remainder on top. Spread level and run the tip of a teaspoon from the centre to the outer edge in a circular movement to make a pretty ridged effect.

Makes one 7 inch (17.5cm) sandwich cake

4 oz (100g) self-raising flour
1 level teaspoon baking powder
4 oz (100g) soft light brown sugar
4 oz (100g) soft creaming margarine
1 teaspoon coffee essence
2 eggs
1 oz (25g) chopped walnuts
pale coffee fudge frosting (page 250)

Cocoa fudge cake

*Makes one 7 inch (17.5cm)
sandwich cake*

4 oz (100g) self-raising flour
1 level teaspoon baking powder
4 oz (100g) castor sugar
4 oz (100g) soft creaming
    margarine
1 rounded tablespoon cocoa
    powder
2 tablespoons boiling water
2 eggs
few drops of vanilla essence
chocolate fudge frosting (page 250)

Heat the oven to 350°F (180°C) or Gas no. 4. Grease two 7 inch (17.5cm) sandwich cake tins and line the bases with greased greaseproof paper. Sift the flour and baking powder into a mixing bowl and add the sugar and creaming margarine. Blend the cocoa with the boiling water in a small bowl. Add to the flour mixture along with the eggs and vanilla essence. Mix together with a wooden spoon, then beat well for 1 minute until batter is smooth.

Divide mixture equally between the prepared tins and spread level. Place in the centre of preheated oven and bake for 25 minutes. Allow to cool in tins for 2 minutes, then turn out on to a wire rack and leave until completely cool. Sandwich cake layers with half the frosting and spoon remainder on top. Spread level and rough up frosting with the tip of a knife.

Lemon syrup cake

*Makes one 11 × 7 inch
(27.5 × 17.5cm) cake*

6 oz (175g) self-raising flour
1 level teaspoon baking powder
pinch of salt
4 oz (100g) soft creaming
    margarine
4 oz (100g) castor sugar
finely grated rind of 1 lemon
2 large eggs
1 oz (25g) coarsely chopped
    walnuts
2 tablespoons milk

Lemon syrup
juice of 1 lemon
4 oz (100g) icing sugar

Heat the oven to 350°F (180°C) or Gas no. 4. Grease an 11 × 7 inch (27.5 × 17.5cm) baking tin and line the base and shorter sides with a strip of greased greaseproof paper long enough to overlap the sides. Sift the flour, baking powder and salt into a mixing bowl. Add the soft creaming margarine, sugar, finely grated lemon rind, eggs, walnuts and milk. Mix together with a wooden spoon, then beat well for 1 minute until batter is smooth. Turn mixture into prepared tin and spread level. Place in the centre of preheated oven and bake for 40–45 minutes. Meanwhile, combine lemon juice and icing sugar in a bowl. Set in a warm place so that sugar dissolves in the juice.

Prick all over the surface of the hot cake with a fork. Spoon warm lemon syrup over the entire surface of the hot cake. Leave in the tin until completely cool, preferably overnight. Loosen unlined sides and, holding the paper ends, lift out cake. Remove paper and cut in 24 pieces.

Variation **Orange syrup cake:** Use the grated rind and juice of 1 orange in place of the lemon.

Cutting cakes

Cutting into delicate cakes need not be difficult if you follow my instructions: you will need a long, sharp knife (not serrated), a tall jug of hot water and a damp sponge. Dip the knife in the hot water until the blade warms through, then shake off the water and cut into the cake. The hot knife blade will quickly melt its way through the filling, making a clean cut that does not tear the delicate texture. Wipe the blade with the sponge before making the next cut. I always cut the cake in serving portions before presenting it at the table to make serving quick and easy.

Dutch apple cake

Heat the oven to 400°F (200°C) or Gas no. 6. Grease an 11 × 7 inch (27.5 × 17.5cm) baking tin and line the base and shorter sides with a strip of greased greaseproof paper long enough to overlap the sides. Sift the flour, baking powder and salt into a mixing bowl and stir in the sugar. Blend the egg with the milk and oil and pour into the flour mixture. Mix together with a wooden spoon, then beat well for 1 minute until batter is smooth. Spoon mixture into the prepared tin and spread level.

Peel, core and thinly slice the apples. Spread the butter over the cake batter using a pastry brush. (The easiest way to melt the butter is to put it in a small mixing bowl in the heating oven.) Arrange the apple slices over the surface of the cake. Mix the sugar and cinnamon and sprinkle this over the apples. Place in the centre of preheated oven and bake for 35 minutes. Allow to cool in the tin for 2 minutes. Loosen unlined sides and, holding the paper ends, lift out cake and remove the paper. Serve hot with vanilla ice cream or leave until completely cool and serve cold.

Makes one 11 × 7 inch (27.5 × 17.5cm) cake

6 oz (175g) self-raising flour
1 level teaspoon baking powder
pinch of salt
3 oz (75g) castor sugar
1 egg
6 tablespoons milk
2 tablespoons oil

Apple topping
1 lb (450g) dessert apples
1 oz (25g) melted butter
2 oz (50g) castor sugar
½ level teaspoon ground cinnamon

Rhubarb streusel cake

Heat the oven to 350°F (180°C) or Gas no. 4. Grease a 9 inch (22.5cm) spring-clip tin. Trim the rhubarb stalks and cut in 1 inch (2.5cm) lengths. Sift the flour for the streusel topping into a bowl, add the butter in pieces and mix together with two table knives using a scissor-like movement until the mixture looks like coarse crumbs. Add the sugar and set aside.

Sift the flour and salt for the cake on to a plate. Cream the butter and sugar in a mixing bowl until soft and light. Lightly mix the eggs and vanilla essence and add to the creamed mixture a little at a time, beating well after each addition and adding a little of the flour along with the last addition of egg. Gently fold half the remaining flour into the mixture with a metal spoon. Add the rest of the flour and the milk and mix until blended.

Spoon cake mixture into the prepared tin and spread level, then cover with the rhubarb. Sprinkle the topping evenly over the fruit. Place in the centre of preheated oven and bake for 1 hour. Allow to cool in the tin before opening sides. Dust with icing sugar and serve with whipped cream. This cake is best when served 24 hours after making.

Variations **Gooseberry streusel cake:** Top and tail 1 lb (450g) green gooseberries and use in place of the rhubarb.

Apple streusel cake: Peel, core and thinly slice 1 lb (450g) cooking apples and use in place of the rhubarb.

Makes one 9 inch (22.5cm) cake

1 lb (450g) rhubarb
6 oz (175g) self-raising flour
pinch of salt
4 oz (100g) butter
4 oz (100g) castor sugar
2 eggs
½ teaspoon vanilla essence
1–2 tablespoons milk
icing sugar, for dusting

Streusel topping
4 oz (100g) self-raising flour
3 oz (75g) butter
3 oz (75g) castor sugar

Madeira cake

*Makes one 6 inch (15cm)
round cake*

6 oz (175g) plain flour
2 oz (50g) self-raising flour
6 oz (175g) soft creaming
   margarine
7 oz (200g) castor sugar
4 eggs
finely grated rind of ½ lemon
1 piece citron peel

Heat the oven to 350°F (180°C) or Gas no. 4. Grease a 6 inch (15cm) round cake tin, and line with greased greaseproof paper. Sift the flours into a mixing bowl. Add the soft creaming margarine, sugar, eggs and finely grated lemon rind. Mix together with a wooden spoon, then beat well for 1 minute until batter is smooth. Turn mixture into prepared cake tin and spread level. Place in the centre of preheated oven and bake for 30 minutes.

Rinse the sugary coating from the citron peel and pat dry in absorbent paper. Carefully place the peel on top of cake. Then lower oven temperature to 325°F (160°C) or Gas no. 3 and bake for a further 1 hour – making 1½ hours total baking time. Allow to cool in the tin for 5 minutes, then turn out on to a wire rack.

Almond cake

Makes one 8 inch (20cm) cake

5 oz (150g) self-raising flour
pinch of salt
3 oz (75g) ground almonds
8 oz (225g) butter
8 oz (225g) castor sugar
4 eggs
few drops of almond essence
icing sugar, for dusting

Heat the oven to 350°F (180°C) or Gas no. 4. Generously grease an 8 inch (20cm) round cake tin. Sift the flour and salt on to a plate, add the ground almonds and set aside.

Cream the butter and sugar in a mixing bowl until soft and light. Mix together the eggs and almond essence and add to the creamed mixture a little at a time, beating well after each addition and adding a little of the dry ingredients along with the last addition of egg. Gently fold half the remaining dry ingredients into the mixture with a metal spoon. Add the rest of the dry ingredients and mix until blended.

Turn mixture into the prepared tin and spread level. Place in the centre of preheated oven and bake for 1 hour. Allow to cool in the tin for 5 minutes, then turn out on to a wire rack and leave until completely cool. Dust with icing sugar. This cake keeps well.

Queen cakes

Makes 9 cakes

3 oz (75g) self-raising flour
pinch of salt
1½ oz (40g) currants
2 oz (50g) butter
2 oz (50g) castor sugar
1 egg
finely grated lemon rind
1–2 tablespoons milk

Heat the oven to 350°F (180°C) or Gas no. 4. Generously grease 9 fluted cake moulds set on a baking tray or a tray of bun tins. Sift the flour and salt on to a plate and set aside. Arrange currants in the base of prepared tins.

Cream the butter and sugar in a mixing bowl until soft and light. Mix the egg and finely grated lemon rind and add to the creamed mixture a little at a time, beating well after each addition and adding a little of the flour along with the last addition of egg. Gently fold half the remaining flour into the mixture with a metal spoon. Add the rest of the flour and the milk and mix to blend.

Spoon mixture into the prepared tins. Place in the centre of preheated oven and bake for 15–20 minutes. Allow to cool in the tins for 2 minutes. Then, turn out of moulds to cool completely.

Glacé cupcakes

Heat the oven to 375°F (190°C) or Gas no. 5. Place 18 paper baking cases in trays of patty tins. Sift the flour and salt on to a plate and set aside.

Cream the butter and sugar in a mixing bowl until soft and light. Lightly mix the eggs and vanilla essence and add to the creamed mixture a little at a time, beating well after each addition and adding a little of the sifted flour along with the last addition of egg. Gently fold half the remaining flour into the mixture with a metal spoon. Add the rest of the flour and the milk and mix until well blended.

Spoon mixture into the paper cases, filling them about two-thirds full. Place above centre in preheated oven and bake for 15–18 minutes. Lift cases on to a wire rack to cool. Top each cupcake with a teaspoon of glacé icing and a sliver of glacé cherry.

Variations **Fruit cupcakes:** Add 2 oz (50g) sultanas to the cake batter but do not ice.

Chocolate cupcakes: Combine 1 level tablespoon cocoa powder with 1 tablespoon boiling water and add to the creamed butter and sugar. Top cupcakes with chocolate fudge frosting (page 250).

Makes 18 cupcakes

5 oz (150g) self-raising flour
pinch of salt
4 oz (100g) butter
4 oz (100g) castor sugar
2 eggs
few drops of vanilla essence
1–2 tablespoons milk
glacé icing (page 248)
glacé cherries, to decorate

Glacé fruit cake

Rinse the sugary coating from the cherries, pineapple, ginger and citron peel in warm water and pat dry in absorbent paper. Cut cherries in quarters and chop the pineapple, ginger and citron peel. Put fruit into a mixing bowl and add the sultanas and chopped walnuts. Sift the flours and salt on to a plate. Add 2 heaped tablespoons of the sifted flour to the fruit and mix together well. Set remaining flour aside.

Heat the oven to 325°F (160°C) or Gas no. 3. Grease an 8 inch (20cm) round cake tin and line with greased greaseproof paper. Cream the butter and sugar in a mixing bowl until soft and light. Mix the eggs and finely grated lemon rind and add to the creamed mixture a little at a time, beating well after each addition and adding a little of the flour along with the last addition of egg. Gently fold in the remaining sifted flour with a metal spoon, then add the fruit mixture and sherry or milk and mix until blended.

Spoon mixture into the prepared tin, spread level and hollow out the centre slightly. Place in the centre of preheated oven and bake for 1½ hours. Then lower oven temperature to 300°F (150°C) or Gas no. 2 and bake for a further 1½–2 hours. Allow to cool in tin for 30 minutes, then turn out and leave for 24 hours. Wrap in kitchen foil and store for at least 1 week or up to a month.

Makes one 8 inch (20cm) cake

4 oz (100g) glacé cherries
4 oz (100g) glacé pineapple
4 oz (100g) crystallized ginger
4 oz (100g) citron peel
4 oz (100g) sultanas
4 oz (100g) chopped walnuts
6 oz (175g) plain flour
4 oz (100g) self-raising flour
½ level teaspoon salt
8 oz (225g) butter
8 oz (225g) castor sugar
4 eggs
finely grated rind of 1 lemon
3 tablespoons sherry or milk

Farmhouse fruit cake

Makes one 7 inch (17.5cm) cake

6 oz (175g) self-raising flour
pinch of salt
1 level teaspoon mixed spice
4 oz (100g) butter
4 oz (100g) soft light brown sugar
2 eggs
6 oz (175g) mixed dried fruits
1 oz (25g) chopped candied peel
1 oz (25g) chopped walnuts
3 tablespoons milk

Heat the oven to 350°F (180°C) or Gas no. 4. Grease a 7 inch (17.5cm) round cake tin and line with greased greaseproof paper. Sift the flour, salt and mixed spice on to a plate and set aside.

Cream the butter and sugar in a mixing bowl until soft and light. Break up the eggs with a fork and add to the creamed mixture a little at a time, beating well after each addition and adding a little of the sifted flour along with the last addition of egg. Add the mixed dried fruits, candied peel, chopped walnuts, remaining flour and the milk and mix until blended.

Spoon mixture into the prepared tin, spread level and hollow out centre slightly. Place in the centre of preheated oven and bake for 45 minutes. Then lower oven temperature to 325°F (160°C) or Gas no. 3 and bake for a further 30 minutes – about 1½ hours total baking time. Allow to cool in tin for 30 minutes, then turn out on to a wire rack and leave until completely cool.

Christmas cake

Makes one 8 inch (20cm) cake

4 oz (100g) glacé cherries
4 oz (100g) chopped candied peel
8 oz (225g) currants
8 oz (225g) sultanas
8 oz (225g) seedless raisins
2 oz (50g) blanched chopped
  almonds
10 oz (275g) plain flour
1 level teaspoon salt
1 level teaspoon mixed spice
8 oz (225g) butter
8 oz (225g) soft light brown sugar
4 eggs
1 tablespoon black treacle
½ teaspoon vanilla essence
2 tablespoons brandy or milk

Rinse the sugary coating from the cherries in warm water and pat dry in absorbent paper. Cut cherries in quarters and put into a mixing bowl. Add the chopped candied peel, currants, sultanas, seedless raisins and almonds. Sift the flour, salt and mixed spice on to a plate. Add 2 heaped tablespoons of the flour mixture to the dried fruit and mix together well. Set remaining flour aside.

Heat the oven to 300°F (150°C) or Gas no. 2. Grease an 8 inch (20cm) round cake tin and line with greased greaseproof paper. Cream the butter and sugar in a mixing bowl until soft and light. Mix the eggs, black treacle and vanilla essence and add to the creamed mixture a little at a time, beating well after each addition and adding a little of the sifted flour along with the last addition of egg. Gently fold in the remaining sifted flour with a metal spoon. Add the fruit mixture and brandy or milk and mix until blended.

Spoon mixture into the prepared cake tin, spread level and hollow out the centre slightly. Place in the centre of preheated oven and bake for 1½ hours. Then lower oven temperature to 275°F (140°C) or Gas no. 1 and bake for a further 2½ hours. Allow to cool in the tin for 30 minutes, then turn out and leave for 24 hours. Wrap in kitchen foil and store for at least 1 week or up to a month.

To finish, cover with vanilla almond paste (page 251). Allow to dry for at least 1 day or up to 5 days, then cover with royal icing (page 252) or American frosting (page 253) and decorate.

Gingerbread

Heat the oven to 350°F (180°C) or Gas no. 4. Grease a 7 inch (17.5cm) square baking tin and line the base and two opposite sides with a strip of greased greaseproof paper long enough to overlap the sides. Sift the flour, bicarbonate of soda, salt, ginger and cinnamon into a mixing bowl and set aside.

Gently heat the cooking fat, sugar, golden syrup and treacle in a saucepan until the fat has melted, then blend together. Allow to cool until the hand can be comfortably held against the side of the pan. Lightly mix the eggs and milk and stir into the melted mixture. Add the mixture to the sifted flour and beat with a wooden spoon until batter is smooth. Stir in the sultanas.

Pour mixture into the prepared tin and spread level. Place in the centre of preheated oven and bake for 50–60 minutes until well risen and firm to the touch. Allow to cool in the tin for 30 minutes. Loosen unlined sides and, holding the paper ends, lift out cake and place on a wire rack to cool completely. Wrap cake in kitchen foil and store for 2 days before serving, or store for 1 week if you prefer a sticky gingerbread.

Variation: Omit the sultanas and sprinkle flaked almonds over the batter before baking. Or use 4 oz (100g) drained and chopped preserved ginger in place of the sultanas.

Makes one 7 inch (17.5cm) square cake

**8 oz (225g) plain flour
1 level teaspoon bicarbonate of soda
½ level teaspoon salt
3 level teaspoons ground ginger
1 level teaspoon ground cinnamon
3 oz (75g) white cooking fat
4 oz (100g) castor sugar
4 oz (100g) or 2 rounded tablespoons golden syrup
4 oz (100g) or 2 rounded tablespoons black treacle
2 eggs
5 tablespoons milk
4 oz (100g) sultanas**

Moist chocolate cake

Heat the oven to 350°F (180°C) or Gas no. 4. Grease a 7 inch (17.5cm) shallow square baking tin and line the base and two opposite sides with a strip of greased greaseproof paper long enough to overlap the sides. Sift the flour, cocoa powder, baking powder and bicarbonate of soda into a medium-sized mixing bowl and set aside.

Gently heat the butter, sugar and golden syrup in a saucepan until the butter has melted, then blend together. Allow to cool until the hand can be comfortably held against the side of the pan. Lightly mix the egg, vanilla essence and milk and stir into the melted mixture. Add the mixture to the sifted flour and cocoa and beat with a wooden spoon until batter is smooth.

Pour mixture into the prepared tin and spread level. Place in the centre of preheated oven and bake for 30–35 minutes until well risen and firm to the touch. Allow to cool in the tin for 2 minutes. Loosen unlined sides and, holding the paper ends, lift out cake and place on a wire rack to cool completely. Remove the paper. Slice the cake horizontally, sandwich with half the frosting and spread the remaining over the top. When frosting has set, cut the cake in 9 pieces.

Makes one 7 inch (17.5cm) square cake

**4 oz (100g) plain flour
½ oz (15g) cocoa powder
½ level teaspoon baking powder
¼ level teaspoon bicarbonate of soda
1½ oz (40g) butter
2 oz (50g) castor sugar
4 oz (100g) or 2 rounded tablespoons golden syrup
1 egg
¼ teaspoon vanilla essence
3 tablespoons milk
pale chocolate fudge frosting (page 250)**

Honey cake

*Makes one 11 × 7 inch
(27.5 × 17.5cm) cake*

7 oz (200g) self-raising flour
pinch of salt
5 oz (150g) butter
4 oz (100g) soft light brown sugar
6 oz (175g) clear honey
1 tablespoon water
2 eggs
flaked almonds, for sprinkling

Heat the oven to 350°F (180°C) or Gas no. 4. Grease an 11 × 7 inch (27.5 × 17.5) baking tin and line the base and shorter sides with a strip of greased greaseproof paper long enough to overlap the sides. Sift the flour and salt on to a plate and set aside.

Gently heat the butter, soft brown sugar, honey and water in a saucepan until the butter has melted, then blend together. Allow to cool until the hand can be comfortably held against the side of the pan. Then beat in the eggs one at a time. Add the sifted flour and beat with a wooden spoon until batter is smooth.

Pour into the prepared baking tin and spread level. Sprinkle with flaked almonds. Place in the centre of preheated oven and bake for 30–35 minutes, until well risen and firm to the touch. Allow to cool in the tin for 30 minutes. Loosen unlined sides and, holding the paper ends, lift out cake and place on a wire rack to cool completely. Remove paper and cut cake in 24 squares.

Cinnamon iced gingerbread

*Makes one 10 × 8 inch
(25 × 20cm) cake*

8 oz (225g) self-raising flour
½ level teaspoon bicarbonate of
  soda
3 level teaspoons ground ginger
1 level teaspoon ground cinnamon
4 oz (100g) butter
4 oz (100g) soft light brown sugar
4 oz (100g) or 2 rounded
  tablespoons black treacle
2 oz (50g) glacé cherries
2 eggs
5 tablespoons milk
4 oz (100g) sultanas
2 oz (50g) chopped candied peel

Icing
8 oz (225g) icing sugar
¼ level teaspoon ground cinnamon
juice of ½ orange

Heat the oven to 350°F (180°C) or Gas no. 4. Grease an 10 × 8 inch (25 × 20cm) roasting tin and line the base and shorter sides with a strip of greased greaseproof paper long enough to overlap the sides. Sift the flour, bicarbonate of soda, ginger and cinnamon into a mixing bowl and set aside.

Gently heat the butter, soft brown sugar and treacle in a saucepan until the butter has melted, then blend together. Allow to cool until the hand can be comfortably held against the side of the pan. Meanwhile, rinse the sugary coating from the glacé cherries in warm water, pat dry in absorbent paper and chop them. Lightly mix the eggs and milk and stir into the melted mixture. Add the mixture to the sifted flour and beat with a wooden spoon until batter is smooth. Stir in the sultanas, chopped peel and glacé cherries.

Pour mixture into the prepared tin and spread level. Place in the centre of preheated oven and bake for 1 hour, until well risen and firm to the touch. Allow to cool in the tin for 30 minutes. Loosen unlined sides and, holding the paper ends, lift out cake and place on a wire rack to cool completely. Remove the paper.

Sift the icing sugar and cinnamon into a mixing bowl. Add sufficient orange juice to mix to a stiff consistency. Set bowl over a saucepan of hot (not boiling) water and stir until icing coats the back of a wooden spoon. Pour the icing over the gingerbread and spread evenly. When icing has set cut gingerbread in 24 squares.

Jam and cream sponge

Heat the oven to 375°F (190°C) or Gas no. 5. Grease an 8 inch (20cm) layer cake tin. Dust the base and sides with equal parts flour and castor sugar and shake out excess. Sift the flour twice on to a plate and set aside in a warm place.

Crack the eggs into a mixing bowl and stir in the sugar. Set the bowl over a saucepan one quarter filled with hot (not boiling) water and whisk until the mixture leaves a good trail as it drops from the whisk. Remove bowl from the heat. Sift the flour evenly over the mixture and gently fold it in with a metal spoon, adding the water when the flour is half blended to lighten the mixture.

Pour the mixture into the prepared tin and spread level. Place in the centre of preheated oven and bake for 20–25 minutes, until the sponge feels springy to the touch. Allow to cool in the tin for 2 minutes. Loosen the sides of the sponge, turn out on to a wire rack and leave until completely cool.

Whip the cream until soft peaks form. Slice sponge horizontally and sandwich with the jam and whipped cream. Dust the top with icing sugar and chill for at least 1 hour for the sponge to absorb moisture and the cream to firm.

Variations **Chocolate sponge:** Use 1 level tablespoon cocoa powder in place of 1 level tablespoon of the flour.

Trifle sponge: Use this sponge (unfilled) for trifles; the open texture readily soaks up fruit juices or flavouring sprinkled over the surface.

Makes one 8 inch (20cm) sponge cake

3 oz (75g) plain flour
3 oz (75g) castor sugar
2 eggs
1 tablespoon tepid water
icing sugar, for dusting

Filling
¼ pint (150ml) double cream
1 tablespoon raspberry jam

illustrated facing page 256

Sponge cake (*made with oil*)

A sponge cake made with oil tends to have a more open and crumbly texture. Heat the oven to 375°F (190°C) or Gas no. 5. Grease an 8 inch (20cm) layer cake tin. Dust the base and sides with equal parts flour and castor sugar and shake out excess.

Sift the flour and baking powder into a mixing bowl and stir in the sugar. Put the oil, milk and eggs into a small bowl or jug and mix together well. Pour into the flour mixture and stir with a wooden spoon until creamy, then beat well for 1 minute.

Pour the mixture into the prepared tin and spread level. Place in the centre of preheated oven and bake for 35–40 minutes until the sponge feels springy to the touch. Allow to cool in the tin for 2 minutes. Loosen the sides of the sponge, turn out on to a wire rack and leave until completely cool. Slice sponge horizontally and sandwich with the jam. Dust the top with icing sugar.

Makes one 8 inch (20cm) layer cake

5 oz (150g) self-raising flour
1 level teaspoon baking powder
4 oz (100g) castor sugar
6 tablespoons oil
3 tablespoons milk
2 eggs
1 tablespoon raspberry jam
icing sugar, for dusting

Soft sponge fingers

Makes 24

2½ oz (65g) plain flour
2 eggs
1 egg white
2½ oz (65g) castor sugar
extra castor sugar, for sprinkling.

Heat the oven to 350°F (180°C) or Gas no. 4. Line two baking sheets with greaseproof paper, fixing paper with a smear of cooking fat under each corner. Sift the flour twice on to a plate and set aside in a warm place.

Crack the 2 eggs into a mixing bowl and add the egg white and castor sugar. Set the bowl over a saucepan one quarter filled with hot (not boiling) water and whisk until the mixture leaves a trail as it drops from the whisk. Remove bowl from the heat and whisk for a further 1 minute – mixture must be very well beaten. Sift the flour evenly over the surface and gently fold it in with a metal spoon.

Spoon the mixture into a large nylon piping bag fitted with a ½ inch (1cm) plain nozzle and pipe 3 inch (7.5cm) lengths on to the prepared sheets. Sprinkle over extra castor sugar. Place in preheated oven and bake for 10–12 minutes until light brown. Place the sheets of greaseproof paper with sponge fingers attached on a damp cloth, then peel off sponge fingers. Transfer to a wire rack and leave until completely cool. They can be stored in an airtight tin for up to 3 days. Serve with fruit desserts or syllabubs.

Sponge flan

Makes one 8 inch (20cm) sponge flan

2 oz (50g) plain flour
2 oz (50g) castor sugar
2 eggs

Heat the oven to 375°F (190°C) or Gas no. 5. Generously grease an 8 inch (20cm) sponge flan tin. Dust the base and sides with equal parts flour and castor sugar and shake out excess. Sift the flour twice on to a plate and set aside in a warm place.

Crack the eggs into a mixing bowl and stir in the sugar. Set the bowl over a saucepan one quarter filled with hot (not boiling) water and whisk until the egg and sugar mixture leaves a good trail as it drops from the whisk. Remove bowl from the heat. Sift the flour evenly over the mixture and gently fold it in with a metal spoon.

Pour the mixture into the prepared tin and spread level. Place above centre in preheated oven and bake for 18–20 minutes, until the sponge feels springy to the touch. Allow to cool in the tin for 2 minutes. Loosen the sides of the sponge, turn out on to a wire rack and leave until completely cool.

Serve filled with fresh raspberries or strawberries topped with a jelly glaze (page 183). Or fill with a drained 11 oz (237g) tin of crushed pineapple topped with an arrowroot glaze (page 183). The flavour is extra nice if a little sherry or kirsch is sprinkled on the sponge before filling with fruit.

French madeleines

Heat the oven to 400°F (200°C) or Gas no. 6. Brush two sheets of 12 madeleine shapes with melted butter, then flour lightly and tap out excess flour. Sift the flour twice on to a plate and set in a warm place. Melt the butter in a saucepan and allow it to cool slightly.

Crack the eggs into a mixing bowl and stir in the sugar and vanilla essence. Set the bowl over a saucepan a quarter filled with hot (not boiling) water and whisk until the mixture leaves a good trail as it drops from the whisk. Remove bowl from the heat and whisk for a further 1 minute. Sift the flour evenly over the surface and gently fold it in with a metal spoon. When the flour is almost completely blended, stir in the warm (not hot) butter and blend. Spoon the mixture into prepared tins filling them level. Place in preheated oven and bake for 10–12 minutes. Turn out on to a wire rack and leave until completely cool. These will keep for at least a week in an airtight tin.

Makes 24

2 oz (50g) plain flour
2 oz (50g) unsalted butter
2 eggs
2 oz (50g) castor sugar
few drops vanilla essence

Swiss roll

Heat the oven to 425°F (220°C) or Gas no. 7. Grease a 12 × 8 inch (30 × 20cm) Swiss roll tin and line the base and shorter sides with greased greaseproof paper. Sift the flour twice on to a plate and set aside in a warm place.

Crack the eggs into a mixing bowl and stir in the sugar. Set the bowl over a saucepan one quarter filled with hot (not boiling) water and whisk until the mixture leaves a good trail as it drops from the whisk. Remove bowl from the heat. Sift the flour evenly over the surface and gently fold it in with a metal spoon.

Spoon mixture into the prepared tin and spread level. Place above centre in preheated oven and bake for 7–8 minutes until the sponge feels springy to the touch. Loosen unlined sides and turn out on to a lightly sugared cloth, then carefully peel off the greaseproof paper. Allow to cool for 3–4 minutes, then trim away the crisp edges from the long sides. (If these are left on, the sponge tends to crack when rolled up.) Spread the jam over the sponge and roll up starting with the short end furthest away. Turn the end of the warm sponge in tightly to start with, then draw the roll towards you using the cloth to help roll it tightly. Allow to cool.

Variations: To fill a Swiss roll with buttercream or whipped cream fillings, roll up the sponge and cloth together and leave until completely cool. Then unroll, remove the cloth, spread with cream filling and roll up again. Chill until filling sets before cutting.

Chocolate swiss roll: Use 1 level tablespoon cocoa powder in place of 1 level tablespoon of the flour, omit the jam and fill with ¼ pint (150ml) whipped double cream.

Makes one 12 inch (30cm)
Swiss roll

2 oz (50g) plain flour
2 eggs
2½ oz (65g) castor sugar
2 tablespoons raspberry jam

How to fill, frost and decorate a cake

Filling

● Make sure filling is of a texture that will not drag up the crumbs on a soft cake. Good cake fillings are jam, whipped cream, buttercreams or fudge frostings.

● Spread a jam layer thinly, having removed any large lumps of fruits. Stir the jam well, particularly commercial ones, or warm it slightly so it has a soft spreading consistency.

● To cut cake layers horizontally – hold the knife horizontally and cut turning the cake not the knife. Never stand cake on its side.

● Keep cake layers together when you split them so you can match them again when it's assembled.

Frosting

● Brush away loose crumbs with a pastry brush. If cake has a peak you can slice it level.

● For frosting the top only, put cake on any flat surface; if sides are to be coated as well place the cake on an upturned plate to act as a turntable and you can rotate it as you work. Or, if cake is to be covered with a thin icing, set it on a wire rack over a dinner plate to catch the drips.

● For coating with glacé icing scoop all the icing to one side of the bowl, hold bowl near the cake and quickly spoon all the icing on to the top of the cake. Spread icing to edges with a palette knife and avoid touching up the top.

● Hold palette knife horizontally when coating the top and vertically when coating the sides. Push icing along so blade has no chance to touch cake surface and pick up crumbs.

● Buttercream or fudge frostings are usually put on the top of cakes only; swirl frosting with a palette knife or table knife or spread the frosting smoothly using a palette knife, then make criss-cross lines with the prongs of a fork. If you dip a knife in a jug of hot water (shake off drips) you can make a really smooth surface for piping any decorations on top.

● Use delicate pastel colours for coating cakes; dark colours are best used in small quantities for decorations. Add colouring carefully – use an eye dropper, tip of a skewer or measure drops of colouring into the bottle cap before you add it to the mixture.

● To prevent warm icings from setting too quickly while coating small cakes, stand the bowl over a pan of warm water while you work.

● Gauge the consistency of icing carefully: icing to coat the top and sides will need to be thinner than for coating the top only.

Decorations

● Simple ideas are more effective, especially if you are a beginner. Practise piping decorations on an upturned plate before piping on the cake. The icing can be scraped off before it hardens and returned to the bowl for using again.

● Get the decorations ready before you ice the cake, especially if the icing sets quickly as with American frosting.

● To make a rough finish on a cake, coat the cake all over, then using a palette knife or large table knife slap the surface sharply all over, pulling the knife away quickly and drawing the frosting up to points.

● *Desiccated coconut* looks pretty sprinkled on buttercream or glacé icings. Spread it out in the grill pan and toast it under a hot grill for 1–2 minutes. Or, shake coconut in a jar with a few drops of food colouring.

● *Glacé fruit* should be first rinsed in warm water to remove the sugary coating, then dried. For a quick finish, use finely chopped glacé cherries and angelica. Arrange in alternating colours on whirls of buttercream or whipped cream.

● *Glacé cherry* halves look pretty, but take a cook's tip and instead of using a whole cherry cut in half, cut thin slices off rounded sides to make 3–4 neater, smaller pieces of cherry.

● *Angelica leaves* are made by first cutting the angelica in ¼ inch (5mm) strips, then cutting each strip diagonally. Use the 'leaves' with glacé cherry halves to make pretty decorations.

Chocolate decorations

● Use plain chocolate for decorations because it sets hard and its deep colour makes a better contrast with cake toppings than milk chocolate does.

● *To melt chocolate:* Chocolate scorches easily and should not be melted over direct heat. Instead, break the chocolate into a bowl set over a saucepan of hot (not boiling) water and stir occasionally until chocolate melts. Any drops of water or moisture from steam will spoil chocolate causing it to become grainy. A flake of unsalted butter or white cooking fat added to chocolate will thin it to a piping consistency.

● *Chocolate rolls:* Pour melted chocolate on to a marble slab or formica top. Using a palette knife, spread the chocolate, gather it up and spread again when it will be on the point of setting. Then using a long sharp knife, push chocolate forwards and at an angle so chocolate curls into neat rolls as the chocolate is shaved off the surface; the secret is to shave the chocolate when it is just on the point of setting.

● *Quick curls:* Using a vegetable peeler, shave a bar of chocolate to make tiny curls for sprinkling on cakes and desserts.

● *Chocolate cut-outs:* When chocolate sets it takes on the texture of the surface it is spread out on. For cut-outs, spread the chocolate over the shiny side of kitchen foil. Leave until almost set and using a sharp knife, mark squares or diamonds. Chill until quite firm, then peel back foil and pick up the shapes; the side against the shiny foil will have a high gloss. These are pretty on whipped cream toppings and dessert cakes.

● *Chocolate leaves:* Pick fresh rose leaves, choosing ones that are undamaged and with good vein markings. Wash, then dry them with absorbent paper. Using a knife tip spread melted chocolate in a thin layer to coat the underside of each leaf. Chill with chocolate side up until quite firm. Carefully peel the rose leaf off the hardened chocolate. Use to decorate chocolate or coffee flavoured cakes or cold puddings.

● *Chocolate cases:* Select firm cake baking cases, not flimsy decorative ones used for serving cakes, and put a teaspoon of melted chocolate into the base. Using the back of the teaspoon, spread chocolate to completely coat the inside. Turn chocolate coated cases upside down on a plate or baking tray and chill until quite firm. If you place these upside down it encourages the chocolate to flow to the rim and strengthens the part that is most fragile and liable to break. When chocolate is set, carefully peel off the paper baking case leaving chocolate mould intact. These look charming filled with a scoop of ice cream or syllabub.

How to make and use a paper piping bag

● A small pointed bag made from greaseproof paper makes a perfectly adequate piping bag for making simple cake decorations. In fact, I find a paper piping bag allows much more control and it's easy to change colours or nozzles by simply starting with a new bag.

● Cut a 10 inch (25cm) square of greaseproof paper and cut in half diagonally to make two triangles. Fold one triangle in half and open out. Hold the triangle with the longest side towards you; curl left side around so the edge aligns with the fold and corners meet at top. Holding the points together, make a cone by bringing the remaining corner right around so all points are together. Secure bag by folding the three corners over twice.

● These bags can be used with or without an icing nozzle. To use the bag without a nozzle, put the icing in the bag, fold it closed and snip a tiny hole at the point. To use the bag with a nozzle, snip off the end a little less than ½ inch (1cm) from the tip and put the nozzle into the bag – it should just appear through the opening. Then fill bag with icing.

● Bags should only be half filled with icing – if too full the icing will ooze out when pressure is applied. After filling bag, fold over the top, then bring corners into centre and fold over again.

● Hold piping bag in the palm of your hand with piping end between your first and second fingers. The pressure to bear is brought by pressing with thumb on the top and squeezing bag gently. Guide the hand holding the bag with your other hand when piping to steady the piping.

Glacé icing

To coat one 7–8 inch (17.5–20cm) layer cake

6–8 oz (175–200g) icing sugar
about 2 tablespoons water
¼ teaspoon vanilla essence
few drops of food colouring
(optional)

Using a fine nylon sieve, sift the icing sugar into a medium-sized mixing bowl. Add sufficient hot water to mix to a thick paste. Then add the vanilla essence, food colouring, if using it, and more hot water and stir until icing leaves a trail when dropped from the spoon. Alternatively, mix to a thick paste with cold water. Add vanilla essence and colouring, if using it, and set the bowl over a saucepan half-filled with hot (not boiling) water. Stir until icing feels pleasantly warm and leaves a trail when dropped from the spoon. Then use glacé icing for coating a cake or as a feather icing for cakes.

Variations **Fruit glacé icing:** Use fresh orange or lemon juice in place of the water (especially with cakes that have the rind in the ingredients). The lemon flavouring will counteract the sweetness of the icing.

To use glacé icing

For coating

● Mixing glacé icing with hot water (or heating the bowl) ensures that the icing sets to a dry, glossy finish, but work quickly once you start using it.

● Place simple cake decorations in place when icing has stopped flowing but before it sets. Decorations added after the icing has set will crack the surface.

● Leave cake layers for about 1 hour before moving the cake. By this time the icing will have set completely.

● For coating tops of sandwich cakes, use half the quantity of icing and make a fairly thick consistency by using less water. Scoop icing to one side of the mixing bowl and, holding the bowl close to the cake surface, pour on to the centre of the cake. Using a palette knife, spread icing to within ¼ inch (5mm) of the cake edge.

● For coating top and sides of layer cakes, set cake on a wire cooling rack with a plate underneath to catch the drips. Make icing to a soft consistency that flows easily. Scoop icing to one side of the mixing bowl and, holding the bowl close to the cake surface, pour on to the centre of the cake. Using a palette knife, generously spread icing right to the edge of the cake and allow it to run down the sides. Then with knife held vertically, spread icing on the sides.

● For coating small cakes, choux puffs, or eclairs, glacé icing can be dropped on to small cakes from a teaspoon and carefully spread using the tip of the spoon. Or, tilt the mixing bowl of icing so icing runs deep on one side and, holding cakes by the base, dip the top of each one in the icing. Drain for a moment so excess icing flows back into the mixing bowl and turn turn right way up. Take care not to allow crumbs to fall into the icing if using this method.

For feather icing

Use 1–2 teaspoons of the icing for piping; add a few drops of food colouring to make a deep shade and adjust consistency with icing sugar to make a piping consistency. Spoon into a small paper piping bag. Quickly spread remaining icing on cake with palette knife. Snip end of piping bag and quickly pipe parallel lines across the cake about 1 inch (2.5cm) apart.

● While coating and piping are still wet, draw a skewer or tip of a knife across icing at right angles to piped lines. Repeat in opposite direction. Leave to set.

Coffee fondant icing

Sift the icing sugar into a warmed mixing bowl. Put the water, instant coffee and granulated sugar into a saucepan. Stir over low heat until the sugar has dissolved. Bring to the boil and draw off the heat. Pour on to the icing sugar and using a wooden spoon, beat to a smooth, soft consistency. Use while warm – this fondant icing sets very quickly.

Variation **Chocolate fondant icing:** Use 1 oz (25g) cocoa powder instead of the instant coffee. Reduce the amount of icing sugar to 6 oz (175g).

To top 12 cream puffs or eclairs

8 oz (225g) icing sugar
3 tablespoons water
1 teaspoon instant coffee
1 oz (25g) granulated sugar

Buttercream

Put the butter in slices into a warmed bowl and cream until softened. Sift the icing sugar on to a plate. Add half the sugar to the butter and beat until light, then gradually beat in the remaining half. Add the vanilla essence and food colouring, if using it, then beat again until soft and creamy. Use to fill and frost cakes or pipe pretty decorations on to small cakes.

Spread buttercream over the top of the cake and swirl it using the end of a round bladed knife or teaspoon. Or you can drag the back of a fork across the frosting in parallel lines to make a pretty pattern. A smooth flat top is nice if you are going to decorate it with rosettes of buttercream; use a knife that has been dipped in hot water (shake off the drips) to smooth the rough surface.

Variations: Beat in 1 tablespoon single cream or milk for a softer consistency. To sandwich two 7–8 inch (17.5–20cm) layer cakes use only 2 oz (50g) butter and 3 oz (75g) sifted icing sugar and a few drops of vanilla essence.

Lemon buttercream: Omit the vanilla essence and use ¼ teaspoon lemon essence or 2 tablespoons lemon curd and add a few drops of yellow food colouring, if liked.

Orange buttercream: Omit the vanilla essence and use ¼ teaspoon orange essence. Or for a fresh flavour, use 1 tablespoon lemon curd and the finely grated rind of ½ orange. Add a few drops of orange food colouring, if liked.

Chocolate buttercream: Break up 2 oz (50g) plain chocolate and melt in a bowl set over warm water. Allow to cool slightly, then beat into the buttercream.

Coffee buttercream: Omit the vanilla essence and use 2 teaspoons coffee essence or 2 teaspoons instant coffee dissolved in 1 teaspoon hot water.

To fill and frost one 7–8 inch (17.5–20cm) layer cake

4 oz (100g) unsalted butter
6 oz (175g) icing sugar
¼ teaspoon vanilla essence
few drops of food colouring (optional)

249

Chocolate fudge frosting

To fill and coat one 7–8 inch (17.5–20cm) layer cake

4 oz (100g) icing sugar
1 oz (25g) cocoa powder
1½ oz (40g) butter
2 tablespoons water
2 oz (50g) castor sugar
few drops of vanilla essence

Sift the icing sugar and cocoa powder into a mixing bowl and set aside. Put the butter, water, castor sugar and vanilla essence into a saucepan and stir over low heat until sugar has dissolved, then bring just to the boiling point and draw off the heat. Pour the hot syrup into the sifted ingredients and mix until smooth.

Smooth coating: Stir gently until frosting is thick enough to coat the back of a wooden spoon. Then quickly pour over the cake and smooth the sides.

Roughed-up coating: Continue stirring with a wooden spoon until frosting is thick enough to leave a good trail. Spread on cake and rough-up surface with a knife. At this stage icing can be used to sandwich cake layers.

Pale fudge frosting: Leave the frosting until completely cool. Then beat with a wooden spoon until pale and fudgy. Spread over cake and swirl the surface with a knife.

For large cakes combine icings at different stages, if liked. Sandwich cake layers with a pale fudge frosting and spread the top with a smooth coating, for example.

Coffee fudge frosting

To fill and coat one 7–8 inch (17.5–20cm) layer cake

7 oz (200g) icing sugar
1½ oz (40g) butter
2 tablespoons water
1 oz (25g) castor sugar
2 teaspoons coffee essence

Sift the icing sugar into a mixing bowl. Put the butter, water, castor sugar and coffee essence into a saucepan and stir over low heat until the sugar has dissolved, then bring just to the boiling point and draw off the heat. Pour the hot syrup into the sifted icing sugar and mix until smooth. Then proceed as for chocolate fudge frosting above to make the consistency you require.

Variation **Vanilla fudge frosting:** Omit the coffee essence and use ¼ teaspoon vanilla essence.

Apricot glaze

1 oz (25g) granulated sugar
1 tablespoon water or lemon juice
2 heaped tablespoons apricot jam

Put the sugar and water or lemon juice into a saucepan and stir over low heat until the sugar has dissolved. Sieve the apricot jam into the pan and stir until blended. Bring to the boil, then lower the heat and simmer for 2–3 minutes until the glaze hangs in heavy drops from the spoon. The trick is to simmer the glaze to a point when it will set to a dry non-sticky surface on cooling.

A brushing of hot apricot glaze provides a base covering for small cakes as it holds down the crumbs. It's also used to help almond paste stick to a fruit cake. It's easiest made in small quantities although a confectioner will often prepare a large amount because it keeps well.

Vanilla almond paste

Sift the icing sugar on to a square of greaseproof paper. Add the ground almonds and set aside. Put the egg and castor sugar into a mixing bowl and set over a saucepan one quarter filled with hot (not boiling) water. Whisk until light in colour and pleasantly warm to the touch. Draw off the heat, remove bowl from saucepan and whisk in the vanilla or almond essence.

Stir in the sifted icing sugar and ground almonds with a wooden spoon and mix to a stiff paste. Turn mixture on to a work surface generously dusted with extra sifted icing sugar and knead until smooth, pliable and not sticky, working in the icing sugar as necessary. Wrap in cling film and leave to rest for at least 1 hour before rolling out. Use to cover Christmas cake or birthday cakes.

Variation: To cover one 9 inch (22.5cm) cake, increase weighed amounts to 8 oz (225g), use 1 egg plus 1 egg yolk and 1 teaspoon vanilla or almond essence.

To cover top and sides of one 7–8 inch (17.5–20cm) cake

6 oz (175g) **icing sugar**
6 oz (175g) **ground almonds**
1 egg
6 oz (175g) **castor sugar**
½ teaspoon **vanilla or almond essence**
extra sifted icing sugar, for kneading

To cover a Christmas or birthday cake

● Brush the cake with hot apricot glaze (page 250) which holds down any loose crumbs and helps almond paste to stick to the cake.

● Divide the almond paste into two portions: one-third for the top and two-thirds for the sides.

● Dust work surface with castor sugar so almond paste rolls out easily. Roll out smaller portion to a circle to fit top of the cake. Turn cake over on to rolled out almond paste and press paste on gently. Trim surplus paste and leave cake upside down.

To make decorations

● Knead a few drops of food colouring into the almond paste. Use pink or yellow for flowers, green for leaves and red for holly berries.

● Roll coloured almond paste out thinly on a board lightly dusted with icing sugar. Leave for 10 minutes to allow almond paste to stiffen slightly.

● *Flowers:* cut small circles of almond paste with a 1 inch (2.5cm) cutter or use the round base of an icing nozzle. Pinch each circle on one side to make a petal shape. Arrange petals in groups of four or six, with pinched edges to the centre, to make up a flower. These look pretty on a birthday cake.

● Using a piece of string, measure the circumference of the cake and cut to exact length. Roll out rest of almond paste to a rope the length of the string, then, using a rolling pin, flatten rope to equal the depth of the cake.

● Trim edges straight, then roll cake along strip of almond paste until sides are covered. Turn cake right way up.

● Cover cake with greaseproof paper or a tea-cloth and put in a dry place for 1–5 days, otherwise oils from almond paste can discolour the icing topping.

● *Leaves:* cut rolled almond paste into ½ inch (1cm) strips and then cut each strip diagonally to make diamond shapes. Mark veins on the leaves with the tip of the knife. For making holly leaves for Christmas cakes first cut a spiky leaf pattern from a stiff plain postcard and use as a guide to cut leaves. Pinch the points and neaten edges, then rest leaves over a pencil to give them a realistic curl as they harden.

● *Holly berries:* roll a small piece of almond paste into a thin rope no thicker than a pencil. Cut rope in small pieces and roll each to a round ball. When hard arrange berries with holly leaves.

Royal icing

To coat top and sides of one 8–9 inch (20–22.5cm) cake

¾–1 lb (350–450g) icing sugar
2 large egg whites
pinch of cream of tartar or squeeze of lemon juice
1 teaspoon glycerine (optional)

Using a nylon sieve, sift the icing sugar on to a square of greaseproof paper. Whisk the egg whites and cream of tartar or lemon juice in a mixing bowl until frothy but not stiff. Using a wooden spoon, beat in half the sifted icing sugar, one-third at a time. Then beat very thoroughly for 10 minutes, until the mixture becomes light and fluffy and can be drawn up to a soft peak with the spoon.

Gradually beat in remaining icing sugar and glycerine, if using it. Cover with a cold damp cloth and leave for at least 1 hour. (If icing is used straightaway air bubbles will spoil the smooth surface of the cake.) Alternatively, make icing in an electric mixer: crack the egg whites into the mixer bowl, add the cream of tartar or lemon juice and lightly mix at low speed. Gradually add half the sifted icing sugar while still at low speed. Increase speed to medium and beat for 5 minutes, or until icing is light and fluffy. Remove bowl from mixer and beat in remaining icing sugar and the glycerine by hand.

Using royal icing

● Cakes coated with royal icing must have a base of almond paste (page 251), otherwise cake will stain the white icing.

● Choose a silver cake board that is about 2 inches (5cm) wider in diameter than the cake. With the tip of a knife, spread a dab of icing in the centre of the cake board and fix cake in position. Leave for about 20–30 minutes for icing to harden, then cake will stay firmly in place.

● Set cake placed on the board on an upturned plate to make a turntable. For elaborate work a proper cake turntable is a great help.

● Reserve a small amount of icing for decoration and spoon the rest on top of the cake. With a palette knife smooth the icing over top and around sides of cake as evenly as possible.

● Dip a long, straight bladed knife in hot water (shake off drips) and draw blade in one continuous move across the cake top to level. Repeat if necessary to make a smooth surface.

● To level the sides use a pastry or icing scraper held upright and at an angle sloping towards you. Run the scraper around the sides of the cake in one easy sweep by revolving the turntable. Don't press too hard or the scraper will go through to the almond paste. Repeat if necessary to get a smooth finish. A serrated plastic scraper gives a pleasing ridged effect.

● When a square cake is being iced it's best to cover the sides one at a time, removing surplus icing from the corners with a sharp knife.

● Immediately prick any air bubbles on the surface of the icing with a pin before icing sets.

● To make a roughed-up surface, tap the icing smartly with the flat blade of the knife and quickly draw the blade away. You can also do this on the parts of the silver cake board that are showing.

● Store iced cake for 1–2 days to allow time for the icing to dry before putting on piped decorations, then any mistakes can be easily scraped off and you can start again.

● Keep bowl of icing covered all the time with a damp cloth or icing will dry out. After use soak icing nozzle in a teacup of hot water to remove royal icing which would otherwise harden and block the nozzle.

How to pipe with royal icing

● To make a guide for piping decorations, draw the design on a piece of greaseproof paper cut to the shape of the cake. Then place the paper on top of the cake and using a pin, prick out the design.

● It's not necessary to have a large number of nozzles. Fine, medium and large writing, or plain, nozzles can be used for making straight lines and dots. Rosette nozzles can be used for piping shell edges, stars and rosettes.

● Get the consistency of royal icing just right and the work will be easier. With writing nozzles use a consistency similar to that for coating: the icing will pull up to soft points with a spoon. Star nozzles require a stiffer consistency: the icing should pull up to stiff points with a spoon – piped stars that are too soft will just flatten.

● Any icing that is badly piped can be lifted off and returned to the bowl if the base coat is dry.

To make piped decorations:

Lines: place the tip of a plain nozzle on the surface where the line is to start. Apply light pressure to the piping bag and when the icing starts to come from the nozzle, lift the icing about ½ inch (1cm) above the surface and move the bag in the direction of the line. About ½ inch (1cm) short of the place where the line is to end, release the pressure on the bag and lower the tip of the nozzle back on to the surface. Then lift nozzle away.

Dots: place the top of a plain nozzle on the surface and hold the bag upright. Apply light pressure to the piping bag and release pressure when dot is the size you require, then lift bag away.

Stars: same treatment applies for stars. Hold a rosette nozzle close to the surface with bag upright. The size of the star will be determined by the pressure on the bag. Release pressure before you lift the bag away to avoid a long tail on the star. Stars should be flat on cake surface and not lifted up to a point.

Rosettes: place the tip of a rosette nozzle on the surface and hold bag upright. Apply light pressure and move nozzle in a tight enclosed circle. Release pressure before you lift the bag away. A series of rosettes look pretty on the border of a cake.

Shells: place the tip of a rosette nozzle on the surface and hold the bag at an angle just above the cake surface. Apply light pressure to the piping bag until icing begins to come out, then pull bag to the right drawing nozzle along the surface and release the pressure so you draw icing to a thin tail. A shell border is made by piping shells individually but starting each new one over the tail of the previous one so shells look as though they are all joined together.

American frosting

Put the sugar and water into a saucepan and stir over low heat until the sugar has dissolved. Remove sugar grains from the sides of the pan with a wet pastry brush. Bring the sugar syrup to the boil and boil rapidly (without stirring) until it reaches 242°F (117°C) on a sugar thermometer, or soft ball stage. Draw the pan off the heat.

Whisk the egg whites in a mixing bowl until stiff peaks form. Pour the hot syrup in a slow steady stream on to the whisked whites, whisking all the time to immediately incorporate. The frosting will become thick and light. Continue whisking until frosting becomes a light fluffy texture like cotton wool. Spread quickly over cake and rough-up surface with a knife.

To cover one 8 inch (20cm) cake

1 lb (450g) granulated sugar
¼ pint (150ml) cold water
2 egg whites

Biscuits

How to make better biscuits

● Measure ingredients accurately, particularly the liquid – too much makes a dough that's soft and too sticky to handle.

● Use butter when making biscuits because the flavour of the fat is important; where bicarbonate of soda is listed in the recipe, remember it acts as a raising agent, so don't leave it out.

● It is important that you make the indicated number of biscuits; should you finish with more or less than the recipe states, your biscuits may be too small or too large and the baking time will then be affected.

● If you have more than one baking sheet among your kitchen equipment then you have an advantage; it's quicker and more accurate if you can spoon out, cut or mould all the mixture at the same time and to do this you will need 2–3 baking sheets.

● Because they are thin, biscuits bake quickly so watch baking times carefully – use an oven timer.

● All biscuits are fragile, so handle carefully; some varieties are very soft when newly baked and need 1–2 minutes to cool on the sheet. A palette knife or fish slice is handy for lifting them off the baking sheet; slide biscuits on to a wire rack and leave them until cool and crisp.

● Biscuits keep well in an airtight tin, but make sure they are quite cold first and don't put any in a tin with cake or they will absorb the moisture and soften.

● Instead of using wooden spoons for rolling brandy snaps, I bought a broom handle from the ironmonger and had it cut into 6 inch (15cm) lengths. The snaps are easier to roll up and they are larger, allowing more room for the filling. But having a lot of round sticks doesn't mean that more snaps can be baked at a time – they become crisp so quickly that you must work quickly to roll them. Bake only the number specified in the recipe at a time.

Cookies

Makes 36

8 oz (225g) self-raising flour
¼ level teaspoon salt
4 oz (100g) butter
8 oz (225g) demerara sugar
1 egg

Coconut currant cookies
1 oz (25g) desiccated coconut
1 oz (25g) currants

Chocolate walnut cookies
1 oz (25g) plain chocolate
1 oz (25g) finely chopped walnuts

illustrated facing page 257

Sift the flour and salt on to a plate. Cream the butter in a mixing bowl until soft and light. Add the sugar and mix together well. Break up the egg with a fork and beat into the mixture a little at a time. Add half the sifted flour and mix to a soft paste, then add the remaining flour and mix to a soft dough. Divide the dough in half.

Add the coconut and currants to half the dough and on a lightly floured work surface, shape into a fat roll. Cover and leave to rest for 10 minutes. Meanwhile, break the chocolate into small nibbly pieces and add to the other half of dough along with the chopped walnuts. Shape into a fat roll on the work surface. Cover and leave to rest for 10 minutes.

Heat the oven to 350°F (180°C) or Gas no. 4. Divide each roll into 18 equal pieces and shape into balls. Arrange on greased baking sheets about 1 inch (2.5cm) apart. Place in preheated oven and bake for 12–15 minutes, or until light brown. Swap the sheets during baking, if necessary, so cookies bake evenly. Allow to cool on the baking sheets for 1 minute, then loosen with a palette knife and transfer to a wire rack. Leave until completely cool.

Rolled oat cookies

Heat the oven to 350°F (180°C) or Gas no. 4. Put the butter, sugar and golden syrup or treacle into a saucepan and stir over low heat until blended. Allow to cool slightly. Sift the flour, bicarbonate of soda and salt into a mixing bowl and stir in the rolled oats and walnuts, then add the slightly cooled mixture and mix to a dough.

Spoon out 36 rounded teaspoons of the mixture and shape into balls about the size of a walnut. Place 12 on each of three greased baking sheets, spacing them well apart to allow for spreading. Place in preheated oven and bake for 15 minutes, or until lightly browned. Swap sheets during baking, if necessary, so cookies bake evenly. Allow cookies to cool on the baking sheets for 1 minute, then loosen with a palette knife, transfer to a wire rack and leave until completely cool.

Makes 36

4 oz (100g) butter
4 oz (100g) demerara sugar
2 oz (50g) or 1 rounded tablespoon golden syrup or treacle
4 oz (100g) self-raising flour
½ level teaspoon bicarbonate of soda
pinch of salt
4 oz (100g) rolled oats
1 oz (25g) finely chopped walnuts

Chocolate chip cookies

Heat the oven to 375°F (190°C) or Gas no. 5. Grease three baking sheets. Sift the flour, bicarbonate of soda and salt on to a plate.

Cream the butter, soft brown sugar and castor sugar in a mixing bowl until soft and light. Lightly mix the egg and vanilla essence and beat into the creamed mixture a little at a time. Stir in half the flour mixture and mix to a smooth paste. Add remaining flour, walnuts and chocolate drops and mix to a dough.

Drop 12 teaspoons of the mixture on to each greased baking sheet, spacing them well apart to allow for spreading. Place in preheated oven and bake for 12 minutes, or until golden brown. Swap the sheets during baking, if necessary, so cookies bake evenly. Allow cookies to cool on the baking sheets for 1 minute, then loosen with a palette knife and transfer to a wire rack. They will become crisp on cooling.

Makes 36

6 oz (175g) plain flour
¼ level teaspoon bicarbonate of soda
pinch of salt
4 oz (100g) butter
3 oz (75g) soft light brown sugar
3 oz (75g) castor sugar
1 egg
few drops of vanilla essence
4 oz (100g) chocolate drops for cooking
1 oz (25g) finely chopped walnuts

Gingersnaps

Heat the oven to 350°F (180°C) or Gas no. 4. Grease three baking sheets. Put the butter, sugar and golden syrup into a saucepan and stir over low heat until blended. Allow to cool slightly. Sift the flour, bicarbonate of soda, salt and ginger into a mixing bowl, then add the slightly cooled mixture and mix to a soft dough.

Spoon out 36 rounded teaspoons of the mixture and shape into balls about the size of a walnut. Place 12 on each greased baking sheet, spacing them well apart to allow for spreading. Place in preheated oven and bake for 15 minutes. (Watch baking because these biscuits easily burn.) Allow gingersnaps to cool on the baking sheets for 1 minute, then loosen with a palette knife and transfer to a wire rack. Allow to cool until crisp and crunchy.

Makes 36

4 oz (100g) butter
4 oz (100g) castor sugar
4 oz (100g) or 2 rounded tablespoons golden syrup
8 oz (225g) plain flour
1 level teaspoon bicarbonate of soda
pinch of salt
1 level teaspoon ground ginger

illustrated facing page 257

Shortbread

Makes 8–10 fingers or petticoat tails or one large mould

4 oz (100g) plain flour
2 oz (50g) rice flour
4 oz (100g) unsalted butter
2 oz (50g) castor sugar

Heat the oven to 375°F (190°C) or Gas no. 5. Sift the flour and rice flour (if difficult to obtain make up the quantity with plain flour) on to a pastry board. Cream the butter and sugar in a mixing bowl until soft and light. Turn creamed mixture on to the sifted flour and work ingredients together with the fingertips to a smooth dough.

Shortbread fingers: Pat or roll dough out to a strip about ½ inch (1cm) thick. Place on ungreased baking sheet and crimp the edges with floured fingers. Prick all over with a fork and mark into finger shapes with a knife – do not cut through.

Petticoat tails: Divide dough in half and pat or roll out each portion to a circle about ¼ inch (5mm) thick. Place on ungreased baking sheet and crimp the edges with floured fingers. Prick all over with a fork and mark into triangles – do not cut through.

Shortbread mould: Use half or all the dough according to the size of mould. Dust mould with extra rice flour and shake out excess. Press shortbread dough into the mould with floured fingers. Tap sharply to loosen edges and turn on to an ungreased baking sheet, then lift off the mould.

Place in the centre of preheated oven and bake for 10 minutes. Then lower oven temperature to 325°F (160°C) or Gas no. 3, and bake for a further 10 minutes for fingers and petticoat tails or 20–25 minutes for a shortbread mould. Allow to cool on baking sheet for 5 minutes, then transfer to a wire rack and leave until completely cool. Break shortbread fingers or petticoat tails along marked lines.

Almond petits fours

Makes 36

5 oz (150g) ground almonds
6 oz (175g) castor sugar
2 egg whites
few drops of almond or vanilla
    essence
glacé cherries, angelica or flaked
    almonds, to decorate
castor sugar, for sprinkling

Put the ground almonds, sugar and egg whites into a mixing bowl and stir with a wooden spoon to make a thick paste, then add the almond or vanilla essence. Set the bowl over a saucepan one quarter filled with hot (not boiling) water and beat until mixture softens and feels warm to the touch. Draw off the heat.

Heat the oven to 350°F (180°C) or Gas no. 4. Line two baking sheets with greaseproof paper – a smear of fat under corners will fix paper to trays. Spoon mixture into a nylon piping bag fitted with a rosette nozzle and pipe rosettes on to the prepared baking sheets. Decorate each one with pieces of glacé cherry, angelica or flaked almonds and sprinkle with castor sugar. Place in preheated oven and bake for 15 minutes. Swap baking sheets, if necessary, so they bake evenly. Transfer the greaseproof paper to a damp cloth and peel off the petits fours. Leave until completely cool.

Illustrated: Jam and cream sponge, page 243

Cigarettes russes

Heat the oven to 400°F (200°C) or Gas no. 6. Generously oil two baking sheets or line them with non-stick parchment paper. Grease four wooden spoon handles. Melt the butter in a saucepan, draw off the heat and keep warm. In a mixing bowl break up the egg whites with a fork and stir in the sugar. Sift the flour over the mixture and gently fold it in with a metal spoon, then fold in the melted butter.

Drop 4 teaspoons of the mixture on to a prepared baking sheet, spacing them well apart. Using the tip of the teaspoon, spread each blob thinly to a neat round shape. Sift over icing sugar to lightly dust.

Place the baking sheet in centre of preheated oven and bake for 5 minutes, or until pale brown at the edges. Meanwhile, prepare next batch. Immediately lift off biscuits with a palette knife and roll 1 around each wooden spoon handle. As soon as biscuits are crisp (about 3 minutes) they can be slipped off the spoons to allow for the next batch. Serve with fruit desserts or ice cream.

Makes 24

2 oz (50g) butter
2 egg whites
2½ oz (65g) castor sugar
2 oz (50g) plain flour
icing sugar, for dusting

Brandy snaps

Sift the flour and ginger on to a plate. Cream the butter in a mixing bowl until soft and light. Add the sugar, golden syrup and sifted flour and mix to a rough dough. Turn on to a clean work surface and pat down with the palm of the hand once or twice until smooth. Cover with upturned mixing bowl and allow dough to rest in a cool place for at least 30 minutes.

Heat the oven to 375°F (190°C) or Gas no. 5. Generously oil two baking sheets or line them with non-stick parchment paper and grease three wooden spoon handles. Divide dough into 24 equal pieces and roll them into balls. Place 3 on a prepared baking sheet, spacing them well apart to allow for spreading. Flatten each one slightly with the palm of the hand. Place above centre in preheated oven and bake for 8–10 minutes, until golden brown and bubbling. Meanwhile, prepare next batch; put them in the oven as you take baked ones out. Allow snaps to cool for 1 minute to firm up slightly. Slide a palette knife under each one, lift off the tray and immediately wrap each one, smooth side in, around a greased wooden spoon handle. As soon as snaps have set, slide them off the handles and allow to cool.

About 1 hour before serving, whip the cream until soft peaks form. Put into a nylon piping bag fitted with a rosette nozzle and pipe a little cream into both ends of each brandy snap.

Makes 24

2 oz (50g) plain flour
½ level teaspoon ground ginger
2 oz (50g) butter
4 oz (100g) castor sugar
2 oz (50g) or 1 rounded tablespoon golden syrup
½ pint (300ml) double cream

Illustrated: rear: Gingersnaps (page 255) and langues de chat (page 258)
foreground: Cookies (page 254), cigarettes russes (see above)
and refrigerator biscuits (page 259)

Langues de chat

Makes 48

2 oz (50g) butter
2 oz (50g) castor sugar
2 egg whites
2 oz (50g) plain flour

illustrated facing page 257

Heat the oven to 425°F (220°C) or Gas no. 7. Grease two or three baking sheets with white cooking fat. Cream the butter and sugar in a mixing bowl until soft and light. Break up the egg whites with a fork and beat into the creamed mixture a little at a time, adding a little of the flour along with the last addition of egg. Then fold in remaining flour with a metal spoon.

Put mixture into a nylon piping bag fitted with a ¼ inch (5mm) nozzle. Pipe 2½ inch (6cm) lengths on to the prepared baking sheets, spacing them about 1 inch (2.5cm) apart. Bake in batches. Place in centre of preheated oven and bake for 4–5 minutes, or until biscuits are tinged with brown, then loosen with a palette knife and transfer to a wire rack. They will crisp up as they cool. Serve with ice cream and sorbets.

Variation **Tulip biscuits:** Increase the amount of sugar in the mixture to 2½ oz (65g). Drop 2 teaspoons of the mixture on to a prepared baking sheet. Using the tip of the teaspoon, spread to make circles about 4 inches (10cm) in diameter. (Do not be tempted to make more than two at a time as the biscuits quickly harden.) Bake until tinged with brown, then quickly loosen with a palette knife and press each one into a teacup. Leave for 1 minute until crisp. Remove them from the teacups to allow for next batch. These dainty biscuits are good filled with ice cream, sorbets, fresh fruit or whipped cream. Makes 12. *Illustrated facing page 225.*

Wine biscuits

Makes 30

6 oz (150g) plain flour
pinch of salt
4 oz (100g) unsalted butter
3 oz (75g) castor sugar
1 egg yolk
1 tablespoon dry sherry

Topping
1 egg white
castor sugar
flaked almonds

Sift the flour and salt on to a plate. Cream the butter and sugar in a mixing bowl until soft and light. Lightly mix the egg yolk and sherry and beat into the creamed mixture. Add half the sifted flour and mix to a soft paste, then add remaining flour and mix to a soft dough. Turn on to a floured work surface and shape into a roll about 2 inches (5cm) in diameter. Wrap in kitchen foil and chill for several hours until firm.

Heat the oven to 375°F (190°C) or Gas no. 5. With a sharp knife, slice biscuit roll into rounds about ¼ inch (5mm) thick. Arrange rounds about ½ inch (1cm) apart on greased baking sheets. Lightly beat the egg white and brush the rounds with it, then sprinkle with sugar and flaked almonds. Place in preheated oven and bake for 10–12 minutes, or until browned. Swap sheets during baking, if necessary, so biscuits bake evenly. Allow to cool on baking sheets for 2 minutes, then loosen biscuits with a palette knife and transfer to a wire rack. Leave until completely cool and serve with fruit desserts.

Refrigerator biscuit roll

Sift the flour and salt on to a plate. Cream the butter and sugar in a mixing bowl until soft and light. Lightly mix the egg and vanilla essence and beat into the creamed mixture. Add half the sifted flour and mix to a soft paste, then add remaining flour and the walnuts and mix to a soft dough. Turn on to a floured work surface and shape dough into a roll about 2 inches (5 cm) in diameter. Wrap in kitchen foil and chill for several hours until firm. (The dough will keep for 2 weeks in refrigerator.)

Heat the oven to 375°F (190°C) or Gas no. 5. With a sharp knife, slice biscuit roll into rounds about ¼ inch (5 mm) thick. Arrange rounds about ½ inch (1 cm) apart on greased baking sheets. Place in preheated oven and bake for 10 minutes, swapping the sheets during baking, if necessary, so biscuits bake evenly. Allow to cool for 2 minutes, then loosen biscuits with a palette knife and transfer to a wire rack. Leave until completely cool.

Variations: This basic biscuit dough is good with any variety of added dried fruits or nuts. Use finely chopped toasted hazelnuts, chopped seedless raisins or chopped glacé cherries in place of the walnuts. Or try any of these excellent combinations: chopped plain chocolate with chopped walnuts, chopped roasted peanuts with seedless raisins, chopped glacé cherries with chopped almonds or chopped dates with desiccated coconut. Use 1 oz (25 g) of each to make up the 2 oz (50 g) required to replace the walnuts in the recipe. You can make a variety of refrigerator biscuit rolls to serve at coffee morning parties.

Makes 36

8 oz (225g) plain flour
pinch of salt
4 oz (100g) butter
5 oz (150g) castor sugar
1 egg
½ teaspoon vanilla essence
2 oz (50g) finely chopped walnuts

illustrated facing page 257

Florentines

Heat the oven to 350°F (180°C) or Gas no. 4. Generously oil two baking sheets or line them with non-stick parchment paper. Put the sugar, almonds, flour, butter, cream and candied fruits into a saucepan and stir over low heat until blended.

Drop 6 teaspoons of the mixture on to each prepared baking sheet and flatten each heap slightly with wetted fingers so biscuits bake in a round shape. Place in preheated oven and bake for 10 minutes, or until golden. Swap the baking sheets half-way through baking time, if necessary. Allow to cool on the baking sheets for 1–2 minutes until just beginning to harden. Lift off biscuits with a palette knife, slide on to a wire rack and leave until completely cool. Bake remaining mixture in the same way.

Break chocolate into a small mixing bowl and place over a saucepan one quarter filled with hot (not boiling) water. Stir until chocolate has melted. Using a pastry brush or knife, coat the flat side of each florentine with chocolate and leave until set.

Makes 24

2 oz (50g) castor sugar
2 oz (50g) flaked almonds
1 level tablespoon plain flour
1½ oz (40g) butter
2 tablespoons single cream
2 oz (50g) finely chopped mixed
  glacé cherries, angelica and
  candied peel
2 oz (50g) plain chocolate

Oatcakes

Makes 24

8 oz (225g) medium oatmeal
2 oz (50g) plain flour
¼ level teaspoon bicarbonate of
  soda
1 level teaspoon salt
1 oz (50g) butter
1 oz (50g) white cooking fat
about 1–2 tablespoons boiling
  water
extra oatmeal, for kneading

illustrated facing page 49

Heat the oven to 375°F (190°C) or Gas no. 5. Put the oatmeal into a mixing bowl and sift in the flour, bicarbonate of soda and salt. Mix together well. Cream the butter and white cooking fat on a plate to soften and blend, add in pieces to oatmeal mixture and rub in with the fingertips. Then, mix with a table knife, adding just enough boiling water (from the kettle) to make a soft, but not sticky dough.

Turn dough on to a board sprinkled with extra oatmeal and knead to a smooth rolling consistency. Divide dough in 4 equal portions and roll out each one to a circle about ¼ inch (5mm) thick. Rub surface with oatmeal to whiten, then cut each circle into 6 triangular oatcakes. Alternatively, roll out dough about ¼ inch (5mm) thick, rub surface with oatmeal to whiten and then cut into rounds with a 2 or 3 inch (5 or 7.5cm) round cutter.

Arrange oatcakes on ungreased baking sheets. Place in preheated oven and bake for 20 minutes, or until dry and crisp at the edges. Swap baking sheets, if necessary, so oatcakes bake evenly. Transfer to a wire rack and leave until completely cool. Store in an airtight container. Serve with cheese, especially a soft cream cheese or curd cheese which are delicious with the crunchy oatcake texture.

Digestive biscuits

Makes 24

6 oz (175g) wholemeal flour
2 level teaspoons baking powder
pinch of salt
2 oz (50g) medium oatmeal
2 oz (50g) butter
1½ oz (40g) white cooking fat
1½ oz (40g) castor sugar
3 tablespoons milk

Heat the oven to 400°F (200°C) or Gas no. 6. Put the wholemeal flour, baking powder, salt and oatmeal into a medium-sized mixing bowl and mix together. Cream the butter and white cooking fat on a plate to soften and blend. Add to the flour mixture in pieces and rub in with the fingertips. Stir in the sugar, then add the milk and mix to a rough dough.

Turn on to a floured work surface and knead just long enough to remove the cracks. Cover dough with upturned mixing bowl and leave to rest for 10 minutes. Roll out dough about ¼ inch (5mm) thick. Cut in rounds with a 2½ inch (6cm) cutter. Press trimmings together and re-roll, then cut out more rounds. Place on greased baking sheets and prick the surfaces all over with a fork. Place in preheated oven and bake for 12 minutes, or until lightly brown. Swap baking sheets, if necessary, so biscuits bake evenly. Allow to cool for 2 minutes on baking sheets, then transfer to a wire rack. These have a coarse texture and are delicious spread with butter or served with cheese.

11

Breads

Ranging from simple scones and teabreads to the
more hearty yeast loaves and rolls, you'll find
breadmaking surprisingly easy if you use the right
ingredients and follow a few basic rules.

Breads

Scones

Scones are a simple form of bread that relies on a chemical raising agent to give them their light texture. They are best eaten newly made.

Ingredients

Flour: To give scones their light open texture a 'soft' flour with a low gluten content is used. (Gluten is what gives yeast breads their elasticity and firmness.) Both plain and self-raising flours are soft flours – never use strong white flour. Wholemeal flour is also good for making scones.

● For the lightest scones use plain flour with a mixture of bicarbonate of soda and cream of tartar in the proportions of 8 oz (225g) plain flour to 1 level teaspoon bicarbonate of soda (alkali) and 2 level teaspoons cream of tartar (acid).

● Or use plain flour and baking powder in the proportions of 8 oz (225g) plain flour with 4 level teaspoons baking powder. Self-raising flour may be used but always add baking powder in the proportions of 8 oz (225g) self-raising flour to 2 level teaspoons baking powder.

Raising agent: Bicarbonate of soda is the chemical substance which causes scones to rise in the oven. It activates immediately on the addition of a liquid which is why scones must be quickly mixed and put straight in the oven. If used alone without a neutralizing acid substance the resulting scones would have a very unpleasant taste. So cream of tartar, which is acidic, is used together with bicarbonate of soda. The most convenient way to add both of these ingredients to the mixture is to use baking powder, a substance containing both the alkaline bicarbonate of soda and an acid reacting powder such as cream of tartar.

Liquid: Buttermilk or sour milk provide some of the acid required to neutralize the bicarbonate of soda so the proportion of cream of tartar is reduced when these liquids are used. Otherwise, ordinary milk is used. With cheese scones, water is used because the cheese contains milk.

● To make scones richer and lighter add 1 egg to the milk but reduce the amount of milk by about 4 tablespoons.

How to make better scones

● Sift flour and raising agent thoroughly through a fine sieve. If the bicarbonate of soda is lumpy measure on to the palm of your hand and press out lumps before sifting with the flour.

● A little butter rubbed into the dry ingredients will help keep scones fresh for a day.

● Add liquid all at once and use the blade of a knife or a fork to mix the dough; both are cooler and mixing is quicker than with a wooden spoon.

● Adding 1 tablespoon natural yoghurt to the milk for mixing will give you lighter scones.

● A teaspoon of golden syrup added to Scotch pancakes encourages them to cook to an even golden brown.

● Press dough together with your fingertips and handle it lightly. Unlike a bread dough the gluten in the flour must not be developed and this will happen if the dough is over-mixed.

● Take care not to roll scone dough too thinly. It's always safer to pat or press scone dough out with your hands; if you use a rolling pin it's very easy to make the dough too thin.

● Thoroughly heat oven and put scones to bake as soon as mixed because the raising agent starts to work when liquid is added. The oven must be hot to give scones a lift – when baked they should have doubled in height.

● For floury oven scones with a soft crust, use a flour dredger to sprinkle flour on baking sheet. Arrange scones on the floured sheet and dust with flour before baking.

● For a glossy finish on oven scones, arrange scones on greased baking sheet; then brush tops with milk or mixed milk and egg.

● Place oven scones close together on baking sheet to make soft touching sides. To make the sides firm, place them at least ½ inch (1cm) apart.

Oven scones

Makes 12

8 oz (225g) plain flour
1 level teaspoon bicarbonate of soda
2 level teaspoons cream of tartar
pinch of salt
1½ oz (40g) butter
1½ oz (40g) castor sugar
¼ pint (150ml) milk

Heat the oven to 425°F (220°C) or Gas no. 7. Sift the flour, bicarbonate of soda, cream of tartar and salt into a medium-sized mixing bowl. Add the butter in pieces and rub in with the fingertips. Stir in the sugar.

Make a well in the flour mixture and pour in the milk. Using a table knife, mix together until dough is soft, but not sticky. Turn on to a floured board and knead about 3 times just to smooth the underside. Turn dough smooth side up and pat or roll out to a thickness of ½ inch (1cm).

Using a 2 inch (5cm) floured round cutter, cut 12 rounds. Press together the trimmings and use to make the last few. Arrange scones on a floured baking sheet and dust the tops with extra flour. Immediately place above centre in preheated oven and bake for 10–12 minutes until well risen and light brown. Transfer to a wire rack and allow to cool for 15 minutes, then split and butter for serving.

Variations: For softer and richer scones, use 1 lightly beaten egg mixed with enough milk – about 4 tablespoons – to equal ¼ pint (150ml). To make sultana scones, add 2 oz (50g) sultanas along with the sugar.

Wheaten Scones: Use half wholemeal flour and half plain flour. Sift plain flour, then add unsifted wholemeal flour to the bowl.

Wholemeal date scones

Heat the oven to 425°F (220°C) or Gas no. 7. Put the flour, baking powder and salt into a medium-sized mixing bowl. Add the butter in pieces and rub in with the fingertips. Stir in the sugar and dates.

Make a well in the flour mixture and pour in the milk. Using a table knife, mix together until dough is soft, but not sticky. Turn on to a floured board and knead about 3 times just to smooth the underside. Turn dough smooth side up and pat or roll out to a thickness of ½ inch (1cm).

Using a 2 inch (5cm) floured round cutter, cut 12 rounds. Press together the trimmings and use to make the last few. Arrange scones on a floured baking sheet and dust the tops with extra flour. Place above centre in preheated oven and bake for 10–12 minutes, or until well risen.

Makes 12

8 oz (225g) wholemeal flour
4 level teaspoons baking powder.
pinch of salt
2 oz (50g) butter
1 oz (25g) castor sugar
2 oz (50g) chopped dates
¼ pint (150ml) milk

Cheese scones

Heat the oven to 425°F (220°C) or Gas no. 7. Sift the flour, baking powder and salt into a medium-sized mixing bowl. Add the butter in pieces and rub in with the fingertips. Stir in the grated cheese.

Make a well in the flour mixture and pour in the water. Using a table knife, mix together until dough is soft, but not sticky. Turn on to a floured board and knead about 3 times just to smooth the underside. Turn dough smooth side up and pat or roll out to a thickness of ½ inch (1cm).

Using a 2 inch (5cm) floured round cutter, cut 12 rounds of dough. Press together the trimmings and use to make the last few. Arrange scones on a greased baking sheet and brush with milk or egg and water. Immediately place above centre in preheated oven and bake for 10–12 minutes until well risen and golden brown. Hot cheese scones are marvellous for a coffee morning party. Or split in half and top them with cream cheese and tomato or egg slices for tea.

Variation: For softer and richer scones, use 1 lightly beaten egg mixed with enough water – about 4 tablespoons – to equal ¼ pint (150ml).

Makes 12

8 oz (225g) self-raising flour
2 level teaspoons baking powder
pinch of salt
1 oz (50g) butter
2 oz (50g) grated hard cheese
¼ pint (150ml) water
milk or egg and water, for glazing

How to cook better soda scones and Scotch pancakes (dropped scones)

These are cooked over direct heat, first on one side, then on the other. An old-fashioned iron girdle or heavy iron frying pan is used – a flat base for cooking them is essential.

● The pan should be gently and thoroughly heated before cooking the scones. Put pan on to heat first thing.

● Knowing when the temperature is right is part of the skill of making perfect scones. Hold your hand about 1 inch (2.5cm) above the pan surface and you should feel the heat. For soda scones the heat is more gentle than for Scotch pancakes, which are cooked more quickly.

● For soda scones sprinkle the pan with flour. If flour immediately browns, the heat is too high. Brush off the flour and lower the heat. Remove the pan and allow it to cool a little, then test again.

● For Scotch pancakes, sprinkle a little water on the hot surface and if it skips about in small balls before evaporating the heat is right. Then grease the pan.

● To grease the pan take a piece of absorbent kitchen paper, twist it into a mushroom shape and dip the larger end in a saucer of oil. Grease pan between each batch. Never use butter for greasing as it easily burns.

● Don't overcrowd cooking surface – allow room for turning the scones. Use a palette knife to lift up scones to have a look – they should be golden when cooked. When colour is right, use palette knife to turn them over. A fish slice will do at a pinch.

● Drop batter from a tablespoon or dessertspoon according to size of scone required. Always drop batter from the tip of the spoon to make perfect round Scotch pancakes.

Soda scones

Makes 8

8 oz (225g) plain flour
1 level teaspoon bicarbonate of
    soda
2 level teaspoons cream of tartar
pinch of salt
6 fl oz (175ml) milk

Slowly heat a girdle or heavy-based frying pan. These scones must be mixed quickly and should be cooked immediately. Sift the flour, bicarbonate of soda, cream of tartar and salt into a medium-sized mixing bowl.

Make a well in the flour mixture and pour in the milk. Using a table knife, mix together until dough is soft, but not sticky. Turn on to a floured board and knead about 3 times just to smooth the underside. Turn dough smooth side up and divide in half. Pat or roll out each portion to a circle a little less than ½ inch (1cm) thick and cut each circle in quarters with a floured knife.

Dust the hot girdle or pan with flour, place 1 circle of scones on the baking surface and cook for 4–5 minutes. Turn them over with a palette knife and cook for a further 4–5 minutes until scones are dried right through. Tip them on their sides to dry the edges before removing from the pan. Brush off browned flour and sprinkle with fresh flour before cooking the remaining scones. Serve at once. These are like a plain bread – you might have them for breakfast in Scotland. They are delicious sliced and spread with butter and marmalade.

Scotch pancakes

Sift the flour, baking powder and salt into a medium-sized mixing bowl. Stir in the sugar and make a well in the centre. Mix together the egg, golden syrup and milk and pour into the centre. Gradually draw the flour into the liquid by stirring all the time with a wooden spoon until all the flour has been incorporated, then beat well to make a smooth batter.

Slowly heat a girdle or heavy-based frying pan and grease the pan surface. (Use a piece of crumpled absorbent kitchen paper that has been dipped in a saucer filled with oil). Drop dessertspoons of the mixture on to the hot surface and cook for about 3 minutes, or until bubbles burst on the surface and the underside is golden. Turn pancakes over with a palette knife and cook for a further 1 minute. Keep warm and soft between folds of a cloth while cooking the remainder. Serve warm with jam and butter. Any unbuttered pancakes can be stored in an airtight container when cold and will keep fresh for a second day.

Makes 24

8 oz (225g) self-raising flour
2 level teaspoons baking powder
½ level teaspoon salt
1½ oz (40g) castor sugar
1 egg
1 teaspoon golden syrup
8 fl oz (225ml) milk

Waffles

Sift the flour, baking powder and salt into a medium-sized mixing bowl. Stir in the sugar. Make a well in the centre and crack in the eggs and about half the milk. Gradually draw the flour into the liquid by stirring all the time with a wooden spoon until all the flour has been incorporated, then beat well to make a smooth batter. Stir in the remaining milk, vanilla essence and melted butter, then pour batter into a jug.

Thoroughly heat a waffle iron – this takes about 10 minutes and if you are using a manual waffle iron, remember to turn it to heat both sides. Brush the waffle iron with melted butter or oil and pour in about 2 tablespoons of the batter. (When you close the lid it spreads so don't use too much.) Cook for about 1–2 minutes – a little longer if using a manual iron – until the steaming stops. If using a manual iron don't forget to turn it over to cook the other side. When waffle is done, loosen with a fork and turn out. Reheat waffle iron, grease and pour in batter for next waffle. Continue until all are cooked.

Serve waffles with sugar or honey and cream. Or top with a dusting of icing sugar, whipped cream and fresh strawberries, or ice cream and hot chocolate sauce.

Variation: To make savoury waffles omit the castor sugar from the recipe. Serve savoury waffles topped with fried eggs, grilled bacon rashers or sausages. They are also very good with slices of ham or chicken in a sauce.

Makes 12

6 oz (175g) plain flour
3 level teaspoons baking powder
pinch of salt
1 oz (25g) castor sugar
2 eggs
½ pint (300ml) milk
few drops of vanilla essence
2 oz (50g) melted butter

How to make better pancakes

● Pancakes can be prepared ahead and then heated through with savoury fillings, or filled on the spot with fruits for dessert. Unfilled pancakes keep for several days in the refrigerator.

● Use a proper pancake pan which is made of heavy iron and is 6 inches (15 cm) in diameter. It has very short sides which make it easier to turn and handle pancakes. An omelette pan is the best alternative.

● Grease the hot pan completely, using a pad of absorbent paper which you dip in a saucer of oil (kept right beside you). Grease the pan before cooking each pancake. Don't use butter.

● Aim for the centre of the pan when pouring in batter from a jug or ladle. Then quickly tilt pan in all directions to spread batter thinly. It's good wrist work that makes thin pancakes.

● Cook for a few minutes until underside of pancake is golden, then turn with a spatula and cook the other side for only a few seconds.

● An enriched pancake batter with melted butter or oil added is the one to use if you want to reheat pancakes.

● When filling pancakes have the more attractive side – the one cooked first – on the outside. For thick fillings, spread a little filling down the centre, then carefully roll up the pancake or fold the pancake in an envelope shape and turn it over on the plate. With thin fillings, spread the filling over the entire pancake and fold in thirds.

Pancakes

Makes 12

4 oz (100g) plain flour
pinch of salt
1 egg
1 tablespoon melted butter or oil
½ pint (300ml) milk

Sift the flour and salt into a mixing bowl and make a well in the centre. Crack the egg into the well, add the melted butter or oil and half the milk. Gradually draw the flour into the liquid by stirring all the time with a wooden spoon until all the flour has been incorporated, then beat well to make a smooth batter. Stir in the remaining milk. Alternatively, beat all ingredients together for 1 minute in a blender or food processor. Pour batter into a jug and leave to stand for about 30 minutes. Stir again before using.

Thoroughly heat, then lightly grease a small heavy-based frying pan or omelette pan. (Use a piece of crumpled absorbent paper that has been dipped in a saucer filled with oil.) Add about 2 tablespoons of batter from the jug and immediately tilt pan so batter evenly coats the base. Brown lightly on one side, then turn and brown second side. Transfer at once, best side down, to a warmed plate. (When pancake is rolled best side will be on the outside.) Cook remaining pancakes in the same way.

To keep pancakes hot (or to reheat), put a soup plate over a pan of simmering water and as each pancake is prepared stack it on the plate. Keep covered with a second plate or, better still, employ an old-fashioned trick by putting a pad of damp muslin over the stack and they won't get soggy.

Variation **Wholemeal pancakes:** Use 4 oz (100g) wholemeal flour and ½ level teaspoon salt. Cover and leave batter to stand for at least 1 hour before using.

Sweet fillings

● Sprinkle hot pancakes with sugar, then squeeze over lemon juice to sharpen flavour and roll up.

● Spread with warm jam – black cherry, apricot, strawberry and raspberry preserve are my favourites. Warm the jam with a squeeze of lemon juice. Roll or fold pancakes in thirds, dust with icing sugar and serve with cream or ice cream.

● Mashed banana (with lemon juice) folded into whipped cream is delicious. Use 4 bananas with the juice of ½ lemon and ¼ pint (150ml) double cream. Fill pancakes and dust with icing sugar. In summer use mashed strawberries in place of the bananas.

Savoury fillings

● Fill pancakes with hot ratatouille, then dot with butter and sprinkle with grated cheese.

● Roll pancakes around cooked asparagus or leeks cut lengthways. Serve with a rich cheese sauce and an extra topping of grated cheese.

● Fill with tinned salmon in a cheese sauce with a little chopped onion softened in butter added. Or try tuna in a parsley sauce flavoured with a squeeze of lemon and freshly milled pepper.

● Fill pancake with mushrooms cooked in butter and garlic, seasoned with salt and pepper and mixed with a dash of cream then fold in an envelope shape.

Traditional Yorkshire pudding

Sift the flour and salt into a mixing bowl and make a well in the centre. Add enough water to the milk to make ½ pint (300ml). Crack the egg into the well and add one-third of the liquid. Gradually draw the flour into the liquid by stirring all the time with a wooden spoon until all the flour has been incorporated, then beat well to make a smooth batter. Add the remaining liquid and beat again to aerate the batter. Leave to stand for 20 minutes.

Put the dripping or cooking fat into a medium-sized baking tin or roasting tin and place on the top shelf of an oven heated to 425°F (220°C) or Gas no. 7 for 5 minutes. When really hot, remove from the oven, stir the batter and quickly pour into the tin to a depth of a little less than ½ inch (1cm). Then bake for 40 minutes, or until well risen, crisp and golden with a creamy layer inside.

Serves 4

4 oz (100g) plain flour
¼ level teaspoon salt
1 egg
8 fl oz (225ml) milk
1 oz (25g) beef dripping or white
    cooking fat

Small Yorkshire puddings

Sift the flour and salt into a mixing bowl. Beat together the egg and milk, then pour into the flour and whisk until smooth and creamy. Stir in the water and leave to stand for at least 20 minutes.

Generously grease 8 tartlet tins and place on the top shelf of an oven heated to 425°F (220°C) or Gas no. 7 for 5 minutes. When really hot, remove from the oven, stir the batter and pour into the hot tins. Bake for 15 minutes, or until well risen, crisp and golden. Give the tin a sharp tap to loosen the puddings and turn out.

Makes 8

4 oz (100g) plain flour
pinch of salt
1 small egg
2 tablespoons milk
3–4 tablespoons water
½ oz (15g) beef dripping or white
    cooking fat

Teabreads

Teabreads are made using self-raising or plain flour and a chemical raising agent. The fat is rubbed in with the fingertips so there's no tiresome creaming of the butter and sugar. Teabreads are nice alternatives to plain bread, but not so rich as cake.

● Use loaf tins in preference to deeper bread tins for baking. Loaf tins come in two standard sizes, a large 9 × 5 × 3 inch (22.5 × 12.5 × 7.5cm) tin and a small 8 × 4 × 2 inch (20 × 10 × 5cm) tin. These tins make teabreads that are an attractive shape and size.

● Test teabreads as you would a cake. Slip a skewer between bread and tin for a moment to warm it, then push it into the centre of the bread. When pulled out the skewer should be clean. When baked the top will be firm and the sides will have shrunk away from the tin.

● Bake teabreads the day before and they will slice without crumbling. Wrap cooled teabreads in kitchen foil and you will find they keep for about 1 week. Serve them sliced and buttered for children's teas or for packed lunches and picnics.

Banana teabread

Makes 1 large loaf

4 oz (100g) glacé cherries
8 oz (225g) self-raising flour
½ level teaspoon salt
4 oz (100g) butter
6 oz (175g) castor sugar
4 oz (100g) sultanas
1 oz (25g) coarsely chopped
   walnuts
1 lb (450g) ripe bananas
2 eggs

illustrated facing page 272

Heat the oven to 350°F (180°C) or Gas no. 4. Grease a 9 × 5 × 3 inch (22.5 × 12.5 × 7.5cm) loaf tin and line the base and shorter sides with a strip of greased greaseproof paper long enough to overlap the sides. Rinse the sugary coating from the glacé cherries in warm water, pat dry in absorbent paper and cut in quarters. Set aside. Sift the flour and salt into a medium-sized mixing bowl.

Add the butter in pieces and rub in with the fingertips. Stir in the sugar, sultanas, walnuts and glacé cherries. Peel and mash the bananas and add to the mixture along with the eggs. Beat well with a wooden spoon to make a smooth batter.

Spoon mixture into the prepared tin and spread level. Place in the centre of preheated oven and bake for 1–1¼ hours. Allow to cool in the tin for 20–30 minutes, then loosen unlined sides and, holding the paper ends, transfer to a wire rack and leave until completely cool. Remove the paper. Serve sliced and buttered.

Fruit teabread

Makes 1 large loaf

9 oz (250g) self-raising flour
1 level teaspoon bicarbonate of
   soda
½ level teaspoon salt
½ level teaspoon mixed spice
4 oz (100g) butter
½ pint (300ml) cold strong tea
6 oz (175g) mixed dried fruits
4 oz (100g) castor sugar

Heat the oven to 350°F (180°C) or Gas no. 4. Grease a 9 × 5 × 3 inch (22.5 × 12.5 × 7.5cm) loaf tin and line the base and shorter sides with a strip of greased greaseproof paper long enough to overlap the sides of the tin. Sift the flour, bicarbonate of soda, salt and mixed spice into a medium-sized mixing bowl.

Put the butter, cold tea, mixed dried fruits and sugar into a saucepan and stir over low heat until the butter has melted and the sugar has dissolved, then draw off the heat. Allow to cool until the hand can be comfortably held against the side of the pan. Then stir into flour mixture and mix together with a wooden spoon. Spoon mixture into the prepared loaf tin and spread level. Place in the centre of preheated oven and bake for 1 hour. Allow to cool in the tin for 10 minutes, then loosen unlined sides and, holding the paper ends, transfer to a wire rack and leave until completely cool. Remove the paper. Serve sliced and buttered.

Yorkshire fruit bread

Heat the oven to 350°F (180°C) or Gas no. 4. and grease two 9 × 5 × 3 inch (22.5 × 12.5 × 7.5cm) loaf tins. Line the base and two shorter sides of each tin with a strip of greased greaseproof paper long enough to overlap the sides. Rinse the sugary coating from the glacé cherries in warm water, pat dry in absorbent paper and cut in quarters. Set aside. Sift the flour, salt and mixed spice into a large mixing bowl.

Add the butter or margarine in pieces and rub in with the fingertips. Stir in the sugar, currants, sultanas and glacé cherries. Lightly mix the eggs and milk, add to the mixture and beat well with a wooden spoon to make a smooth batter.

Divide the mixture equally between the prepared tins and spread level. Place in the centre of preheated oven and bake for 1 hour. Allow to cool in the tin for 10 minutes, then loosen unlined sides and, holding the paper ends, transfer to a wire rack and leave until completely cool. Remove the paper. Serve sliced and buttered. These loaves keep well.

Makes 2 large loaves

4 oz (100g) glacé cherries
1 lb (450g) self-raising flour
1 level teaspoon salt
1 level teaspoon mixed spice
8 oz (225g) butter or margarine
8 oz (225g) castor sugar
8 oz (225g) currants
8 oz (225g) sultanas
4 eggs
¼ pint (150ml) milk

Date and walnut bread

Heat the oven to 350°F (180°C) or Gas no. 4. Grease a 9 × 5 × 3 inch (22.5 × 12.5 × 7.5cm) loaf tin and line the base and shorter sides with a strip of greased greaseproof paper long enough to overlap the sides. Sift the flour and salt into a medium-sized mixing bowl.

Add the butter in pieces and rub in with the fingertips. Stir in the sugar, chopped walnuts and chopped dates. Lightly mix the eggs, treacle and milk. Add to the flour mixture and beat well with a wooden spoon to make a smooth batter.

Spoon mixture into the prepared tin and spread level. Place in the centre of preheated oven and bake for 1 hour. Allow to cool in the tin for 10 minutes, then loosen unlined sides and, holding the paper ends, transfer to a wire rack and leave until completely cool. Remove the paper. Serve sliced and buttered.

Makes 1 large loaf

12 oz (350g) self-raising flour
½ level teaspoon salt
2 oz (50g) butter
4 oz (100g) soft light brown sugar
2 oz (50g) chopped walnuts
4 oz (100g) chopped dates
2 eggs
1 tablespoon black treacle
8 fl oz (225ml) milk

illustrated facing page 272

Malt teabread

Makes 1 large loaf

12 oz (350g) self-raising flour
1 level teaspoon salt
1 oz (25g) butter
2 oz (50g) soft light brown sugar
4 oz (100g) sultanas
2 oz (50g) chopped walnuts
4 oz (100g) or 2 rounded
** tablespoons malt extract**
2 oz (50g) or 1 rounded tablespoon
** black treacle**
¼ pint (150ml) milk
2 eggs

Heat the oven to 350°F (180°C) or Gas no 4. Grease a 9 × 5 × 3 inch (22.5 × 12.5 × 7.5cm) loaf tin and line the base and shorter sides with a strip of greased greaseproof paper long enough to overlap the sides. Sift the flour and salt into a medium-sized mixing bowl.

Add the butter in pieces and rub in with fingertips. Stir in the sugar, sultanas and chopped walnuts. Warm the malt extract, treacle and milk in a saucepan and stir to blend ingredients, then mix in the eggs. Add to the dry ingredients and beat well with a wooden spoon to make a smooth batter.

Spoon mixture into the prepared tin and spread level. Place in the centre of preheated oven and bake for 1 hour. Allow to cool in the tin for 10 minutes, then loosen unlined sides and, holding the paper ends, transfer to a wire rack and leave until completely cool. Remove the paper. Serve sliced and buttered.

Gifts and sales
Teabreads are ideal to take to a neighbour's coffee morning or the local bring-and-buy sale. You can bake them a few days in advance (and they freeze well, too). Just make sure the teabread is completely cool, then peel of the baking paper and wrap in cling film. Tie a pretty ribbon round the bread and you have a lovely gift to give.

Besides the simple fruit and nut teabreads, try a sticky gingerbread (page 241), honey cake (page 242), almond cake (page 238), or farmhouse fruit cake (page 240). None of these has fancy toppings which make wrapping or transport difficult, and all stay fresh for several days or more so you can rest assured that when eaten they will be as good as the day you baked them.

Honey teabread

Makes 1 large loaf

12 oz (350g) self-raising flour
½ level teaspoon salt
1 level teaspoon ground mixed
** spice**
2 oz (50g) butter
2 oz (50g) soft light brown sugar
4 oz (100g) currants
6 oz (175g) or 3 rounded
** tablespoons clear honey**
1 egg
¼ pint (150ml) water
flaked almonds, to decorate

Heat the oven to 350°F (180°C) or Gas no. 4. Grease a 9 × 5 × 3 inch (22.5 × 12.5 × 7.5cm) loaf tin and line the base and shorter sides with a strip of greased greaseproof paper long enough to overlap the sides. Sift the flour, salt and mixed spice into a medium-sized mixing bowl.

Add the butter in pieces and rub in with the fingertips. Stir in the sugar and currants. Mix together the honey, egg and water with a fork. Add to the dry ingredients and beat well with a wooden spoon to make a smooth batter.

Spoon mixture into the prepared tin and spread level. Sprinkle the top with flaked almonds. Place in the centre of preheated oven and bake for 1 hour. Allow to cool in the tin for 10 minutes, then loosen unlined sides and, holding the paper ends, transfer to a wire rack and leave until completely cool. Remove the paper. Serve sliced and buttered.

Illustrated: Banana teabread and date and walnut bread, pages 270 and 271

Orange nut bread

Heat the oven to 350°F (180°C) or Gas no. 4. Grease a 9 × 5 × 3 inch (22.5 × 12.5 × 7.5cm) loaf tin and line the base and shorter sides with a strip of greased greaseproof paper long enough to overlap the sides. Sift the flour and salt into a medium-sized mixing bowl.

Add the butter in pieces and rub in with the fingertips. Stir in the sugar, walnuts, candied peel and grated orange rind. Mix together the eggs, milk and orange juice in a small bowl. Add to the dry ingredients and beat well with a wooden spoon to make a smooth batter.

Spoon mixture into the prepared tin and spread level. Place in the centre of preheated oven and bake for 1 hour. Allow to cool in the tin for 10 minutes, then loosen unlined sides and, holding the paper ends, transfer to a wire rack and leave until completely cool. Remove the paper. Serve sliced and buttered.

Makes 1 large loaf

12 oz (350g) self-raising flour
½ level teaspoon salt
2 oz (50g) butter
3 oz (75g) castor sugar
2 oz (50g) chopped walnuts
2 oz (50g) chopped candied peel
finely grated rind and juice of 1 orange
2 eggs
1 pint (600ml) milk

Brown soda bread

Heat the oven to 425°F (220°C) or Gas no. 7. Put the wholemeal flour in a large mixing bowl. Sift in the plain flour, bicarbonate of soda and salt. Add the butter in pieces and rub in with the fingertips. Blend the yoghurt with the milk.

Make a well in the flour mixture and pour in the yoghurt and milk. Then, using a table knife, fold in until dough is soft but not sticky. Turn on to a board dusted with wholemeal flour and knead about 3 times just to smooth the underside. Turn dough smooth side up and flatten with the hand to a round about 1½ inches (3cm) thick.

Place dough on a lightly floured baking tray. Using a floured knife, cut a deep cross on top, which allows soda bread to bake evenly. Immediately place above centre in preheated oven and bake for 30–35 minutes, or until well risen. The baked loaf should sound hollow when tapped on the base. Transfer to a wire rack. For a soft crust, wrap hot bread in a clean cloth. Leave until completely cool. Serve sliced and buttered – this bread does not keep.

Variation **White soda bread:** Omit the wholemeal flour and increase the plain flour to 1 lb (450g).

Sweet soda bread: Omit the wholemeal flour and increase the plain flour to 1 lb (450g). Add 4 oz (100g) currants and 1 oz (25g) castor sugar to the dry ingredients before mixing in the yoghurt and milk.

Makes 1 large loaf

12 oz (350g) wholemeal flour
4 oz (100g) plain flour
1 level teaspoon bicarbonate of soda
1 level teaspoon salt
2 oz (50g) butter
¼ pint (150ml) natural yoghurt
¼ pint (150ml) milk

Illustrated: Granary cob, page 277

273

Yeast Breads

Ingredients

Flour: Using the right flour is an important start. Strong white flour is the best for breadmaking as it absorbs liquid easily and develops quickly with kneading into a firm, elastic dough that rises well to make a loaf with a good volume. White flour for breadmaking is usually labelled 'strong' on the packet. A recipe for bread given on the reverse side of the packet is also an indication that it's the right kind of flour. Wholemeal (or wholewheat) flour is milled from the whole grain and includes the wheatgerm and the bran with nothing taken away during processing. This flour produces a brown bread with a nutty flavour and a closer texture because the presence of the wheatgerm and bran retards the stretching qualities of the gluten. Wheatmeal flour usually has an extraction rate on the packet indicating that 80–90% of the original grain remains and that the coarsest particles of bran have been removed. Wheatmeal flour is more digestible and makes a lighter textured loaf than wholemeal. Granary flour is a special blend of wholemeal flour that includes malted wheat and rye. It is very coarse and flavoursome and can be used in place of wholemeal flour in bread recipes.

Sugar: This is the food yeast needs in order to grow. In plain bread doughs, yeast finds sufficient natural sugar in the flour for fermentation. In sweet bread recipes extra sugar is added for flavour. Sometimes a little sugar (it can be treacle, honey or ordinary sugar) is added to yeast to start it working, particularly when reconstituting dried yeast granules. Too much sugar slows yeast down.

Salt: An essential ingredient that you must not forget. Salt gives flavour, strengthens the gluten and controls the yeast by preventing it from fermenting too quickly. Unsalted doughs are sticky and rise too fast. The correct proportions to use in a bread dough are 1–2 level teaspoons salt per 1 lb (450g) flour or ½–1 oz salt per 3 lb (1.4kg) flour. Too much salt slows yeast down.

Fat: Lard, white cooking fat, butter and margarine are used in breadmaking. Not an essential ingredient but if a little is rubbed into the flour, it softens the crumb to provide a finer texture and also improves the keeping qualities of the baked loaf. Proportions are about ½ oz (15g) per 1 lb (450g) or 1–2 oz (25–50g) per 3 lb (1.4kg) in a plain bread dough. Rich bun doughs have a higher proportion of fat in order to make a softer texture. For some continental breads, butter is softened or melted and added at a later stage in the recipe. A high proportion of fat slows yeast down.

Liquid: The liquid used for mixing a dough can be water or a mixture of milk and water. Milk improves the food value and encourages a good colour on the crust. Water gives bread a chewier texture and a crisp crust. About ½ pint (300ml) liquid to 1 lb (450g) flour is an average quantity, but you will find that wholemeal flour requires a little more liquid than white flour because the bran in wholemeal flour is thirsty and absorbs more liquid. In rich doughs, an egg is used as part of the mixing liquid. Egg improves the keeping quality and makes the baked bread very light and soft in texture.

Yeast: This is what makes bread rise. Fresh yeast should be creamy in colour and break into nice chunky pieces without being crumbly. A lump of yeast will keep in a tied polythene bag for 4–5 days in a cool place or 2–3 weeks in the refrigerator. Fresh yeast should be first mixed into a cupful of tepid liquid and it will quickly dissolve. There is no need to cream fresh yeast with sugar.

Dried yeast is just as effective if used properly. Dried yeast will keep for 3 months in the storecupboard so long as the tin or sachet is kept tightly closed. Easy blend dried yeast can be added to recipes directly with the flour – follow packet instructions.

Dried yeast granules must be reconstituted first and require a mixing liquid of about 110°F (43°C), or hand-hot (a drop on the wrist feels hot but not burning). Mix 1 teaspoon castor sugar, honey or treacle into 1 teacupful of the recipe liquid, sprinkle in the yeast granules and stir with a fork. Then set in a warm place for about 15 minutes until the liquid is frothy.

If dried yeast does not froth up to give a lively brew, the yeast is stale and should not be used. When using dried yeast in a recipe remember that it is more concentrated than fresh yeast. When a recipe calls for fresh yeast only half the amount of dried yeast should be used: 1 oz (25g) fresh yeast equals ½ oz (15g) or 1 level tablespoon dried yeast and ½ oz (15g) fresh yeast equals 2 level teaspoons dried yeast.

Four steps to perfect bread dough

1. Mixing: Two different methods are used for mixing a bread dough.

● *Straight dough method:* This is the one found in most cookery books; it's simple and straightforward. Using this method the flour is mixed with the salt and any fat used is rubbed in with fingertips. The yeast is blended with part of the recipe liquid, then immediately mixed into the dry ingredients with the rest of the liquid to make a rough dough in the mixing bowl.

● *Sponge and dough method:* With this method, which is especially good if using dried yeast, two-thirds of the flour is mixed with the salt and any fat used is rubbed in with fingertips. The yeast is blended with all the water and the remaining third of the flour to make a batter which is allowed to ferment for about 30 minutes, when it becomes frothy or spongy. Then the yeast batter, or sponge, is mixed into the dry ingredients to make a rough dough in the mixing bowl. This method gives the yeast a lively start and shortens the time that is required for the bread dough to ferment or rise.

● With both methods, a wooden fork is best for mixing yeast liquid evenly through the flour. Otherwise, use a wooden spoon.

2. Kneading: Kneading helps develop the gluten in the flour which is what makes bread dough elastic, essential for good bread.

● Turn the bread dough out of the mixing bowl on to an unfloured work surface. If a wholemeal or wheatmeal bread dough is a little sticky, use a little extra flour for dusting the surface.

● Push the dough down and away from you with the palm of the hand, then gather up the dough and push out again. You can afford to be quite firm and brisk at this stage. A bread dough will appear rough and sticky at first but as you knead the gluten gains strength and elasticity and the dough develops a smooth surface.

3. Fermenting or rising: This is the period when the yeast works to aerate the dough.

● Shape the kneaded dough into a ball and return it to the mixing bowl. Make sure the bowl is large enough to allow the dough to rise properly.

● The dough must be covered to prevent the surface from becoming dry. Place the bowl of dough inside a roomy polythene bag and tie tightly; the dough will retain its warmth and moisture.

● The kitchen table is the place to leave the dough to rise as a slow rising at room temperature makes the best bread. The dough is ready when doubled in size and when a floured finger pressed into the dough leaves an imprint.

4. Knocking back: When you knock back a risen dough you distribute the gas bubbles and even out the texture.

● Turn the risen dough out on to an unfloured work surface and press all over with the knuckles to flatten it.

● Gather the knocked back dough into a ball, then cover with cling film and leave it to rest for a further 10 minutes and you'll find it's easier to shape it into the bread you require.

Freezing homemade bread

● Baking batches of bread and rolls makes sense if you have a freezer. White bread and rolls with soft floury crusts, wholemeal, wheatmeal, granary and enriched breads such as currant bread, bridge rolls and poppy seed plaits freeze best. The keeping quality of plain white and wholemeal loaves is improved if you double the amount of fat used in the recipe.

● Freshly baked bread must be completely cool before freezing. Place loaves or rolls in freezer bags and tie closed – bread must be wrapped and covered like any other food.

● For best results, allow loaves to thaw at room temperature for about 2–3 hours; rolls take about 1–2 hours. Bread will keep for 6 months in the freezer but mine never lasts that long. I bake a batch of loaves at the weekend, put them in the freezer and take one out at a time, and I have fresh bread every day of the week.

How to make better bread

● Slow rising at room temperature gives the best texture and flavour to your bread. In hot weather keep the bowl of dough away from direct sunlight and when weather is very cold the bowl of dough can be kept at an even temperature by standing it over a saucepan of warm water.

● Keep your dough covered with a piece of polythene to prevent a skin forming. This applies particularly to a dough not baked in a tin. While shaping one loaf keep other piece of dough covered.

● Warm the bread tins before using – a warm dough placed in cold tins will result in an unevenly risen bread. Always brush tins with melted lard or white cooking fat so the bread won't stick.

● When bread loaves go into a hot oven the sudden heat causes a rapid expansion of the dough – bakers call this 'oven spring'; make certain you allow sufficient space between oven shelves for the bread to rise without touching the rack above.

● Bake all breads, white bread in particular, to a really attractive golden crust. For an extra crusty finish, turn white bread loaves out of the tins and return to the oven for a further 5 minutes.

● When bread is baked, loaves or rolls should sound hollow when the bottom is tapped sharply with the knuckles. Allow baked bread to cool on wire racks, not in the tins. Delicate breads, like currant bread, are best cooled lying on their sides.

White tin loaves

Makes 3 small loaves or 1 large and 1 small loaf

½ oz (15g) fresh yeast or 2 level teaspoons dried yeast and 1 level teaspoon castor sugar
18 fl oz (500ml) tepid water
1 lb 14 oz (875g) strong white flour
3 level teaspoons salt
½ oz (15g) white cooking fat or lard
salted water, for glazing (optional)

Dissolve the fresh yeast in ¼ pint (150ml) of the water. If using dried yeast, have the water hand-hot, stir in the sugar and sprinkle in the yeast. Set dried yeast mixture in a warm place for 10–15 minutes until frothy. Sift the flour and salt into a large mixing bowl. Add the fat and rub in with the fingertips.

Add the yeast together with the remaining tepid water to the flour mixture and mix to a rough dough. Turn on to an unfloured work surface and knead for 10 minutes until smooth and not sticky. Shape into a ball, return to the mixing bowl and set inside a roomy polythene bag. Leave at room temperature for about 1½ hours, or until dough has doubled in size.

Turn dough out and knock back. Divide into thirds (or into two-thirds and one-third if making 1 large and 1 small loaf). Knead each dough into a round, loosely cover with cling film and leave to rest for 10 minutes. Flatten each dough to an oblong and pull and flap dough to elongate, then turn sides over middle and roll up tightly. Place dough seam side down in greased bread tins. Cover with cling film and set in a warm place for about 30 minutes, or until dough has risen ½ inch (1 cm) above the rims of the tins.

About 15 minutes before baking, heat the oven to 450°F (230°C) or Gas no. 8. Brush the tops of risen bread with salted water if a crusty top is liked, or dust with flour for soft tops. Place in preheated oven and bake small loaves for 30–35 minutes and large loaf for 35–40 minutes. Turn out on to a wire rack and leave until completely cool.

White cob loaves

Sift 10 oz (275g) of the flour into a mixing bowl. Dissolve the fresh yeast in the tepid water; if using dried yeast, have the water hand-hot and sprinkle in the yeast. Stir in the sugar. Pour into the flour and whisk to make a smooth batter. Set in a warm place for 20 minutes until frothy.

Sift the remaining flour and the salt into a large mixing bowl. Add the fat in pieces and rub in with the fingertips. Stir the yeast batter, add to the flour mixture and mix to a rough dough. Turn on to an unfloured work surface and knead for 10 minutes until smooth and not sticky. Shape into a ball, return to the bowl and set inside a roomy polythene bag. Leave at room temperature for ¾–1 hour or until the dough has doubled in size.

Turn out the risen dough and knock back. Divide dough in quarters and knead each piece into a round. Loosely cover with cling film and leave to rest for 10 minutes. Then knead each piece again, shaping into tight rounds. Place in pairs on greased baking sheets, loosely cover, and set in a warm place for about 30–40 minutes or until well risen and puffy.

About 15 minutes before baking, heat the oven to 450°F (230°C) or Gas no. 8. Brush the tops of risen loaves with salted water if a crusty top is liked, or dust with flour for a soft top. Make 3 slashes on each loaf. Place in preheated oven and bake for 25–30 minutes. Transfer loaves to a wire rack and leave until completely cool.

Variations: **Granary cobs:** Use 10 oz (275g) strong white flour to mix with the yeast and 1 lb 6 oz (625g) granary flour in place of the remaining flour, but do not sift. Shape as for white cob loaves, omitting the slashes.

Wheatmeal cob loaves: Use 10 oz (275g) strong white flour to mix with the yeast and 1 lb 6 oz (625g) wholemeal flour in place of the remaining flour. Add 1 tablespoon black treacle to the water for mixing to get a delicious flavour. Omit the sugar. Shape as for white cob loaves, but before final rising, brush the tops with water and sprinkle with bran sifted from wholemeal flour or use kibbled or cracked wheat (coarsely cut wheat grains). Set wheatmeal cobs in a warm place until well risen before baking.

Bloomer loaves: Turn out risen dough and knock back. Divide dough in 3 portions and shape each one into a round. Cover and leave to rest for 10 minutes. Flatten each dough to an oblong, pull and flap to elongate, then turn sides over middle and roll up tightly by the long side to make a narrow roll about 8 inches (20cm) long. Place on greased baking sheets with seam underneath. Cover loosely with cling film and set in a warm place for 40 minutes, or until dough is well risen and puffy. Using a sharp knife, cut 6–8 diagonal slashes across each top. Brush with salt water and bake for 30–35 minutes, or until crusty and brown.

Makes 4 cob loaves

2 lb (900g) strong white flour
½ oz (15g) fresh yeast or 2 level
teaspoons dried yeast
1 pint (600ml) tepid water
1 level teaspoon castor sugar
½ oz (15g) salt
1 oz (25g) white cooking fat or lard
salted water, for glazing (optional)

Granary cob illustrated facing page 273; wheatmeal cob loaf illustrated facing page 304

Crusty rolls

Makes 12

½ oz (15g) fresh yeast or 2 level
    teaspoons dried yeast and 1 level
    teaspoon castor sugar
½ pint (300ml) tepid water
1 lb (450g) strong white flour
2 level teaspoons salt
½ oz (15g) white cooking fat or
    lard
starch glaze (page 281)
poppy seeds or sesame seeds, for
    sprinkling

Dissolve the fresh yeast in half the water. If using dried yeast, have the water hand-hot, stir in the sugar and sprinkle in the yeast. Set dried yeast mixture in a warm place for 10–15 minutes until frothy. Sift the flour and salt into a large mixing bowl. Add the fat in pieces and rub in with the fingertips.

Add the yeast together with the remaining tepid water to the dry flour mixture and mix to a rough dough. Turn on to an unfloured work surface and knead for 10 minutes until smooth and not sticky. Shape into a ball, return to the mixing bowl and set inside a roomy polythene bag. Leave at room temperature for about 1½ hours, or until dough has doubled in size.

Turn the risen dough out on to an unfloured work surface and knock back. Divide dough into 12 pieces. Using the palm of the hand, roll each piece into a ball. Press down hard at first and then ease up. Place rolls on a greased baking sheet about 1 inch (2.5cm) apart. Loosely cover with cling film and set in a warm place for 30 minutes or until risen and puffy.

About 15 minutes before baking, heat the oven to 450°F (230°C) or Gas no. 8. Brush tops of risen rolls with starch glaze and sprinkle with poppy seeds or sesame seeds. Place above centre in preheated oven and bake for 20 minutes. Transfer rolls to a wire rack and leave until completely cool.

Variations **Brown and serve rolls:** These rolls are very convenient if you have a freezer. They are baked at a lower oven temperature long enough for them to bake through but not brown. The second baking browns them and takes only a few minutes. Leave rolls unglazed and dust with flour. Bake in an oven heated to 300°F (150°C) or Gas no. 2 for 20 minutes. Allow to cool on a wire rack. Chill overnight (or freeze packed in polythene bags). Place rolls on ungreased baking sheets. Bake in an oven heated to 425°F (220°C) or Gas no. 7 for 10 minutes until heated through and browned. Bake frozen rolls for 20 minutes.

Pitta bread: Turn risen dough out and knock back. Divide dough in 12 equal portions and round up each one to a smooth ball. Dust with flour and leave to rest for 10 minutes. Heat the oven to 450°F (230°C) or Gas no. 8 and put 2–3 ungreased baking sheets in the heating oven. On a well floured work surface, roll each portion of dough to an oval 5–6 inches (12.5–15cm) long. Dust with flour and place on hot sheets. Immediately put them in preheated oven and bake for 8–10 minutes when they will puff up. Split each pitta bread open as soon as you remove them from the oven, then leave them covered with a cloth so crust stays soft. Serve pitta bread warm (or reheated) as pockets for kebabs, slivers of cheese, grilled bacon, egg mayonnaise or your own delicious salad mixtures – great for picnics and snack meals.

Wholemeal bread

Dissolve the fresh yeast in half the water and stir in the treacle. If using dried yeast, have the water hand-hot, stir in the treacle and sprinkle in the yeast. Set dried yeast mixture in a warm place for 10–15 minutes, or until frothy. Mix the flour and salt in a large mixing bowl. Add the fat in pieces and rub in with the fingertips.

Add the yeast together with the remaining tepid water to the flour mixture and mix to a rough dough. Turn on to an unfloured work surface and knead for 5–8 minutes until smooth and not sticky. Shape into a ball, return to the bowl and set inside a roomy polythene bag. Leave at room temperature for 40 minutes, or until dough has doubled in size.

Turn risen dough out and knock back. Divide dough in thirds. Knead each dough into a round. Loosely cover with cling film and leave to rest for 10 minutes. Flatten each dough to an oblong, pull and flap dough to elongate, then turn sides over middle and roll up tightly. Sprinkle the insides of greased bread tins with cracked wheat, if using it. Place dough seam side down in prepared tins. Loosely cover with cling film and set in a warm place for 40 minutes, or until dough has risen 1 inch (2.5cm) above the rims of the tins.

About 15 minutes before baking, heat the oven to 425°F (220°C) or Gas no. 7. Place loaves in preheated oven and bake for 30–35 minutes. Rub the tops of the hot loaves with buttered paper if a soft crust is liked. Turn out on to a wire rack and leave until completely cool.

Variations **Wholemeal cobs:** Shape each piece of dough into a tight round and place on greased baking sheets. Leave plain or brush tops with salted water and sprinkle with cracked wheat or bran sifted from wholemeal flour. Loosely cover with cling film and set in a warm place for 30 minutes, or until well risen and puffy. Bake for 20–25 minutes.

Wholemeal bread rolls: Divide the dough in 24 equal portions and roll each piece into a ball. Place rolls on greased baking sheets, spacing them about 1 inch (2.5cm) apart. Brush with salted water, then sprinkle with extra wholemeal flour or with bran sifted from the flour. Loosely cover with cling film and set in a warm place for 30 minutes, or until well risen and puffy. Bake for 15–20 minutes.

Makes 3 small loaves or cobs

1 oz (25g) fresh yeast or 1 level
   tablespoon dried yeast
1 teaspoon black treacle
18 fl oz (500ml) tepid water
2 lb (900g) wholemeal flour
3 level teaspoons salt
2 oz (25g) white cooking fat or lard
cracked wheat, for sprinkling
   (optional)

The Grant loaf

Makes 3 small loaves

1¾ lb (800g) stoneground
  wholemeal flour
2 level teaspoons salt
¾ oz (20g) fresh yeast
½ oz (15g) soft dark brown sugar
1¼ pint (700ml) tepid water

This recipe for a wholemeal loaf is very easy and quick to make. The recipe was developed by Mrs Doris Grant, a pioneer of the wholefood movement. Success depends on having the flour and baking tins thoroughly warmed and the yeast frothy so that it works quickly.

Put the flour and salt into a large mixing bowl and set in a warm place along with three greased bread tins until thoroughly warmed. Dissolve the yeast in ¼ pint (150ml) of the water and stir in the sugar. Set in a warm place for 10 minutes until frothy.

Add the yeast together with the remaining water to the dry ingredients and mix to a wet, slippery dough. Spoon at once into the warmed bread tins. Loosely cover with cling film and set in a warm place for about 40 minutes, or until the dough has reached the tops of the tins.

About 15 minutes before baking, heat the oven to 375°F (190°C) or Gas no. 5. Place risen loaves in centre of oven and bake for 50–60 minutes. Turn out on to a wire rack and leave until completely cool. This bread keeps for about 5 days.

Wheatmeal baps

Makes 12

1 oz (25g) fresh yeast or 1 level
  tablespoon dried yeast and 1 level
  teaspoon castor sugar
½ pint (300ml) tepid milk and
  water (half and half)
8 oz (225g) strong white flour
2 level teaspoons salt
8 oz (225g) wholemeal flour
½ oz (15g) white cooking fat or
  lard

Dissolve the fresh yeast in half the liquid. If using dried yeast, have the liquid hand-hot, stir in the sugar and sprinkle in the yeast. Set dried yeast mixture in a warm place for 10–15 minutes until frothy. Sift the strong white flour and salt into a mixing bowl and add the wholemeal flour. Add the fat and rub in with fingertips.

Add the yeast together with the remaining tepid liquid to the flour mixture and mix to a rough dough. Turn on to an unfloured work surface and knead for about 10 minutes until smooth. Shape into a ball, return to the mixing bowl and set inside a roomy polythene bag. Leave at room temperature for about 1 hour, or until dough has doubled in size.

Turn risen dough out and knock back. Roll out the dough to a thickness of ½ inch (1cm). Using a 3 inch (7.5cm) floured round cutter, cut 12 circles of dough. Place on greased baking sheets, 6 per sheet. Loosely cover with cling film and set in a warm place for about 20 minutes, or until risen and puffy.

About 15 minutes before baking, heat the oven to 425°F (220°C) or Gas no. 7. Dust baps with wholemeal flour. Place in preheated oven and bake for 15 minutes. Transfer baps to a wire rack and leave until completely cool. Serve with a cold supper of chicken or ham or with hot soup. They're ideal for a packed lunch, too – fill them with cheese, tomato, egg or salami and lettuce.

Poppy seed plaits

Sift the flour and salt into a mixing bowl. Add the butter and rub in with the fingertips. Dissolve the fresh yeast in ¼ pint (150ml) of the liquid. If using dried yeast, have the liquid hand-hot, stir in the sugar and sprinkle in the yeast. Set dried yeast mixture in a warm place for 10 minutes, or until frothy.

Add yeast together with remaining tepid liquid to dry ingredients and mix to a rough dough in the bowl. Turn on to an unfloured work surface and knead for about 10 minutes until smooth and not sticky. Shape into a ball, return to the bowl and set inside a roomy polythene bag. Leave at room temperature for about 1 hour, or until dough has doubled in size.

Turn risen dough out and press all over with the knuckles to knock back. Divide dough in half. Then further divide each dough portion in three and roll each portion to a rope of about 12 inches (30cm) long. For each loaf, pinch three dough portions together at one end, then plait into a loaf shape. Place a loaf on each of two greased baking sheets and brush with beaten egg. Loosely cover with cling film and set in a warm place for about 30 minutes, or until risen and puffy.

About 15 minutes before baking, heat the oven to 425°F (220°C) or Gas no. 7. Glaze risen bread with egg again and sprinkle generously with poppy seeds. Place in preheated oven and bake for 30–35 minutes. Transfer loaves to a wire rack and leave until cool. This is a nice bread to serve at a cheese and wine party or a buffet supper.

Makes 2 plaited loaves

1 lb 8 oz (675g) strong white flour
3 level teaspoons salt
1 oz (25g) butter
1 oz (25g) fresh yeast or 1 level tablespoon dried yeast and 1 level teaspoon castor sugar
¾ pint (400ml) mixed tepid milk and water (half and half)
beaten egg, for glazing
2 tablespoons poppy seeds

Starch glaze

For a crisp crust on plain white bread you can use a specially prepared starch glaze which keeps the surface of the dough soft during the early part of baking and dries to a crusty finish similar to that which you get on the old-fashioned baker's loaf.

Blend 1 level tablespoon cornflour to a paste with 1 tablespoon cold water and make up to ½ pint (300ml) with boiling water from the kettle. Stir well as you add the boiling water so the glaze thickens evenly. Leave until cool. Then using a pastry brush, paint the glaze thinly over the tops of white tin loaves, cobs, bloomers or rolls before baking. You will find sesame seeds or poppy seeds will stick to the dough nicely if you are going to use them for decoration.

Fruited malt bread

1 lb (450g) strong white flour
1 level teaspoon salt
1 oz (25g) white cooking fat
8 fl oz (225ml) tepid water
2 oz (50g) or 1 tablespoon malt extract
2 oz (50g) or 1 tablespoon black treacle
1 oz (25g) fresh yeast or 1 level tablespoon dried yeast
4 oz sultanas

Sift flour and salt into a mixing bowl. Add the fat and rub in with the fingertips. Combine the water, malt extract and black treacle in a bowl and stir in the fresh yeast to blend. If using dried yeast, have the water with malt extract and black treacle hand-hot, sprinkle in the yeast and set in a warm place for 10–15 minutes, or until frothy.

Add the yeast liquid to dry ingredients and mix to a rough dough in the bowl. Turn on to an unfloured work surface and knead for about 10 minutes until smooth and not sticky. If dough is too sticky sprinkle with a little flour while kneading. Shape into a ball, return to the bowl and set inside a roomy polythene bag. Leave to stand at room temperature for about 2 hours, or until dough has doubled in size – malt bread takes longer to rise than other breads.

Turn risen dough out and knock back. Scatter sultanas over the surface of the dough and knead to mix them through the dough. Divide dough in half. Flatten each piece to an oblong, pull and flap dough to elongate, then turn sides over middle and roll up tightly. Place dough seam side down in well greased bread tins. Loosely cover with cling film and set in a warm place for 50 minutes until dough has risen to the top of the tins.

About 15 minutes before baking, heat the oven to 400°F (200°C) or Gas no. 6. Place loaves in preheated oven and bake for 30–35 minutes. Rub tops of baked loaves with buttered paper. Turn out on to a wire rack and leave until completely cool.

Currant bread

1 lb (450g) strong white flour
1 level teaspoon salt
½ level teaspoon mixed spice
1 oz (25g) fresh yeast or 1 level tablespoon dried yeast
8 fl oz (225ml) tepid milk and water (half and half)
1 oz (25g) castor sugar
2 oz (50g) butter
1 egg
2 oz (50g) currants
1 oz (25g) finely chopped walnuts

Sift 4 oz (100g) of the flour into a small bowl. Sift the remaining flour, the salt and mixed spice into a large mixing bowl and set aside in a warm place. Dissolve the fresh yeast in the tepid liquid. If using dried yeast, have the liquid hand-hot, stir in 1 teaspoon of the sugar and sprinkle in the yeast. Pour the yeast liquid into the 4 oz (100g) flour and whisk to make a smooth batter. Set aside in a warm place for 20 minutes until frothy.

Add the butter in pieces to the large mixing bowl of sifted flour and rub in with the fingertips, then add remaining sugar. Break up the egg with a fork, add to the flour mixture along with the yeast batter and mix to a rough dough. Turn on to an unfloured work surface and knead for about 10 minutes until smooth and not sticky. (Add a little extra flour if the dough is too sticky to handle.) Shape into a ball, return to the mixing bowl and set inside a roomy polythene bag. Leave at room temperature for 1 hour, or until dough has doubled in size.

Turn the risen dough out and knock back. Sprinkle the currants and walnuts over the dough and knead to mix them into the dough. Divide the dough in half and shape into rounds. Loosely cover with cling film and leave to rest for 10 minutes. Flatten each half to an oblong, pull and flap dough to elongate, then turn sides over middle and roll up tightly. Place loaves seam side down in two greased bread tins. Loosely cover and set in a warm place for about 30 minutes or until dough has risen ½ inch (1cm) above the rim of the tins.

About 15 minutes before baking, heat the oven to 425°F (220°C) or Gas no. 7. Place risen loaves in the centre of preheated oven and bake for 30–35 minutes. Turn out and rub the hot bread tops with buttered paper to give a soft shiny finish. Currant bread is also delicious with a little glacé icing (page 248) on top and day-old slices are delcious toasted.

Variation: For an unusual effect, divide the dough in 10 pieces and shape each piece into a neat round. Place 5 pieces of dough in a row in each loaf tin. Cover and leave to stand in a warm place until risen and puffy. Glaze with beaten egg and bake for 25–30 minutes.

Finishes for loaves and rolls

There are many ways of making bread look professional. Some finishes are applied before bread is baked, others when bread comes out of the oven.

Soft crust: Use for white tin loaves, cobs or rolls.

● Using a flour dredger, dust bread with flour before baking.

● For brown bread and rolls dust with bran sifted from wholemeal flour, especially nice on cob loaves.

● Rolls or baps can be brushed with milk and then dusted with flour.

● Cover plain rolls with a cloth when hot from the oven.

● A buttered paper or melted butter can be rubbed or brushed over white, currant or milk bread loaves or enriched buns when hot from the oven.

Crisp crust: Only plain white loaves or rolls will achieve a really crisp crust.

● These can be brushed over with salt water (1 teaspoon salt dissolved in 1 tablespoon cold water) before baking.

● Use a starch glaze (page 281) to paint over loaves or rolls before baking.

● Use 1 egg white lightly mixed with 1 tablespoon water and a pinch of salt to paint white bread and rolls before baking.

Shiny crust: Use for milk breads and all enriched rolls and buns.

● Lightly mix 1 egg with a pinch of salt and paint over tops before baking to make extra golden crust.

Seed crust: Any loaves or rolls brushed with salt water, starch glaze or egg can be sprinkled with poppy seeds or toasted sesame seeds for an attractive finish. Seeds need a wet surface to stick on bread or rolls.

Slashed crust: The tops of white bread loaves can be cut decoratively. Slashes extend the crust area and make loaves look pretty. Make sure you use a very sharp knife or razor blade and slash bread just before baking. Wholemeal or wheatmeal breads are never slashed because the dough is too fragile – it would just collapse.

Bridge rolls

Makes 24

½ oz (15g) fresh yeast or 2 level
  teaspoons dried yeast and 1 level
  teaspoon castor sugar
8 fl oz (225ml) tepid milk and water
  (half and half)
1 lb (450g) strong white flour
1 level teaspoon salt
2 oz (50g) butter
1 egg
beaten egg, for glazing
poppy seeds, for sprinkling

Dissolve the fresh yeast in the liquid. If using dried yeast, have the liquid hand-hot, stir in the sugar and sprinkle in the yeast. Set dried yeast mixture in a warm place for 10–15 minutes until frothy. Sift the flour and salt into a mixing bowl. Add the butter in pieces and rub in with the fingertips.

Break up the egg with a fork, add to the flour mixture along with the yeast and mix to a rough dough. Turn on to an unfloured work surface and knead for about 10 minutes until smooth and not sticky. Shape into a ball, return to the mixing bowl and set inside a roomy polythene bag. Leave at room temperature for about 1½ hours, or until dough has doubled in size.

Turn out risen dough and knock back. Divide dough into 24 pieces and shape each piece into a smooth ball. Using the palms of the hands, elongate dough pieces to a fat cigar shape. Place about ½ inch (1cm) apart (so sides will touch when risen) in neat rows on two greased baking sheets – make 2 rows of 6 rolls on each sheet. Brush with a little beaten egg. Loosely cover with cling film and leave in a warm place for about 30 minutes or until risen and puffy.

About 15 minutes before baking, heat the oven to 425°F (220°C) or Gas no. 7. Brush rolls with beaten egg again and sprinkle with poppy seeds. Place in preheated oven and bake for 15–20 minutes until golden. Transfer rolls to a wire rack and leave until completely cool, then separate rolls.

Savarin

Serves 6–8

6 oz (175g) strong white flour
½ level teaspoon salt
½ oz (15g) fresh yeast
6 tablespoons tepid milk
2 eggs
3 oz (75g) butter

Syrup
6 oz (175g) castor sugar
½ pint (300ml) water
thinly pared rind of ½ lemon
juice of 1 lemon
3 tablespoons rum or brandy

Thoroughly grease a 1½ pint (900ml) ring mould. (Use your fingers – they get into the small corners which is important if a fluted mould is used.) Sprinkle a little flour into the mould and shake it all over to coat, then shake out excess.

Sift the flour and salt into a mixing bowl and make a well in the centre. Dissolve the yeast in the milk. Lightly beat the eggs and stir into the yeast liquid. Pour into the centre of the flour. Sprinkle a little of the flour in the bowl over the liquid. Cover and leave in a warm place for about 20 minutes, or until the yeast breaks the surface and looks spongy.

Melt the butter in a saucepan over low heat and allow to cool until warm to the touch. Add to the bowl and mix ingredients together with a wooden spoon, then beat well to make a soft glossy batter that falls in sheets from the spoon. Pour into the prepared mould and spread level. Cover and leave at room temperature for 1 hour, or until the mixture has risen to the top of the tin.

About 15 minutes before baking, heat the oven to 400°F (200°C) or Gas no. 6. Place risen dough in the centre of preheated oven and bake for 20–30 minutes. Test by piercing the centre with a warmed skewer – if the skewer comes out clean, the savarin is baked. Allow to cool in the tin for 5 minutes, then turn out on to a wire rack. Wash and dry the savarin mould.

Put the sugar, water and thinly pared lemon rind for the syrup into a saucepan. Stir over low heat until the sugar has dissolved. Bring to the boil, then lower the heat and simmer for 5 minutes. Draw off the heat and add the lemon juice and rum or brandy. Pour the hot syrup into the cleaned mould and return the savarin to the mould so that it floats on the syrup. After about 15 minutes the savarin will have soaked up the syrup and settled back into the mould. Chill until ready to serve, then turn on to a serving dish. Serve whipped cream separately. Savarin is marvellous with a fresh fruit salad.

Variation: If using dried yeast, use 2 level teaspoons yeast and 1 level teaspoon castor sugar. Have the milk hand-hot, stir in the sugar, sprinkle in the yeast and leave in a warm place for about 15 minutes. Then mix in the beaten eggs and add to the flour.

Pizza

Dissolve the fresh yeast in the water. If using dried yeast, have the water hand-hot, stir in the sugar and sprinkle in the yeast. Set dried yeast mixture in a warm place for 10–15 minutes.

Sift the flour and salt into a mixing bowl. Make a well in the centre, pour in the yeast, add the oil and mix to a rough dough. Turn on to an unfloured work surface and knead for 10 minutes until smooth and not sticky. Return to the mixing bowl and set inside a roomy polythene bag. Leave at room temperature for about 1 hour, or until dough has doubled in size.

Turn the risen dough out on to an unfloured work surface and knock back. Divide dough in half. Roll out each dough to a circle about 12 inches (30cm) in diameter and slide on to greased baking sheets. Alternatively, place flattened dough on each of two greased 12 inch (30cm) pizza pans and press with the fingertips, making the edge slightly thicker than centre. Brush both pizza bases with a little oil.

Drain and chop the tomatoes and spread over the pizza bases. Peel and slice the onions and separate into rings. Arrange onions on the tomatoes and sprinkle over the grated cheese. Season with salt and pepper and sprinkle with the herbs. Garnish the pizzas with anchovy fillets and black olives or sweet pickled prunes. Leave pizzas to stand in a warm place for about 15 minutes. Heat the oven to 425°F (220°C) or Gas no. 7. Place pizzas in preheated oven and bake for 25–30 minutes. Serve hot cut in slices.

Makes two 12 inch (30cm) pizzas

½ oz (15g) fresh yeast or 2 level teaspoons dried yeast and 1 level teaspoon castor sugar
½ pint (300ml) tepid water
1 lb (450g) strong white flour
2 level teaspoons salt
1 tablespoon oil
extra oil, for brushing

Topping
1 × 1 lb 12 oz (850g) tin peeled tomatoes
2 onions
8–10 oz (225–275g) grated mature Cheddar cheese
salt and freshly milled black pepper
2 level teaspoons dried mixed herbs
2 × 1¾ oz (50g) tins anchovy fillets
12 black olives or sweet pickled prunes (page 306)

Garlic bread

Serves 6–8

2 Vienna loaves

Garlic butter
4 oz (100g) butter
1 tablespoon hot water
1 clove garlic
salt
2 tablespoons chopped parsley

Cut the Vienna loaves in slices at an angle, but do not cut completely through the loaf.

Cream the butter with the hot water to soften. Crush the garlic, remove the papery coating and, using a knife blade, mash to a purée with a little salt. Beat into the butter along with the chopped parsley. Generously spread the butter on each slice of bread. Any left over can be spread over the tops. Wrap each loaf in kitchen foil and chill for at least 1 hour.

Heat through for 20 minutes in an oven heated to 425°F (220°C) or Gas no. 7. For a very crisp finish, open up the foil and return loaves to the oven for a few minutes. Serve hot.

Variation **Herb bread:** Cream the butter with a squeeze of lemon juice and beat in the parsley and 1 tablespoon chopped chives. Omit the garlic.

Reheating bread

● Warm bread is always nice to serve with salad and snack meals. Put uncovered crusty loaves in an oven heated to 400°F (200°C) or Gas no. 6 for 5 minutes to warm and crisp them. Crusty rolls need only 2–3 minutes. Pitta bread can be reheated by placing under a hot grill for 2–3 minutes.

● Slightly stale loaves can be freshened by loosely wrapping them in kitchen foil and placing in an oven heated to 425°F (220°C) or Gas no. 7 for 5–10 minutes. Let bread cool in the wrapping and serve warm. Rolls or scones can be placed in a baking tin and covered closely with kitchen foil. Breads reheat without drying out and will emerge as freshly baked; they are best served warm, not hot.

● Frozen bread can be wrapped loosely in kitchen foil and placed in an oven heated to 400°F (200°C) or Gas no. 6 for 45 minutes to thaw. Frozen rolls will take 15 minutes. Let bread cool a little in the foil wrapping and serve warm. Remember, sliced bread can be toasted from frozen.

● Home-made bread is wonderful toasted – it becomes so crisp and crunchy without drying out. Try using home-made bread for toasted cheese sandwiches – it will make all the difference.

Home-made breadcrumbs

Soft white breadcrumbs are easier to make in a blender or food processor. Tear the soft part of fresh white bread slices into pieces and drop them through the centre hole on to the whirling blades. Make only small quantities at a time. Fresh breadcrumbs must be used straight away or they can be stored in a polythene bag in the freezer. If a white loaf stales, then crumb it and store in the freezer. The breadcrumbs will remain free flowing and can be used frozen. These are the breadcrumbs to use for stuffings, bread sauce and cheese toppings.

Toasted breadcrumbs are made from pieces of stale bread which have been baked in a slow oven until hard and golden. Melba toast or biscottes crushed with a rolling pin are ideal if you like natural looking crumbs for coating rather than the prepared golden coloured varieties you buy. Put toasted bread in a roomy polythene bag and crush with a rolling pin. Tip into an airtight container and they will keep well in the storecupboard. Use for coating fish and other foods for frying.

Sandwiches

Bread

● A fresh crusty loaf can be put in the refrigerator for a few hours which makes it easier to slice.

● For making rolled or pinwheel sandwiches very fresh sliced bread is best so bread won't break when rolled.

● Use a variety of breads. A brown or wheatgerm loaf has a lighter texture and is easier to cut thinly than a wholemeal loaf which tends to be crumbly. A combination of white and brown slices is pretty. Continental rye breads are particularly nice with meat and ham and those with caraway seed in the mix are very good with cheese. Currant bread and malt bread make delectable sweet sandwiches.

Butter or margarine

● For easy spreading allow butter or margarine to stand at room temperature to soften. Or cream butter or margarine so you can spread it thinly and evenly.

● For large scale sandwich making, soften butter by beating 1 tablespoon hot water into 4 oz (100g) butter. This is best done in a blender or food processor and makes a spread that is easy to handle and more economical.

● Flavoured butters will improve the taste. Try adding a little made English mustard to butter and use for roast beef or cheese sandwiches; horseradish butter is good for tongue. Add finely grated orange rind for ham or chicken, grated cheese for tomato, lemon juice for seafood, and anchovy paste or chopped chives for egg fillings.

Fillings

● For closed sandwiches combine soft and crisp ingredients to make contrasting flavours and textures.

● With meat fillings use several thin slices instead of a single thick one for a better taste.

● Remember fillings that make bread soggy or limp don't travel well.

● Use very smooth spreads for pinwheels and rolled sandwiches.

● For open sandwiches include salad ingredients that have lots of eye appeal.

● Using a flexible spatula, butter all slices right to the edge so butter acts as waterproof coating and prevents fillings from making bread soggy. Crisp lettuce leaves also serve this purpose.

● You can butter a stack of bread in advance if you place bread slices with buttered sides facing. Keep stacks to about 8 slices so bread is easy to separate again.

● Place filling on one slice of every pair, covering bread right to the edge. Do not over-fill – use about the same thickness filling as the bread slice.

● Close each sandwich with matching slice and leave crusts on all but the daintiest sandwiches; crusts help keep sandwiches fresh.

Wrapping sandwiches

Keep sandwiches with different fillings separate from each other so they don't take on other flavours.

● Set each sandwich (cut in halves or quarters) in centre of a square of waxed paper or kitchen foil (greaseproof paper is porous so must be over-wrapped with kitchen foil). To keep them moist top sandwich stack with a lettuce leaf, then bring opposite ends of wrapping together over centre and fold edges on top of sandwich stack, then tuck ends under. Wrapped like this the sandwiches can be refrigerated overnight.

● Those arranged on plates should be covered with cling film – no damp cloth please!

Finishing touches

● Make sandwiches look appetizing – a sprig of watercress or a sprinkling of scissor-snipped salad cress always looks fresh.

● Top sandwich stacks with a gherkin fan, a crisp spring onion, or wedges of tomato or hard-boiled egg.

● Parsley sprigs or trimmed radishes always look pretty placed around the edge of any sandwich arrangement.

Lunch or supper sandwiches

Delicious fillings between slices of fresh buttered bread are ideal for a picnic, a packed lunch or a supper snack. Follow good sandwich making techniques for the perfect assembly job and choose from these tasty fillings. Remember that all go perfectly between buttered soft baps as well.

● Wafer thin slices of salami or slicing sausages such as Mortadella with crisp lettuce or, better still, coleslaw from the delicatessen.

● Chopped cooked chicken or turkey mixed with chopped apple, chopped celery and mayonnaise; top with crisp lettuce.

● Thinnest slices of ham with sweet cucumber pickle (page 307), lamb with mint jelly, turkey with cranberry jelly or rare roast beef with horseradish; top with crisp lettuce.

● Sardines mashed with lemon juice, then mixed with chopped hard-boiled egg and plenty of freshly milled pepper.

● Taramasalata has a good flavour; or use home-made kipper or smoked salmon pâté – top with lettuce.

● Sliced home-made meat loaf with a little mustard and sprigs of watercress; leftover cold hamburger is good, too.

● Hard-boiled eggs chopped while still hot and mixed with butter – about ½ oz (15g) to 4 eggs – so butter melts. Add mayonnaise to bind, seasoning and chopped chives or watercress. As the filling cools in the sandwich, the butter sets and prevents the egg from falling out.

● Flaked salmon with chopped cucumber and mayonnaise or flaked tuna with chopped apple and mayonnaise; top with crisp lettuce.

● Peeled ripe tomatoes, seeds removed, mashed and mixed with grated Cheddar cheese to absorb tomato juices and a good seasoning of salt and freshly milled pepper.

● Cream cheese (Demi-sel is nice) blended with butter until smooth – use half and half – seasoned with salt and pepper and mixed with dressed drab or chopped prawns; top with crisp lettuce.

● Seasoned cream cheese or cottage cheese with sliced crisp radishes and lettuce. Cottage cheese and cream cheese are also tasty flavoured with horseradish.

● Marinated kippers (page 68), cut in bite-sized pieces, with onion rings and crisp lettuce.

● A thin smear of raspberry jam and sliced banana with lemon juice squeezed over.

Crusty rolls or French sticks:

Sandwiches made with crusty rolls and French sticks are extra special. Split almost through and butter generously. Fill a french stick, then slice crossways for serving. Try some of these fillings:

● Slices of ham, crisp lettuce, slices of tomato and thin slivers of Camembert cheese.

● Slices of rare roast beef, crisp lettuce and thinly cut onion rings.

● Slices of salami, slices of tomatoes, lettuce leaves and spring onions.

● Thin slices of Brie – try the blue and the herb-flavoured varieties – with crisp lettuce and thinly sliced cucumber.

● Slices of cold chicken with crisp fried bacon rashers, lettuce and tomato.

Open sandwiches

For a buffet lunch open sandwiches are ideal. They look fresh and pretty. For open sandwiches you start with a base of thinly sliced rye bread (buy it in packets at a delicatessen). Rye bread has a close texture and will take the weight of the toppings, or you can use a firm textured brown bread. Then the ingredients are interestingly arranged so that the bread base is hardly visible. Meat should be very thinly sliced so it can be arranged in folds to give the sandwich height, and on each open sandwich a suitable garnish is added to give colour. They are quite easy to make if you avoid making too many kinds; just four to six varieties will make a handsome display at a buffet. Allow two or three per person and remember guests will need a knife and fork for eating them.

Decide what you are going to use as toppings and assemble all the ingredients before you start. They can be made in advance and will keep quite fresh for a few hours if covered with cling film and left in a cool place. Open sandwiches look pretty displayed on a large old-fashioned ashets or you can unroll kitchen foil down the centre of a buffet table and set them out on that.

● Start by spreading bread slices to the edge with butter. Leave crusts on brown bread slices. Cut large bread slices in half; small slices of Hovis bread are a good size. Place a crisp lettuce leaf on the base and add a topping chosen from any of the following:

● Thinly sliced ham in folds, topped with a spoonful of potato salad and a garnish of a cucumber twist.

● A sliced hard-boiled egg (use an egg slicer) arranged to cover the base, topped with a slice of tomato and a spoonful of mayonnaise garnished with black lumpfish caviar.

● Thin fillets of smoked trout or smoked mackerel lifted off the bone and arranged across the lettuce base. Top with soured cream horseradish sauce (page 122) and a lemon twist.

● Thin slices of smoked salmon in folds topped with a strip of cold scrambled egg (let cooked eggs cool under a light weight so they flatten) and a sprinkling of snipped salad cress and a lemon twist.

● Prawns arranged in neat rows on the lettuce, topped with a spoonful of mayonnaise and garnished with a lemon twist and sprig of parsley.

● Overlapping thin slices of Danish blue or Mycella cheese topped with seeded black grapes.

Club sandwiches

Fillings placed between three slices of bread make a club sandwich. Use white or brown bread, either plain or toasted, and there are endless varieties of fillings. Club sandwiches are bulky so you have to secure them with a wooden cocktail stick and cut them diagonally for serving. This type of sandwich makes a complete light meal.

Use thinly sliced bread and have fillings ready in advance. If you are making club sandwiches with toast work fast so that toast is still crisp and hot when served. Place the second, or middle, slice of bread buttered side up and the top slice buttered side down on the filling. Choose from among the following:

● Spread hot toast or bread with butter and top with sliced chicken and a lettuce leaf. Cover with second slice. Add tomato slices and grilled bacon. Cover with third slice.

● Spread hot toast or bread with butter and top with crisp slices of grilled bacon and a lettuce leaf. Cover with second slice. Add a thin slice of processed cheese and tomato slices. Cover with third slice.

● Spread hot toast or bread with butter and top with slices of hard-boiled egg and a lettuce leaf. Cover with second slice. Add a thin slice of ham and a slice of tomato. Cover with third slice.

● Spread hot toast or bread with butter and top with slices of liver pâté and a sliced dill pickle, then a lettuce leaf. Cover with second slice. Add sliced hard-boiled egg. Cover with third slice.

Party sandwiches

Pretty rolled or pinwheel sandwiches look tempting for a special occasion and make delightful cocktail party snacks. For fancy rolled or pinwheel sandwiches trim the crusts and flatten bread slices slightly with a rolling pin before filling and rolling them.

Rolled sandwiches: Use trimmed slices from a small loaf and butter the slices right to the edge. Place filling about ½ inch (1cm) in from the edge and fold bread over filling. Then roll up tightly. Pack rolled sandwiches close together, so they keep their shape, and chill to set the butter and filling. Try these fillings:

● Asparagus tips – tinned asparagus are ideal – arranged so tips slightly overlap the bread and show at one end. Use brown bread.

● Fresh crisp watercress rolled in buttered bread slices with a touch of Marmite – allow the leaf ends to show.

● Cooked chipolata sausages rolled up in buttered bread slices with a touch of mustard. Trim sausages and bread at each end, then garnish by dipping ends in grated Parmesan cheese or finely chopped parsley.

Pinwheel sandwiches: Buy an unsliced brown or white loaf. Using a long sharp knife, cut off all the crusts except the bottom, then cut bread in thin slices lengthways. If you like, put the trimmed but unsliced loaf in the freezer for 30 minutes and you will find it easier to cut the bread in slices. Run a rolling pin over each slice to prevent the bread from cracking when it is rolled. Butter each slice right to the very edge, then spread with a smooth filling so bread rolls easily. Starting from one short end, roll up each slice. Wrap rolls individually in kitchen foil, twisting the ends like a cracker, and refrigerate for several hours to set butter and filling. Cut chilled rolls in ½ inch (1cm) slices. Choose from among these fillings:

● Liver pâté blended with half as much butter and some chopped green olives. Use white bread.

● Softened cream cheese mixed with chives, chopped walnuts or chopped prawns and parsley, seasoned with salt and pepper. Use brown bread.

● Thin slices of smoked salmon flavoured with lemon juice. Season with pepper. Use brown bread.

● For an unusual green filling mash a ripe avocado with lemon juice to preserve the colour, and add a good seasoning of salt and pepper. Spread over white bread slices.

● Stilton cheese mashed to a paste with equal parts of softened butter. Use white bread.

Arrange sliced pinwheel sandwiches in a variety of colours (or all of one kind) on a platter garnished with crisp celery stalks. Smoked salmon pinwheels look good arranged around a vandyked lemon half in the centre of the serving plate.

French toast or fried sandwiches

French toast is simply slices of trimmed white bread dipped in beaten egg and fried in butter until golden brown on both sides. The egg keeps the sandwich from absorbing too much butter, making it less greasy than an ordinary fried sandwich. Use any of the following fillings:

● Thin ham or processed cheese slices. Marmite on its own is delicious.

● Mozzarella cheese with a seasoning of salt and pepper – an Italian favourite.

● Flavoured cream cheese, or a tasty meat paste.

● Jam is nice – sprinkle the tops with sugar for serving – red jam such as raspberry is pretty.

To make 2 sandwiches: In a shallow dish lightly mix 2 eggs with 2 tablespoons milk and a seasoning of salt and pepper. Dip both sides of each sandwich into the egg mixture. Then add to 2 oz (50g) hot and foaming butter in a frying pan. Fry until crisp and brown on one side, then turn to cook the other side. Cut each sandwich in half. Serve on a warmed serving plate with a side dish of sweet pickle or relish.

12

Preserves

Larder shelves lined with home-made jams,
jellies, pickles or chutneys take pride of place in
any kitchen. Old favourites are always popular,
but try some of the more unusual ones for
interesting and delicious flavour combinations.

Preserves

Jams, jellies and marmalade

For good jam and jelly making there's nothing that beats the traditional preserving pan. Jam and jelly mixtures froth up when sugar is added; the sloping sides and sheer size of a preserving pan allow for this. A nut of butter added to a boiling mixture helps to reduce frothing, but it's very important to boil fast to obtain a set in the shortest possible time. A big pan lets you do this without any risk of spilling over – stainless steel or aluminium is best. You can use it for marmalade, sweet pickles and acid chutneys as well.

There are two stages in the making of jams and jellies and it's important to observe both carefully. First a gentle simmer in a measured quantity of water breaks down fruit and extracts the natural setting agent called pectin. With jellies you really must crush the fruit with the back of a wooden spoon. I sometimes use a potato masher to crush fruits like quinces. The initial cooking tenderizes the fruit; sugar added too soon will make tough skinned fruits chewy. Next the fruit is boiled rapidly to obtain a set quickly, which will give your preserve the best flavour and brightest colour. Very acid fruits will reach setting point in about 10 minutes, but most mixtures take 15–20 minutes. I set my kitchen timer to observe this meticulously and, at the same time, have a few saucers chilled in the refrigerator to cool a test sample down as quickly as possible.

Testing for a set is simply cooling a small sample of the boiled fruit mixture to see if it will set. A sugar boiling thermometer is a help and tells you that the jam is ready when the temperature reads 220°F (105°C), but the saucer test is the most reassuring. Allow a little jam, marmalade or jelly to drip on the chilled saucer and cool for a few minutes. Then push the drop with your finger and if setting point has been reached, the jam will wrinkle. While waiting for the test sample to cool be sure to have the pan off the heat – it will do no harm at all. If the test is negative you can return the pan to the heat and boil briskly for a few more minutes before testing again.

How to make better jams and jellies

● Don't fall for the mistaken, but widely held idea, that any old fruit will do. It won't. For good jams and jellies, the fruit should be sound and slightly underripe.

● For jams, prepare fruit according to type and remember that stones which are difficult to remove will float in the jam and can be removed with a perforated spoon. A bonus for jelly making is that there's no initial preparation of fruit because fruit is always strained in a jelly bag.

● Granulated sugar is excellent – you don't have to buy expensive preserving sugar. Castor and brown sugar produce a lot of scum and are not recommended. Sugar will dissolve more quickly if you warm it first.

● If you lightly grease the preserving pan with buttered paper before you start, this will help prevent the jam from sticking to the pan; a nut of butter stirred in just before bringing jam to the boil helps to reduce frothing. I sometimes add a nut of butter when the jam is taken off the heat because it helps disperse the scum.

● Scald the jelly bag first by pouring boiling water through it, then the fruit juices run through the bag and do not soak into it.

● Don't squeeze the jelly bag to speed up the dripping juices or you will have a cloudy mixture.

● To skim jam or jelly, allow it to cool for a moment, then push the scum to one side of the pan. Use a perforated spoon that has been dipped in boiling water for lifting it out.

● Stand jars on a board or folded newspaper. They might crack on a cold surface when hot jam or jelly is poured in. Wipe pots of jam clean with a damp cloth while jars are still hot – it's much easier. Immediately cover each jar with a waxed disc (supplied with pack of jam covers), then with Cellophane covers, either when very hot or quite cold. Avoid covering jams when they are warm or condensation will develop under the cover which encourages mould. Wet one side of the Cellophane cover with a damp sponge. Place covers over the hot jars wet side upwards. Pull tightly and secure cover to jar with an elastic band. When the jam cools the covers will be as tight as a drum.

Using frozen fruits: Fruit must be prepared according to type before it is put in the freezer. Pack fruits without sugar in quantities that correspond with the recipe you intend to use. Follow your recipe, adding the fruit while still frozen. In the case of tough skinned fruit such as gooseberries and blackcurrants, simmer fruit in water as recipe indicates. For soft fruits where no water is used put frozen fruit directly into the pan with about 4 tablespoons water just to start the cooking process. Once the fruit is thawed proceed with recipe in usual way.

Strawberry jam

Makes 5–6 lb (2.3–2.7kg)

4 lb (1.8kg) strawberries
3½ lb (1.6kg) granulated sugar
juice of 2 large lemons

Include a few strawberries that are slightly underripe. Crush half the fruit (choose larger berries for this) in the base of a preserving pan. Add remaining fruit and cook gently for about 15 minutes to soften fruit and allow some of the water to evaporate.

Add the sugar and stir until dissolved, then add the lemon juice. Bring to the boil and boil rapidly for about 15–20 minutes. Draw off the heat and test for a set. Skim the surface and allow jam to cool for 30 minutes, to ensure an even distribution of the strawberries. Stir once, pour into warmed jars and cover.

Rhubarb and ginger jam

Trim the rhubarb stalks and cut in 1 inch (2.5cm) lengths before weighing the quantity required. Place the rhubarb and sugar in a large mixing bowl in alternate layers.

Bruise the ginger and tie in a muslin bag together with the thinly pared lemon rind. Add to the fruit along with the juice of the lemons. Drain the preserved ginger or rinse the sugary coating from crystallized ginger in warm water. Finely chop the ginger and add to the bowl. Cover with a cloth and leave to stand overnight. The sugar will begin to dissolve in the juices drawn from the rhubarb.

Pour the rhubarb mixture into a preserving pan. Slowly bring to the boil, stirring occasionally, until the sugar has dissolved. Boil rapidly for about 15 minutes. Draw off the heat and test for a set. Skim the surface and discard the muslin bag. Pour into warmed jars and cover.

Makes 5 lb (2.3kg)

4 lb (1.8kg) rhubarb (weight after preparation)
4 lb (1.8kg) granulated sugar
1 oz (25g) dried root ginger
thinly pared rind and juice of 2 large lemons
3 oz (75g) preserved ginger in syrup or crystallized ginger

Gooseberry and orange jam

Top and tail the gooseberries and put them into a preserving pan. Add the water, finely grated orange rind and orange juice. Simmer gently for about 30 minutes, crushing the fruit occasionally with the back of a wooden spoon, until gooseberries are tender.

Add the sugar and stir until dissolved. Bring to the boil and boil rapidly for about 10 minutes. Draw off the heat and test for a set. Skim the surface. Pour into warmed jars and cover. The subtle hint of orange in this recipe greatly enhances the flavour of the gooseberries.

Variation: If the orange is omitted increase the water used to 1 pint (600ml).

Makes 6 lb (2.7kg)

3 lb (1.4kg) green gooseberries
¾ pint (400ml) water
finely grated rind and juice of 2 oranges
3½ lb (1.6kg) granulated sugar

Summer jam

Top and tail the gooseberries and put them into a preserving pan along with the water. Simmer gently for about 30 minutes, crushing the fruit occasionally with the back of a wooden spoon, until tender. Add the strawberries and raspberries and reheat until simmering.

Add the sugar and stir until dissolved. Bring to the boil and boil rapidly for about 10–15 minutes. Draw off the heat and test for a set. Skim the surface. Leave to stand for 5 minutes, then stir once and pour into warmed jars and cover.

Makes 6 lb (2.7kg)

2 lb (900g) gooseberries
½ pint (300ml) water
1 lb (450g) strawberries
1 lb (450g) raspberries
4 lb (1.8kg) granulated sugar

Uncooked strawberry jam

Makes 3½ lb (1.6kg)

1¼ lb (550g) strawberries
2 lb (900g) castor sugar
2 tablespoons lemon juice
4 fl oz (125ml) bottled pectin

This is a mixture of crushed strawberries and sugar set with pectin. As there is no cooking the fresh strawberry flavour is superb. Put the strawberries into a mixing bowl and crush them with the back of a wooden spoon. Add the sugar and lemon juice. Leave to stand at room temperature for about 1 hour, stirring occasionally, until the sugar has dissolved.

Add the liquid pectin (half bottle) and stir for 2 minutes to mix thoroughly. Pour into small freezerproof containers to within ½ inch (1cm) of the rims. Leave to stand for 24 hours until set. Then seal containers and freeze.

To use: Thaw overnight in the refrigerator. Once thawed the jam will keep for 1–2 weeks stored in refrigerator. Stir before serving. Spread on hot toast or scones or use as a thick sauce for ice cream.

Variation **Uncooked raspberry jam:** Use fresh raspberries in place of the strawberries.

Raspberry jam

Makes 6 lb (2.7kg)

4 lb (1.8kg) raspberries
4 lb (1.8kg) granulated sugar

Pick over the raspberries, but do not wash them. Put about one quarter of the fruit into a preserving pan and crush the fruit with the back of a wooden spoon to release some of the juices. Add remaining fruit and cook gently until the juices run.

Add the sugar and stir until dissolved. If a seedless jam is liked, press the fruit and juices through a nylon sieve and return to the rinsed pan. Bring to the boil and boil rapidly for about 6–8 minutes. Draw off the heat and test for a set. Skim the surface. Pour into warmed jars and cover.

Plum jam

Makes 7 lb (3.2kg)

4 lb (1.8kg) plums
¾ pint (400ml) water
4 lb (1.8kg) granulated sugar

Cut plums in half following the line of the fruit, twist to separate and remove the stones. Put plums and water into a preserving pan and simmer gently for 10–20 minutes until fruit is tender. Meanwhile, crack 12 stones and remove inner kernels. Blanch the kernels for 1 minute, then drain and set aside.

Add the sugar to the plums and stir until dissolved. Bring to the boil and boil rapidly for about 15–20 minutes. Draw off the heat and test for a set. Skim the surface and stir in plum kernels – they add a subtle almond flavour to the jam. Pour into warmed jars and cover.

Blackcurrant jam

Strip the berries from their stalks with a fork and put them into a preserving pan. Add the water and simmer gently for about 30 minutes until the skins are tender.

Add the sugar and stir until dissolved. Bring to the boil and boil rapidly for about 10 minutes. Draw off the heat and test for a set. Skim the surface. Pour into warmed jars and cover. Blackcurrants are very high in pectin which means they give a higher yield of jam in relation to the amount of fruit used.

Makes 5 lb (2.3kg)

2 lb (900g) blackcurrants
1 pint (600ml) water
3 lb (1.4kg) granulated sugar

Blackberry and apple jam

Peel, core and slice the apples into a saucepan. Add half the water and cook gently until soft. Put the blackberries into a preserving pan, add remaining water and simmer gently until tender. If a seedless jam is liked, press the blackberries through a nylon sieve and return to the rinsed pan.

Add the apples and sugar to the blackberries and stir over low heat until the sugar has dissolved. Bring to the boil and boil rapidly for about 15 minutes. Draw off the heat and test for a set. Skim the surface. Pour into warmed jars and cover.

Makes 5 lb (2.3kg)

1½ lb (700g) cooking apples
½ pint (300ml) water
2 lb (900g) blackberries
3 lb (1.4kg) granulated sugar

Old-fashioned apple jelly

Coarsely chop the apples, discarding any damaged parts. Put into a preserving pan and add the water (should be just enough to cover) and pared lemon rind or cloves. Simmer gently for about 1 hour until quite soft. As fruit softens, stir occasionally and crush the fruit with the back of a wooden spoon (extracts pectin).

Ladle the softened fruit and juices into a scalded jelly bag and leave the fruit to drip for several hours. Measure strained juice into the rinsed preserving pan and for every 1 pint (600ml) juice add 1 lb (450g) granulated sugar. Stir over low heat until sugar has dissolved. Bring to the boil and boil rapidly for about 10 minutes. Draw off the heat and test for a set. Skim the surface. Pour into warmed jelly jars and cover.

Variations **Crab-apple jelly:** Use 4 lb (1.8kg) coarsely chopped crab-apples, leaving small ones whole. Pot quickly as crab-apple jelly sets very fast. Crab-apples produce a pretty pink jelly.

Redcurrant and raspberry jelly: Use 2 lb (900g) raspberries and 2 lb (900g) redcurrants and omit the lemon (or cloves). These two fruits make a good partnership – you get a marvellous colour from the raspberries and a good set from the redcurrants.

Makes 5 lb (2.3kg)

4 lb (1.8kg) cooking apples
2 pints (1.1 litres) water
thinly pared rind of 1 lemon or 4–6 cloves
granulated sugar (see recipe)

Herb jelly

Makes 4 lb (1.8kg)

3 lb (1.4kg) cooking apples
1½ pints (900ml) water
about 6 sprigs fresh mint, parsley,
    thyme or sage
¼ pint (150ml) malt vinegar
granulated sugar (see recipe)
3–4 tablespoons finely chopped
    mint, parsley, thyme or sage – the
    one chosen above

Coarsely chop the apples, discarding any damaged parts, and put them into a preserving pan. Add the water and a small bunch of herbs tied together. Simmer gently for 1 hour until fruit is very soft. As apples soften, stir and mash well to reduce them to a pulp. Add the vinegar and cook for a further 5 minutes.

Ladle softened fruit and juices into a scalded jelly bag and leave fruit to drip for several hours. Measure strained juice into the rinsed preserving pan and for every 1 pint (600ml) juice add 1 lb (450g) granulated sugar. Stir over low heat until sugar has dissolved. Bring to the boil and boil rapidly for about 10 minutes. Draw off the heat and test for a set. Skim the surface. Add the chopped herb and allow jelly to cool for 5–10 minutes, or until a skin forms on the surface. Stir once, then pour into warmed jelly jars and cover. You will find **mint jelly** goes well with lamb, **thyme jelly** with chicken, **sage jelly** with pork and **parsley jelly** with ham. The vinegar produces a delicious sweet-sour flavour.

Rowan jelly

Makes 5 lb (2.3kg)

3 lb (1.4kg) rowan-berries
1 lb (450g) crab-apples or cooking
    apples
2 pints (1.1 litres) water
granulated sugar (see recipe)

To the unsuspecting, rowan jelly will taste very astringent – it's a jelly that is traditionally served with venison and other game. The pretty clusters of rowan-berries are best picked in late autumn when they have full colour. They need some crab-apples or sour cooking apples to get a good set.

Trim stalks from rowan-berries and coarsely chop the apples, discarding any damaged parts. Put the fruit into a preserving pan and add the water (should be sufficient to cover). Simmer gently for about 1 hour until soft. As fruit softens, stir occasionally and mash fruit with the back of a wooden spoon (extracts pectin).

Ladle the softened fruit and juices into a scalded jelly bag and leave fruit to drip for several hours. Measure strained juice into the rinsed preserving pan and for every 1 pint (600ml) juice add 1 lb (450g) granulated sugar. Stir over low heat until sugar has dissolved. Bring to the boil and boil rapidly for about 10 minutes. Draw off the heat and test for a set. Skim the surface. Pour into warmed jelly jars and cover.

Testing for pectin

Pectin is a kind of natural gum which is found in the cell walls of fruit and is vital for a good set. Simmering fruit gently helps to extract pectin. If you want to test your preserve for pectin content do it after cooking the fruit and before adding the sugar. Or before straining if making a jelly.

Take a teaspoon of the liquid in the pan and put it in a teacup. Let it cool for a moment, then add 3 teaspoons methylated spirit and shake gently together. If the juice forms a single clot the preserve will set perfectly. Several small clots means the mixture needs a little longer simmering to get a more concentrated juice. Discard test sample.

Quince jelly

Quinces turn yellow when ready for picking and can be quite difficult to see in a tree with yellow autumn leaves. They are as hard as wood but quickly turn to pulp like cooking apples, and they make a pink jelly that has a sharp flavour.

Coarsely chop the quinces and put them into a preserving pan. Add 4 pints (2.4 litres) of the water and the lemon juice. Simmer gently for about 1 hour until fruit is very soft. As quinces soften, squash them with the back of a wooden spoon (extracts pectin).

Ladle fruit and juices into a scalded jelly bag and leave fruit to drip for 30 minutes. Then remove pulp from the bag and return to the rinsed pan along with the remaining 2 pints (1.1 litres) water. (Quinces are so high in pectin that pulp can be reboiled for a second extraction.) Simmer for 30 minutes, then ladle back into the jelly bag for a second straining.

Measure all the strained juice into the rinsed preserving pan and for every 1 pint (600ml) juice add 1 lb (450g) granulated sugar. Stir over low heat until sugar has dissolved. Bring to the boil and boil rapidly for 10 minutes. Draw off the heat and test for a set. Skim the surface. Pour into warmed jelly jars and cover. Add a spoonful of quince jelly to any cooked apple mixture to sweeten and flavour, or serve it with roast pork or game.

Makes 6 lb (2.7kg)

4 lb (1.8kg) quinces
6 pints (3.5 litres) water
juice of 1 lemon
granulated sugar (see recipe)

Cranberry orange preserve

Pick over the cranberries and discard any bruised or soft berries. Put them into a saucepan together with the grated orange rind. Add enough water to the juice of the orange to make ½ pint (300ml) and add to the pan. Slowly bring to the boil, then lower the heat and simmer for 10 minutes, stirring occasionally with a wooden spoon. The cranberries will pop and the mixture will cook to a thick pulp.

Press cranberries and juice through a nylon sieve. Return the purée to the rinsed saucepan and add the sugar. Stir over low heat until the sugar has dissolved. Bring to the boil, then lower the heat and simmer for 5 minutes. Pour into warmed jars and leave until completely cool. Cover and store in a cool place. This preserve keeps for 1 month. Cranberries have a delicious flavour and are popular in America where this recipe originates. Serve with roast turkey or ham.

Fills 4 × 8 oz (225g) jars

1 lb (450g) fresh or frozen cranberries
finely grated rind and juice of 1 orange
1 lb (450g) granulated sugar

How to make better marmalade

● Fruit peel must be simmered until quite tender before the sugar is added. When ready, a piece of cooked peel squeezed between the fingers will feel quite soft.

● Pectin is found in pith, pulp and pips of citrus fruits (bitter oranges have plenty), so it's very important that the trimmed pith should be chopped for better extraction and tied in a loose muslin bag (so water circulates) together with pips and added to the pan. Simmering extracts pectin. After simmering, squeeze bag between two dinner plates over the pan to extract all the juice.

● Fast boiling is the secret of a good flavour and set. Test marmalade after 15 minutes and then every 5 minutes after that. Draw the pan off the heat before you test – it will do no harm at all.

● Don't pot marmalade straight away unless you like all the peel at the top of the jar. Allow hot marmalade to cool for about 20 minutes when a skin will form on the surface. Stir once and the peel will hang suspended in the jelly, then pour into jars.

● Cover marmalade with waxed discs and a clean cloth when hot. Seal with Cellophane covers when cold – to reduce risk of condensation which encourages mould.

● Use the whole fruit method to make a chunky marmalade. Oranges can be boiled whole and chopped after cooking. This is also the method to use with frozen oranges – no need to thaw.

● For an improved flavour in any orange marmalade recipe, coarsely crush 1 tablespoon coriander seeds, tie in a muslin bag and suspend in the pot with the simmering oranges or peel. The flavour is deliciously aromatic. Discard the muslin bag before adding the sugar to the recipe.

Orange marmalade (*whole fruit*)

Makes 8 lb (3.7kg)

3 lb (1.4kg) bitter oranges
4½ pints (2.7 litres) water
6 lb (2.7kg) granulated sugar
juice of 2 lemons

Scrub the oranges and pick off the small disc at the stalk end. Put whole or frozen oranges into a large saucepan with 4 pints (2.4 litres) of the water. Cover with a pan lid and simmer gently for 2 hours until oranges are quite soft – test with a sharp knife.

Using a perforated spoon, transfer softened oranges to a mixing bowl. Reserve the cooking liquid. When cool enough to handle, cut fruit in half, scoop out pith and pulp with pips and put into a separate saucepan. Add the remaining ½ pint (300ml) water and simmer for 10 minutes. Meanwhile, coarsely or finely chop softened orange peel according to texture liked. Alternatively, pass the cooked peel through a mincer which results in even-sized, very finely chopped peel. (A blender or food processor may chop the peel too finely.)

Add the cut peel to the reserved cooking liquid. Strain the liquid from the pith and pips into the pan and add the sugar and lemon juice. Stir over low heat until the sugar has dissolved. Bring to the boil and boil rapidly for about 15 minutes. Draw off the heat and test for a set. Skim the surface. Allow to cool for 15–20 minutes, then stir once and pour into warmed, dry jars. Cover and seal.

Variation **Dark chunky marmalade:** Add 1 tablespoon black treacle (for bitter flavour) along with the sugar. If you like, a proportion of brown sugar can be used. Replace not more than one quarter of the total amount of sugar with brown sugar. It froths and causes a lot of scum. Cut the peel coarsely, to go with a bitter flavour.

Orange marmalade (*fine cut*)

Scrub the oranges and pick off the small disc at the stalk end. Halve the oranges and squeeze out juice and pips. Cut the peel in quarters and cut away any thick white pith. Finely shred the peel. Coarsely chop the white pith and tie in a loose muslin bag along with pulp and pips. Put shredded peel, orange and lemon juice, muslin bag of pith, pulp and pips, and water into a preserving pan. Bring to the boil, then lower the heat and simmer gently, uncovered, for 1½–2 hours until peel is quite tender.

Squeeze the bag of pith and pips between two dinner plates over the pan to extract juice. Add the sugar and stir until dissolved. Bring to the boil and boil rapidly for about 15 minutes. Draw off the heat and test for a set. Skim the surface. Allow to cool for 15–20 minutes, then stir once and pour into warmed, dry jars. Cover and seal.

Makes 10 lb (4.5kg)

3 lb (1.4kg) bitter oranges
juice of 2 lemons
6 pints (3.4 litres) water
6 lb (2.7kg) granulated sugar

illustrated facing page 304

Marmalade (*pressure cooker*)

A pressure cooker cuts down on the cooking time for the oranges, but remember the pressure gauge and lid are only used for cooking the fruit. After the first stage, the cut-up fruit and sugar are boiled for a set in the uncovered pan.

Scrub the fruit and pick off the small disc at the stalk end. Remove the trivet and place the whole oranges in the pressure cooker base. Add 2 pints (1.1 litres) of the water and cover with the cooker lid. Bring to High (15 lb) pressure and hold for 20 minutes, then slowly reduce pressure.

Using a perforated spoon, transfer softened oranges to a mixing bowl. Reserve the cooking liquid. When cool enough to handle, cut fruit in half, scoop out the pith, pulp and pips and put into a separate saucepan. Add the remaining 1 pint (600ml) water and simmer for 30 minutes. Meanwhile, chop softened peel either coarsely or finely, according to texture liked.

Add the chopped peel to the reserved cooking liquid in the pressure cooker base. Strain the liquid from the pith and pips into the cooker and add the sugar, lemon juice and treacle, if using it. Stir over low heat until the sugar has dissolved. Bring to the boil and boil rapidly for about 15 minutes. Draw off the heat and test for a set. Skim the surface. Allow to cool for 15 minutes, then stir once and pour into warmed, dry jars. Cover and seal.

Makes 6 lb (2.7kg)

2 lb (900g) bitter oranges
3 pints (1.7 litres) water
4 lb (1.8kg) granulated sugar
juice of 2 lemons
1 tablespoon black treacle
   (optional)

Chutneys and pickles

Attitudes to home-made chutneys and pickles have changed. It's not a case of using up a glut of vegetables or fruit any more. Smaller batches of tastier, more unusual mixtures are popular now.

● The first thing to get sorted out are the jars and covers. Vinegar is the preservative in chutneys and if jars are not sealed airtight it will evaporate and chutney will shrink and dry out. Cellophane covers will not do. You can use jam jars if you tie squares of preserving skin (Porosan) on top – one sheet will cut into as many squares as you are likely to need.

● The old-fashioned way is to use paraffin wax (available at chemists'). When paraffin wax is warmed in a saucepan it melts and becomes clear. On cooling it becomes brittle and white like candle wax. To use it you must first tie a grease-proof paper cover over each jar of chutney, then dip a square of double thickness muslin into melted paraffin wax and tie it over the top. Or attractive wide-necked jars with tight-fitting corks can be used as long as you boil the corks and put a layer of greaseproof paper between the contents of the jar and the cork – expensive but nice if chutney is given as a gift.

● For pickles the presence of excess water in vegetables or fruit weakens flavour, dilutes vinegar concentration and therefore the keeping qualities. To get rid of excess water, vegetables can be either sprinkled with salt or soaked in salt solution. For dry salt, prepared vegetables are put in a deep bowl or colander with salt sprinkled between the layers – allow 1 oz (25g) coarse cooking salt per 1 lb (450g) vegetables. Cover and leave for 24 hours. Then rinse in fresh cold water and drain thoroughly. For a salt solution (brine) dissolve 8 oz (225g) coarse cooking salt in 4 pints (2.4 litres) cold water in a deep bowl. Add prepared vegetables and keep them submerged by covering with a plate. Leave for 24 hours, then rinse in fresh cold water and drain thoroughly.

● Spices make an important contribution to the flavour of a chutney. Those not to be left in the chutney can be tied in muslin with a long string tied to the pan handle to make removing bag easy. A 3 inch (7.5cm) wide bandage is good to use for making small bags.

● Vinegar and sugar are two of the main ingredients in chutney and the types used vary with the recipe. Malt vinegar used with brown sugar makes a rich, dark mixture, but in some recipes distilled white vinegar and granulated sugar are used to keep the colours bright. On the other hand, cider vinegar gives chutney added flavour. Remember to use a stainless steel or aluminium pan (not copper or brass) when cooking with vinegar. Metal lids must have a plastic lining if used. If a sieve is used it must be nylon – all these are important because the reaction of acid to metal alters flavours.

● Onion is a regular ingredient in chutney recipes and because vinegar has a hardening effect on raw onion, I find results are better if the chopped onion is simmered for 5 minutes, then drained and added to the ingredients.

● Chutneys are cooked slowly for a long time in order to reduce the mixture right down to a pulp and drive off excess water. It is easy to tell when the mixture is ready: a wooden spoon drawn across the mixture should leave a trail.

● Bottle chutneys when hot and cover immediately. You'll find most chutneys improve with a short storage period before serving.

Spiced vinegar: Spiced vinegar adds flavour to straightforward pickled vegetables like onions and it perks up chutney recipes too. You can buy it or make your own. For the best flavour soak whole spices tied in muslin in vinegar for at least 1 month. Shake the bottle occasionally.

For a quicker method, add 1 oz (25g) pickling spice to 2 pints (1.1 litres) vinegar. Put the vinegar in a mixing bowl, cover with a plate, and set over a saucepan of cold water. Slowly bring the water to the boil and draw off the heat. Leave to stand for at least 3 hours to infuse the vinegar and spices. Then strain.

Herb vinegar: A herb vinegar is easy to make. Push a few sprigs of fresh herbs into a bottle of wine vinegar and store for at least 1 week before using, though the flavour will improve with longer keeping. I just top up with more vinegar as it is used – the herb continues to add flavour to the vinegar for months.

Pickled onions

To peel small pickling onions quickly, trim a slice from both ends and put onions into a mixing bowl. Pour over boiling water to cover and leave to soak for 5 minutes, then drain and the skins will slip off easily. Mix together the salt and water to make a brine. Pour the brine over the onions in a bowl to cover. Leave onions to soak for 24–48 hours – the longer soaked, the crisper they will be. Keep them below the surface of the brine by placing a plate on top.

Put vinegar and pickling spice into a bowl and cover with a plate. Set bowl over a saucepan one quarter filled with cold water and bring the water to the boil. Draw off the heat and leave to infuse for 2 hours, then strain.

Drain the onions and rinse thoroughly. Pack the onions neatly and tightly into one or more jars. Push in a few bay leaves for flavour and appearance. Any water that settles in the bottom of the jar during packing should be poured off. Pour over cold spiced vinegar to completely cover the onions. Seal airtight and store for 3–4 months before using.

Variations **Sweet pickled onions:** Dissolve 4 oz (100g) granulated sugar in the spiced vinegar. Add onions to sweetened vinegar and simmer for 10 minutes, then pack into jars. Store in a cool place for at least 1 month before serving.

Pickled eggs: Hard boil 12 eggs for 8 minutes from cold, then shell and submerge in cold water and leave until completely cool. Pack neatly into jars and pour over cold spiced vinegar. Seal airtight. After 6 weeks these are ready to eat and are very good for picnics.

Makes 4 lb (1.8kg)

4 lb (1.8kg) pickling onions
4 oz (100g) coarse salt
2 pints (1.1 litres) water
2 pints (1.1 litres) malt vinegar
1 oz (25g) pickling spice
few bay leaves

Mustard pickles

Peel the onions. Cut the cauliflower in florets. Peel and cut the marrow in bite-sized pieces. Chop the cucumber in bite-sized pieces. String the runner beans and cut in 1 inch (2.5cm) lengths. Put the vegetables into a large mixing bowl. Mix the salt and water to make a brine. Pour the brine over the vegetables to cover. Leave to soak for 24 hours with a plate on top of the vegetables to hold them below the brine. Then drain and thoroughly rinse.

Put the flour, sugar, mustard powder and turmeric into a large saucepan. Blend with a little of the vinegar, then stir in the rest of the vinegar. Stir over low heat until sauce thickens. Add the vegetables and cook for 5 minutes, or for a softer pickle cook for 10 minutes. Draw off the heat. Lift out vegetables with a per-forated spoon and pack into warmed jars, taking care to evenly distribute the different vegetables. Pour sufficient sauce into each jar to cover. Seal when cold. Store in a cool place for 1 month before serving.

Makes 5–6 lb (2.3–2.7kg)

1 lb (450g) pickling onions
1 small cauliflower
1 lb (450g) marrow
½ cucumber
8 oz (225g) runner beans
8 oz (225g) coarse salt
4 pints (2.4 litres) water

Mustard sauce
3 oz (75g) plain flour
6 oz (175g) castor sugar
2 oz (50g) mustard powder
½ oz (15g) turmeric
2 pints (1.1 litres) distilled white
    vinegar

Mint sauce

Makes about 12 fl oz (750ml)

4 oz (100g) fresh mint
½ pint (300ml) distilled white
**   vinegar**
6 oz (175g) granulated sugar

Strip mint leaves from their stems. Rinse and shake dry or pat dry in absorbent paper. Finely chop the mint with a stainless steel knife (prevents discoloration) and put into a mixing bowl.

Put the vinegar and sugar into a saucepan and stir over low heat until the sugar has dissolved. Bring to the boil and draw off the heat. Stir vinegar into the mint and leave until completely cool. Spoon mint sauce into one or more clean screw-topped jars. Cover tightly and store in a dark place.

To serve: Spoon out required amount and mix with additional vinegar to taste.

Apricot chutney

Makes 4 lb (1.8kg)

1 lb (450g) dried apricots
1½ lb (700g) onions
8 oz (225g) sultanas
1 pint (600ml) malt vinegar
finely grated rind and juice of 2
**   oranges**
2 level teaspoons salt
1 level teaspoon turmeric
½ level teaspoon ground cinnamon
1 tablespoon mustard seed
1 lb (450g) soft light brown sugar

Soak the apricots overnight, then drain. Peel and finely chop the onions. Put onions into a saucepan and pour over cold water to cover. Bring to the boil, then lower the heat and simmer for 5 minutes until tender. Meanwhile, coarsely chop the apricots and put into a large saucepan. Drain the onions and add to the apricots along with the sultanas, half the vinegar, the finely grated rind and juice of the oranges, salt, turmeric, cinnamon and mustard seed. Simmer gently for 30 minutes until apricots are softened.

Dissolve the sugar in the remaining vinegar and add to the pan. Simmer gently for about 2 hours until quite thick. Pour into warmed jars and cover.

Variation: Add 2 oz (50g) chopped walnuts before potting.

Plum chutney

Makes 4 lb (1.8kg)

1 lb (450g) onions
2½ lb (1.1kg) plums (dark red or
**   purple)**
2 lb (900g) cooking apples
1 pint (600ml) cider vinegar
2 level teaspoons salt
1 piece dried root ginger
1 teaspoon whole cloves
1 teaspoon whole allspice
1 teaspoon black peppercorns
1 lb (450g) soft light brown sugar

Peel and finely chop the onions. Put onions into a saucepan and pour over cold water to cover. Bring to the boil, then lower the heat and simmer for 5 minutes until tender. Meanwhile, halve and stone the plums and peel, core and coarsely chop the apples. Put plums and apples into a large saucepan. Drain the onions and add to the pan. Add half the cider vinegar and the salt and simmer gently for about 30 minutes until fruit is softened.

Meanwhile, bruise the ginger and tie in a muslin bag along with the spices. Put into a separate saucepan and add the remaining cider vinegar and the sugar. Stir over low heat until the sugar has dissolved. Bring to the boil, then lower the heat and simmer for 5 minutes. Draw off the heat and allow the flavours to infuse for 30 minutes, then discard the muslin bag.

Add sweetened vinegar to the softened fruit and continue to cook gently for about 2 hours until chutney is quite thick. Pour into warmed jars and cover.

Illustrated: Fine cut marmalade and wheatmeal cob loaf, pages 301 and 277

Ripe tomato chutney

Peel and finely chop the onions. Put onions into a saucepan and pour over cold water to cover. Bring to the boil, then lower the heat and simmer for 5 minutes until tender. Meanwhile, scald tomatoes and peel the skins. Chop tomato flesh and put into a large saucepan. Drain the onions and add to the tomatoes. Simmer for 10 minutes until liquid has reduced and mixture is thick. (Ripe tomatoes have a high percentage of water and must be well reduced, otherwise there is a danger that the added vinegar, which is the preservative, will be diluted and the finished chutney will not keep.) Add half the vinegar, the salt and the spices and simmer for 30 minutes until thick.

Dissolve the sugar in the remaining vinegar and add to the mixture. Simmer gently for a further 1–2 hours until quite thick. Pour into warmed jars and cover.

Makes 4 lb (1.8kg)

8 oz (225g) onions
6 lb (2.7kg) ripe tomatoes
½ pint (300ml) distilled white vinegar
3 level teaspoons salt
pinch of mixed spice
pinch of cayenne pepper
2 level teaspoons paprika
12 oz (350g) granulated sugar

Apple chutney

Peel and finely chop the onions. Put onions into a saucepan and pour over cold water to cover. Bring to the boil, then lower the heat and simmer for 5 minutes until tender. Meanwhile, peel, core and coarsely chop the apples, discarding any damaged parts. Put apples into a large saucepan and add the vinegar. Drain the onions and add to the apples along with the sugar, sultanas, ground ginger, salt and cayenne pepper, if using it.

Stir over low heat until the sugar has dissolved. Bring to the boil, then lower the heat and simmer gently for about 2 hours until quite thick. Pour into warmed jars and cover.

Makes 4 lb (1.8kg)

1 lb (450g) onions
3 lb (1.4kg) cooking apples
2 pints (1.1 litres) malt vinegar
1½ lb (700g) soft light brown sugar
6 oz (175g) sultanas
1 oz (25g) ground ginger
1 level teaspoon salt
¼ level teaspoon cayenne pepper (optional)

Salted runner beans

When there are a lot of runner beans it is worthwhile salting beans (if you have no freezer), but a word of warning: use only fresh, tender young beans. Do not wash the beans unless necessary and if you do, dry them well. String and thinly slice the beans.

3 lb (1.4kg) fresh young runner beans
1 lb (450g) coarse salt

Place a layer of salt in the bottom of a large earthenware crock or glass jar. Add a layer of beans and continue in alternate layers with the salt, pressing each layer down well and finishing with a layer of salt. As the beans shrink, the liquid will make a brine which preserves the beans. More beans and salt can be added to the crock but each time finish with a layer of salt. When the crock is full, cover with a lid.

To use: Soaking overnight is unnecessary if you thoroughly rinse the required amount of beans. Put them into a saucepan and cover with fresh cold water, bring to the boil, then drain. Add the beans to a pan of boiling unsalted water and cook until tender.

Illustrated: How to cut a Brie – shown on a 'pepper' Brie, page 327

Sweet pickles

● Sugar is added to vinegar and spices for sweet pickles – they are the perfect partner for cold meats. Sweet pickles have a delicate balance of flavours and lovely colours. They taste sharp but not at all sour, which is why I like them.

● Sweet pickles don't need to be sealed airtight. I put my sweet pickles in attractive jars and set them directly on the table to spoon on to a plate of cold meats such as ham, beef or chicken. Most recipes are made with fruit although my own favourite is made with cucumber. I find sweet pickles keep right through to the next season when I make a fresh batch.

● Spices are important in sweet pickles so don't leave any out. A health food store is always a good source and a big supermarket is pretty reliable. Stick cinnamon is used a lot as is dried root ginger (which needs to be cracked, or bruised, with a rolling pin) and turmeric which keeps cucumber pickle a beautiful green – surprising because it's actually bright yellow. I always keep allspice, cloves and mustard seed in my larder.

● The preparation is simple: fruits or vegetables are simmered in spiced vinegar and sugar until tender. Then they are transferred to jars. The vinegar syrup is boiled to concentrate the consistency and flavour before it is poured over the fruits. A concentrated syrup will draw natural juices from the fruits and achieve the right balance of flavour during storage. During the first few weeks you may see a separation of heavy syrup at the base and thinner liquid at the top – just give the jar an occasional shake to evenly redistribute the syrup. Sweet pickles are best left for a month or two before using.

Sweet pickled apricots

Makes 4 lb (1.8kg)

4 lb (1.8kg) fresh ripe apricots
2 lb (900g) granulated sugar
1 pint (600ml) distilled white vinegar
2 teaspoons whole cloves
2 teaspoons whole allspice
3 × 1 inch (2.5cm) pieces stick cinnamon

illustrated facing page 96

Remove the stalks from the apricots. Cut in half following the line of the fruit, twist to separate and remove stones. Put the sugar and vinegar into a preserving pan and stir over low heat until the sugar has dissolved. Add the cloves and allspice to the pan along with the cinnamon and prepared apricots.

Simmer gently for 10–20 minutes until fruit is tender. Draw off the heat and, using a perforated spoon, transfer apricots and spices to storage jars. Return the pan of syrup to the heat and boil rapidly for 10 minutes to reduce the liquid and concentrate the flavour. Pour syrup over the fruit – there should be sufficient to cover. Cover tightly when cold.

Sweet pickled prunes

Makes 8 oz (225g)

8 oz (225g) prunes
½ pint (300ml) malt vinegar
¼ pint (150ml) water
8 oz (225g) soft light brown sugar
2 inch (5cm) piece stick cinnamon

Put the prunes into a mixing bowl and add the vinegar, water, brown sugar and stick cinnamon. Cover with a cloth and leave to stand overnight when the prunes will soften and the sugar will dissolve in the liquid.

Put the contents of the bowl into a saucepan. Simmer gently for 10 minutes until prunes are tender. Draw off the heat and, using a perforated spoon, transfer prunes to a plate, allow to cool slightly, then remove the stones. Put prunes into a storage jar. Return the pan of syrup to the heat and bring just to the boil. Pour syrup over the prunes – there should be sufficient to cover. Cover tightly when cold. These are invaluable to have in the larder but they can be used straight away. Use them to garnish pizza, open sandwiches or meat terrines.

Sweet cucumber pickle

Thinly slice the cucumbers. Peel and thinly slice the onions. Arrange in alternating layers in a mixing bowl, sprinkling salt between each layer. Cover with a weighted plate and leave to stand for 3 hours. After this time the cucumber and onion will be swimming in liquid. Pour away the salty liquid and thoroughly rinse and drain the vegetables.

Put the vinegar, sugar and spices into a saucepan. (Despite its colour, the turmeric will turn this pickle a bright green; without it the pickle would be a dull grey colour.) Stir over low heat until the sugar has dissolved. Add the cucumber and onion. Bring to the boil and boil for 1 minute only – so vegetables remain crisp – and draw off the heat. Using a perforated spoon, transfer cucumbers, onion and mustard seed to storage jars.

Return the pan of syrup to the heat and boil rapidly for 10 minutes to reduce the liquid and concentrate the flavour. Pour syrup over the vegetables – there should be sufficient to cover. Cover tightly when cold. This pickle is especially nice with cheese and biscuits or a raised pork pie.

Makes 4 lb (1.8kg)

3 large cucumbers
2 large onions
2 oz (50g) salt
1 pint (600ml) cider vinegar or
    distilled white vinegar
1 lb (450g) granulated sugar
½ level teaspoon ground turmeric
¼ level teaspoon ground cloves
1 tablespoon mustard seed

illustrated facing page 96

Marrow in ginger syrup

Marrow is very watery so it has to be brined; it also overcooks easily. Peel the marrow, cut in half lengthways and scoop out the seeds, then cut in bite-sized pieces. Put into a mixing bowl layered with the salt. Leave to stand for 24 hours, then thoroughly rinse. Blanch in a saucepan of boiling water for 2–3 minutes. Drain at once and return to the rinsed mixing bowl.

Put the sugar and vinegar into a saucepan. Bruise the ginger and tie in a muslin bag. Add to the pan along with the pared lemon rind. Slowly bring to the boil, stirring to dissolve the sugar. Pour syrup over the marrow, cover with a plate and leave to stand for 24 hours.

Put marrow with syrup into a saucepan and simmer for 5 minutes until marrow is translucent. Using a perforated spoon, transfer marrow to storage jars, discarding the muslin bag and lemon rind.

Return the pan of syrup to the heat and boil rapidly for 10 minutes to reduce the liquid and concentrate the flavour. Pour syrup over the fruit – there should be sufficient to cover. Cover jars tightly when cold.

Makes 4 lb (1.8kg)

2 lb (900g) marrow (weight after
    preparation)
2 oz (50g) coarse salt
1 lb (450g) granulated sugar
½ pint (300ml) distilled white
    vinegar
1 oz (25g) dried root ginger
thinly pared rind of 1 lemon

Pickled oranges

Makes 2 lb (900g)

6 medium-sized oranges
½ pint (300ml) distilled white
 vinegar
1 lb (450g) granulated sugar
8 whole cloves
1 teaspoon whole allspice

illustrated facing page 96

Cut the oranges in ¼ inch (5mm) slices or cut them in wedges. Discard any pips. Put into a saucepan and pour over cold water to cover. Bring to the boil, then lower the heat and simmer gently for 1 hour, or until tender. Test the peel by squeezing a piece between the fingers – it should be quite soft. Using a perforated spoon transfer oranges to a mixing bowl.

Put the vinegar, sugar and spices into a saucepan and stir over low heat until the sugar has dissolved. Bring to the boil and add the orange slices, then lower the heat and simmer gently for 30 minutes until slices appear glazed. Draw off the heat and, using a perforated spoon, transfer oranges and spices to storage jars.

Return the pan of syrup to the heat and boil rapidly for 10 minutes to reduce the liquid and concentrate the flavour. Pour syrup over the fruit – there should be sufficient to cover. Cover tightly when cold.

Spiced pears

Makes 4 lb (1.8kg)

4 lb (1.8kg) pears
1 piece dried root ginger
2 teaspoons whole cloves
2 teaspoons whole allspice
2 × 1 inch (2.5cm) pieces stick
 cinnamon
2 lb (900g) granulated sugar
1 pint (600ml) malt vinegar
2–3 pieces thinly pared lemon rind

Conference pears should be used for this recipe. Peel and halve the pears, then scoop out cores with a teaspoon. As you prepare the fruit, place in a bowl of cold water with a little lemon juice or salt added to prevent discoloration. Bruise the ginger, crush the cloves and allspice and tie them in a muslin bag along with the stick cinnamon.

Put the muslin bag, sugar and vinegar into a large saucepan and stir over low heat until the sugar has dissolved. Add the pears and thinly pared lemon rind. Simmer gently for 15–20 minutes until tender. Draw off the heat and discard muslin bag. Using a perforated spoon, transfer pears to storage jars.

Return the pan of syrup to the heat and boil rapidly for 10 minutes, to reduce the liquid and concentrate the flavour. Pour syrup over the fruit – there should be sufficient to cover. Cover tightly when cold.

Cranberry and orange relish

Serves 6

8 oz (225g) cranberries
1 small orange
8 oz (225g) castor sugar

Pick over the cranberries and discard soft berries and the stalks. Cut up the unpeeled orange and discard pips. Pass cranberries and orange pieces through the coarse blade of a mincer or chop in a food processor.

Transfer cranberries and orange to a mixing bowl and stir in the sugar. Leave to stand for at least 30 minutes so sugar dissolves in the fruit juices. This uncooked relish has a marvellous fresh flavour. Serve it with hot or cold roast turkey or ham.

Mincemeat

Peel, core and coarsely chop the apples – do not use juicy cooking apples as they may cause mincemeat to ferment.

Pass the apples, raisins, sultanas and candied peel through a mincer into a mixing bowl. Or chop ingredients in a food processor. Add the currants, brown sugar, mixed spice, ginger, nutmeg, shredded beef suet and finely grated rind and juice of the lemons. Mix together thoroughly with a wooden spoon. Cover and leave to stand overnight.

Stir the mincemeat, then pack into clean, dry jars. Cover with a waxed-paper disc and a good moistureproof cover – screw caps or preserving skin (Porosan). In the old days a greaseproof paper cover painted with beaten egg white was used. Store in a cool place for at least 6 weeks. Stir before using as juice tends to settle at the bottom of jars.

Variation: Add 2 tablespoons brandy, or stir in a little brandy at the time of using it.

Makes 6 lb (2.7kg)

1 lb (450g) dessert apples (weight after preparation)
8 oz (225g) seedless raisins
8 oz (225g) sultanas
4 oz (100g) candied peel
1 lb (450g) currants
1 lb (450g) soft light brown sugar
1 level teaspoon mixed spice
½ level teaspoon ground ginger
¼ level teaspoon ground nutmeg
12 oz (350g) shredded beef suet
finely grated rind and juice of 2 lemons

Lemon curd

Put the sugar and finely grated lemon rind into a mixing bowl and using a wooden spoon, crush together so that sugar takes on the flavouring oils from the lemon. Add the butter and lemon juice. Set over a saucepan one quarter filled with simmering water until the butter has melted and the sugar has dissolved.

Break up the eggs with a fork and strain into the bowl. Cook gently, stirring frequently, until thick and creamy. This will take 20–25 minutes if yolks only are used or 10–15 minutes if whole eggs are used. Pour at once into small jars and seal while hot. Home-made lemon curd tastes better than anything you can buy, but make it in small quantities because it's not something that keeps well.

Variation: Make a luscious lemon filling for sponges by folding 4 tablespoons lemon curd into ¼ pint (150ml) lightly whipped double cream – especially suitable for jam and cream sponge (page 243).

Makes 1½ lb (700g)

8 oz (225g) castor sugar
finely grated rind and juice of 3 lemons
4 oz (100g) butter
4 egg yolks or 3 whole eggs

Bottling fruits

Bottling is a method of preserving best used for fruits only. You can bottle any fruit but it makes sense to choose fruits like pears, plums and peaches, which do not freeze successfully. Bottling works on the basis that the fruit is sterilized then hermetically sealed. Bottled fruit keeps indefinitely and is ready to serve or use in pies and puddings, just like canned fruit, only bottles look prettier on the larder shelf.

The only initial expense is the jars, but if you take care of them (see they don't get chipped or cracked) they will serve you well over and over again. I use the traditional Kilner jars with a lacquered metal lid (washer is attached) and a plastic screw band to secure the lid during sterilization. Proper preserving jars have nice wide necks that make it easy to pack in the fruit. For family servings the medium-sized 1 lb (500ml) jars are the most useful.

For bottling you need good quality sound fruit which you prepare according to type, just as if you were going to poach or stew it. Fruits that discolour or turn brown are best dropped into water with a little lemon juice added as they are prepared. You will find that fruits keep the best colour and flavour if they are bottled in a sugar syrup. Make this by dissolving 8 oz (225g) sugar in every 1 pint (600ml) water and boiling the

Time in a 300°F (150°C) or Gas no. 2 oven for not more than		
Preparation of fruit	*4 × 1 lb (500ml) jars.*	
Apples: cut in slices and pack quickly. Bottle apple slices in layers with blackberries, if liked.	30–40 minutes	
Apricots: Cut fruit in half following the line of the fruit, then twist halves to separate. Remove kernels from stones and crack a few to add to the fruit. Pack fruit quickly to prevent discoloration.	50 minutes	
Blackberries: Pick over and discard any hard or underripe fruit. Remove hulls and carefully examine fruit for grubs.	30 minutes	
Blackcurrants: Blackcurrants bottle better than redcurrants which lose their colour. Strip berries from stems with a fork, and use only ripe blackcurrants.	40 minutes	
Cherries: Bottle cherries that are firm but ripe. Acid varieties give best results. Remove stalks but leave stones in for best flavour.	50 minutes	
Damsons: Leave fruit whole. Remove stalks and wipe off any bloom from the skin as it would make the syrup cloudy. Rinse in cold water.	50 minutes	
Gooseberries: Choose acid green fruit. Pick over and top and tail, slicing off a small piece to allow syrup to penetrate.	35 minutes	
Loganberries: Pick over fruit carefully and gently. Hull and carefully examine for grubs.	30 minutes	
Peaches: Scald in boiling water for 1 minute then plunge in cold water and peel the skins. Halve and remove the stones. Pack quickly to prevent discoloration.	50–60 minutes	
Pears: Use dessert pears only. Peel, halve and then scoop out cores with a teaspoon. Put fruit as prepared in water with lemon juice added to prevent discoloration, and cover with an upturned plate to keep submerged. Drain and pack quickly.	60–70 minutes	
Plums: Bottle Victoria plums when just turning pink. Or use greengages. Halve and remove stones as for apricots and wipe off bloom.	Whole plums 40–50 minutes Halved plums 50–60 minutes	
Rhubarb: Bottle tender pink stalks of early rhubarb. Trim and cut in 1–2 inch (2.5–5cm) lengths. Pour boiling syrup over fruit and leave overnight. Strain and reheat syrup for pouring over packed fruit.	25 minutes	
Raspberries: Handle fruit with care to prevent damage. Do not wash. Hull and carefully examine for grubs.	25 minutes	

syrup for 2 minutes. Have a panful of syrup ready-made before you start preparing the fruit so you can get on with the job quickly once you start. For every 1 lb (500ml) jar you will need to allow a generous ¼ pint (150ml) prepared syrup, but if you don't have quite enough it's easy to make up a little extra at the last minute.

For the home cook, using the oven is the best method; this way you can prepare a few jars in a relatively short space of time. All you need is a sturdy baking tray that fits 4 × 1 lb (500ml) jars – the maximum to process at one time. Line the baking tray with folded newspaper to catch any overflow of syrup. You can process more bottles by preparing the next batch while the previous one is in the oven.

● Heat the oven to 300°F (150°C) or Gas no. 2.

● Rinse the jars in hot water but do not dry them (fruit slips in more easily) and pack the prepared fruit very neatly so you fit in as much as possible.

● Place the jars on the lined baking tray about 2 inches (5cm) apart to allow hot air to circulate. Then slowly pour in the boiling syrup to within 1 inch (2.5cm) of the tops.

● Immediately put on sealing disc (but not screw caps) and place tray of jars in preheated oven.

● When processed, remove jars from the oven one at a time and place on a wooden board or folded newspaper. Immediately close lids, place on screw caps and screw tightly.

● Leave to cool overnight – don't place hot jars on a cold surface as jars may crack – a chopping board is ideal. Then test the seal by unscrewing caps and lifting each jar by the lid. As the contents cool a vacuum forms underneath and should be strong enough to hold it on. When you use the fruit you must prise the lid open and release the vacuum.

Bottled fruit salad

Prepare the syrup first. Put the sugar and water into a saucepan and stir over low heat until the sugar has dissolved. Bring to the boil and boil for 2 minutes, then draw off the heat.

Halve and stone the plums. Halve the grapes. Scald peaches in boiling water for 1 minute. Drain and plunge into cold water. Peel the skins, halve and remove stones. Halve and peel the pears. Scoop out cores with a teaspoon and cut each half in half lengthways. (Keep pears submerged in cold water with lemon added to prevent discoloration.)

Have the jars hot and pack a selection of fruit into each one. Arrange jars about 2 inches (5cm) apart on a baking tray lined with newspaper. Bring syrup back to the boil and fill each jar to within 1 inch (2.5cm) of the tops. Cover jars with lids (but not screw bands). Place in the centre of an oven heated to 300°F (150°C) or Gas no. 2 and leave them for 1½ hours. Remove from oven and hermetically seal jars by screwing on caps tightly. Leave until quite cold then test seal before storing.

Fills 4 × 2 lb (900g) jars

1½–2 lb (700–900g) Victoria
  plums
8 oz (225g) seedless green grapes
6 ripe peaches
4–6 ripe dessert pears

Syrup
1 lb (450g) granulated sugar
2 pints (1.1 litres) water

Preserved peaches

1 lb (450g) granulated sugar
½ pint (300ml) water
12 ripe peaches
½ pint (300ml) brandy

Put the sugar and water into a saucepan and stir over low heat until sugar has dissolved. Bring to the boil, then simmer for 5 minutes. Draw off the heat.

Using a perforated spoon, dip the peaches one at a time into a saucepan of boiling water and leave for 30 seconds. Drain and immediately transfer to a bowl of cold water. Peel, halve and stone the peaches. Prick peaches deeply all over with a fine skewer. Add to the pan of hot sugar syrup and bring to the boil, then lower the heat and simmer gently for 5 minutes.

Carefully lift out peaches with a perforated spoon and pack them into a large earthenware crock or glass jar. Pour over the syrup, filling to a little over half full. Top up with the brandy to cover the peaches completely. Cover tightly and store in a cool place. Peaches may rise in jars at first but as they become saturated with syrup they will sink again at which time they are ready for serving. They make a delicious dessert served with cream and will keep for up to 6 months.

Tutti-frutti

Fresh summer fruits when they come into season can be preserved with sugar and brandy. After a month the various fruit flavours will have combined with the sugar and brandy to form a delicious fruit syrup that can be used to soak trifle sponges or served over ice cream. The syrup is also nice served as an after-dinner liqueur with coffee – it is not at all too sweet. Use it to flavour a glass of chilled white wine in the same way you would use cassis.

In the middle of summer I gather fresh strawberries and place them in layers with an equal weight of sugar in an earthenware crock. (You can also use one of those really big knob-stoppered glass jars.) Then I pour over brandy to completely immerse the fruit. As the season progresses, I add stoned dark cherries with a few of the cracked kernels added to give a subtle almond flavour. Finally, I add raspberries.

The only rule to remember is that you use exactly as much sugar as fruit and pour over brandy to cover each time. Without it the fruit would ferment. Give a good stir each time more fruit and sugar is added and keep the jar covered and in a cool place. A piece of cling film placed over the top as well as the lid is a good idea. Store for at least 1 month before using. I have a jar of strawberries flavoured with rum in my larder that I've had for 2 years. The syrup is a deep burgundy and the mellow flavour is exquisite.

13

Confectionery

Sweetmaking requires accuracy and patience as
well as a flair for presentation. It can be very
rewarding to serve your own sweets and you can
make lovely gifts for friends.

Confectionery

How to make better sweets

● Before you start have tins, cutters and colourings required ready. Measure your ingredients accurately.

● Dissolve the sugar in the water before bringing to the boil – the syrup should look quite clear. Get rid of any stray sugar crystals by washing down the inside of the saucepan with a pastry brush that has been dipped in cold water.

● Use a small pan for making a sugar syrup – you have more control. Use a large pan for fudges with other ingredients added, particularly milk, as syrup froths up and may boil over.

● Boil sugar syrups to the right temperature or stage without stirring – exceptions are when recipes contain milk or cream, both of which are liable to catch.

● A sugar boiling thermometer will give you the most accurate results; one with a clip will fasten to the saucepan side. Make sure the bulb is immersed in the boiling syrup.

● Fudges are stirred after cooking to encourage a smooth texture. This is called graining; allow mixture to cool to 110°F (45°C), then stir with a wooden spoon. When ready the mixture thickens, begins to sound gritty in the pan and loses its shine. Pour at once into moulds or tin before it sets in the pan.

● Grease tins or moulds with butter and make sure you use metal tins or trays because they stand up to the heat of boiled syrup or fudge mixtures. Use mild flavoured vegetable or corn oil for greasing surfaces of plates or trays for recipes such as praline, sugared walnuts and glacé grapes.

Sugar boiling and temperatures

Many recipes in this section are made using a boiled sugar syrup. The sugar is first dissolved in water over low heat until clear. It is very important to start with a clear syrup and the sugar completely dissolved. The syrup is then brought to the boil. The temperature required depends on the type of sweet being made. A sugar boiling thermometer removes the guesswork.

When taking a temperature reading make sure that the bulb of the thermometer is immersed in the hot syrup. Read the temperature at eye level. You'll have to bend down to look. As soon as the temperature is reached draw the pan off the heat and cool the bottom of the pan in cold water for a few seconds to stop the heat of the pan sending the sugar syrup up another degree.

Temperature	Stage
212°F (100°C)	Temperature of boiling water. Keep the sugar thermometer ready for use in a pan of boiling water. Check the reading on the thermometer for accuracy.
230°F (110°C)	*Thread:* test by dipping a cold fork in the hot syrup; when a drop falls from the prong a fine thread will form.
240–245°F (116–118°C)	*Soft ball:* when a little syrup dropped into a saucer of cold water can be gathered into a soft ball that flattens when rolled between the fingers.
250°F (120°C)	*Hard ball:* when a little syrup dropped into a saucer of cold water can be gathered into a hard ball that holds its shape when rolled between the fingers.
300°F (150°C)	*Crack:* when a little cold syrup dropped into a saucer of cold water immediately hardens and snaps easily. The colour of the syrup at this stage is a pale straw, showing that it is beginning to caramelize.
310°F (155°C)	*Caramel:* the syrup turns brown in colour.

Fresh cream fudge

Makes 1¼ lb (550g)

1 lb (450g) granulated sugar
¼ pint (150ml) water
2 oz (50g) or 1 rounded tablespoon
   golden syrup
¼ pint (150ml) double cream
½ oz (15g) butter
1 teaspoon vanilla essence

Butter a 7 inch (17.5cm) shallow square baking tin. Put the sugar and water into a large saucepan and stir over low heat until the sugar has dissolved, then add the golden syrup. Bring to the boil and boil, without stirring, until the temperature on a sugar thermometer reaches 230°F (110°C). Add half the cream and boil, stirring occasionally, until temperature reaches 238°F (115°C). Then add remaining cream and boil until temperature reaches 240°F (116°C), stirring occasionally to prevent mixture from sticking to the pan. Draw off the heat, add the butter in pieces and the vanilla essence.

Allow mixture to cool to 110°F (45°C), then stir with a wooden spoon until the mixture begins to grain. Then quickly pour into the prepared tin. When surface has set, mark fudge in squares. Leave until completely cool, then turn out and break in squares.

Variations **Chocolate cream fudge:** Add 2 oz (50g) broken plain chocolate and only ½ teaspoon vanilla essence along with the butter.

Coffee cream fudge: Add 2 teaspoons coffee essence and 1 oz (25g) chopped walnuts along with the butter. Omit the vanilla essence.

Almond and raisin cream fudge: Add ½ teaspoon almond essence, ½ oz (15g) chopped blanched almonds and 1 oz (25g) seedless raisins along with the butter. Omit the vanilla essence.

Glacé grapes

Wash the grapes and pat dry in absorbent paper. Then snip grapes off the bunch in pairs, leaving a short stalk attached to them. Set fruits on absorbent paper to make sure they are absolutely dry.

Put the sugar and water into a saucepan and stir over low heat until sugar has dissolved. Add the golden syrup and bring to the boil. Boil rapidly without stirring until sugar boiling thermometer shows a reading of 300°F (150°C) or crack stage. Draw the pan off the heat and allow bubbles to subside.

Work quickly and, using a fork, dip the pairs of grapes into the syrup to coat them completely. Drain for a moment over the pan and then place on an oiled baking tray or plate. Set the first grapes dipped at the end of the tray furthest from you to avoid dripping syrup over dipped fruits as you add more to the tray. Leave until cold and set hard. Then place in paper petits fours cases for serving. These do not keep and are best eaten on the day of making.

Makes about 1 lb (450g)

1 lb (450g) black or green grapes
1 lb (450g) granulated sugar
¼ pint (150ml) water
2 oz (50g) or 1 rounded
   tablespoon golden syrup

Coconut ice

Butter a 7 inch (17.5cm) shallow square baking tin. Put the sugar and water into a saucepan and stir over low heat until the sugar has dissolved. Bring to the boil and boil rapidly, without stirring, until the temperature on a sugar thermometer reaches 240°F (116°C), or soft ball stage. Draw off the heat and allow the bubbles to subside.

Add the vanilla essence, coconut and cream and stir gently until the mixture thickens and is a little cloudy. Pour half the mixture into the prepared tin and spread level. Quickly colour the remaining mixture pink with the food colouring. Pour mixture over the mixture in the tin and spread level. Leave until completely cool and set firm. Then turn out and cut the coconut ice in squares.

Makes 1½ lb (700g)

1 lb (450g) granulated sugar
¼ pint (150ml) water
1 teaspoon vanilla essence
3 oz (75g) desiccated coconut
1 tablespoon single cream
few drops of pink food colouring

illustrated facing page 320

Pink marshmallows

Makes 24

6 tablespoons cold water
2 level tablespoons powdered
   gelatine
1 lb (450g) granulated sugar
½ pint (300ml) water
1 teaspoon golden syrup
1 teaspoon raspberry or strawberry
   essence
few drops of red food colouring
2 egg whites
pinch of salt

For dusting
2 oz (50g) icing sugar
1 oz (25g) cornflour

Butter an 11 × 7 inch (27.5 × 17.5cm) baking tin. Put the water into a small bowl, sprinkle in the gelatine and leave to soak. Put the sugar and water into a saucepan and stir over low heat until the sugar has dissolved, then add the golden syrup. Bring to the boil and boil, without stirring, until the temperature on a sugar thermometer reaches 240°F (116°C), or soft ball stage. Draw off the heat and allow bubbles to subside.

Add the soaked gelatine and stir until dissolved. (The heat of the pan will be sufficient.) Pour the hot syrup into a mixing bowl and leave until warm to the touch. Using a rotary beater or electric whisk, beat the sugar syrup until very light and thick. Whisk in the essence and food colouring. Whisk the egg whites with the salt until stiff peaks form and gently fold them into the mixture using a metal spoon. Pour the mixture into the prepared tin to a depth of about 1 inch (2.5cm). Leave overnight to set.

Sift the icing sugar and cornflour on to a sheet of greaseproof paper and dust a little over the top of the marshmallow mixture. Loosen one corner of the mixture and pull the sheet of marshmallow out on to the bed of sugar. Using a sharp knife, cut in 1 inch (2.5cm) squares. Roll marshmallows in the dusting sugar as they are cut. Store in an airtight tin.

Fruit jellies

Makes 1¼ lb (550g)

1 lb (450g) granulated sugar
¼ pint (150ml) water
¼ level teaspoon cream of tartar
7 tablespoons water
2 level tablespoons powdered
   gelatine
½ level teaspoon citric acid
1 teaspoon raspberry, lemon or
   orange essence
few drops of food colouring
castor sugar, for dusting

Butter a 7 inch (17.5cm) shallow square baking tin. Put the granulated sugar and ¼ pint (150ml) water into a saucepan and stir over low heat until sugar has dissolved. Dissolve the cream of tartar in 1 tablespoon of water and add to the pan. Bring to the boil and boil, without stirring, until the temperature on a sugar thermometer reaches 240°F (116°C), or soft ball stage.

Meanwhile, put 5 tablespoons of cold water into a small bowl, sprinkle in the gelatine and leave to soak for 5 minutes. Draw the pan of syrup off the heat and allow bubbles to subside. Add the soaked gelatine and stir until dissolved. (The heat of the pan will be sufficient.) Dissolve the citric acid in 1 tablespoon of water and add to the syrup along with the essence and a few drops of food colouring. Choose a colour that corresponds with the fruit-flavoured essence.

Pour at once into the prepared tin. Leave overnight until set firm. Spread a layer of castor sugar over a sheet of greaseproof paper. Loosen one corner of the jelly mixture and pull out of the tin, turning it over on to the sugar base. Cut in 1 inch (2.5cm) squares. Immediately dip cut edges in castor sugar to prevent them from sticking. Store in an airtight tin.

Candied orange sticks

Make sure you remove the orange peel in neat pieces so it can be cut in strips. Do this by first cutting a small slice from the top of each orange, then mark the peel in quarters with a sharp knife. Soak the peel overnight in salted cold water, then drain. Put the peel into a saucepan and pour over cold water to cover. Slowly bring to the boil, then drain. Repeat boiling and draining to remove all the salt. Then return to the rinsed pan, pour over fresh cold water to cover, and simmer for 20 minutes until tender. Drain and cut peel in thin strips with scissors.

Put the sugar and water into a saucepan and stir over low heat until sugar has dissolved, then add the orange strips. Bring to boil, cover with a lid, then simmer gently for 20–30 minutes until peel is glazed. Drain well. Toss orange sticks in granulated sugar and separate the pieces with a fork. Spread in a single layer on waxed paper and leave to dry overnight in a warm place. Store in an airtight tin.

Variations: You can prepare this with leftover peel from grapefruits. It makes a charming sweetmeat. Or, chop it and use as an edible decoration for cakes and desserts.

Makes 1 lb (450g)

peel of 3 large oranges
8 oz (225g) granulated sugar
4 tablespoons water
extra granulated sugar, for coating

Brandy balls

Break the chocolate in a medium-sized mixing bowl and add the unsalted butter. Set the bowl over a saucepan one quarter filled with hot (not boiling) water and heat, stirring occasionally, until chocolate and butter are melted and blended. Draw off the heat and stir in the egg yolk.

Sift the icing sugar into a mixing bowl. Crush the sponge fingers in a polythene bag with a rolling pin and add to the sugar. Stir in the walnuts. (These must be very finely chopped and are best grated in a Mouli grater.) Add the dry ingredients to the melted chocolate along with the brandy and stir with a wooden spoon to blend thoroughly. Chill for 15 minutes until firm. Sift icing sugar for dusting on to a square of greaseproof paper.

Scoop out teaspoons of the brandy ball mixture and roll into balls the size of a walnut – divide the mixture first, then roll. As each one is shaped, roll in sifted icing sugar to coat. Chill until firm. The flavour improves considerably if they are allowed to mature for 48 hours in a covered tin. Store in the refrigerator. A pretty jar filled with brandy balls makes a lovely gift.

Variations: Use rum in place of the brandy, or use bourbon, which will make these sweets especially delicious. Roll the brandy balls in finely chopped walnuts or in cocoa powder mixed with a little icing sugar.

Makes 36

4 oz (100g) plain chocolate
2 oz (50g) unsalted butter
1 egg yolk
4 oz (100g) icing sugar
16 sponge fingers
4 oz (100g) finely chopped walnuts
3 tablespoons brandy
icing sugar, for dusting

illustrated facing page 320

Chocolate truffles

Makes 24

6 oz (175g) icing sugar
1 oz (25g) cocoa powder
1 level tablespoon golden syrup
1 tablespoon milk
1 tablespoon rum
1½ oz (40g) butter

For dusting
2 level tablespoons cocoa powder
1 level tablespoon icing sugar

Sift the icing sugar and cocoa powder for the truffles into a mixing bowl. Put the golden syrup (measure with a tablespoon dipped in boiling water so excess syrup runs off and you get an accurate measure), milk, rum and butter into a saucepan and stir over low heat until blended, then bring to the boil and pour at once into the sifted mixture. Beat with a wooden spoon until soft and smooth. Leave until completely cool, then beat again until fudgy. Chill until firm.

Sift together the cocoa powder and icing sugar for dusting on to a square of greaseproof paper. Scoop out rounded teaspoons of the truffle mixture and roll into balls. The easiest way to do this is to scoop out the right number and place on a chilled baking sheet. They can then be rolled quickly and lightly. Drop truffles as they are shaped on to the sweetened cocoa powder and shake the paper to coat them all over. Carefully place in petits fours cases. Store in the refrigerator.

Variation **Coffee-flavoured truffles:** Use 2 tablespoons milk and replace the rum with 2 level tablespoons instant coffee powder.

Marzipan strawberries

Makes 36

6 oz (175g) icing sugar
6 oz (175g) ground almonds
6 oz (175g) castor sugar
1 egg
½ teaspoon almond essence
few drops of green, red and yellow
   food colouring

For dusting
icing sugar
castor sugar

For modelling marzipan fruits a cooked marzipan is used because it is easier to handle and less likely to go oily. Sift the icing sugar on to a plate and add the ground almonds. Put the castor sugar and egg into a mixing bowl and set over a saucepan one quarter filled with hot (not boiling) water. Whisk until pale in colour and warm to the touch. Draw off the heat. Add the almond essence and ground almond mixture and mix to a smooth paste with a wooden spoon.

Turn mixture on to a work surface dusted with icing sugar. Add green food colouring to one quarter of the mixture and colour the remaining paste with red and yellow food colouring to make a deep strawberry shade. Knead the mixtures separately until smooth and evenly coloured. Wrap in waxed paper or cling film and leave to stand for 1 hour.

Roll the strawberry-coloured marzipan into a sausage shape and cut in 36 slices. Roll each slice into balls, tapering one end to make a strawberry shape. Roll out the green marzipan thinly and, using a star-shaped aspic cutter, cut 36 shapes. Using a matchstick, push a tiny star into the top of each strawberry, then roll each strawberry in castor sugar. Place in petits fours cases.

Illustrated: Selection of home-made sweets – coconut ice, brandy balls and marzipan strawberries, see above, and pages 317 and 319

Crystallized flowers and petals

Gum tragacanth is a powder available from chemists' and the rosewater is too, although the latter should be easily found in large food stores. You will also need tweezers to hold the flowers or leaves and a darning needle to separate the petals from flower heads. Put the gum tragacanth in a small screw-topped jar and add the rosewater. Cover and leave for 6–8 hours in a warm place for the powder to dissolve. Give the jar an occasional shake.

Snip stems of flowers to about 1 inch (2.5cm) long; separate rose petals (small ones are best) or divide mint leaves leaving on a short stem for holding. Using a paint brush, brush each flower head, petal or leaf on both sides with the solution of gum tragacanth. Dip flower heads in castor sugar or sprinkle petals or leaves on both sides with sugar. Use the darning needle to carefully separate petals on the flower head if they have stuck together. Place on a wire rack (slip flower stems through the gaps) and leave for 24 hours in a warm place to dry. Snip stems on flowers level with heads. These will keep for several months in an airtight tin and can be used to make edible decorations for cakes or desserts.

Variation: This is a more convenient method but items will only keep for about 1 month: lightly mix 1 egg white and 1 teaspoon water with a fork. Use the egg mixture to coat flowers or leaves in the same way as the tragacanth solution. Then dip them in castor sugar and leave to dry.

¼ level teaspoon gum tragacanth
2 tablespoons triple distilled
    rosewater
1 small bunch primroses, wild
    violets, rose petals or mint leaves
castor sugar, for sprinkling

Orange and lemon flavoured sugars can be used in place of ordinary sugar to give a zesty fruit flavour to dishes. Grate the rind of 1 orange or lemon on the finest possible grater and mix with castor sugar, allowing 4 oz (100g) sugar per 1 orange or lemon. Using a wooden spoon, work the sugar and rind together. The sugar will take on the colour of the fruit and absorb flavouring oils. Spread the sugar out on a square of greaseproof paper or kitchen foil and set in a warm place to dry. Crush any lumps and store in a covered jar.

● Use flavoured sugar instead of ordinary castor sugar when making sandwich cakes.

● Use lemon sugar in apple pie and orange sugar to sweeten any dessert recipe using rhubarb.

● Either is nice sprinkled over pancakes.

● Make sugared rims on individual serving glasses to add a lovely touch to serving ice creams or sorbets, especially lemon or orange sorbets.

Sugared fruits make a pretty buffet table centrepiece especially when they are combined with citrus fruits and walnuts in their shells. Small bunches of sugared grapes look pretty as a garnish on cold ham and tiny clusters of redcurrants are lovely on desserts.

All you will need is an egg white and castor sugar for coating plus fruits that have been washed, dried and polished with a cloth. The egg white should only be broken up with a fork until runny – not beaten which would add volume to it. Sprinkle a bed of castor sugar over a sheet of greaseproof paper. Brush the fruit with the egg white – I use a small paint brush. It's best not to paint the entire surface of apples and pears: a streaked effect running from stalk downwards is more attractive. Roll the fruit in the bed of sugar to give a pretty frosted look. The sugary coating will quickly dry.

Sugared grapes: Have grapes in small clusters of 2 or 3. Dab the top of each grape with egg white, then roll the fruit in the bed of sugar.

Illustrated: Vin chaud, page 334

Peppermint creams

Makes 48

1 lb (450g) icing sugar
½ level teaspoon cream of tartar
1 egg white
few drops of oil of peppermint or 1
    teaspoon peppermint essence
few drops of green food colouring
    (optional)

This is an uncooked fondant. Sift the icing sugar and cream of tartar on to a work surface. In a mixing bowl, break up the egg white with a fork. Gradually beat in about one-third of the sifted sugar with a wooden spoon to make a stiff paste. Add a few drops of oil of peppermint or the peppermint essence and a few drops of food colouring, if using it.

Turn mixture on to the remaining icing sugar. Using the fingertips, gradually knead in as much sugar as is required to make a smooth, pliable fondant. Then roll out fondant about ¼ inch (5mm) thick. Using a small round 1 inch (2.5cm) cutter, cut 48 circles of fondant. Arrange on trays lined with waxed paper and leave to stand overnight to dry. When firm they can be lifted off the paper.

Sugared walnuts

Makes 8 oz (225g)

8 oz (225g) walnut halves
8 oz (225g) granulated sugar
finely grated rind and juice of 1
    orange

Grease a small cake tin or large plate. Spread the walnuts on a baking tray and place in the centre of an oven heated to 350°F (180°C) or Gas no. 4 for about 5 minutes until walnuts become crisp and hot.

Meanwhile, put the sugar into a medium-sized saucepan. Make up the orange juice to ¼ pint (150ml) with water. Add to the pan and stir over low heat until sugar has dissolved. Bring to the boil and boil, without stirring, until the temperature on a sugar thermometer reaches 240°F (116°C), or soft ball stage. Draw off the heat and allow bubbles to subside.

Add the grated orange rind and hot walnuts. Stir with a wooden spoon until thick and creamy. Quickly turn on to the prepared tin or plate and separate nuts with a fork. Leave until completely cool. Store in an airtight tin.

Variation: Use chopped walnuts and separate mixture into clusters using two forks.

Praline

Makes 8 oz (225g)

4 oz (100g) granulated sugar
4 oz (100g) almonds in skins

Put the sugar and almonds into a heavy-based saucepan or frying pan and cook over moderate heat, stirring all the time, until the mixture is golden brown and the nuts are glazed. Quickly pour mixture on to an oiled baking tray and leave until completely cool and hard. Then break in pieces and finely crush the praline with a rolling pin.

Praline will keep for 6 months stored in an airtight tin or screw-topped jar. It adds a most delicious flavour to mousses or ice creams. Sprinkle praline over trifle, custard puddings or dessert cakes.

14

Special Occasions

A few good ideas on what to serve plus a little time spent on advance planning will turn your entertaining into relaxing occasions that will allow you to spend time with your guests.

Special Occasions

Planning a better menu

● A good menu has the right balance, not too many rich foods or too many bland foods. Dishes should include contrasts of colour, flavour and texture.

● Plan a party menu based on dishes you know – the ones you cook well are the ones to choose.

● Consider dishes in relation to each other so you avoid a sequence of rich sauces, or worse still, cream in every course.

● Balance heavier courses with others of a lighter nature so that the menu as a whole is not too filling.

● Make use of seasonal foods, then your menus will vary with the time of the year.

● Work out what you can cook beforehand. It's suprising how many dishes actually benefit from being made in advance. At least one, if not two, courses can be made in advance.

● The index of ideas on the following pages is not a list of all the recipes in the book. It is intended to serve as suggestions to prompt your own thoughts and help plan your menus.

● Savoury recipes are very versatile: for instance, some first courses would also make a light main dish; but as a main dish they may not go so far so you might have to increase the quantities.

● When serving numbers that require a recipe to be doubled (a buffet is a good example), bear in mind that, in some cases, it is better to cook a recipe twice, rather than double the ingredients when the volume of mixture can become difficult to handle.

● Never feel obliged to offer an enormous choice of foods; plenty of a few dishes is often more appealing than an overwhelming variety.

● Do try out new recipes – on the family please! A recipe is only new the first time you make it; if it's a success you have another addition to your repertoire and you can extend it to the dinner party table.

First course

I like to keep first courses simple if my main course involves a lot of work. On the other hand, I go for something a little elaborate if I'm serving simple grilled or roast dishes. Many first courses can be prepared in advance.

● Don't hesitate to buy in a first course if that helps. Smoked fish is always a good choice.

● Any meat or fish pâté will actually taste better after 24 hours. A surface covering of melted butter or cling film will help retain the moisture.

● A savoury mousse will improve in texture with overnight refrigeration. They have lovely colours and there's a variety to choose from.

● Prepare a home-made soup that just needs reheating and if cream is to be added, stir it in just before serving.

● Go for a salad mixture in an oil and vinegar dressing that doesn't include lettuce. You get a lovely blend of flavours if the mixture has time to marinate and there's no risk of lettuce wilting.

Main course

I find it easier to choose the main course first – it's usually a tricky one – then it's not too difficult to add on a first and last course. Sometimes it's re-assuring to go for a dish that will keep hot without spoiling, and by using attractive oven-to-table ware you can avoid last minute dishing up.

● Try a meat dish in a sauce or gravy, such as oriental beef, chicken paprika, or a beef curry. Or try a chicken Provençal, which stays moist and succulent; flavours will develop if made in advance.

● An exotic casserole such as beef in beer, a spicy goulash or a casserole of game makes a good main course. Casseroles can often be made in advance and reheated.

● Moussaka and lasagne can be made in advance and just reheated.

● If you are serving a dish that needs last minute attention (and there's no need to rule out a particular favourite), have everything ready right down to the chopped garnish, then all you have to do is assemble it.

Vegetables

Plain cooked vegetables should be served as soon as they are cooked. But if you like everything to be ready beforehand there are ways to get round it.

● A ragout of vegetables, which requires slow cooking, such as a mixture of aubergines and tomatoes or red cabbage with apple is a good idea.

● Bake or braise vegetables in oven-to-table ware. Try braised celery, stuffed tomatoes, peas cooked in the French style with lettuce and spring onions or scalloped potato slices.

● Cook green vegetables until just tender, then drain and plunge into cold water to arrest cooking and retain colour. Just before serving plunge them into boiling water and bring back to the boil. Toss in hot butter and serve.

● Cook rice 24 hours ahead and refrigerate. To reheat, spread rice in a thin layer in a buttered dish. Add a few flakes of butter, cover with kitchen foil and place in an oven heated to 350°F (180°C) or Gas no. 4 for 20 minutes. Stir with a fork before serving.

● Cook noodles or spaghetti ahead, drain and plunge into cold water. Just before serving, plunge into boiling water for 1 minute. Then drain and toss with a lump of butter.

Desserts

Very filling or rich meats need only a simple dessert. But luxurious desserts can be an impressive finish to a meal and many benefit by being made in advance; some only need last minute assembling.

● Any fruit compote or cooked fruit mixture will taste better after 24 hours. No need to refrigerate.

● A dessert cake soaked in a flavoured syrup becomes moister and more delectable the longer it stands. Make it in advance and leave overnight in the refrigerator.

● Meringue layers can be baked days ahead and kept in an airtight tin. Fill with whipped cream and fruit about 2 hours before serving.

● Make a spectacular ice cream and transfer from freezer to refrigerator just before the meal.

Timing

If you calculate the timing of each dish, you'll know just when to start each dish in relation to the others, and you'll finish with everything ready together. Note down timing beside the recipe.

● A cooked main dish that is cold from the refrigerator will take 20–30 minutes longer to heat up than one at room temperature. Take it out at least 1 hour beforehand and you'll find it easier to judge the reheating time.

● Reheating times required will depend on the size of the dish and the number of dishes. Several dishes absorb a lot of oven heat and time required will be about half as much again. Deep dishes take longer to heat through than shallow ones.

● Starting from room temperature, an average-sized casserole will take 40 minutes to become bubbling hot. More closely packed dishes like lasagne take 1–1½ hours. Best oven temperature for reheating is 350°F (180°C) or Gas no. 4.

● Cover meat dishes that are to be kept hot with a lid or kitchen foil to reduce drying out. Best oven temperature for keeping foods hot is 250°F (120°C) or Gas no. ½.

● A double boiler is useful for keeping food hot, but if you have more than one pan to keep hot, pour boiling water into a large shallow roasting tin and arrange pans of food in the tin.

● Salads and cold puddings should be taken from the refrigerator about 30 minutes before serving; cheeses must be allowed to stand at room temperature for at least 1 hour.

● Don't get caught out with cold serving plates for hot food. If there's no space left to warm them, pop the whole lot into a washing up bowl of piping hot clean water; it takes only a moment to dry them again.

Presentation

The look of the meal counts as much as the taste. You owe it to yourself to present food looking fresh and inviting.

● Keep the garnish on dishes to a minimum; many dishes don't need any at all if there are pretty accompaniments.

● Cold roast meats sliced wafer thin will look more appetizing if rolled, folded or curled in cones. Include a selection of delicatessen meats for a variety of textures and colours.

● Mix vegetables after cooking but before serving. Diced carrots with peas, Brussels sprouts with small onions, and peas with sliced mushrooms are pretty combinations that taste delicious too.

● Lemon wedges with the thin length of the wedge dipped in chopped parsley or slices of lemon sprinkled with chopped parsley are a nice garnish for fish.

● Arrange clusters of sugared grapes (page 321) round cold ham or cold roast turkey – they look mouth watering. If you place the clusters on crisp lettuce they stand out more.

● Cut delicate cheesecakes, meringue layers or gateaux into serving portions before taking to the table – it's easy if you know how (page 236).

● Spotless, shining dishes are important. If oven-to-table ware develops any cooking stains, rub them away before taking to the table. Use salt, which acts as an abrasive, and the damp corner of a tea towel.

● Develop your own theme for serving meals. For me, it's white porcelain serving dishes. I have built up a collection of all shapes and sizes and the white allows food colours to show off dramatically.

Cutting a Brie

A clever cutting technique for a whole Brie will transform it into even-sized serving portions. Using a long sharp knife, first divide cheese by cutting a series of concentric circles, then cut in wedge-shaped portions. Separate the pieces a little but leave the cheese in position. This is wonderful to serve at a buffet and ensures that the cheese will remain looking attractive as guests help themselves. Those peppercorn studded Bries are really impressive and this technique works equally well with any similar-shaped cheese. *Illustrated facing page 305.*

Dinner parties

Buffets

Spring buffet

Summer buffet

Autumn buffet

Winter buffet

Extras for barbecue parties

Picnic suggestions

Gift ideas

Party punch

Makes 15 glasses

3 lemons
small piece dried root ginger
2 pints (1.1 litres) water
6 whole cloves
2 inch (5cm) piece cinnamon stick
1 oz (25g) China tea
8–12 oz (225–350g) granulated
    sugar
1 × ½ bottle (375ml) rum

Pare the rind from 2 of the lemons using a vegetable peeler and bruise the ginger. Put into a large saucepan along with the water, cloves and cinnamon. Bring to the boil, then stir in the tea and draw off the heat. Cover with a pan lid and allow the flavours to infuse for 5 minutes, then carefully strain into a punch bowl.

Add the sugar and stir until dissolved. Squeeze the juice from the 2 pared lemons, strain into the bowl and add the rum. Slice the remaining lemon and float the slices on top. Serve warm. The tea gives a lovely golden colour to this winter drink. The punch is also good served chilled.

Sangria

Makes 10 glasses

1 lemon
1 orange
1 tablespoon castor sugar
2 tablespoons brandy
1 × 70cl bottle light red wine
½ pint (300ml) soda water

Slice the lemon and orange and put them into a tall jug. Add the sugar and brandy and allow fruit to marinate for about 15 minutes. Add the red wine and chill. Just before serving, stir in the soda water.

Variation: Use lemonade in place of the soda water to make a sweeter flavour. For a party, double the quantities and use a bottle of champagne in place of the soda water.

Bowle

Makes 18–20 glasses

1 lb (450g) ripe strawberries
1–2 tablespoons castor sugar
1 wine glass brandy
2 × 70cl bottles hock or moselle
1 × 70cl bottle sparkling white
    wine or champagne

Hull the strawberries and slice them into a punch bowl. Add the sugar, brandy (which draws out the aroma of the fruits) and 1 bottle of hock or moselle. Leave to marinate for at least 1 hour. Chill the remaining wine thoroughly.

Just before serving, add the remaining wine and the bottle of sparkling wine or champagne. This makes a lovely drink at a summer garden party.

Variation: Use sliced peaches in place of the strawberries, or use half strawberries and half peaches – the wine takes on the flavour of the fruits used.

Fruit cup

Makes 15 glasses

1 pint (600ml) lemonade
1 pint (600ml) undiluted orange or
    lemon squash
1 pint (600ml) dry cider
orange or lemon slices, to garnish

Combine the lemonade, undiluted orange or lemon squash and cider in a tall jug and chill well. Carefully pour into a punch bowl and add slices of fresh orange or lemon.

Variation: Use fruit cup to make refreshing drinks. Pour a measure of vodka, rum or gin over ice in tall glass tumblers, then top up with fruit cup. They will taste and look like some exotic cocktail, particularly if you provide long straws and hook slices of fruit on the rims of the glasses.

Sparkling fruit cup

Squeeze the juice from the lemons and set aside. Put the lemon peel with pith into a mixing bowl along with the sugar. Boil the water and pour it over the lemon peel and sugar. Stir to dissolve the sugar and leave until completely cool.

Strain the mixture into a serving jug, add the reserved lemon juice and the orange juice and chill. Just before serving, stir in chilled ginger ale or ginger beer and garnish with a few orange slices. This is a refreshing drink to serve at a children's party.

Makes 15 glasses

2 lemons
4 oz (100g) castor sugar
1 pint (600ml) water
1 pint (600ml) orange juice
1 pint (600ml) ginger ale or ginger
  beer
orange slices, to garnish

Bitter lemon drink

Squeeze the juice from the lemons and set aside. Put the lemon peel with pith into a large mixing bowl and add the sugar and citric acid. Boil the water and pour it over the lemon peel and sugar. Stir to dissolve the sugar and leave until completely cool.

As the peel softens press it occasionally with a wooden spoon to extract all the flavour. Squeeze and discard the lemon peel. Add the reserved lemon juice and strain the syrup into 2 × 1 litre lemonade bottles. Cover with screw caps and store in a cool place for up to 2 weeks.

To serve: Fill one-third of a glass with syrup, add ice and top up with water or soda water. Hook slices of lemon on the rims of the glasses, if liked. Or place a slice of lemon in each glass, add a few drops of grenadine syrup, then add the bitter lemon syrup and top up with soda water.

Makes 24 glasses

2 lemons
1½ lb (700g) castor sugar
1 oz (25g) citric acid
2 pints (1.1 litres) water
lemon slices, to garnish (optional)

Keeping party drinks cool and pretty

Decorative ice cubes: Take a tip and make ice cubes with water that has been boiled and allowed to cool. Boiled water freezes clear while water straight from the tap goes cloudy. Mint leaves, segments of orange or lemon, raspberries, grapes, melon balls or olives can be set in the ice tray before adding the water.

Ice cubes in bulk: When you need a quantity of ice cubes for a drinks party, you can make them ahead if you have a freezer. Turn ice cubes on to a baking tray and space them apart so they do not touch. Place in the freezer long enough for the outside surface to freeze dry – about 15 minutes. Tip into a large freezer bag, tie closed and store in the freezer. Make as many cubes as you need and they'll stay quite free flowing.

Frozen orange and lemon slices: Cut as many slices as you like of fresh lemons or oranges. Arrange flat on a baking tray and open freeze until quite firm. Tip into a freezer bag, tie closed and freeze. Add the frozen slices to drinks – they cool the drinks and add flavour at the same time.

Ice blocks: Remember an ice block will not thaw as quickly as ice cubes in chilled wine or fruit cups and it will float attractively on the surface. Freeze water in a small ring mould – add mint leaves, melon balls, strawberries, raspberries, orange or lemon slices to make ice look pretty. To remove a frozen block from mould wrap a hot wet cloth round outside of upturned mould for a few seconds and ice will slide out. Add to a wine cup just before serving.

Fresh lemonade

Makes 4–6 glasses

3 lemons
4 oz (100g) castor sugar
1½ pints (900ml) water

Thinly pare the lemon rind using a vegetable peeler and squeeze the juice from the lemons. Put lemon rind and sugar into a bowl. Boil the water and pour it over the lemon rind and sugar. Stir to dissolve the sugar and leave until completely cool. The pared rind gives a good colour and fresh flavour. Add the lemon juice and strain the lemonade into a jug. Chill well. Serve in ice-filled tumblers.

Variations **Mint lemonade:** Use old-fashioned garden mint and place bruised mint leaves in the jug before straining in the lemonade. Bruising mint leaves with a wooden spoon and a pinch of sugar helps release flavouring oils. Garnish with sprigs of mint and add a dash of crème de menthe, if liked.

Pink lemonade: Add just enough grenadine syrup to each serving glass to give a delicate pink colour. Add a cocktail stirrer and put a maraschino cherry on the end of the stick. Children will love this.

Iced coffee

Serves 6

2 oz (50g) ground coffee
1½ pints (900ml) boiling water
2–3 tablespoons castor sugar
chilled milk or single cream, for serving

Choose a dark continental roast. Make the coffee any way you like, but the filter method is best because it makes a clear brew with no grounds. Sweeten to taste with the sugar while hot. Allow to cool, then chill.

Pour into ice-filled glasses, top up with chilled milk or cream and stir to mix. Freshly brewed and chilled coffee has an astringent and very refreshing taste. This is a marvellously cooling drink you can serve any time by keeping a jug of chilled black coffee ready-made in the refrigerator.

Variations: A dash of rum or brandy added to iced coffee is delicious. Or add a scoop of vanilla ice cream. The ice cream floats and you'll need straws for the coffee and a spoon for the ice cream.

Vin chaud

Makes 10 glasses

1 × 70cl bottle red wine
½ pint (300ml) water
6 oz (175g) castor sugar
3 lemons
2 inch (5cm) piece stick cinnamon

illustrated facing page 321

Put the wine, water and sugar into a saucepan. Thinly pare the rind from 1 lemon using a vegetable peeler, add to the pan along with the cinnamon. Very slowly bring just to the boil, stirring to dissolve the sugar. Draw off the heat, cover with a lid, and allow flavours to infuse for 10 minutes. Then remove the cinnamon stick, otherwise the flavour will be too strong.

Meanwhile, peel the lemons and cut away all the white pith, then slice. Put a slice into each glass. Ladle the warm spiced wine into each glass and serve.

Special touches

Using wine

● You don't need anything grand, just an inexpensive wine that you would be happy to drink. Wine boxes are especially handy for cooks.

● Wine that's cooked loses its alcohol content, but leaves behind a subtle flavour that makes all the difference; you'll find wine goes naturally with fresh fruits too.

● In general, fish and white meats are cooked in white wines and meat and game are usually reserved for reds, but there are always exceptions to the rule.

● Try the most straightforward way when cooking steaks or escalopes: deglaze the hot frying pan with a few tablespoons of wine and let it bubble up while you stir and scrape up coagulated pan juices. Then pour the juice over the meat before you serve it.

● Use wine for baking fish in the oven, then use the liquid to make a sauce.

● A little red wine and fresh herbs makes an excellent and simple marinade for meat. Leave meat to marinate for at least 1 hour. Then use the meat to make a casserole with the wine as part of the stock.

● Dry vermouth, which has a delicate herb flavour, can deputize for wine in a recipe; it's more concentrated so dilute it with an equal quantity of water. It's especially good when used to make fish and chicken dishes.

● For a macedoine of fruits, slice peeled fresh peaches and arrange in layers with sliced strawberries, using 4 oz (100g) sugar per 1 lb (450g) fruit. Add a glass of wine to get the juices flowing and marinate for 1–2 hours, then add a dash of cognac for the finishing touch. Choose a pretty glass dish and arrange fruit in layers to show contrasting colours.

● Soak dried fruits in sherry or sweet white wine, then use in traditional puddings such as bread and butter pudding; wine-plumped fruit is great for fruit cakes, especially at Christmas.

● Decant unfinished wine into smaller bottles, then tightly cork and it will keep for several days. Or freeze wine in ice cube trays and you can drop a cube into a casserole any time.

Using cream

● Cream adds a smooth, rich texture to dishes and greatly enhances the flavour. Make sure you use the right cream for the dish you are making.

● The type of cream is determined by the amount of fat in it – each has a specified minimum content.

● *Double cream* has a minimum fat content of 48 per cent and is the most versatile. Use whipped double cream for syllabubs where flavouring ingredients are added or as a rich pouring cream – it floats perfectly on hot Irish coffee. *Whipping cream* has a minimum fat content of 30 per cent and will whip to a good light volume. It can be used for cake toppings or pastry fillings or for floating on chilled soups. However, it will not hold added ingredients without separating.

● To whip double or whipping cream, have the cream well chilled and the bowl and beater as cold as possible. If you keep cream chilled the fat is firm and you get a better volume. Use a roomy mixing bowl and a wire balloon whisk. Whip double cream to soft peaks for folding into dishes, then the cream blends in smoothly and evenly.

● You can extend double cream by whipping it with an equal quantity of single cream. Or, if yours is extra thick double cream, it can be thinned down for whisking by adding 3 tablespoons milk to each ¼ pint (150ml) cream to make it lighter. To flavour whipped double cream, try adding 1 level tablespoon vanilla sugar to ¼ pint (150ml) double cream to make *chantilly cream*. To really impress your dinner guests, add 1 tablespoon brandy or another liqueur and spoon on to desserts. Always add flavouring to cream before whipping; this way you avoid overbeating the cream in order to fold in the flavouring.

● Make the quickest and easiest cream sauce by heating double cream seasoned with salt and pepper and a touch of lemon juice and add 1 tablespoon chopped fresh green herbs. Pour the sauce over vegetables or fish.

● *Single cream* has a minimum fat content of 18 per cent; single cream will not whip but is an ideal cream for adding to soups and sauces and for serving with desserts. *Half cream* has a minimum fat content of 12 per cent and is a thinner pouring cream best used on fruit or cereals.

● Cream gets thinner when it is heated so add single cream to enrich dishes after cooking. Double cream, on the other hand, can be boiled and if used in a sauce, be sure to boil the liquid ingredients (usually wine or pan drippings) until syrupy to make a concentrated flavour and to avoid over diluting the cream, then add the cream and bring just to the boil.

● A liaison of 3 tablespoons double or single cream and 1 egg yolk is a good way of adding texture and colour to a pale sauce: stir in at the last minute, then heat for about 1 minute until sauce thickens. Do not allow to boil or egg will overcook.

● *Soured cream* is a single cream soured commercially with a lactic culture. It has a thick but soft consistency and a sharp refreshing taste. Soured cream cannot be whipped, but for thickest consistency it should be spooned from the carton without stirring. Add soured cream to salad dressings or blend with mayonnaise in equal parts to make a light textured topping. Use soured cream as a base for dips or spoon it over fruit pies.

● Most cream sold commercially is pasteurized and will not sour naturally; you can sour fresh cream by adding 1–2 teaspoons lemon juice to ¼ pint (150ml) double cream and leave covered at room temperature for 15 minutes.

● Fresh cream should be kept in the refrigerator; once opened, it should be kept covered as it can easily pick up the flavours of other foods. *Long life cream* is heat treated to sterilize. It will keep for 6 months in the store cupboard but once opened it should be treated as fresh cream and refrigerated.

● *Crème fraîche* is double cream which has a slightly acid taste because it is soured naturally in much the same way as yoghurt. It's richer than our soured cream and keeps well in the refrigerator. The French use *crème fraîche* for spooning on fruits or fruit tarts and in sauces too, since it can be brought to the boil. You can easily make it yourself. Start with fresh double cream and use soured cream, buttermilk or natural yoghurt to sour it:

Turn ½ pint (300ml) double cream into a saucepan and heat to 110°F (43°C) – slightly over blood heat (a drop on the wrist should feel hot but not burning). Pour into a screw-topped jar. Add 1 tablespoon soured cream, buttermilk or natural yoghurt. Cover jar and shake for 1 minute. Leave to stand at room temperature for at least 8 hours, or until cream is thick, then chill. *Crème fraîche* will keep for 2–3 weeks stored in the refrigerator.

Using nuts

Almonds are the nuts we know best and use the most; sweet almonds come largely from Spain. Most trees in this country yield bitter almonds which should not be eaten.

● Shelled almonds have brown skins which are easily removed if the nuts are first blanched in boiling water for a few minutes; then slip the almonds out of their skins while still warm. Newly blanched almonds are soft and easier to chop, flake or shred.

● To toast almonds, spread the nuts on a baking tray and place under a hot grill for a few minutes to brown – watch them, they easily scorch.

● For salted almonds, add blanched nuts to hot oil in a shallow pan and fry gently until golden. Drain and while hot, toss in salt; if you use sea salt you can be more generous with it.

Brazil nuts have an exceptionally hard shell which encloses what I believe to be a most delicious nut. When fresh these nuts have an ivory smoothness and rich flavour.

● If you put Brazil nuts in the freezer for a few hours you'll find them easier to crack.

● The shelled nut is delicious eaten plain with the ends dipped in salt. Or, for the sweet-toothed, it can be dipped in melted chocolate.

● Make a pretty decoration for a trifle or mousse by shaving slices lengthways with a vegetable peeler. Then toast under the grill and shavings will curl up and tinge with brown – they look and taste delicious.

Chestnuts should never be mixed with other nuts in a bowl as they cannot be eaten straight from the shell without cooking. The ones we eat are the fruit of the sweet chestnut tree. They are usually served as a vegetable (page 145) or made into a sweetened purée (page 220).

● Roasting chestnuts in the ashes of an open fire is traditionally done in winter. Make sure you slash the outer brown skin with a knife to avoid explosions. Peel when hot and eat with a sprinkling of salt.

Hazelnuts, being very hard, are one of the crunchiest of all nuts. You can buy them whole, shelled, chopped or ground. Our own Kent cobnut is a variety of hazelnut; they have a green and brown lacy outer coating and look pretty heaped on a dish and passed with the cheese tray. Provide nut crackers and allow guests to crack their own.

● Whole shelled hazelnuts have a brown feathery skin around the kernel. Spread nuts on a baking tray and place under the grill for a few minutes; tip hot nuts into a tea towel, rub together and the skins will flake off. A further few minutes under the grill to toast the skinned nuts will give them a more pronounced flavour.

● For use in cooking, skinned whole hazelnuts are best ground in a Mouli grater because they are difficult to chop. Beware of grinding them for too long in a blender as they become oily and form a paste.

● Try using hazelnuts instead of almonds to make praline (page 322); toasted chopped hazelnuts are also good sprinkled on ice cream.

Peanuts are also called groundnuts and come from the same family as green beans. They are rich in oil and provide peanut, or arachide, oil much used for cooking on the Continent, particularly for deep frying because it has a high smoke point.

● The high oil content in peanuts means that when finely ground, they will form a paste or spread – the popular peanut butter.

● Peanuts are an economical way to add protein and a delicious flavour to a number of dishes. I like to toss salted peanuts in coleslaw. They are also good added to rice dishes and lend their flavour very well to a cold chicken salad. Add peanuts just before serving so they do not lose their crunch.

Pecans are closely related to walnuts and have something of their flavour. The pecan nut is from a species of hickory tree which grows in North America. They are popular for their pretty reddish brown colour and delicious flavour, but they are expensive and imported on a limited scale because pecan trees have a two-year cycle for bearing fruit and supplies can vary considerably.

● Many American recipes use pecans, especially in baking; the best substitute is walnuts.

Pistachio nuts are dainty little nuts that come from the Mediterranean. They have a bright green kernel and sweet aromatic flavour. The pretty green colour encourages their use in confectionery and for decorating desserts.

● For use in the kitchen, the outer brown skin must be removed. To do this, blanch nuts in boiling water for 1 minute and pop them out of their skins while warm. Use whole or chopped.

● Pistachio nuts are also available salted in their shells and are delicious as a cocktail nut.

Walnuts in the shell look pretty combined with fruits for a table centre-piece. As they are very oily they turn rancid quickly and should be eaten soon after buying and not allowed to wither inside the shell.

● Shelled walnuts can be chopped, but it is quicker to snip them with a pair of scissors. For cooking, buy the less expensive walnut pieces; for finely grated nuts a Mouli grater is invaluable.

● Walnuts are good in savoury dishes – add chopped nuts to cream cheese with chives or sprinkle them in salads. Chopped walnuts are delicious in cakes and teabreads, especially banana teabread (page 270).

Index

References to a recipe, or to a variation of a recipe, are shown in **heavy** type.